BEWARE
OF THE BULL

BEWARE
OF THE BULL

The Enigmatic Genius
of Jake Thackray

Paul Thompson
John Watterson

Scratching Shed Publishing Ltd

First published by Scratching Shed Publishing Ltd in 2022
Registered in England & Wales No. 6588772
Registered office: 47 Street Lane, Leeds, West Yorkshire. LS8 1AP
www.scratchingshedpublishing.co.uk
ISBN 978-1838489984

Provenance of cover image unknown.
Page 1: Publicity shot for BBC radio folk show, 1976 © BBC

The Bull
Words and Music by Jake Thackray
Copyright © 1983 Noel Gay Music Company Limited
International Copyright Secured All Rights Reserved
Reprinted by Permission of Hal Leonard Europe Ltd.

The Black Swan
Words and Music by Jake Thackray
Copyright © 1967 Noel Gay Music Company Limited
Copyright Renewed
International Copyright Secured All Rights Reserved
Reprinted by Permission of Hal Leonard Europe Ltd.

The Last Will And Testament of Jake Thackray
Words and Music by Jake Thackray
Copyright © 1967 SGO Music Publishing Limited
and Leola Music Limited Copyright Renewed
All Rights Administered by BMG Rights Management (US) LLC
All Rights Reserved Used by Permission
Reprinted by Permission of Hal Leonard Europe Ltd.

A catalogue record for this book is available from the British Library.

Typeset in Caslon
Printed and bound in the United Kingdom by
Short Run Press Ltd
Bittern Road, Sowton Industrial Estate, Exeter. EX2 7LW
Tel: 01392 211909   Fax: 01392 444134

For Jake.
With thanks for all the silvery laughter.

Contents

Publicity photo,
Jake Thackray,
1969 concert
programme.
Mid Pennine Arts

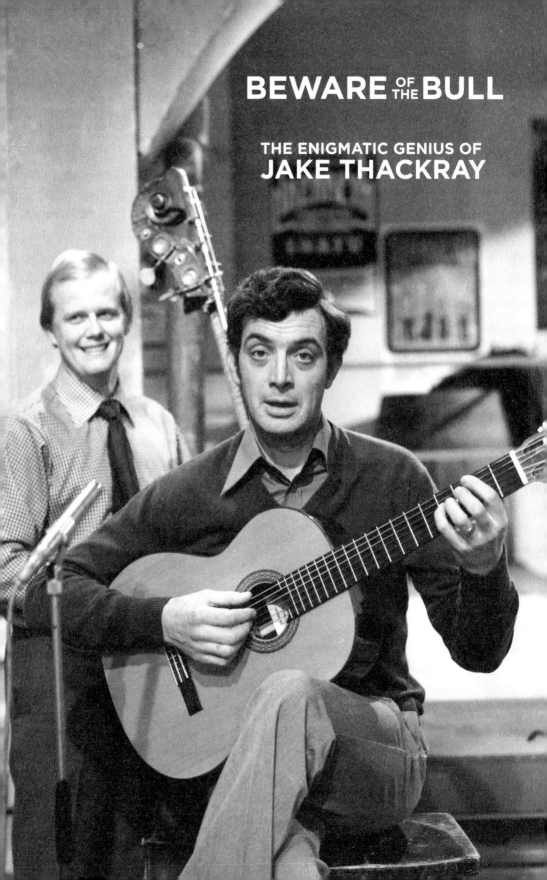

BEWARE OF THE BULL

THE ENIGMATIC GENIUS OF JAKE THACKRAY

Introduction

Beware of the Bull

'These well-known men, so over-glorified,
There's one of them here, his name's on the poster outside.
And he is up here like this, and you are all down there.
Remember his cock and his bull, and mutter "Beware!"'

Jake Thackray, *'The Bull'*

Jake Thackray looked out at 1,800 empty seats. In a couple of hours' time, here in the main auditorium of Fairfield Halls, Croydon, one of the largest concert venues in Britain, he would be performing to a sell-out crowd. Beside him on the stage stood Alex Armitage, his young agent.

'It's very big, isn't it?' Jake said, and Alex agreed.

At which, the star turn headed quietly to his dressing room.

Twenty minutes before curtain-up and with the hall filling nicely, a watchful stage doorkeeper then approached Alex with some news: Mr Thackray had just left the building.

His agent wasn't unduly concerned, and explained that Jake had probably gone out for a cigarette. 'I don't think so,' said the doorkeeper. 'He was carrying his guitar and his suit bag.'

In great alarm, Alex dashed outside. He reached Jake's car just as it was reaching the car park exit and threw himself in front of it. 'The closest I have ever come to getting run over,' he would later recall. But having blocked Jake's escape, he now had to talk him out of the vehicle, which wasn't going to be easy. 'Jake really didn't want to do the show. He thought it was too big for him. He thought the audience wouldn't like him. He thought they would laugh, but not in a good way.' Alex had to work hard and fast to calm Jake's nerves and convince him that he should perform: 'The argument I used that night was that when the house lights were down and the spotlight was on him, Jake wouldn't know that he wasn't in a folk club with one hundred people.' Eventually, Jake stepped reluctantly out of his green Renault 18 and returned to the stage, starting a few minutes late. 'And, of course, he was sensational,' said Alex. 'He had 1,800 people absolutely in the palm of his hand.'

The above incident took place in February 1977, when Jake's career was on the crest of a second wave. At the start of the year, his beautifully written fourth studio album, *On Again! On Again!*, had gone into record shops and, in a real coup for Alex and his father, Richard, who headed their agency, Noel Gay Artists, its release coincided with Jake's return to television for a five-month residency on one of the BBC's most popular programmes, *That's Life!*. Artistically and commercially, the planets were in alignment. It was hardly a surprise that the Fairfield Halls concert was sold out.

By this time, Jake had been a household name for almost a decade. Having been talent-spotted by the BBC, he'd swapped his teacher's mark-book and chalk in Leeds for the bright lights of London. He had recorded his songs at Abbey Road studios (rubbing shoulders with the Beatles, who became fans), and made countless appearances on the BBC's popular late Saturday night TV show *Braden's Week*, establishing a national reputation. Over the years, he'd had plenty of practice dealing with his nerves, performing week after week in folk clubs and theatres, singing live to millions on television and radio, and even, on occasion, appearing on stage in front of royalty, with such greats as Louis Armstrong and Tony Bennett following him on the bill. But Jake would remain prey to stage-fright and self-doubt throughout his career. As his friend, singer-songwriter, Harvey Andrews, observes: 'The slightest heat used to scald him in life.'

Jake Thackray was a complex man, and it wasn't just nerves that almost derailed him that evening in 1977. He hated the physical remoteness of venues like Fairfield Halls and the lack of intimacy with his audience, notwithstanding his extraordinary gift for making audiences in the biggest, coldest arenas feel as though they were in the cosy backroom of a pub. Furthermore, he was a genuinely modest and self-effacing man who not only shunned celebrity but positively despised and distrusted it.

A dyed-in-the-wool socialist, he saw no reason at all why he should be put above anyone else, had no desire whatsoever to be put on a pedestal.

Given which, in many ways it was remarkable that Jake ever stepped into the spotlight in the first place. He was both a reluctant and accidental star, someone whose extraordinary and original talent drew others to champion his cause, taking him down a path he'd never planned to travel, nor thought through. He was not only ambivalent about his career as a performer, but also the quality of his writing. The low self-esteem from which he suffered had roots in his childhood. In later years he'd apologise to audiences for every aspect of his performance, embarrassed at having to perform songs loved by his fans, but which he regarded as trivial. Jake was genuinely and utterly dismissive of some of his cleverest, most entertaining writing. He would not – or could not – accept or believe that he was a great, uniquely gifted artist.

And yet, from the off, it was clear to anyone who heard him perform that Jake was an original and singular talent. His songs had an unusual mixture of qualities: they could be hilarious, moving, satirical, irreverent, bawdy and anarchic, sometimes all within the same song. They were the work of a writer who was a master storyteller and had a poet's love and command of language and form; a writer who employed a rich vocabulary and made artful use of vulgarity, word play and innuendo. His songs celebrated life in all its earthy vibrancy, replete with love, sex, booze and unseemly behaviour, as well as an irreverent attitude to religion and death, and a healthy disrespect for authority, snobbery and hypocrisy. Jake used his observer's eye to immortalise the mundane: country buses, jumble sales, the personal and agony aunt columns at the back of newspapers and magazines. He populated his songs with extraordinary and fanciful versions of ordinary people: gypsies, village bobbies, scallywags, drunks, tedious in-laws, farm-hands, Salvation Army girls, lonely spinsters, accident-prone relatives. He took ephemeral, crude jokes and re-moulded them into timeless and beautifully-crafted musical delights, ending with punchlines that remain hilarious however often the song is heard.

Of course, there were songwriters before Jake whose work displayed some of those same qualities. However, whilst the innuendo which laced his songs was reminiscent of George Formby and music hall, in Jake's skilled hands it was altogether more nuanced and sophisticated. The sharpness of wit and satirical bite of his humour invited comparisons with American musician Tom Lehrer, but Jake's writing was imbued with a compassion that Lehrer's lacked. Furthermore, whilst Jake's subject matter and themes were as quintessentially English as the work of Flanders and Swann, his writing had much more edge, marked by a lack of deference for the Establishment. Jake combined tremendous technical and poetic skill with a unique imagination and attitude.

It wasn't just Jake's writing that made him stand out; so did every other aspect of his performance. His choice of instrument immediately declared that he was not a member of the pop or folk mainstream: aside from Jake and Leonard Cohen, his Canadian contemporary, very few English-speaking singers before or since have accompanied themselves on a nylon-strung, classical guitar. This unusual choice was married to a memorable delivery: Jake had a striking appearance, with handsome, distinctive facial features, but he sang in a pointedly detached manner, with a deadpan, lugubrious expression, and only the occasional, knowing glint in his eyes. In addition, his singing was out of the ordinary: blessed with a rich baritone and outstanding diction (vital, given the verbal gymnastics involved in some of his lyrics), his was an idiosyncratic, clipped style, prompting one reviewer for *The Times* to declare that 'he sings as if he was about to swallow a soft egg whole'.

Furthermore, in an era when many entertainers felt under pressure to disown their regional accent, Jake's tones and turns of phrase were unapologetically northern and Yorkshire.

Anyone familiar with French music would immediately identify that the greatest influence upon Jake came not from England, nor America, but France, where he spent three hugely formative years. As a songwriter and performer Jake's approach was unmistakably Gallic. In France, he found the inspiration that made him a truly unique cultural hybrid – a Yorkshire chansonnier.

The anarchism running through Jake's work like lettering in a stick of Scarborough rock can be traced to his upbringing in the terraces of Leeds, where he knew first-hand what poverty looked like and how privilege could lead to injustice. 'In Jake's songs there is an impatience with, and attack on, the British class system,' observes author Neil Gaiman. 'I would take Jake Thackray over the entire British kitchen sink drama trend of the 1950s and early 1960s. There is never any point in any of his songs where you find yourself looking up to anybody. We are all on the same level in his songs. If anyone appears to be more important than anyone else in the song, then there are signals that they shall be taken down a notch by the end of it.'

During his heyday, millions recognised Jake's power to entertain, but few acknowledged his real stature as a writer. In large part this is down to the fact that he was soon trapped by the one-song-per-show television format that brought him fame, pigeonholed as 'that bloke who sings funny songs on the telly'. Also at play are a failure to appreciate both the breadth and depth of Jake's writing, and the intellectual snobbery that leads to humorous writing not being taken seriously as art.

His record producer, Norman Newell, was never in any doubt as to how special Jake's talent was: 'One day he will be recognised as one of the greatest writers of all time. He is a complete and utter natural. The magic of T.S. Eliot lives on forever, and Jake's work is just as good. Maybe I am overdoing the praise, but I really mean it... I thought he was a genius, and I still do.'[1] He also told the lyricist Don Black that he had met many brilliant people in his life, but only two geniuses: Noël Coward and Jake Thackray.

Newell's prediction is beginning to come true. Thackray is admired by a host of literate songwriters, including Don Black, Benjamin Clementine, Jarvis Cocker, Thea Gilmore, Cerys Matthews and Alex Turner. Neil Gaiman is in no doubt as to Jake's originality: 'There's nothing else like him, there's nobody else like him. Once you've heard enough of his songs, you realise there is nobody else doing anything like that. There was nobody else doing slices-of-life songs that were stories.'

The tale of Jake's own life is fascinating, from his humble working-class childhood in Leeds, being brought up under the watchful eye of a devout Catholic mother and bullying father, through to his lonely death in self-imposed obscurity in South Wales and a simple gravestone near the tomb of a Catholic martyr. It is the story of a shy, bright and creative boy whose life would be transformed both by the Jesuits and a post-war grammar school revolution that took him to one of England's top universities. It is the story of a risk-taker who would head abroad, fall in love with French culture and choose to live in

Algeria during wartime. It is the story of an inspirational, creative, unorthodox teacher who wrote songs for his own amusement and took his guitar into the classroom. It is the story of a northern provincial whom the BBC executives in London eventually recognised as hot property, but whose relationship with show business would never be easy. It is the story of a man who turned his back on fame and chose a different path. It is the story of a man who remained genuinely loved and hugely admired by many, even after he let them down. It is the story of a man who left us with ninety or so extraordinary, idiosyncratic songs which deserve to be heard, sung and studied for decades to come. It is the story of a fantasist and master storyteller who would never have believed his own story deserved to be told.

He was wrong. Let the story begin.

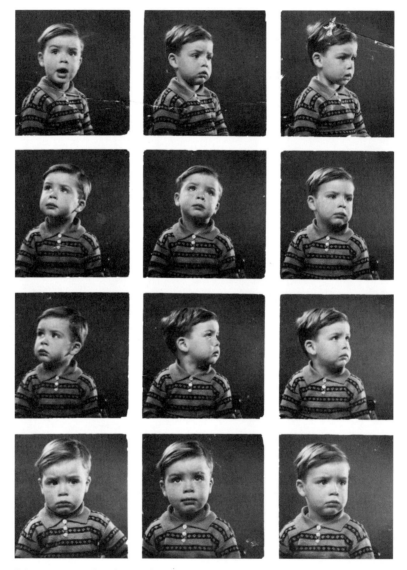

Jake practising lugubrious looks in 1941.   *Thackray family*

Up My Family Tree

'Here is the gritty old city of Leeds
Which is not as it seems
From the tops of the ridges.
It is gaunt and greedy and grim in the face,
Unyielding, unlovely, a flat black place,
And its only merited saving grace
Is the people who live in the city of Leeds.'

– Jake Thackray, '*Gritty Old City of Leeds*'

Jake's roots in the West Riding of Yorkshire ran deep, and he presented himself as a proud and unapologetic northerner. At the start of his performing career he was billed as the 'Leeds schoolteacher', and this remained as important to his sense of identity as the northern vowels he steadfastly refused either to disguise or lose. Set alongside this, the cynical views he expressed in 'Gritty Old City of Leeds' (written for a radio documentary in 1980) come as a real surprise, but the origins of this ambivalence, as with so many other conflicted aspects of his complex personality, lie in his upbringing.

In his song 'Family Tree', Jake revels in the fact that his ancestry is 'lurid', declaring proudly that there is 'no blue blood, no nobility'. This is true enough: his family line was working-class, through and through. However, anyone hoping to glean further truths about the Thackrays from the song's colourful catalogue of family rogues and their dubious achievements will be greatly entertained, but sorely disappointed. Everything (and almost everyone) in 'Family Tree' is invented.[1]

This is characteristic of Jake's writing. He was at pains to reveal little of himself in song, and preferred to create glorious flights of fantasy, populated with memorable characters who were the product of an extraordinary and highly original imagination. This shy, self-deprecating man would always rather we look at his fictional creations than him.

Occasionally, however, he does provide a fleeting glimpse of people in his life. 'Personal Column' contains one such moment. The song's amusing catalogue of newspaper small ads and personal notices includes a message from a Mrs Ivy Armitage, publicly thanking all those who showed her 'kindnesses when times were hard.' Ivy Armitage was the maiden name of Jake's mother. She was a woman with a strong sense of what was proper and belonged to a generation which might indeed have spoken of thanking people for 'kindnesses'. Certainly, she had known hard times throughout her life.

Ivy May Armitage, known in the family as Molly, was born into a working-class family in Halifax in 1901, the seventh of nine children. The eldest, Mary Louisa, was 13 years her senior, the youngest, Joseph (the only boy), eight years her junior. In 1911 the family was living at 161 St Stephens Terrace in Copley, near Halifax, alongside the Brighouse to Sowerby Bridge railway line. Molly's father was a horse driver for Halifax Corporation's health department, while all her older sisters, including 12-year-old Josephine, were working as 'twisters' or 'spinners' at Copley Mill, the woollen mill at the end of their street. When Jake's wife, Sheila, met some of them in the 1960s, they all struck her as clever, but they would have received only a basic education. In all likelihood Molly joined them at the mill when she left school, aged 12.

Copley Mill was opened in the nineteenth century by Edward Akroyd, a wealthy Victorian industrialist who, out of a sense of Christian duty, built small, stone-built terraces for his workers in model villages at Copley and the less modestly named Akroydon.[2] Most of the houses were in tightly-packed rows, lacking even back yards, and the Armitages had the good fortune to live in a slightly larger end-of-terrace. Nevertheless, life for such a large family, squeezed into five rooms, would have been tough. So too would the highly repetitive, manual tasks the girls were forced to endure in noisy, stifling conditions during shifts of up to 60 hours a week. From a very young age the Armitage girls would have known hard work.

By the time of the 1921 census, 19-year-old Molly was a brush maker in Halifax, and much had changed in the family. Her father was dead, most of her older sisters had left home and she was living with her mother, three siblings and a brother-in-law in a terraced house in Skircoat Green, one mile from Copley. The family remained here for many years, and one of Jake's earliest memories was of visiting Skircoat Green when he was five, after his grandmother's death.

Jake's father, Ernest, also came from a working-class family, albeit one very different from Molly's. He was born in 1900 in a terrace in Pinfold Lane, Armley, a working-class district of Leeds. Although his home was small, it was much less crowded than Molly's because he only had one sibling. His father was the caretaker at the local Conservative Club, and by the time Ernest was eleven his mother worked there part-time as well. Underpinning the difference between the two households was religion: the Armitages were Catholic, while the Thackrays were Protestant.

In September 1916, an Ernest Thackray, possibly Jake's father, became an assistant postman in Leeds. In 1918, Ernest definitely became eligible for military conscription but did not receive the call-up in wartime. He did spend 14 months in the Sherwood Foresters' regiment after the war, however, and possibly served in Ireland in 1920, during the brutal Irish War of Independence. This might be what led Jake to believe that his father had been a member of the notorious and brutal Black and Tans,[3] the constables recruited into the Royal Irish Constabulary to help with policing and the suppression of the IRA.[4] It was a belief that would only have been reinforced by Ernest's behaviour towards Molly and their children.

In January 1921, at the age of 20, Ernest joined the West Riding Constabulary. The job had many attractions: it was secure, relatively well paid and came with accommodation or a housing allowance, along with a good pension. He would remain a policeman for the next 25 years, serving out his time unremarkably, aside from one career-changing event.

Initially Ernest worked on the beat in the mill town of Sowerby Bridge, but in 1925 transferred to the divisional offices in Halifax, where he met Molly. In Jake's weekly column for the *Yorkshire Post* in the 1990s, he wrote that his mother was working as a flower-shop girl in Skircoat Green at this time, and that his parents met at Thirsk races, but caution is needed: Jake's journalism, like his songs, is full of fantasy. In the same article he claimed that Molly and Ernest were both excellent cricketers.

Given their characters, Ernest and Molly seem an unlikely couple. Ernest was a stern and unemotional man, with no obvious religious faith; in later years, at least, he was an alcoholic who could be volatile and violent towards his family. Molly, by contrast, was a devout Catholic whose dry sense of humour was tempered by a strong sense of propriety. Perhaps there was a degree of pragmatism in their decision to marry: whatever her feelings may have been for Ernest, in an era of mass unemployment, marrying a policeman offered her the prospect of financial security. Furthermore, she was not getting any younger: at the time of their wedding in December 1927, she was 26, which was relatively old for a bride at that time. She would have required a bishop's permission to marry a non-

Catholic, and she would also have had to promise that she would raise her children in the Catholic faith. She kept that promise fastidiously.

In 1928, Ernest was transferred to Barnsley and became a village constable in Hunshelf and Hoyland Common. In the same year, Molly had their first child, Michael, who was joined three years later by a brother, Richard. In 1936, Ernest was transferred again, this time to the village of Rawdon, near Leeds, where the family lived at 2 Park View Terrace. The two-up, two-down house was small with only a back yard, but it was on a spacious road and, with a park nearby and views across the hills, it was a pleasant place in which to raise a young family.

On 27th February 1938, seven years after Richard was born, Molly gave birth in Hyde Terrace maternity hospital, Leeds, to her third child, Jake. Or rather John Philip, as he was christened; he would only start calling himself Jake in his early 20s. (And as far as Molly was concerned, he would always be John Philip.) Apparently it was not an easy delivery, his survival touch and go, reflecting perhaps the nature of medical care then, and the fact that Molly was relatively old. Happily, mother and child came through. Molly didn't return to work: in the 1939 register her occupation is recorded as 'unpaid domestic duties', i.e. she was a housewife, as was customary then for most women bringing up a family.[5]

Jake was 18 months old when war came. Undoubtedly the war years would have been difficult for the Thackrays, with rationing and other hardships exacerbated by the anxiety of living near a major industrial city and the heightened risk of air raids. However, at least Ernest's occupation as a policeman meant that he was not called up.

Court records show he was assiduous in his duties, including enforcing the law to protect the war effort. Two months after its outbreak he arrested a man for 'failure to obscure a light during a blackout'. This was subject to strict observance everywhere, but especially in Rawdon, since it neighboured an enormous, elaborately camouflaged aircraft factory in Yeadon, which would have been a prime target for bombing.[6]

Ernest initially had a good war, and in 1941, after 20 years of service, was promoted to the rank of sergeant (2nd class). Along with increased pay and status came other benefits: he was transferred to picturesque Boston Spa, a few miles from Wetherby, east of Leeds, and the family moved into a house in the nearby village of Clifford. Here, surrounded by countryside, air raids posed less of a threat, and Molly would doubtless also have been pleased to be bringing up her sons in a community with a strong Catholic identity: the small village, built to house flax-mill workers, boasted a large Catholic church, a convent and two Catholic schools. Life, it seems, was looking up.

Court reports in the *Yorkshire Post* show that the newly-promoted Sergeant Thackray remained busy, dealing with drink-drivers, road traffic accidents, drunk and disorderly behaviour and car theft. But then in 1942, when Jake was four, something happened which had a profound impact on Ernest's career, family circumstances and, quite possibly, his youngest son's world view.

In April 1942, Ernest, assisted by a constable, was on traffic duty at Wetherby racecourse. To smooth the traffic flow at the end of the race meeting, a temporary one-way system was established, but one obstinate driver refused to accept the instruction to turn left, complaining that it would take him a few miles out of his way.

The driver was a wealthy and influential man. Kenneth Parkinson was what Jake would later call a 'big wig', and well on his way to becoming an even bigger wig in the future. He was also very well-connected: his father-in-law was a peer of the realm. Given this, he was a man whom some might have allowed to turn right, but not Sergeant Thackray or his constable. Parkinson initially tried to argue his case, before appearing to follow their direction. However, after going 100 yards, he turned around and tried once more to drive on to

Wetherby. He was pulled up again, and Sergeant Thackray removed the keys from the ignition. Reluctantly, Parkinson agreed to follow the officers' direction, but not before being booked.

The case came to court in May 1942 and the proceedings were reported in the *Yorkshire Evening Post*. Parkinson's father-in-law, Lord Bingley, was on the bench that day but withdrew because of the obvious conflict of interest, as did another magistrate. However, the two remaining justices failed to agree a verdict, and so a re-hearing was ordered, and the two policemen presented their evidence to the new bench. At this point Parkinson decided to avoid further humiliation and submitted a letter, pleading guilty to a technical offence. He was fined £5, a sizeable sum, roughly equivalent to a week of Sergeant Thackray's wages.

Thackray family legend has it that Ernest and his family paid a much higher price than Parkinson following this run-in. Within two months of the court case, Ernest had been demoted to the rank of constable. There is no evidence that this was connected to the court case, and it is entirely possible that he was demoted for another reason, perhaps related to his alcoholism. Nevertheless, given the timings, it is easy to see why the Thackrays assumed the events were linked.

Ernest's demotion hit the family hard. He and Molly now had to raise their children on reduced wages.[7] Years later, Jake would speak of the hardship: 'We were a working class family in Leeds... and money wasn't very, sort of, obviously left lying around... there wasn't a lot of it about.'[8] Along with the financial impact, he vividly remembered the upheaval caused by Ernest being repeatedly transferred to different districts. In July 1942 the family moved to Marsden, near Huddersfield, and then, only a month later, to Pudsey, on the outskirts of Leeds. His final transfer was to Morley, another suburb of Leeds. By the late 1950s, Molly had lived in no fewer than 12 houses.

Whatever the real story behind Ernest's demotion, the

legend was powerful and its formative impact upon young Jake would have been profound: he would have grown up believing that his family's lot had been made harder by members of the establishment closing ranks and punishing his father (and, indirectly, the family) for embarrassing one of their own.

Set against this background, it is hardly surprising that such a strong, anti-establishment attitude peppers Jake's writing, and that he takes every opportunity to mock deference and vent his spleen at entitlement or privilege. He channels these feelings to great comic effect in songs such as 'The Brigadier' and 'Pass Milord the Rooster Juice', but they find their most powerful and brilliant expression in his late masterpiece, 'The Bull'. The song serves as his manifesto:

> Beware of the bull! The dancing cock is right;
> Beware of whoever looks down upon you from a height.
> Beware of His Honour, His Excellence,
> His Grace, His Worshipful,
> Beware of His Highness, because of the bull.
> For if the boss, the chief, the chap at the top,
> Should let a single lump of claptrap drop;
> The greater the weight and the height he is,
> The harder it will go,
> With a grander splat on the bleeders below.

Alongside his father's demotion, another enduring issue growing up was Ernest's behaviour. He was a cold and stern man and, as was common then, when he meted out discipline at home, he did so physically, as Jake's wife, Sheila, recalled: 'I heard Jake and his brothers talking about their early life, and it wasn't a happy, easy time, when they were young. [Their father] was a hard man, an unpredictable man... not loving. None of them have the memory of him telling them that he loved them. He was more likely to knock them about.'[9] Ernest's actions were exacerbated by his alcoholism, which made him more volatile.

Jake grew up when people didn't talk openly about what went on behind closed doors. Nevertheless, the euphemistic language used by friends and neighbours cannot disguise their real concerns. One neighbour described Ernest's conduct towards 'Mrs Thackray' as 'objectionable in the extreme'.[10]

Molly's close friend and fellow church-goer, Teresa Burke,[11] would say that she had 'a very poor opinion' of Mr Thackray. 'If she said that of someone,' says her son, Paddy, 'then that was really damning. She said that he gave Molly a hard time, but wouldn't go into details.' Vince Dobson, a childhood friend of Jake's, also read the signs: 'I think his father was a bit of a hard man. Jake didn't mention anything specific, but as a child you pick up these vibes. I think his father might have given his mother a bit of a hard time on occasions.'

By February 1946, after 25 years' service, Ernest had had enough of life as a constable and retired at the earliest possible opportunity. The impact on the family was again significant: his pension was half his constable's salary.[12] They also lost the benefit of police-funded accommodation, implications perhaps softened by the fact that Jake's oldest brother, Michael, had by then left school and was working in a bank.

In June 1946, the family moved to a rented house at 90 Burley Lodge Road in Headingley, which was within walking distance of St Michael's College, where Jake's other brother, Richard, was a pupil. The terraced property only had a small, open back yard, overlooked by tenement blocks, but with its bay windows, four bedrooms (two of which were in the attic) and cellar, it was larger than most in the neighbouring streets. However, nothing could hide the fact that the address was right on the doorstep of Kirkstall, one of Leeds' poorest districts, dominated by rows of back-to-back terraced slums, with shared toilets and gas-powered streetlights.

Kirkstall had a terrible reputation. It was not a place in which to walk after dark. For eight-year-old Jake, the contrast between life here and in leafy Rawdon and Boston Spa was stark. In 1981, he would tell BBC Radio 2's John Dunn how much he disliked Leeds initially, and was even blunter in an interview with Paul Vallely in 1973: 'I was brought up in a nasty part of Leeds... We had hard times in Leeds.'[13]

Jake lived in Burley Lodge Road for more than a decade, and by the end of the 1940s was the only child in the house. Michael had left the bank to begin training for the priesthood and Richard had joined the merchant navy. For years, therefore, he was left to bear the brunt of his father's behaviour with only his mother there to give him support. The house was not a happy one in which to grow up. Paddy Burke only visited once, but it made a lasting impression: 'It was quite a forbidding place. It was rather dark inside and there didn't seem to be a lot of fun there.' Vince Dobson agrees, but doesn't think that it was entirely down to Ernest: 'It wasn't a happy, jovial household. It was fairly sombre. Part of that, I think, might have been because Jake's mother was very religious.'

Unsurprisingly, when friends visited, Jake preferred to play outdoors. Even at the age of ten or eleven, his creativity left a strong impression on Vince: 'I marvelled at his imaginative games. The *Just William* books by Richmal Crompton greatly influenced him and he devised *Just William* games, allocating each of us a part. Jake was always William. We would play these games in the council park on Burley Road, just up the road from his home, followed perhaps by a five-mile trail through Headingley to get into Hawksworth Wood for more exciting and imaginative games, always accompanied by sandwiches and drinks of lemonade.'

After his retirement, Ernest supplemented his pension by getting a job as a school caretaker. He seems to have cut a rather solitary figure in the community. The area had a large Catholic population and church attendance was high, but he didn't accompany his family to Mass. The neighbours' children found him a grim-jawed, taciturn and intimidating man, as young Elaine Howey, who lived two doors along from the

Thackrays in the early 1950s, recalls: 'Jake's dad was a right grumpy old bruiser, and in the road we used to hear him yelling inside the house. Each morning he would set off on his ancient push bike, standing on one pedal, with a fag-butt hanging out of the corner of his mouth, and coast down the cobbles of the back street, which was very narrow and pierced by ginnels between the tenements and terraces. We made sure we kept out of his way. We were terrified of him.'

It seems that Ernest could manage his behaviour (or be managed by Molly, perhaps) on those occasions when Jake's school friends visited. Basil Foot, who stayed with the family during the Easter holidays in 1951, found Ernest friendly, happily paying up when he lost a bet with Basil over a Featherstone Rovers rugby league match. Another school friend, Don Stoker, who met Ernest briefly in 1955, remembers him as a cheerful enough man who talked enthusiastically about visiting the Great Yorkshire Show; he told Don the story of a brass-necked scallywag worthy of one of Jake's songs, who drove off with someone else's prize-winning bull, having persuaded the crowd of unwitting bystanders to help him load it onto his trailer.

The depth of the tensions in the household were graphically laid bare for Elaine Howey's family, though, when Jake was a teenager. 'Jake and his dad did not get on,' recalls Elaine. 'They were once fighting, rolling and scrapping on the kitchen lino. Mrs Thackray came and knocked on our door and asked my dad to separate them. They were in the kitchen doorway, and Jake's father was sitting on Jake's chest, throttling him. My dad was going to knock the old chap out... but Jake rolled his eyes backward to put my dad in his gaze and said: "Don't you bloody touch him... I'm going to batter 'im!" In the end, Mrs Thackray hit her husband over the head with a coal scuttle.' The fact Molly had asked Elaine's dad to intervene is a measure of how exceptional the situation was – the normal culture of silence could not be maintained in the face of real danger.

Growing up with such a father cast a long shadow over Jake's life, and the gulf between them continued to the end. Ernest died of alcohol-related cancer in October 1956 when Jake was 18, and their final conversation was almost monosyllabic. As his father faced the prospect of meeting his maker, Jake asked him bluntly: 'Are you okay seeing the Big Man?'

For Molly, the years of marriage to an unloving and volatile alcoholic had been hard and she doubtless had mixed emotions. If his death was met with any sense of relief, it also brought with it financial hardship: all she and Jake now had to live off was her meagre widow's pension, supplemented by what she earned working as a housekeeper for a Catholic priest. Other changes followed: before long, their days at Burley Lodge Road came to an end, and they moved to a small council house three miles away in West Park.

Jake's relationship with his mother is similarly complex and fascinating. Molly was a very good mum, but not one to dote, as young Vince Dobson noticed: 'I wouldn't say he was close to her particularly, but I think he respected her and felt for her, perhaps, because she didn't have the affection of his father.'

By the time Jake entered his teens he had undergone a growth spurt and was a tall, gangling boy, with unusual, rather ungainly facial features. Although he towered over Molly, they were recognisably mother and son, sharing the same very distinctive eyes. Don Stoker, who first met Jake's mother when he and Jake were in the sixth form, saw other similarities: 'I thought Molly was quite reserved, and that she was like Jake in character. She had a lot of culture about her; she read a lot. I thought there was a lot more to Molly. You could miss the richness that was there.'

'She was formidable in that she was clever as well,' recalled Sheila Thackray. 'She didn't parade it or anything, but she was a highly intelligent woman, and you couldn't really get anything past her. She was witty, and she believed in all the Catholic pieties, which can be a bit of a bore really, sometimes. She was so funny, she was so witty, I used to wish that she would sin a bit more!' Sheila could see that Jake inherited many qualities from his mother: 'His mum was a great raconteur as well – lots of stories. I think some of Jake's delight in the weak and the frail or the halt and the lame, that comes from her... She had lots and lots of stories, always chatting to neighbours, but in a really nice way. She used to talk to the sparrows she was feeding as if they were real characters.'

Molly made a memorable impression upon friends and neighbours. 'She was a great character and had a fantastic sense of humour,' says Paddy Burke, 'but if she thought anyone had airs and graces, she would cut them down to size. She was definitely a strong character, and she wasn't a lady to be argued with. At church, she would make it very clear if she didn't approve of something. She was a lovely woman, but everyone was a bit nervous of her.' This matches the experience of Elaine Howey: 'Mrs Thackray was very kind and well known in the parish. She used to go to sales of work (knitting and such like) at Sacred Heart Church and bring back things to give away. She was also very proper; she wasn't a prude, but she liked good manners. If you blasphemed or made a joke about the blessed sacrament, she would tell your parents.' Once, she told Elaine and a friend off because they had been to the cinema and marched them straight off to church, insisting that they go to confession immediately. At a time when trips to the nearby picture house were part of the weekly routine for families in Burley Lodge Road, Elaine doesn't remember ever seeing the Thackrays there.

Molly needed a strong personality, given the husband she had and, diminutive though she was, knew how to manage the men in her family. Jake's brother-in-law, Rick Irons, recalls that even when they were adults Molly could control her sons with a look, and how, in her presence, Jake and his brothers would always defer to their mother.

By the age of 50, Molly was suffering badly from arthritis.

Elaine recalls her seeming prematurely old, as she waddled along the street with swollen ankles, her elbows raised, or pushed a pram, laden with the week's washing, up to the municipal wash-house at Kirkstall Road Baths.[14] It is not surprising, given her condition and her faith, that Molly made the pilgrimage to Lourdes in 1952, on one of the regular trips organised by the Catholic diocese, and in later years she made the pilgrimage with Jake.

Molly's Catholic faith was of great importance to her, a source no doubt of strength and comfort. She wasn't overtly pious, the Thackray house wasn't cluttered with religious pictures or statuettes, but she was devout and sincere in her beliefs and attended Mass daily.

Given such devotion, it is hardly surprising her faith had a tremendous and enduring influence on Jake and his brothers. From the outset, Catholicism played a central part in their lives. As Jake laconically put it in an interview, 'Everybody went to Mass. Even the dog went.'[15] Molly ensured that they attended Catholic schools and both Jake and Michael were to entertain thoughts of the priesthood, the pinnacle of aspiration for many a Catholic mother. Although Jake did not pursue the idea, Michael was a member of a religious order for several years.[16] Pleasing Molly must surely have been part of their motivation.

When Jake was seven, he was confirmed, taking Joseph as his saint's name and receiving first communion at St Joseph's Church in Pudsey, where he also served as an altar boy. Fifty years later, when writing a weekly column for the *Catholic Herald*, he devoted one article to a photo of himself and his brothers taking part in a procession at St Joseph's, to celebrate Victory in Europe Day in May 1945. He paints an amusing and vivid picture of the nature of church life at the time:

> John Philip Jake Thackray is the little 'un in the white shirt
> and black trousers holding his candle and just about to turn
> the corner of the street, and Mary Shaw, with whom he is

having a torrid affair, is the third Child of Mary from the back, in white veil and frock, top left. It never came to anything...

...At St Joseph's we were procession crazy. Any excuse and we were out stomping the streets of our town with best clothes and candles, singing our hymns, sometimes with a silver band and massed thurible swingers with boat bearers and their stocks of incense.

Easter Sunday, of course, and the Whitsuntide Walk. Corpus Christi, Remembrance Sunday to the war memorial and Christmas Eve to the town crib before Midnight Mass. St Joseph's Day was a big religious binge with a picnic on the school meadows and as I remember some country dancing and a bar which opened after the sermon.

I am not inventing this. We were always processing, tramping up and down streets proclaiming our faith and sometimes beating drums. I loved it then, as a little 'un, but whether or not it was a good idea I am not so sure now.

By the time Jake reached the age of nine or ten, his involvement in Catholic-run activities extended far beyond church services and processions, and began to take up most of his weekends. By this time his brother Michael was a novice in the Order of the Cross and Passion and was training at Myddelton Lodge, a sixteenth-century hall near Ilkley. The Lodge also served as a weekend retreat for Catholic men, and young Catholic boys – many of them the brothers of novices – were recruited to help out, doubtless partly in the hope of nurturing them in their Catholic faith. Jake became one of these helpers, along with Vince Dobson and another friend, Brian Rankin, who would eventually become a priest.

Most weekends, therefore, Jake, Vince and Brian would catch the bus to Ilkley on Friday evening or Saturday afternoon and stay over until Sunday, sleeping in the Lodge's dormitory. Their duties included serving at table, working in the kitchens and gardening, and Jake particularly enjoyed helping out on the Lodge's farm. In addition, he served as an altar boy at the

6.30am Mass in the chapel. These early morning services were made more entertaining by Brother Dominic, the Order's chief recruiter, a legendary character who would irreverently imitate the sound of farts on his hand. Jake liked him a great deal.

Domestic and religious duties out of the way, Jake relished the company and freedom that these weekends offered in an environment a world away from the cramped terraces of Kirkstall and his solitary existence in a sombre home. He and his friends ran wild in the woods, built dens, climbed trees, played in barns, went apple scrumping and swam in the river Wharfe. There were games of football and cricket with the novices, and evenings would be spent around an open log fire, telling ghost stories and daring each other to make midnight visits to the spooky sepulchre on the hillside nearby. The spirit of *Just William* was strong.

For Jake, an added bonus was that he had the chance to play a musical instrument. 'When Jake got there at the weekend,' recalls Vince, 'he often went straight to the old, out-of-tune piano. He loved to learn to pick out a tune with one finger.' First, small beginnings, perhaps.

Vince remembers Jake being full of fun, but he was also struck by his unusual way of talking and the fact that, despite being a year his junior, he had views on many subjects which seemed advanced for a boy of ten or eleven. Jake told him about his mother's hard working life, and he seems to have been politically aware at a young age. 'I always sensed a strong socialistic leaning which almost verged on cynicism at times,' says Vince. 'Jake seemed to have early opinions that I certainly didn't have. He was perhaps a bit cynical of anyone who had money. I seem to recall that when we used to walk up to Myddelton Lodge, we'd walk through some really exclusive areas... roads full of large, detached houses. I don't know whether he was in awe of them, or whether he was critical of them. But he certainly gave things like that some thought.'

Molly's strong faith set a clear example for her youngest son.

Jake remained an altar boy until he went to university at the age of 19 and, when he returned to Leeds to teach, he once more accompanied her to Mass. Having spent his childhood immersed in Catholic ritual and communities, he would remain a practising Catholic for the rest of his life. As he would jokingly declare to singer-songwriter John D Loudermilk in 1976, 'I turn up for training every Sunday morning'.

There seems to have been a simple sincerity to Jake's faith. His brother-in-law Rick was struck by his joy at Easter, when he would declare, without flippancy: 'It's Easter! Hooray!' Regular attendance at Mass was very important to him, and on visits to his Anglican in-laws he would head off on his own to church, saying he was getting a 'take-away Catholic'. On tour as a professional musician, he would note in his gig diary which churches he attended, and was determined to attend early morning Mass on Sunday, even if he had been up until the early hours after a concert on Saturday night.

Important as his faith was to him, Jake was intensely private about it, to the extent that in adult life some close friends were genuinely surprised to discover that he went to church; it was something he seemed to keep completely separate from the rest of his life. For many years he completely avoided discussing his religious beliefs with journalists. However, in the mid-1990s, after he started to write his amusing weekly column for the *Catholic Herald*, he was persuaded to give newspaper and television interviews on the subject. His defensiveness and discomfort at having his faith put into the spotlight were obvious: 'It really is rather difficult talking about one's beliefs. It's such a bloody private thing... I still go to church as often as I can, and I love it. I go to church because of the other people who go. When I see their faith, and their sheer, unmitigated virtue – I know that sounds crummy – then I am reinforced in my own belief. Day by day in my daily life, I meet lots of people and I can actually see God in their lives, and I say to myself, this God thing, there must be something in it.'[17]

As well as the sense of community, Jake was attracted by the nature of Catholic worship, stating, 'I love the ritual and I love the performance of having to get there and say prayers and all that.' Involvement in so much highly ritualised, procedural activity from a young age seems to have impacted on other aspects of his life, as well as the lives of his brothers: they all apparently attached tremendous importance to rituals, routines and procedures. Jake would discuss with his wife Sheila the importance of structure in the raising of their children, while in his final years, despite a lifetime's familiarity with church ritual, he wrote obsessively detailed notes to guide him on how to assist the priest at Mass. Oddly, this attention to detail, which extended to precision and perfectionism in his writing, sat cheek by jowl with a chaotic and disorganised approach to other aspects of his life.

In later years, in a rare and illuminating conversation about his faith, Jake told a friend: 'It's my backbone, but it's also my burden.' This burden seems to have included a strong sense of Catholic guilt. When he was challenged in an interview in 1981 to explain why he thought he had been a poor teacher, his answer was telling: 'I am a Roman Catholic, and we have a weekly habit of self-examination and confession. And if you are a skiving teacher, it's an easy enough thing to spot that you are skipping on certain things, that you are doing things badly, that you are skimping, that you are not consistent.'[18]

Strong as Jake's faith was, it wasn't unquestioning, and therefore it seems strange at first sight that he remained in a church which was strongly hierarchical and dogmatic in its teachings. In a television interview in 1995 he put his attitude down to Molly: 'My mother, my mother, believe it or not – this is not a picturesque story, it's a true story – was the best Catholic I've ever known. I mean, I'm not mother-struck, you know. I'm not that sort. But she was such a fine person but also she was a terrific cricket player... and we used to go to church together, and we used to talk a lot, and we used to talk about

God and the church, and she had this thing: she used to say, "Jake, old love, you don't quarrel with God. And you don't quarrel with the cricket umpire. But bloody argue with everybody else." And she always questioned things, and it's a good thing, to question.'[19] Devout as Molly was, she was known to question priests, and even, on occasion, bishops, over the content of their sermons. Jake, it seems, inherited her willingness to challenge, and also her need for the Catholic faith.

When Jake became a songwriter, he wrote several beautiful religious songs. More often than not, however, his writing displayed a decidedly irreverent attitude to religion. In 'The Ballad of Billy Kershaw', 'poor, distracted Catholic' wives rate a humble Yorkshire Lothario's ability to provide sexual healing more highly than Lourdes; in 'Sister Josephine', a burglar hides away from the police in a convent, disguised as a nun, and engages in all manner of outrageous behaviour, including showing 'tenderness' towards the younger nuns; and in 'I Stayed Off Work Today', a swindling bishop tricks a prisoner into drinking holy water to make him 'a proper Christian' and force him to kneel. In 'The Bull', Jake gives powerful expression to his scepticism about the authority of the Church, as he pictures the bull in the pulpit, 'bestride the Holy Lamb' [the crucified Christ], pouring out bullshit. Most irreverent and hilarious of all, however, is 'On Again! On Again!', in which, in response to a husband's prayer that his garrulous wife be struck dumb, the Virgin Mary talks unendingly, leading Jake to sympathise with 'the rest of the family', i.e. the Holy Trinity. When questioned about his approach, Jake would colourfully declare that he felt it was fine for him to take the piss out of God because God took the piss out of him often enough.

Given Molly's faith and her sense of propriety, it is unsurprising that she did not approve of Jake's songs, even if, when he first started writing, she encouraged him and suggested topics. When he became famous, she did nothing to

hide this disapproval from her church-going friends. 'It was
the subject matter she didn't like. She rather disapproved,'
recalls Paddy Burke. 'You see, she was very traditional. For
example, as a Catholic, she wasn't keen on services in English,
and she didn't like lay people being allowed to assist with
Communion; she always insisted on receiving the elements
from the priest.' He was also struck by the fact that Molly rarely
talked about her famous son, but this seemed to Sheila
Thackray to be bound up with her humility: 'She was proud
of him, but when people used to say, "I saw your son on
television last night", she used to say (*assumes a posh voice*), "I
do have three sons". She just wouldn't bask in it.'

Molly remained very down-to-earth to the end of her days,
living out her final years in a high-rise council flat in Leeds.
When she died, Jake felt the loss greatly. However, for all that
he loved and admired her, two of his closest friends in adult
life, Don Burton and Sue Haverly, sensed that he found it hard
to meet her expectations. Don always got the impression that
Jake felt she was hypercritical of him, and Sue thinks that the
career he chose may have been a disappointment to her: 'I got
a feeling that Molly, being of the generation that she was, and
with her background and her Catholicism, probably saw Jake's
occupation as being a bit on the frivolous side really, and
thought that he could really have done much more with his
life.'

Without doubt, his mother's influence on Jake was
profound: she saw to it that he received the education she was
denied, and his faith, values, wit and imagination all owed
much to this remarkable woman. And yet, if he indeed lived
his life believing that he had fallen short of her aspirations,
how great a burden that must have been.

Big Black Gilbert

'I was educated by the Jesuits. I was educated in... I won't
name it because it would, it would embarrass... me...
and the buggers would come and get me...'

– Jake Thackray, 1980

In November 1980, Jake found himself accompanied at one concert by a gifted young jazz guitarist, John Etheridge. Despite having had no time to practise, they both enjoyed the experience and agreed to do it again, only with some preparation this time.

The day spent rehearsing for their next concert was full of laughter and chat, and when John discovered that Jake had gone to a Jesuit school, they began to share experiences. 'We used to compare the beatings we'd had as children, and him describing the terror and fear and the loneliness, and the whole thing that defines you as a child,' recalls John. 'I thought the idea of a Yorkshire Jesuit was wonderful... there's a wonderful tension between things that may have fuelled his humour.'[1]

Given Molly Thackray's commitment to bringing her sons up in her faith, Catholicism was always going to play a central role in Jake's education. Both primary schools he attended were run by the Roman Catholic diocese of Leeds. The Church's influence would have been strong and they would have been

attended almost exclusively by Catholics. In 1942, at the age
of four, he was enrolled at St Joseph's in Pudsey, and in July
1946, following the Thackrays' move to Burley Lodge Road,
he transferred to St Anne's School for Boys, near Leeds'
Catholic Cathedral.[2] It was here that he sat the eleven-plus
exam, gateway to a prized grammar-school education.

Jake would be one of thousands of working-class children
to benefit from the 1944 education reforms that opened doors
previously closed to all but a select few. The new state-funded
secondary system enabled academically able children to attend
grammar schools, regardless of their financial circumstances,
with selection based upon performance in the eleven-plus.
Those set up by local education authorities were free. Privately-
run schools could charge fees, but if parents could not afford
to pay, places might be funded by central or local government
through a direct grant system.

Heads of primary schools were quick to encourage parents
of bright pupils to put them in for the exam, and Molly would
have needed little persuading: she valued education and wanted
the best for her sons. Jake was clever, and for a devout Catholic
the choice of school was obvious – St Michael's College, which
both his brothers had attended. The College was a selective,
direct grant boys' school founded by Jesuits in 1905 to provide
education for the Catholic population of West Yorkshire. The
imposing presence of its buildings on St John's Road, close to
the city centre, was accentuated by its hilltop location. Being
so highly prized, it drew Catholic boys from right across the
county. For Jake, it was but a short, steep walk from home.

Given his parents' limited means after Ernest's retirement,
Jake needed direct-grant funding to attend. To win a 'City
scholarship',[3] as it was known, he not only had to pass the
College's entrance test, but also perform well in the eleven-plus
examination. He did so and in September 1949, at the age of
eleven, joined St Michael's on a free place, along with three
other boys from St Anne's.

'St Michael's had a wonderful mélange of young men from a large range of backgrounds and academic levels,' recalls school friend Vince Dobson, 'and this opened up new ideas, challenges and possibilities to be explored by our inquisitive minds.' The College had high standards and encouraged the boys to excel in all areas, inside and outside the classroom. Pupils were streamed by ability, with a boy's placing in the entrance exam determining which class he joined. The College offered an education from the age of eleven to 18, but with the option for boys to stay on for an additional year in the sixth form ('Scholarship 6th') to prepare for university entrance.

The Jesuit tenet that 'God is to be found in all things', and therefore that all things are worthy of study, resulted in a famously broad and progressive curriculum, and the wide range of subjects studied included Religious Knowledge, French and Latin. This tenet was habitually reinforced in written work. 'Everything you did had to be for the greater glory of God,' said Jake's school friend, Michael Bateson, 'and so on every piece of work you would write A.M.D.G. (Ad Maiorem Dei Gloriam – "to the greater glory of God").' Writing this reminder of the importance of Christian humility became as ingrained as putting the date on work, and Jake would find it a hard habit to break, even in adult life.

In 1949, all the pupils would have been Catholic, and the December edition of *St Michael's Magazine* gives a powerful sense of the strong religious ethos. On the first page are printed those ubiquitous letters, A.M.D.G., and adverts include one recommending that parents should 'ask to see Mr. Malone, the Catholic Optician'. A detailed report on Speech Day, which Jake attended in Leeds Town Hall in November 1949, includes a rousing speech by the College's new Rector (headteacher), Father Doyle, on the virtues of a Catholic education: 'Catholic education is true education, which caters for the whole of man. It is not merely intellectual, but unites as in a single golden pattern the threads of education, intellectual, moral and physical, social and individual, material and spiritual... the splendid training to stern and noble standards which carries man through the tests and trials of this life and into the next.'

In practice, the teaching was strict and focused primarily on imparting knowledge, as Dan Cronin, one of Jake's classmates, recalls: 'At school you did things without question. You weren't encouraged to be questioning. Most of the teachers didn't encourage a critical outlook.' That was a prevailing attitude in schools and society in the post-war era, reflecting how, during wartime, the nation's survival had depended on unquestioning acceptance of – and trust in – authority.

The college magazine records that in 1949 it had 464 pupils taught by eleven priests and 14 lay teachers, of whom three were women. Only nine of 60 boys in the sixth form had stayed on for Scholarship 6th, 'following what is now an enlightened tradition'. The promotion of aspiration is everywhere palpable: that year 'showed a record in the number of University awards - four being gained... six boys were successful in the Civil Service Executive examinations'. St Michael's would grow significantly during Jake's time there, as would the number of boys going on to higher education.

The magazine paints a vivid picture of college life, with reports on a trip to Versailles, dramatic productions, a rambling club, elocution competitions and sporting achievements. The debating society tackled topics such as juvenile delinquency, the reform of spelling and blood sports. However, it apparently 'showed some weakness of judgement in deploring the discovery of America and in denying that children's "Comics" are a bad influence and should be abolished'.

The 1950 edition provides a tantalising glimpse of how young Jake responded to this new environment, when he entered the elocution competition. Overall, the judges report that 'comedy dominated but did not monopolise events, and the opportunity for clear actions as well as speech was not neglected'. Jake's performance is singled out: 'The appeal to bathos was as skilfully made by J. Thackray... whose alarm was false, but whose accent true.' In the event, he was runner-up to his friend, Brian Rankin. The judges' final remarks might be taken as prescient, in terms of Jake's future career: 'In general, contestants avoided monotony, and showed a pleasing sense of rhythm.'

Encouragement to do everything to the greater glory of God was one distinctive feature of college life, the Jesuits' approach to discipline another. 'St Michael's was a forbidding-looking place and had a high standard of education,' says former pupil Geoff Fitchett, 'but the discipline by today's standards was particularly harsh.'

This was an era in which corporal punishment was normal, at home as well as in school. However, Jesuit schools had developed their own unique method of delivering it. The *ferula* ('tolly' to the boys) was a piece of whalebone, 12 to 18 inches long, covered with hard rubber, with a flat surface about two to three inches across. This was administered to the hand in doses of three to 12 strokes. In serious cases the punishment would be 'twice nine' on two hands, but administered on separate days, on account of the hand becoming numb.

Teachers punished misconduct by giving the boy a slip of paper with details of how many strokes he was to get and why. This had to be countersigned by another master, and then the boy had to report within 24 hours to the 'Tolly Office', where the punishment would be administered by one of two discipline masters. 'The tolly was incredibly painful,' recalled Michael Bateson. 'We all hoped that we wouldn't get Father Whittal, nicknamed Bonzo, when we had to go to the Tolly Office. He was enormous. He gave it some stick, did Bonzo.'

The system was intended to be humane, preventing teachers from beating boys in anger, and the requirement for a countersignature theoretically meant that there was an element of peer review. Also, the tolly, being flat, was less likely to cause injury than a cane. However, it was a very cold-blooded system, and the delay between offence and punishment brought with it an agonising psychological element. 'You could receive the tolly for the most trivial thing,' says Geoff Fitchett, 'and the punishment was doubled if you did not go within 24 hours. It gave me nightmares.'

Jake didn't escape the tolly and, at the time, it was simply seen as a normal part of school life. However, in the 1990s, when he wrote a column for the *Yorkshire Post*, he reflected upon corporal punishment and the impact of this treatment upon him. In his rough draft he wrote:

> I went to a flogging school... What this ritual beating did to the Thackray boys when they were young I cannot say unless it was a sort of disdain for pain and humiliation and indifference to those who give orders for the sake of orders and who punish for the sake of punishment ~~and, perhaps, an instinct to take the piss~~.

There may be an element of journalistic hyperbole here, and Jake's classmates might not agree with his characterisation of St Michael's as a 'flogging school'. Nevertheless, the statement, including those eight words he crossed out and removed from the final draft, is revealing. He makes a connection between his treatment at school, his anarchistic leanings and his motivation to write songs like 'The Bull' with its mocking assault on those who lord it over others. Given his experience at the hands of the Jesuits, it is perhaps unsurprising that authority figures in the church would not be safe from his pen.

In concerts, Jake would draw upon his school experiences, taking his audiences on hilarious flights of fancy in his between–songs storytelling, and introducing them to a fictitious Jesuit priest, Big Black Gilbert:

> I was educated in a Jesuit college in the north of England, and there was a man there... you know, as a teacher, he was

outstanding... for... for the method that he discovered. He used to teach children by frightening them, by making them so terrified that they would do anything that he said. He just put the fear of God into everybody. I mean, that was his... that was his trade, that's what they paid him for. He was the Head of the Fear of God Department. His name was Father Harry Gilbert, mainly he was known as Big Black Gilbert... He was filled with rage... It wasn't rage that he was stuffed full with, it was WRATH...[4]

Jake proceeds to paint a wonderfully exaggerated picture of the priest, comically hirsute, stiff with wrath.

In *Jake's Progress*[5], his book of lyrics and stories, we find a similarly evocative and telling picture:

I am a Catholic and when I was ten I was a clever one and got a scholarship to a Jesuit grammar school. Our form master was head of English and he put the fear of God into people. That was his job: fear of God into people. He put a lot into me and, although I've since got rid of some of it, there's still a good bit left. He was a six foot six man with a dark and hairy face.

'In this school, you boys, I am in charge of Finer Feelings,' he bellowed at us. 'This afternoon we have two-and-a-half hours together and you are going to spend it writing literature, LITERATURE! You will write a long composition entitled My Environment. Now, environment you boys is what is ALL around you. Street you live in, house, mam, dad (names and occupations), neighbours (ditto), sisters, brothers, friends...' (He was just a nosey bugger, that's what; he didn't want literature, he wanted information.) Now this essay suited me, for writing it was a way of pretending that I was not at this frightening place but was at my home. My nib was first into the inkwell and away to a racing start. I was first and then second up the aisle for, 'Another piece of foolscap Father please.' 'Good! Good!' he shouted 'Lots of Literature!'

The following week came 'The Handing Back of Essays

with Comments'. He was a man who developed and worked hard on his scorn, flexed it like a bodybuilder does his muscles. And then he used to beat us up with it.

'Stand up Thackray J.,' he roared. 'Full marks for volume (it was an inch thick, my essay), and full marks for imagination. But I wanted the TRUTH! These aren't real people. You've made them up! You've been reading books by Piers Dudgeon and listening to radio plays. These people of yours don't exist.'

I had been living with these people for ten years but if a Jesuit said they didn't exist, they didn't.

Surprisingly, in the summer of 1950, after just one year at St Michael's, Jake left the College. This wasn't in reaction to the tolly, however, and he would return in the sixth form. His life and education now underwent a huge change, as he became a boarder at St David's College, a junior Catholic seminary in North Wales. Evidently, Jake and his mother now thought that he might follow the same path as his brother Michael and train for the priesthood.[6]

What led to this change? Jake may have been inspired by Michael's example, or by those many weekends spent at Myddelton Lodge, in the sociable company of the novices. Perhaps, as was the case for other young Catholics, he was recruited by a priest visiting the parish or his home: this was an era in which priests would 'shoal' good Catholic families into sending their sons to seminaries. Jake wasn't alone in leaving St Michael's for St David's that summer – he was joined by another boy in his year, Michael Fitzpatrick. 'In those days it wasn't unusual for boys educated at Catholic schools to aspire to becoming priests,' says Basil Foot, who became friends with Jake at St David's. Indeed, as seen with Molly, for many Catholic mothers it was one of their dearest wishes to see their son have a calling for the priesthood, and a source of enormous pride. Whatever led to Jake's decision, it would seem that at this time Molly must have felt particularly blessed at the paths being taken by her sons.

St David's was a small seminary for 16 or so boys, housed in Farchynys Hall, near Dolgellau. Nestling in the shadow of the Cader Idris mountain range and a stone's throw from the Mawddach estuary, it was in a beautiful, remote setting. The seminary was run by the Order of the Sacred Heart of Jesus of Bétharram, founded in France in the nineteenth century. 'The seminary was intended to give a decent education to young lads contemplating becoming priests in our Order,' explains Father Austin Hughes, 'but usually less than a quarter ever progressed to the senior seminary for theology.'

Although the Thackrays had limited means, the boarding fees were not an issue, as families were only asked to pay what they could afford. 'If a family could afford very little, then there was no quibble,' says Father Austin. This was because St David's had a wealthy benefactor, the Countess Amy Quarles van Ufford, who lived in Monaco at the Palais du Printemps, in the most exclusive residential district of this most exclusive of principalities. Jake would not forget her generosity, as he would demonstrate one summer, rather unexpectedly, a year after he left St David's.

Jake and Basil Foot did a lot together during the two years Basil was at St David's, exploring the Welsh countryside, climbing Cader Idris and staying with each other's families during the holidays in 1951. 'I don't think Jake and I discussed religious matters unduly,' he says, and perhaps this isn't surprising for two young boys spending so much of their time immersed in a religious environment. However, he remembers that Jake already had a talent for amusing writing: 'He was always very entertaining, even in his young days, with some compositions of his own.'

Living in such a small school community, Jake became friends with boys of all ages. Terry Sheridan, who was three years his senior and would become a priest in the Order, had fond memories of their time together, which included a hitch-hiking trip to France one summer when Jake was 13.[7] The two revelled in the adventure and freedom, despite having little money and no tent. They had to sleep in ditches. This would not be Jake's last such trip, and France would have an enormous impact upon him in the years ahead.

He remained at St David's for four years, sitting 'O' Levels there in 1954. Then, however, he and Michael Fitzpatrick returned to Leeds and joined the sixth form at St Michael's, telling their classmates that St David's had closed. Jake's flirtation with the priesthood was over. We can only imagine how Molly might have felt about this, and whether he had any sense of guilt about her disappointment (real or imagined). Michael Day, who was his friend in the sixth form and at university, believed that he felt under a lot of pressure at home to become a priest, although, with hindsight, is not sure how much of this may have been pressure Jake put on himself. Undoubtedly he had pronounced feelings of personal failure later in his life, and one wonders how much of this was rooted in the idea that he had fallen short in his mother's eyes.

Back in Burley Lodge Road, Jake cut a rather lonely figure to his young neighbour, Elaine Howey, and the other children in the street. Perhaps inevitably, given the years spent at school in Wales, he seemed to have few friends locally, and Elaine also felt sorry for him because he had no siblings at home. She would sometimes see a bookish-looking friend from St Michael's calling at the house, or Jake heading to Burley library at the end of the road with books tucked under his arm.

He soon got involved in college life again. He was a keen and decent footballer, and his efforts for the 3rd XI in the Lower Sixth were praised in its magazine: 'mention must be made of Thackray for his fine work at left half'. The team could boast (A.M.D.G., of course) an impressive goal difference of 48-4 in four matches. Jake was elevated to the 2nd XI the following season, and in Scholarship 6th his elevation in the high jump (clearing an impressive five feet) won him first place on Sports Day. He also took the plunge in swimming galas.

He likewise made his presence felt in lunchtime games on the playground, as Michael Bateson recalled: 'There was a regular football competition called "Scratch 8". Teams of eight players, each led by a sixth-former, who would pick his team from other forms. These games were incredibly hard fought. Jake had very big feet which you tried to stay clear of.' Michael also ruefully remembered boxing with him in the ring in the school attic: 'Jake gave me a real towelling that day.' This would not be the last time Jake donned boxing gloves against a friend – they would reappear at university.

He enjoyed his 'A' Level subjects – English, History and French – and, with his love of reading, was put in charge of the college library. He flourished academically, and in December 1955 achieved a Distinction in his Higher Certificate in Religious Knowledge, which focused on Catholic doctrine. Although the priesthood was not for him, in December 1956 he joined the College's devotional fraternity, the Sodality of Our Lady, committing him to weekly worship. (It is not known whether his commitment extended to confession in the college chapel. Teenage boys would line up each week to confess to the adolescent habit of 'self-abuse', and if two priests were on duty, the more lenient one would always prove the more popular, resulting in a long queue snaking outside his confessional. The boys came up with their own vulgar nickname for this queue.)

For all his success academically, Jake enjoyed mischief when the opportunity presented itself. He and Michael Day were taught Latin for university entrance by the Rector in his study and, when Father Doyle had to leave the room to take phone calls, they would play 'pass the biretta' with his priest's hat, the challenge being not to get caught with it when he returned.

Jake's creativity and sense of fun could brighten the most dismal situation. In 1955 he got a holiday job in the Hygienic Laundry in Armley, working with Tony Adamthwaite, another St Michael's pupil. Conditions in the hot, steamy laundry were oppressive, not least because the supervisor pounced upon any sign of slackness, including toilet breaks. 'It was the nearest I've come to a slave labour camp,' says Tony. The boys were paired up, either end of a sheet-pressing machine, and because it was too noisy to talk, Jake came up with a word-association game to pass the time: 'He said, "Look, let's get through this like this. I'll come up with a song title or movie and you connect with one of the words in the title and bring up something else."' And so they played hours of this word-association tennis, taking turns to holler song and film titles to each other across the steaming sheets. 'The time went quicker because of that,' recalls Tony. 'The take-away memory it gave me was of this really warm personality, the sense of humour, the quick wit, the verbal nimbleness.' Heaven knows what the supervisor made of it all.

One of his closest friends in sixth form was Don Stoker. 'Jake was a quiet lad really, and rather solitary,' says Don. 'He didn't stand out, but he was obviously thinking and reacting. There was a gold mine there, but you had to dig for it.' He was compassionate, with a strong sense of justice; once, when Don impulsively kicked another pupil, he was immediately filled with remorse because he realised that Jake would not have approved. This matches the experience of Chris Jackson, a younger pupil who often walked home with Jake from school: 'In contrast with the way some sixth-formers treated younger boys, Jake was always so nice, so polite, so diffident.'

Jake and Don spent a lot of time together. Like many boys of his age, Jake was an under-age drinker, and he would often head to the pub for at least a couple of pints after school football matches on Saturdays. He had one clear advantage over Don: taller and with more impressive stubble on his face, he found it much easier to get served.

Jake's original and quirky sense of humour was already in evidence. Don recalls him drawing amusing cartoon caricatures of two Roman poets on the blackboard: for shy, bald Horace, he put the outline of the back of a head, with a single strand of hair, while he gave Ovid a comically long nose and wrote under it 'banished for writing racy poems!'.[8] It was also clear that Jake could hold an audience. In a recitation competition he gave a skilful and arresting performance of a poem describing a man taking out a razor. Through his dramatic delivery he lured the audience into thinking that the man was about to cut his throat before, with impressive comic timing, breaking the tension and revealing that he was simply preparing to shave.

His creativity and skill in performance also found an outlet in debating competitions, where he displayed a talent for amusing and unusual lines of argument, as his contribution to the College's Prize Debate in July 1956 indicates. The motion was 'This house deplores the present and would welcome a return to the past,' and Jake spoke on behalf of the Government in favour of the motion:

> J. Thackray (Limehouse) said that the Government were not escapists, indeed they were realists. We were then treated to a German story (straight from the scroll, and in English) of three men in a meadow who were chased by a ferocious bull. The brave but foolish man said, 'Come and get me'; the stupid man said, 'What bull?'; and the brave and wise man said nothing but pressed apace to yonder gate. We must not hide our faces in the sand like ostriches but must use our little grey cells to realise what the present and the future hold for us. Hence, not being idiots, we must return to the past. The Hon. Member then referred to a 'musical evening' (sic) which he had recently attended, when the band played on and on. A thought occurred to him at the time: Where will it all end? We have progressed from the crystal set to the wireless, thence to the 'Telly'; in the space of a few short years we shall have in our front rooms the 'feelies' and the 'smellies'. Soon we shall be engaged in a tooth-and-nail fight with weird little green men from Mars. For the future, then, we have but apprehension; for the present, disappointment; for the past – can it be worse?

He was also writing poetry. He had long loved it, as he later explained: 'When you are eleven or so, you begin to have heroes. Mine were all poets.'[9] His surviving poems are mostly serious, and there is no sign of the original voice he was to find in his songs, nor his interest in human foibles, storytelling and character. However, they do show a talented young man using language with great care and control, as his earliest surviving poem, written when he was 18, reveals:

Love Passing

We deeply our own selves engrave:
In a stone on whose grey face
Is cut the lowly cipher
Of our passing grace.
We mark, as the customary tumours grow,
The lineaments collapse; even below,
The bone crumbles in our dissolving bed;
At once, we are the un-born, living, and long-dead.
Unwrap the winding bandage, and, unsealed,
The balm escapes; exposure works at once
The scars' retraction. Such sores
As the process made, it healed.
We wound, we bleed, and pass, but
In the congealing, mark; we, still, save
Our brief contracting of the human frame
From womb to grave.

As Don Stoker said, he was obviously thinking and reacting. There was a gold mine there.

During these years, Jake shared many adventures with Don that reveal how independent-minded and, at times, reckless he could be. They hitch-hiked, starting, at Jake's suggestion, with practice trips to Blackpool and London. They each had their own technique: Jake's theory was that a hang-dog look would be more effective in getting lifts, while Don used more positive body language and felt vindicated by his greater success.

Sometimes, Don was struck by Jake's odd priorities and lack of concern for himself. On more than one occasion he ran out of money many miles from home, and Don was astonished to learn that he would spend the last of his cash on a packet of Woodbine cigarettes, rather than anything useful.

In the summer of 1955, at the end of the lower sixth, their love of travel and literature led them to undertake their greatest adventure. They both enjoyed the humour of Catholic writer Hilaire Belloc and were inspired by his account of his pilgrimage in *The Path to Rome*, which included walking across the Alps. They decided to emulate him and, leaving Leeds with £20 each in their pockets, spent three weeks hitch-hiking to Rome.

This trip was a tremendous experience. The chances of any driver offering a lift to two teenage boys with large rucksacks was small, so they travelled separately and arranged to meet up every couple of days. Inevitably, this was an uncertain business, and on some occasions the arrangements they made misfired.

After crossing the Channel they booked into a modest charity-run hostel in Calais on a Saturday night. However, in their enthusiasm to make the most of Sunday by attending early morning Mass, they annoyed the warden, who objected to being awoken so early. Feeling they had blotted their copybook, they avoided the hostel on their return journey.

They encountered many perils. Lacking a tent, they had to sleep where best they could, in doorways, ditches, haystacks or under bridges, and as their sleeping bags were thin, the nights were cold. Whenever possible, they slept in the countryside to avoid attracting attention. Jake ended up in a fight with a man on a motorbike, and both boys were solicited, although it is testimony to their innocence that neither understood what was happening.

At Jake's suggestion they travelled to Rome via Monaco on the Côte d'Azur, where he wanted to visit Countess Quarles van Ufford, the benefactor whose generosity had enabled him to attend St David's. Her house was high up on the exclusive

Palais du Printemps, overlooking the famous Corniche in
Monte Carlo, with wonderful views of the sea. After days of
roughing it, Jake and Don were eagerly anticipating a stay in
such luxurious and comfortable surroundings, but they never
got past the door. To their dismay the doorkeeper informed
them that the Countess was away on holiday, and they had to
trudge back down the hill disconsolately to find somewhere
altogether humbler to sleep.

The two friends briefly managed to travel together as they
entered Italy. Don had hitched a ride with gypsies, travelling
slowly in a clapped-out truck. By chance, they passed Jake
walking along. Using his limited Italian, Don managed to
persuade the driver to stop and pick Jake up as well.

Arriving separately in Rome, it took a little time for them
to get back together, so Jake spent his first night there alone,
bedding down in the colonnades of the Vatican. However, at
2.00 a.m. he was discovered by the Pontifical Swiss Guard and
moved on. When he and Don finally met up, they stayed in a
pensione, enjoying the rare luxury of a night in proper beds.

While in Rome, they saw people swimming in the Tiber
and decided to join in, leaving their clothes on the river bank.
However, a crowd soon gathered and a policeman called them
out, as some street urchins had been spotted stealing Jake's
money. Flanked by the crowd, Jake and Don went off with the
policeman in search of the culprits. The policeman clearly
knew his patch: he took them to a dingy house, knocked on
the door and spoke to a man who duly hauled out the guilty
child and started walloping him. Jake shouted, 'You don't have
to kill him! Just give me my money!'

From Rome, Jake and Don continued south to Lake
Albano, where there was an English seminary at which they
hoped to stay. However, as in Monte Carlo, no success: the
Rector had absolutely no interest in accommodating them.
Instead, he directed them to visit the Pope's summer residence,
Castel Gandolfo, which was nearby, and to hear Pius XII's daily

afternoon address. They did so. Molly would have been delighted.

On the return leg of the journey they travelled through Germany, gave the hostel in Calais the widest of berths and caught a ferry at Boulogne, arriving back in England with scarcely a penny to their name. This trip through a continent still rebuilding after the war had been extraordinary, truly the trip of a lifetime. As Don recalls, travelling across Europe in this way, 'you saw the best of people and the worst of people'.

Despite all the time they spent together, Jake remained an enigma to Don: 'He was always a mystery man. He was funny, but he was also shy.' Don's sister took a shine to Jake, and it is revealing that Don was relieved nothing came of it: 'You'd never get your head round Jake. He was so independent, there was such a lot going on inside... I couldn't see Jake being a husband, first and foremost; I thought he would have something else to do.'

In 1956, Jake entered the Scholarship 6th and prepared his university application. The number of boys going to university increased massively during his time at St Michael's, from four in 1949 to 32 in 1957, one of whom would be Jake. The son of the brush maker and policeman was going far.

Jake applied to read English at Hatfield College at the University of Durham. Central to his decision was that the course included the study of both language and literature. He summarised his interests in the personal statement submitted with his application. His 'strong interest in music' came first, but it was 'purely non-technical': he played the piano for his own amusement, enjoyed listening to a variety of classical music and found 'the early forms of jazz interesting'. Reading was his other passion: 'I take great pleasure in contemporary novels:- Evelyn Waugh, Ronald Knox, E. Forster and H.E. Bates and find the American humorists Thurber, Runyon and Benchley delightful: Jane Austen and Dickens I value highly. Keats, Donne and Dylan Thomas are in the main my poetical preferences.' His reading of French literature includes Flaubert, Victor Hugo, Paul Verlaine and Merimée. The impression given is of a serious-minded and well-read young man.

Early in 1957 he travelled to Durham to sit the University's entrance examination papers and attend an interview, which required an overnight stay. In the comfortable surroundings of Hatfield College he shared a room with Eddie Stringer, whom he made a point of telling that he was Roman Catholic. They were both offered a place and would become good friends over the course of the next three years.

Jake finished his academic career at St Michael's in fine fashion. He gained three 'A' levels, achieving distinctions in English Literature and History, and was awarded a College prize for his performance. More importantly, he gained a Leeds Senior City scholarship to fund his university place.

St Michael's had given Jake a good education, enabling him to study at one of the country's best universities, and he was grateful. Nevertheless, years later he expressed candidly his reservations about the part played by religion in his school life:

> If you are Catholic and you have been brought up by the Jesuits, then there must come a point in your life where you are going to say to yourself 'that isn't good enough', or else you are quite content with it, and you stay being Catholic... I've stayed on being Catholic because I quite like it, it suits me, you know... I wouldn't send my children to a Jesuit school. I wouldn't send my children to a Catholic school. I'd prefer for them to go to their own school, and then if I'm any good as a Catholic, they'll spot what's going on. They'll say, 'He's alright. We'll try a dabble at that.'[10]

In their schooling, he had no desire for his children to follow in his footsteps. University would be a very different matter.

What is a Prof?

'Mother said we talked a little differently somehow,
And Father said we dressed a little strange,
A little strange.
And Kirkstall Road and Woodhouse Lane
Were well behind us now;
We'd gone and left them,
How they must be changed.'
– Jake Thackray, 'Those are the Days'

Jake wrote 'Those are the Days' in 1975 for *A Century of Leeds,* a Yorkshire Television programme about Leeds University.[1] This song, which was never released on record, starts by offering a wistful view of student life:

Those are the days we remember best,
Now we grow older.
Those were the days of happiness,
Made of gold.

It then goes through the stages of an undergraduate's life, starting with the farewells at home:

Mother shut the suitcase,
Father stood and said goodbye,
We went and took a room in Chapeltown, Chapeltown.
And we were lost and we were anxious,
We were eager, we were shy;
It took some little time to settle down, settle down.

Jake sings of academic challenge and intellectual awakening, the debates, the flirting, the fallings-out and the growing up, and a running joke is that these rites of passage all take place in pubs:

And we were desperately serious,
We read throughout the night,
We argued all the way down Kirkstall Lane, Kirkstall Lane.
And we beat our fists, we closed our eyes,
We clutched our foreheads tight,
We understood, we were aflame, were aflame.
So it was Shelley in The Skyrack,
Schopenhauer in The Ship;
It was Kafka in The Fenton,
It was murder in The Whip.
And in The Eldon it was Kierkegaard,
And Wittgenstein, of course,
But it was Molly, Molly, Molly in The Packhorse.[2]

It is a well-observed, amusing and poignant piece of writing which combines Jake's intimate knowledge of Leeds boozers with an understanding of the university experience that comes from his three years at Durham. The full lyrics of this and all the other previously unpublished songs are in the appendix.

Jake went up to Durham in October 1957 and he loved his time there. Indeed, when his eldest son Sam was considering his university choices, he encouraged him to apply there.

Looking at its location, it is not hard to see why. England's third-oldest university has a dramatic and beautiful setting, with its colleges nestling in the shadow of Durham Cathedral, at the heart of a medieval city, on a hill encircled by the river Wear. In the 1950s, the contrast with industrial Leeds and the terraced streets of Kirkstall could hardly have been greater.

In addition, Jake's college, Hatfield, was a small, highly sociable community. It was single-sex, as were all the colleges at this time. He was one of only 49 'freshers' in 1957 and, as almost everyone lived in college during their first and third years, they got to know each other well; indeed, even when they went into digs in the second year, they still ate in college. Consequently, for three years he spent his days with a settled group of friends: Eddie Stringer (his room-mate at interview), Malcolm Yorke and Bob Graham, both studying English with him, and several classicists including Michael Day, his class-mate from St Michael's. For a time the group also included a mature overseas student, Zoltan Soos, who'd fled to England after suppression of the Hungarian Uprising in 1956. Alongside their studies they would spend the next three years engaging in the activities Jake described so colourfully in 'Those are the Days', with beer-drinking and getting better acquainted with members of the opposite sex high on the agenda.

Being in such a place, in such company, would have been a liberating experience for Jake. University life was a far cry from Burley Lodge Road, where he had lived, effectively as an only child, for so many years. Initially, Eddie Stringer found him rather quiet and introspective, but he soon developed a great respect for him: 'He was clearly very intelligent, and if you had a different opinion to him, he wasn't aggressive in his arguments; he didn't batter you with his points.'

By the time Jake entered his second year, he was regarded by some freshers in the year below as a bit of a character, and someone to whom people gravitated. Certainly, he had a reckless streak which Malcolm Yorke, who became one of his closest friends, found appealing: 'In some ways he was very sophisticated, but in others he wasn't. He was a dangerous man.

That was what was attractive about him, really. I felt that, with him, you were on the edge sometimes.'

Jake's behaviour could be studiously respectable, as when he joined the library committee in his first year. However, he undoubtedly enjoyed taking risks, as when, with Malcolm in tow, he successfully blagged his way backstage at the university theatre, claiming to be supervising a set of timpani. He also had a love of mischief. One night in college, he sneaked into the communal toilets on his staircase, entered every cubicle in turn, locked the door from the inside and climbed out. Next morning he enjoyed watching the chaos his prank caused.

Hatfield had a reputation for being rather 'hearty' and 'macho' in character, which was partly down to the fact that many of its students came from public schools. If Jake felt uncomfortable about this, he didn't show it. Indeed, despite the great differences in their backgrounds, he got on well with his first-year room-mate, Bob Graham, who had been privately educated. 'Hatfield was a melting pot in which you met people from very different backgrounds,' says Eddie Stringer. 'I don't think that there were any class issues but, in comparison with Leeds, it must have felt very middle-class.' Malcolm who, like Jake, came from a working-class family, thinks that the College's ethos suited them, even if they might both have been somewhat overawed by the environment. What may have made Jake feel more comfortable was being in the company of many former St Michael's pupils.[3]

An indication of the exuberant culture is given by the grandly-titled Quinquereme, a Hatfield initiation ceremony. In a distinctly primeval and savage tradition, freshers were organised into boats and sent off to do battle on the river, armed with buckets of offal and other unmentionable materials. Jake took part, as did Malcolm, who was soon tipped into the river and had a cockerel's severed head rubbed in his face – a memory not easily forgotten. They got involved with other traditions, too: for Rag Week, they paraded on a float decorated with a display promoting contraception, bearing the provocative strap-line 'Buy me and stop one!'

Jake's life in college would have been positively luxurious in comparison with life at home. He ate his meals in the grand hall (ties and gowns obligatory wear at dinner on weekdays), and had a centrally-heated room and cleaner. The bill for his board and lodgings had to be paid up-front each term, which was just as well. He could be guaranteed to have blown the rest of his grant within a month.[4] With a culture of heavy drinking among students, a lot of money was spent on beer, much of it at a favourite pub, The Shakespeare, close to Hatfield, where ale cost a shilling a pint. As Michael Day recalls, Jake would get 'really grown-up drunk'.

Alongside the drinking and socialising, Jake and Malcolm got involved in one of the university's oldest sports: rowing. Ivan Mansley, who was a cox in the rowing club, remembers it well: 'Someone had the bright idea that, instead of recruiting people who had rowed beforehand, the best way forward was to recruit big blokes and teach them to row. Jake was one of these.' At 6ft 3in, he met the requirements and Ivan had a go at coaching him. At first he rowed in a four, but then teamed up with Tom Wingate in a coxless pair. Jake may not have been a natural oarsman, but he rowed with Tom throughout his time at university. The pair hitch-hiked to compete in a regatta in Leeds, and their training paid off in Jake's final year when they won a cup in a Durham University regatta. Much of the credit must go to Tom, who faced the unenviable challenge of getting Jake out of bed and onto the river for training early on Sunday mornings, following Saturday nights spent in Durham's pubs.

Jake had declared his Catholicism to Eddie Stringer when up for interview, and his faith remained important to him. He attended Mass every week and took very seriously the Catholic tradition of no meat on Fridays, as demonstrated memorably on one occasion. 'We had all been out boozing on Thursday night – six or seven pints was the norm – and Jake had bought a pork pie,' says Malcolm Yorke. 'It was late at night and he began to eat it, but Michael Day, who was equally devout, said to him, "It's gone midnight! You can't eat meat!" Jake promptly threw the pork pie away. I was astonished.'

In their second year Jake and Malcolm moved into digs, initially joining four friends in lodgings at the Bridge Hotel, where they honed a skill that would prove useful the following summer. 'There were six of us, just enough for a darts team,' explains Malcolm, 'so most nights we were downstairs, playing darts against the locals, and Jake and I became very expert.' By Christmas 1958, however, the pub landlord had retired, and so the fledgling team had to move on. Jake, Malcolm and two friends ended up sharing a tiny two-bedroom cottage tucked away in the back garden of another house, in which the owner lived; they could only reach the cottage by walking through their landlord's home. The garden offered a commanding view of Durham bus station, some 30 feet below, at the bottom of a precipitous drop.

Jake got himself into a scrape worthy of the character in his song, 'Scallywag', as Malcolm vividly recalls: 'One Saturday night, the rest of us were in bed, and at about one o'clock Thackray came in, in a hurry, jumped into bed and declared, "I've been here all night, ok? I've been here all night." About half an hour later some policemen came hammering on the door and hauled us all out of bed, saying they wanted to see our shoes. We got up and asked what this was all about, and a policeman said, "We're looking for shoes that are wet. It's raining outside and somebody has climbed up the wall from the bus station. There's been some trouble in town and this person is involved."' Fortunately for Jake, he wasn't identified and the police left.

Malcolm never found out what had happened, but thinks a woman was involved. It seems that Jake had done a runner and, finding the landlord's door locked, in his desperation scaled the wall. 'That was a typical scrape for Jake at that time,' says

Malcolm. This reckless quality was to prove a dangerous attraction for other friends in the years ahead. On another occasion, after a night's drinking and in the depths of winter, Jake, Malcolm and Bob Graham went walking on the frozen Wear. If they had gone through the ice, it would undoubtedly have been the end of them.

In the summer of 1959, Jake and Malcolm hitch-hiked to Stratford to see a legendary season of productions by the Royal Shakespeare Company, featuring Laurence Olivier and Paul Robeson, among others. They stayed for three weeks but, as they were short of cash and needed to save what little they had to buy tickets, they roughed it, sleeping in the bandstand in the park next to the theatre, with newspapers as bedding. Each morning they got up early and washed in the Gents' toilets, before heading over to the box office. They chatted up foreign girls to cadge cups of coffee and, staving off hunger, even resorted to scrumping apples. In their hour of greatest need they put to good use the skill they had honed at the Bridge Hotel, playing darts for pints with the locals. This was a high-risk strategy, however: they knew they couldn't afford to lose.

Although Hatfield was all-male, Jake had plenty of opportunities to meet women at Durham. His love life blossomed, helped greatly by the fact he was no longer a gawky, gangly youth. Women were drawn to him. 'Jake was certainly attractive,' recalls Malcolm. 'Some of the girls I knew said, "You know John [Jake] Thackray? Will you invite him to tea? Will you bring him along?"' Malcolm was also struck by how much Jake was drawn to women: 'He was always falling in love. I remember he fell in love while I was president of the debating society, and Jake and I had a debate. The proposition was "The female of the species is more deadly than the male". I proposed it, and he opposed it. In the debate Jake confessed how in love he was; there were one or two occasions when that happened.' However, any woman in his life had to cope with the fact that his feet stank (a cause of great distress for his poor room-mate,

Bob Graham) and, unusually in his social circle, he smoked.[5]
Malcolm doesn't recall Jake ever having a steady girlfriend.

At Hatfield itself, young women were few and far between,
but there was one, an Italian *au pair*, who looked after the
Master of the College's children. Hatfield's undergraduates
lusted after her, but she remained tantalisingly out of reach. Or
so it seemed at the time. After they left university, Jake revealed
to Malcolm that he would go to Mass with her each week,
following which they would head to his room to enjoy more
earthly pleasures. Malcolm was astonished: 'It seems that, in
Jake's head, he had done his confessions, so his slate was clear
for the week. None of us suspected what was going on, but he
succeeded where no one else had.' In the 1990s, when he wrote
a column for the *Catholic Herald*, he would coyly allude to this
au pair in one of his articles.

For all its importance to him in later years, music played
almost no part in Jake's life at Durham. In a college as hearty
as Hatfield, where sport was dominant, there was little music
on offer, and Malcolm never remembers discussing it with him.
His access to music seems to have been limited to occasional
town hall dances, or hearing classical music at the gramophone
club run by Bob Graham.

There was a lot for Jake to enjoy socially at university, but
he also found his academic work stimulating, undoubtedly
benefitting from the company of his fellow English students,
Malcolm and Bob. The three northerners hit it off from the
outset. Bright and competitive, they sparred intellectually.
Indeed, Malcolm and Jake literally sparred on one occasion:
Malcolm boxed for the university, and one day Jake decided to
take him on. Neither would give any quarter, and the fight only
ended when they both collapsed, exhausted.

Jake also benefitted from excellent teaching. Alongside
lectures, his tutorials could be intense because they involved
only two students at a time: the ill-prepared had nowhere to
hide. The most distinguished of his teachers was Professor

Charles Randolph Quirk, who taught him Anglo-Saxon, among other subjects. He was a formidable, highly-respected man, exceptionally dedicated, even being known to work on Christmas Day. By 1959 he had published books on Anglo-Saxon poetry, grammar and Dickens, on his way to becoming one of the world's leading authorities on the English language. Eventually, he would be honoured with a peerage.

Quirk undoubtedly had a real impact on Jake, as is clear from the fact that Randolph Quirke (*sic*) features as a character (along with the Italian *au pair*) in an amusing *Catholic Herald* article written in 1994. He paints a picture of his interrogation by Quirke in a tutorial. As with so much of his writing, fantasy abounds, but his regard for his teacher seems authentic.

'So why, Mr Thackray,' said Professor Randolph Quirke, 'do you go to the Catholic Mass every Sunday and sometimes on a weekday when you hold the views you have just claimed you hold?'

This was in November 1960, at a tutorial in a house off Saddler Street, Durham, at about 11:30 on a Thursday morning.

I was 17 and the Prof was 35. He was wise and slick and he knew it and I was young and slickless and he knew that too.

He was the Professor of Linguistics and never stopped asking us cocky boys from the North Riding what we meant when we used words. He nagged us into language, he nagged us into a kind of honesty. He was a wonderful teacher, Randy Quirky, nag, nag, nag.

I had just delivered to him my definitive essay on Jonathan Swift and his superlative vision of the worthlessness of the human species, the dodgy God who purportedly created it, and the looniness of the religionisers who say they know how to save it. It was pretty hot stuff.

'I cannot but conclude,' I intoned, 'the bulk of your natives to be the most pernicious race of little odious vermin that nature ever suffered to crawl upon the surface of the earth.'

'Gosh, Mr Thackray!' said the Prof, who had heard everything before, 'Who'd have thought it?'

'And furthermore, Swift later remarks,' I was on high intone mode by now 'that we have just enough religion in us to make us hate but not enough to make us love one another.'

The wise man of Saddler Street sat back and lit a fag. 'Yes, Jake lad. Swifty got it on the button. I'd love to have met him, wouldn't you? Young Thackers, you are a young Yorkshire prat but you could not have come across a finer moral sense or an honester, savager, peculiarer, Englisher prose style than that of Dean Jonathan Swift who was an Irishman.

'I think I admire your admiration for the great man. But, but, but. Why do you go to this Mass thing? Come on, pal. You can tell me. Go for it, baby.'

Thus spake the Professor of Linguistics. So I went for it.

I sat back and I lit a fag up too.

If a professor up in Durham could do it so could a young prat from the Ridings. There was a first time for everything.

If he could tell the truth and own up and ask awkward nagging questions, well, bugger me, so could I. Seventeen is the best time to learn how to own up and Professor Randolph Quirke was the best teacher I could have had for the job.

'Sir. I started going to Mass because my mummy and daddy and my brothers went.

'So did my gran and my aunties and all my cousins. We all went. We used to take the dog too.

'I liked the Latin and the plain chant and the costumery and mysteriousness of it all.

'I was the altar boy at the seven o'clock mass before school and was given breakfast by the housekeeper and loved the smell of priestliness mingled with ground coffee and the quietness and stillness of the morning.

'Even now these are among the reasons why I go.

'A more recent reason is that the only other Catholic in my college is Luciana the Master's Italian maid and this is the only occasion when I get to be with her and sometimes touch her.

'At the Jesuit school in Leeds I was taught the Four Proofs

of the Existence of God and even at 12 I didn't believe any of them although I passed the exams on the subject.

'But these days, Professor, I do believe in God and although I do not know exactly why, yet, I think that contrary to any evidence of expectation, I one day shall.

'I do believe, Sir, in the people who believe in God. Including my mummy and daddy and the aunties and the priests and the cardinals, well, some of them, and especially the Italian maid who I believe has got the same hots for me as I am getting for her.

'I believe in a God who gives us the hots, the moral senses and brains, and the indignations, and the capacity to raise our eyebrows, both in church and at tutorials; who gave us professors of language and above all who gave us Jonathan Swifts. Give us another fag.'

In his final year Jake wrote an essay on the language of Swift. The ending gives an insight into his academic confidence and a flavour of his style:

Mankind – and especially the 18th century variety – was for Swift an anomaly. Animal Capax Rationalis. The 'vous-autres' – Pope Steele, later Johnson and even bland Addison entertained a certain animus towards it; a kind of lurking angst that becomes a shriek in Blake and a shudder in Voltaire; their language reveals it – the Augustan language; superbly poised, as Empson says, 'on one leg'! A study of Swift's linguistic instinct would reveal I think a much more composed attitude.

Quirk's feedback is revealing and amusing:

Something too French about this? Well up to standard have no fear!! You give the impression of a man who has all the exits covered with a machine gun. Very comprehensive, very well documented. Usual journalistic bits but you're learning the jargon eh? I wonder should you be in the Lang. Opt. or the Sociology Dept.

And then there are the handwritten scribblings in the margins of the essay, added after it had been returned. These are less erudite but just as revealing. Beneath the title Jake added:

Or ('From one Creeping Jesus to another').

This looks like an amusing dig at himself, and possibly Quirk: a 'creeping Jesus' is someone who makes an ostentatious display of their Catholic faith.

Halfway down the page, Jake has drawn amusing cartoon heads of Troilus and Cressida. Cressida says, 'Oh Gentle Troilus, the nightingale would rather eat his heart than sing of us', to which a bemused Troilus responds simply '?'.

Someone else has left two messages for him:

Nag's Head 5.30 – after training? Bring Beatrice!! I can lend you 5 till next term.

Off to Margaret's for dinner. See you at Boathouse – 1.30...?

So here we have a window on Jake's world at Durham: sharp intellectual engagement, quirky humour, self-deprecating Catholic irreverence, short of cash, and the prospect of a trip to the pub with a girl in tow.

By the time he finished his degree he had gained a strong understanding of English language and literature, and some knowledge of Logic and Philosophy. The forbidding titles of his final papers show the range of his studies: History of the English Language, History and Principles of English Philology, Germanic and Old English Antiquities, Translation and Criticism of Old and Middle English texts, Shakespeare, Literature to 1475 and Literature 1475-1880. Jake took all of this in his stride and graduated in July 1960 with a 2.1 B.A. honours degree. Graduation day, with all its tradition and pomp, was celebrated in the grand surroundings of the Great Hall of Durham Castle, and a photo was snapped of Jake, Malcolm and Bob fooling about, posing as statues on the wall by Hatfield boathouse.

What was the impact of his studies upon Jake? He certainly believed that his time at Durham had been important to his development as a writer, as he impressed upon Ian Gliddon, who became a friend in the 1960s: 'He loved writing, and it was clear that this was the reason he had chosen to go to Durham. I remember he was quite verbose about it being a place where you "do" literature rather than simply studying it.' There is a puzzle here, however, because the English course involved no creative writing, and there is no evidence that Jake did any at university. Malcolm Yorke is not surprised: studying Shakespeare and Donne all day could be oppressive, stifling rather than stimulating creativity. Indeed, Jake told another friend that studying English made it difficult for him even to read for pleasure, because the instinct to analyse everything got in the way. Malcolm wrote pieces for the student newspaper, but was never aware of Jake doing so. Tantalisingly, the paper does contain some anonymous prose contributions whose humour is similar to Jake's but, if they were his work, it would be typical of him not to tell anyone.

Along with 'Those are the Days', we get some sense of what university meant for him through two spoken-word pieces, written and performed on radio in Leeds in 1966. Both were published in *The Listener*. These complementary pen portraits show his flair with language and ability to paint evocative and amusing pictures.

The first answers the question: 'What is a Prof?'

A Prof is crowded lecture rooms on pale winter mornings; he is a scratch of pens, a strain of necks, a drone of seminars, a sweat of finals; scholarship in a baggy suit, knowledge smiling into sherry glasses, research with a pair of rose clippers in his hands; erudition glancing round the town hall toilets after classical concerts. A Prof likes: the Hotel Metropole, his own slim publications, boy scouts, God, the British Council, long and finely chiselled fingers, the syllabus. A Prof does not like: first year students, the Bricklayers' Arms, meaningful conversations, 'University Challenge', second year students, Nobel prizes, Wayne Fontana and the Mindbenders, someone else's fat publications, third year students, visiting lecturers, American universities, you, me, and especially, *you*!

A Prof is a four-letter word on a four-figure salary. A Prof prefers protégés, proselytes, prostrations, politeness, and power. A Prof always professes, but is always very good at pleasing, persuading, posturing, patronizing, pandering, prevaricating, pinching, and pontificating. A Prof has no known means of communication with anybody else, or for that matter with himself. In a five-minute interview he can render you helpless with sleep, awaken your blood lust, rock you half silly with the giggles, forget what he was talking about, forget what you were talking about and that anybody anywhere else has still got anything to talk about.

Nevertheless, at the end of your course when you are tired, embittered, wasted, you will know that it was worth every burbling, bumbling, blathering, humbugging minute of it, for he will come to you with your letters of credit and your testimonials, and he will clutch at your sleeve and his eyes will shine and he will whisper 'what was your name?'

The second is 'What is a student?'

A student is Eternal Youth feeding himself on baked-beans and spot-questions, 'Gaudeamus Igitur' on the back seat of the Rugby coach; High Spirits calling out merry things in the local cinema; a seeker of Wisdom, hoping to goodness that he can get his tenth pint away before they all realize (pardon) that he really only contains four. He is a duffle-coatful of japes, a toggle of hops, a snood of parties.

A student mostly calls himself – Mike, Rick, Dick, Nick,

Jake, Jed, or Guss, and very often Gord. But you can always recognize him – B.A.

A student likes (but kids on he could not give a monkey's for): *Coronation Street*, academic dress, the Penguin Guides, *Reveille*, Acker Bilk, his degree, Blackpool, the Union Committee, his references, Graduation Day, his Mum. A student does not like (but swears that he is only truly happy when contemplating): the look of his future, black coffee, the second stack, ten pints of beer, *Last Year in Marienbad*, the professor's special subject, Dusty Springfield, the look of your future. He has a very bad reputation with the people in whose town he lives, but he is not the free-wheeling, self-inflating lunatic he makes out to be. A student is O.K. And when you are scrubbing words off your pavements, getting down your motor cars from your steeples, reassembling your war memorial, looking for your Lady Mayoress and your lady eagle, and shuddering your way through *The Rag Magazine* at half a crown a stifled sob, remember, yes remember, the Good Cause behind it – because he can't.

But don't despair of him. Forget all the posturing, the bluster, the crawling, the finger, the big deal, all the pussy-footing flim-flam, because one day, one day he will pack his gay little motor car with his bull-fight posters, his Union newspaper clippings and Union Jack ash-trays, his witty collection of municipal road signs and ladies' step-ins, and Vietnam sit-downs, plus his books, and he will return to you, and creep into your arms, and sigh, 'Well, I can always teach.'

'Well, I can always teach.' So goes the orthodoxy, and when Jake left Durham in July 1960, he followed it. But his route would be a distinctly unorthodox one, its influence enormous.

Celebrating graduation with Bob Graham and Malcolm Yorke, July 1960.
Thackray family

Mether

The French Connection

'All these new things, all these new words going into the brain and the diary of a young tyke who hadn't been to church, or paid his bills, or written to his parents. But he was learning; beginning to understand what people were saying...'

– Jake Thackray, **Yorkshire Post,** *1991*

The years Jake spent abroad after leaving Durham are among the most fascinating and important for his development as a songwriter. They are also tantalisingly elusive because witnesses are in short supply and he rarely talked about his experiences, even with his closest friends. What he did say and write about this period in his life is made more complicated by the fact that he loved to mix fact with fiction.

In 1960, long before the free movement of labour was normalised across Europe, working abroad was an unusual path to take. However, for three years Jake lived and worked in the French-speaking world, in France and Algeria. The impact of this experience upon him cannot be overstated. During these years he wrote poetry copiously, fell in love repeatedly and experienced life in a country violently shaking off the chains of Empire. He also drank deep of French culture and encountered for the first time the tradition of *chanson*, in which songs are performed by the singer-poets ('chansonniers') who created them and the poetry of lyrics is of overriding importance. Most significantly of all, he fell deeply in love with the music of one Georges Brassens, widely regarded as the greatest of the chansonniers.

The impact upon Jake's own writing and, ultimately, the direction of his life, would be profound.

Where did the idea of working in France originate? His schoolboy hitch-hiking trips to France and Italy show his sense of curiosity and adventure. Evidently he wanted to experience more of French culture, and he possessed the self-confidence to travel independently, without worrying too much about where the path would take him or how he would get there. Perhaps he read an article in Durham's student newspaper in 1959, enthusiastically proclaiming the benefits of working in France as a language assistant.

The key figure in his decision, however, must have been his brother, Michael, in whose footsteps he was following. After leaving his training for the priesthood in the 1950s, Michael had moved to the continent, where he married a French woman in 1958, before settling in the industrial city of Lille, in northern France. Here he taught English at ICAM, a Catholic university specialising in engineering,[1] and it was here that Jake joined him in the summer of 1960, no doubt using his brother's contacts to find work and accommodation.

With a good degree and some proficiency in French, teaching English provided him with an easy way to pick up work and fund himself. However, while his decision may have been a pragmatic one, it shouldn't come as a surprise: this was a natural choice of profession, bearing in mind his love of his subject and interest in people. Given his Catholic upbringing and education, there may have been a moral imperative behind it as well, and he had Michael's example to follow.

In fact, Jake had initially planned to train as a teacher in

Britain, and one of his tutors was disappointed that he didn't stay on at Durham, writing on his university file: 'I am a little sorry not to have him under my eye during a Dip. Ed.[2] Course, which he is taking at (I think) Bristol. (London did not accept him, and he did not want to stay in Durham.)'

In the summer of 1960 Jake travelled to Lille.[3] During the next three years he would teach not only there but, according to the sleeve notes on his first album, also in Brittany and the Pyrenees, and, for six months in 1961-1962, Algeria. Later, though, he would tell a reporter that he spent most of his time teaching in Lille, dividing his time between four schools.[4] He is known to have taught at a private Catholic high school, L'École Supérieure Professionnelle Ozanam, and Michael seems also to have found him some work as a *lecteur* (language assistant) at ICAM.

Possibly he initially stayed with Michael and his young family in their apartment in the suburbs of Lille, but with space at a premium, it wouldn't have been for long. By May 1961 he was living on Rue Neuve, a bustling street full of shops and cafés, close to the city centre, and within walking distance of L'École Supérieure Professionnelle Ozanam.

Jake quickly discovered that French and English schools were very different. Teachers in France had no responsibility for discipline, and Ian Gliddon remembers him saying that in one school, run by a religious order, a nun was present in all his lessons: 'There was a low, raised platform at front of the classroom for the teacher to stand on. The nuns would make children kneel on the edge of the platform, as a kind of a punishment. Jake didn't like this, and was very critical of their approach, but didn't feel he could intervene.' He also made clear to Ian that he didn't like the fact that teachers had no involvement in after-school activities, such as sport, music and drama: 'He said that, as a teacher, you turned up to your lessons, and then you went away... he preferred the approach in England.' When Jake returned to Leeds to teach in 1963, his involvement in school activities outside the classroom would play an important part in his creative development.

Jake claimed that his French pupils hated him and nicknamed him Wellington. Despite this, he undoubtedly felt a connection with French people and their culture. 'Jake said that the worst thing about being in France was the English ex-patriots, and he didn't like them,' says Ian. 'He didn't think that they were respectful of French culture. He also thought that there were a lot of bores. I think that because he was there, people introduced him to the British community, thinking he'd be happy to eat fish and chips – that was the level Jake would put it on. He much preferred the company of the French.'

In Leeds, as a boy, Jake had played some rugby league for a club in Bramley, and he played the game in France, where he 'lost his enthusiasm along with several front teeth in a friendly match among the excitable Gallic players'.[5] Meeting him on his return to England, his schoolfriend Don Stoker remembers his shock when he broke into a broad smile and revealed his missing teeth. Jake even claimed that he was banned for biting an opponent, but his fanciful imagination may have been at work here. Rugby league wasn't played in northern France, where rugby union held sway, so he probably only played the game while working in the Pyrenees, where rugby league was dominant. Doubtless his political sympathies lay with the working-class form of the game, which in France was the underdog to rugby union, suffering discrimination at the hands of the state for decades. With its links to socialism, it was banned during the war by the Vichy government and had all its assets seized, and for many years afterwards 'Le Jeu à Treize' ('the Game for Thirteen') couldn't even be called rugby.

Teeth were not the only thing Jake lost in France. He also lost his faith temporarily and stopped going to Mass, as he would later explain: 'I didn't believe that I believed. It's an odd process to describe, but it [I] was a young man getting rather smart-arsed and saying "Oh no." On reflection, I think it was a healthy thing to do.'[6] In another interview, recorded in the same month, he put it down to peer pressure: 'I was in a group of people who were my age, who were about twenty-one, twenty-two, twenty-three – women and men, mostly young, but some older. And they took up that I was a Catholic, you know, so they gave me it: (*shrugs and puts on French accent*) "Why are you a Catholeek?" You know, "What eez all this about? Immaculate conception!" You know, all this. It wasn't intimidating, it wasn't aggressive, it was just questioning. So for about three years I pulled out, I didn't go to church anymore.'[7] When Ian Gliddon met him in 1963, he couldn't detect any inkling that he had any religious beliefs. Nevertheless, once Jake was settled back at home with his mother, he started attending Mass again.

In France Jake began to write a lot of poetry, some of which was apparently published in a magazine. A few poems survive, including one written in Lille in September 1960. Titled 'A Villanelle',[8] this love poem is prefaced by four lines by Paul Fort, a French poet who had died a few months earlier. It is serious in tone and has a style reminiscent of Yeats and Auden:

> I took an orange from the street
> And gave it to my heart.
> My heart is thereby none so sweet;
> My love is such as acid on my heart.
>
> Dear love, so cheap it was to meet,
> And as bitter now to part,
> My love is such, as acid on my heart.
>
> To yellow love a sweet sun did impart
> What health? That we can eat
> My heart, is thereby none so sweet.
>
> But slowly our strange lips did greet

Each other; such a foretaste, as tart
My love is, such as acid on my heart.

And then who knows where such loves start?
What sicknesses do we repeat?
My heart, is, thereby, none so sweet?

I took an orange to my heart
And it gave love to eat.
My love is, such as acid, on my heart.
My heart is, thereby none, so sweet.

The poem's vocabulary is simple, but it is used to create some memorable images and there is careful artistry in the re-ordering of repeated words to create new ideas. Jake would later use a similar technique in some of his songs.

Jake was experimenting with his writing and reading widely in French literature. 'Degage qu' J'degage! Bordel!', written at Christmas in 1960, is bawdy and playful in tone. It is prefaced by a quote from Rabelais, the sixteenth-century French comic satirist, and only the first part of the poem survives:

Calliope, Caligula, and Clitoris and HE,
O well sir jaspering the Brompton Road,
Eyedling lamp-posted limbs and for free!
Aleing along, sick-pricking free goad.
For aye! For alack!
Bordel!

Kindly Calliope fingered her mind
And spat on her windwardly thigh;
Caligula didn't seem to mind
(And though Clitoris we couldn't quite find)
Yet HE found a place to lie
Bordel!
And HE found a place to lie.

A man in the Bunch o' Grapes said 'Why...'
But fly holed his doubts and fumbled away.
Bombastard! Chastities, firkins and pie,
Closet ye lips, 'tis boneache day.
For aye! For alack!
Bordel!

Kindly Calliope scratched her knee
And dabbed a compassionate eye.
Caligula seemed inclined to agree
(Though Clitoris we couldn't quite see)

The inventive approach to language (e.g. 'jaspering') is reminiscent of Dylan Thomas, a poet Jake had long admired; the structure is song-like, and the bawdy double entendres ('Clitoris we couldn't quite find') gives a foretaste of what was to come in his songs.

In contrast to this flight of fancy, another undated poem relates directly to Jake's personal experience. Almost nothing is known of the women in his life before 1966, other than that he got engaged several times while in France. He would later speak amusingly of failing his 'interviews' with the families of his French fiancées but, characteristically, revealed little beyond this to anyone. The name of one fiancée is known – Sofia – and he dedicated this poem to her, 'with love and smiles':

Sofia,
– I am in love
As dragons love
That rudely hiss
And scald
And carbonise
What they would kiss
And Burn;
– I am in love

As leopards love
That out of hunger leap
To rip
The flesh
From its soft sleep
And eat;
– I am in love
As eagles love
That drive their eyes
Into the
Waiting sun
And turn eating the skies
And kill.

Sofia,
– I am in love
As towers fall
That crumble sadly
Down and wide display
Their stony ribs
And grey antique decay
To lie;
– I am in love
As rain that fell
From Sunday skies
To darken your bright hair
And soak my heart
Tearing a shadow there
To hurt;
– I am in love
As grey dawns came
To a happy room
Where calm impelled
The morning on
And tranquil people held
Their peace.

This is certainly a powerful expression of love. Jake's use of short lines and regular rhymes enables him to do interesting things, and he develops his ideas and images in a sustained way, through the series of similes focusing on animals and nature.

Sadly, little else is known about his relationship with Sofia. Another undated poem takes the ending of a love affair as its theme, using the refrain 'Lord, have mercy on us'. It is dedicated anonymously 'à elle' ('to her'), and titled 'De Ma Part' ('For My Part'). The dedication and title suggest that it was written while he was in France, so it could be about Sofia.

In addition to poetry, Jake apparently set out to write a novel in French, perhaps inspired by the example of Samuel Beckett.[9] He told Don Stoker of this, who was astonished at the ambition of an enterprise that would require an extraordinary understanding of French language and culture. Admittedly, Jake became so proficient in the language that French people sometimes assumed he was a native speaker, but the project suggests both his ambition and naïveté. He later acknowledged as much when he told a journalist that he had been 'laughed at when producing a novel of 18 chapters in French'.[10] Nothing of the work survives.

During 1961 he returned at one point to Leeds, where a visit to St Michael's earned him a mention in the college magazine. He also decided it was time to move on from Lille. In May he obtained a reference from the director of L'École Supérieure Professionnelle Ozanam, which suggests that he planned to take up a new position at the start of the new academic year. So it's likely that his six months working in Algeria started in September 1961.

Jake's decision to work in Algeria is one of the most intriguing episodes in his years abroad, given that he chose to go there at a time of great upheaval and violence, when the country's long-running war to win its independence from France was coming to a head.

France's conquest of Algeria in 1830 had been marked by massacres, mass rapes and other atrocities, and the bitterness and resentment thus created simmered for decades. However, the Algerian independence movement only gained real momentum after 1945, when French promises of greater self-rule failed to materialise. In 1954, the Algerian National Liberation Front[11] began a guerrilla war that continued until 1962. Although its fighters ('Fellagha' in Arabic) operated in the countryside, the most serious fighting took place in and around the capital, Algiers. The French only retained control through brutal measures, and the ferocity of fighting weakened their will to continue the conflict. A series of political crises followed, leading some to fear that France itself might descend into civil war, and in the face of this emergency Charles De Gaulle, the country's veteran war leader, came out of retirement. A new constitution was approved, giving the Presidency vastly increased powers, and De Gaulle was elected President of the Fifth Republic in 1958.

By the time Jake went to Algeria in 1961, the conflict was reaching its climax. De Gaulle's declaration that Algeria had the right to determine its own future was met with violent resistance from dissident right-wing French army officers in Algiers. They formed a rebel faction, the OAS,[12] which made multiple attempts on De Gaulle's life and carried out terrorist attacks in Algeria and France; between April 1961 and April 1962, they are estimated to have murdered 2,000 people. However, there were atrocities on both sides, including, on the orders of the chief of police, a notorious massacre of peaceful Algerian demonstrators in Paris, many of whose bodies were dumped in the Seine.

Jake was clearly affected by all this, as he would later explain: 'I had a lot of friends who were drafted for the Algerian bit. There's a difference between a stagnant army and a fighting army. It seemed to me – in my early twenties – as though a new emotion had been born. There was a kind of melancholy about these people, but they were tough. I was in Lille. This was between 1960 and 1961. There were the most horrific bloody murders going on. The people who didn't pay their dime to the Liberation Front didn't go on living. It was a kind of protection racket. I can remember catching the tram to school – school started at eight – some of the boys would get on the tram, you know, with little short trousers and tucker boxes. They'd say something like, "We saw another one this morning, Sir, around the corner." Sure enough, around the corner, there'd be a shape under a blanket.'[13]

So, why did he go to Algeria? Visiting the country at such a turbulent time was risky, but he was adventurous and, as his friend Ian Gliddon observes, 'he wouldn't have been worried about his personal safety.' Always curious, it seems likely that he wanted to see for himself and better understand an issue dominating French society and politics at the time. In all this, there can be no doubt as to where his sympathies lay. 'He was certainly left-wing,' says Ian, 'so I'm pretty sure he would have taken the side of the Algerians. He was very much a supporter of the underdog and ordinary people.' He was already a socialist and contemptuous of authority. We can only speculate as to the impact of the Algerian war on the development of these views.

We know a little of his movements in Algeria. He told his friend, Colin Evans, that he taught English at a Jesuit College in Algiers. At one point he stayed at the Abbey of Our Lady of Atlas, a small monastery at Tibhirine, in the Atlas mountains. Run by Trappist monks, it was a place of sanctuary and silence, but it was not insulated from the violence of the times and, in 1959, two of its monks had been kidnapped. Jake's son, Sam, remembers him talking about his time there: 'The monks had either taken a vow of silence or spoke very, very little. One thing they did do was eat cannabis, and they would sit around the dinner table, stoned, or wile away the time in their cells, high. The cannabis made Dad sick, he didn't enjoy the feeling.' Years later, whenever Jake was partying with musicians and offered a spliff, he would recount his experience in Algeria and politely decline.

In 1961 he also visited the city of Sétif where, 16 years earlier, the French had carried out an infamous massacre which had triggered a spate of violence, leading to the deaths of thousands of Algerians. While there, Jake wrote a poignant poem, adopting a style similar to Ted Hughes's 'Crow'. He addresses a Fellagha, an Algerian guerrilla fighter:

Fellagha,
   your field no longer turns
in the sun.
Set so your mouth.
Squat on your old earth. The crow
Will come to wait with you
In your south.
Your blood is run.

Fellagha,
   your eyes no longer
grow on your age.
Prolong this only night.
That glint in the scree is
An officer's badge. Shatter such
Far off light.
Plant only rage.

Fellagha,
   where then are your father
and children now?
Remember blood.
Crouch on your old earth. Wait. Wait
For no rising suns to ease
The ceasing god.
Forget now.

This is a poem written for the underdog, and the reference to the 'officer's badge' suggests the same attitude to authority as can be found in his songs. Jake would return to the theme of the occupier and occupied a decade later in one of his darkest songs, 'The Prisoner', in which he paints harrowing images of dead children, with 'mouths pale with questions' and 'wide eyes still fearful', and suggests that any parent experiencing such a loss would gouge out eyes and curse Jesus Christ. With their compassion for the victims of war and sense of rage at its brutalism, the song and the poem have much in common.

Decades later, in sharp contrast to this poem, Jake would paint a fanciful and comical picture of his time in Algeria in his *Yorkshire Post* column. He starts the article, which focuses on how people develop their understanding of others, with a fictional farewell scene in Leeds, involving both his parents (despite Ernest having been dead for four years). He puts into his mother's mouth the following advice:

'Now then. Listen on old love. Keep your shoes polished and your teeth clean. Remember your fingernails and your socks. Pay bills and keep promises. Catch a cold if you want to, but eat right and not too much supping. Go to church and be right with women.'

He then transports the reader to an uproarious, drunken night in Algiers:

The next thing I am in a dubious bar in Algiers. I have dirty shoes, teeth, nails and socks, but I am having a whale of a time with a tart and a bottle of brandy. I am learning new words.

First on to the top of the table was a Scot with no trousers on. He was my boss at the school where I had got a job and this is what he sang: (he was the Head of English) 'The peeper cam tae oor toon/The peeper ae Dindee...'

Jake populates the rest of his story with an Irishman, an Algerian, a Frenchman, a German and an American, all singing on the table, until it eventually collapses. Everything is obviously fictional apart, perhaps, from his reflections on the impact of his experiences upon him:

> 'All these new things, all these new words going into the brain and the diary of a young tyke who hadn't been to church, or paid his bills, or written to his parents. But he was learning; beginning to understand what people were saying.'

After six months in Algeria, Jake returned to France, where he ended his overseas adventure, as he had started it, in Lille, before moving back to Leeds in the summer of 1963.

The glimpses we have of his time abroad give testimony to his curiosity, sense of adventure bordering on recklessness and desire to live life to the full and learn about the world.

The poems he produced there suggest a reflective writer growing in confidence and ability, absorbing and responding to what he was reading, seeing and hearing.

Years later, he would tell a friend that in France he became 'drunk on the French language'. In fact, he became most intoxicated with French music. The seismic impact it had upon him would alter the course of the rest of his life.

Pip

Tonton Georges

'In France, let me tell you that he is not just... he's not just a household word, he's a household paragraph... I think Georges Brassens is easy, easy, the greatest songwriter in the world, bar none.'

– Jake Thackray, 1981 [1]

Jake had left England in 1960 as someone who only dabbled on the piano, with an unremarkable taste in music. By the time he returned in 1963, he had found his inspiration and desire to become a songwriter and musician. The transformation was so great that when he appeared, guitar in hand, on national television in 1968, his school and university friends were utterly astonished. None of them had seen it coming.

France changed everything.

'I missed out on my blue suede shoes and my rock 'n' roll; I never got that when I was a teeny,' Jake would say in the 1970s.[2] It is hardly surprising that the tidal wave which struck Britain's shores from America in 1955 passed him by. He had spent much of the early 1950s living in the small, isolated community at St David's College, where he would have had limited access to anything other than church music and, when he returned to Leeds for sixth form, it is hard to imagine his straight-laced mother or bullying father tolerating the rebellious tones of 'Rock Around The Clock' or 'Heartbreak Hotel' echoing around the place. Furthermore, record players were luxury items, the records themselves expensive and money was in short supply in the Thackray household.[3]

If Jake was to get a taste for rock 'n' roll, university gave him the freedom to acquire it, but this didn't happen. He was 19 when he went to Durham and, by then, may have felt that he was beyond a form of music that satirist Tom Lehrer suggested should be classified with 'other children's records'. At Hatfield he attended the gramophone club's classical recitals; rock 'n' roll music remained the preserve of the coffee bars and town hall dances on Saturday nights.

It was not until he was 22 and living in France that Jake was bowled over by his own musical tidal wave. *Chanson* was very different from rock 'n' roll and it knocked him off his feet. He doesn't seem to have taken up the guitar until his return to Leeds in 1963, but what he had heard and absorbed was to be hugely important to his development, both as a songwriter and performer.

'I wasn't singing in France then,' he said in an interview, 'I was just teaching. It was only when I came back home I started singing. But I was learning how to write songs. At that period, in the mid-sixties in France, there was a whole swarm of terrific French songwriters, and they were writing different songs from the rock and roll. They were writing songs that were... I don't... when I first heard them, do you know... I couldn't sit down in the chair, I had to stand up and listen to them. They were elegant, they were full of language and terrific tunes and simplicity and wit and comment. And I loved them.'[4]

The musical cultures of France and Britain were very different in the 1950s. In Britain, brass bands, music hall, folk music and dance bands were in decline due to the influence of jazz, swing, blues and rock 'n' roll from America. In post-war France, however, despite the country's reliance on the USA for its reconstruction and defence, the French were determined to recover national pride after the capitulation and collaboration of the war years. They therefore not only mythologised the role of the Resistance in winning the war, but also fiercely defended the nation's cultural identity, including its cinema, language and popular music. Consequently, the American influence was less pronounced in France than in Britain. As Jake would put it, the French scene 'doesn't imitate any other sort of idiom, being based on their own folk music. Also, they were very struck by swing, they didn't seem to take much to bebop. A lot of inspiration for French singers has come from Grappelli and Reinhardt.'[5]

For these reasons the distinctively French tradition of *chanson* remained very strong, helped by the wide variety of venues where it could be performed, including nightclubs, music halls, casinos and theatres. In the post-war period Paris became particularly important culturally, with the presence of writers, thinkers, singers and chansonniers, of whom the most famous was Georges Brassens. It became a place where ideas, poetry and music met, and *chanson* flourished.[6]

In *chanson*, lyrics are of supreme importance, so it is easy to see why it appealed to Jake. The post-war chansonniers who wrote and performed their own work were many and varied in their approach, but poetry, storytelling and emotion all figured prominently. Edith Piaf, the 'little sparrow', who held audiences spellbound with her powerful performances, won international fame with songs like 'Non, Je Ne Regrette Rien'. Jacques Brel, a Belgian, was a huge star in the French-speaking world, and English and American performers like Dusty Springfield and Terry Jacks had hits with translations from his oeuvre, 'If You Go Away' and 'Seasons in the Sun' among them. In his writing, Brel mocked bourgeois society and dealt with many subjects, ranging from love and death to the seedy side of life, including brothels.[7] On stage, he brought to life characters and emotions in dramatic, exhausting performances. Jake became a huge fan of both Piaf and Brel, as well as Gilbert Bécaud and Charles Trenet.[8]

The poet-singer *par excellence*, however, was Brassens, or 'Tonton Georges' ('Uncle Georges'), as he was affectionately known in France. Jake found in him a kindred spirit upon whom he would model his approach to music and stagecraft, and their writing would share many of the same values, attitudes and themes, particularly regarding authority. In short, it is not possible to understand Jake properly without knowing something of the Frenchman. Without Georges Brassens, Jake Thackray would not have been Jake Thackray.

Brassens was already firmly established as one of France's leading chansonniers when Jake first heard his songs. He was born in 1921 in Sète, a working-class port in Southern France. His mother, like Jake's, was a devout Catholic, whilst his father was anti-clerical. Despite being a poor student at school, he developed a love of poetry and writing. In his teenage years he had a brush with the law (the inspiration for some of his songs) and was sent to live with an aunt in Paris, where he studied and wrote poetry and taught himself the piano. Then war came, Paris was occupied, and in 1943 he was conscripted to work in an aircraft factory in Germany. A year later, he absconded while on leave in Paris and hid until the liberation, staying with Marcel and Jeanne Planche, a poor couple whose home lacked even heating and running water. He lived with them for two decades and became Jeanne's lover; she was 20 years his senior.

When the war ended Brassens was jobless. He wrote articles for an anarchist newspaper briefly and published an unsuccessful novel. After spending years writing poetry (some of which was also published), he turned to the guitar and songwriting, only being persuaded to perform his own works when attempts to sell them to popular singers failed. In 1952, he secured a recording contract and his career took off: he went on to write over 200 songs, sell millions of records and have his output covered by numerous French singing stars.

His attitudes and writing were influenced by a longstanding French tradition of flouting convention, which had been given added impetus by the First World War, causing people to question authority, nationalism and capitalism.[9] Although his anarchism and anti-militarism attracted controversy, Brassens became a major cultural figure and his status as one of France's greatest poets was recognised formally in 1967, when he was awarded the prestigious Grand Prix de Poésie by the Académie française. When he died, in 1981, he was a national institution: to this day, his songs are studied in French schools, and countless public buildings, streets, schools and parks are named in his honour. In Paris there is even a tram stop named after him.

Yet for all his success, Brassens remained a man who shunned the spotlight. In his music, as in his lifestyle, he ploughed his own furrow. He stayed with the Planches long after becoming famous and, when he moved out, lived simply and alone, never marrying or co-habiting with his long-term partner, Püpchen. Although he appeared regularly on television and radio, once his career took off he had no need to tour, so stage appearances were limited to occasional sell-out runs at one of the large Parisian music halls close to his apartment. He was therefore able to devote most of his time to reading and writing. He rarely left France, and only performed once in Britain. He never achieved international recognition because he did not court it, and also because his complex, wordy songs, utterly embedded in French culture, are notoriously difficult to translate.

Brassens's approach to performance, unchanged throughout his career, hugely influenced Jake, who saw an honesty in its simplicity. He would stand playing his nylon-strung guitar with one foot placed on a chair, his distinctive, rhythmic, 'oompah' accompaniment complemented only by a double bass. His delivery was completely deadpan and he never spoke during concerts; indeed, Brassens scarcely acknowledged his audience, probably because of nerves. The song was the thing.

His lyrics, like Jake's, are the work of a poet and a craftsman.

They are elegant, poetic and full of literary allusions, and every word is carefully chosen, yet they also use vulgar slang. The inclusion of obscure, archaic French can make them difficult even for native speakers to understand.

Brassens's world view was similar to Jake's: his sympathies lay with the outcast, the underdog and the poor, and his anarchism underpinned his hostility to authority. He often used dark humour and extolled the virtues of good deeds and innocence as a way of attacking hypocrisy and self-righteousness in conservative French society, especially among the religious, the well-to-do and the police. The range of subjects he covered was wide. He sang of the suffering of the poor peasant ('Pauvre Martin'), the outsider who dared to go his own way on Bastille Day ('La Mauvaise Réputation'), and those who gave a helping hand to the outcast ('Chanson pour l'Auvergnat'). He celebrated the simple joys of friendship ('Les Copains d'Abord'), sharing an umbrella with a pretty girl ('Le Parapluie') and getting an erection ('Fernande'). He wrote a moving love song in which he promised his partner he would never propose ('La Non-Demande en Mariage'). In 'La Guerre de 14-18' he declared satirically that the First World War was the ideal war, and in 'Mourir pour des Idées' he attacked the notion that people should be bullied into dying for causes.

One of his earliest and most famous songs, 'Le Gorille', was banned from French state-run radio in 1952. Using highly literary language, it attacks capital punishment and judges, many of whom had served the Vichy régime during the war and condemned members of the Resistance to death. The song tells the tale of a sex-starved gorilla which escapes from a circus cage. Looking for sexual gratification, the animal has to choose between the only two people foolish enough not to run away – an old lady and a judge – and opts to get better acquainted with the latter. Jake would go on to write a brilliant adaptation of the song, demonstrating not only his admiration of Brassens, but also his command of French and skill as a poet.[10]

Jake was not only blown away by Brassens's lyrics, but also his musicality and melodies, which were rooted in jazz: 'Georges Brassens is startling because you're anticipating what's coming next, and then he drives off somewhere else, which is really satisfying. He's very swinging but he still uses a lot of peculiar French lines and minor keys – it's all bloody minor keys with frog singers!'[11] The influence could be seen on Jake's own musical style and chord progressions, albeit that he developed as a guitarist whose subtle and inventive finger-picking far outshone the playing of his musical hero.

In 1971, Jake would tell his friend, Colin Evans, that he 'fell in love with Brassens' after hearing him on French radio: 'It drove me crazy. I listened to him so much.'[12] He knew all his songs and even made his own by-ear transcriptions of the lyrics so he could study them. He saw him in concert,[13] as Sheila Thackray recalled: 'He'd heard Brassens singing, and he'd gone to see him, gone to see a concert, and was so bowled over by this... My memory is that he told me he'd gone to knock on the stage door, and Brassens had been welcoming to him – this was the story – and encouraging, and said, "If you want to write, you'll do it." And he certainly was his influence.'[14]

In time, Jake and Brassens would become friends, and for one magical night they would appear on the same stage.

This musical love affair endured for the rest of Jake's life. Without Brassens, it is doubtful he would have turned to songwriting, or developed as the writer and performer he became. With Brassens as his role model he would become something unique – a Yorkshire chansonnier, creating and performing a body of work rooted in the north country of England, and yet whose poetic approach and musical style were recognisable to anyone familiar with the Frenchman.

Jake's songs and performance would bring his audiences within touching distance of Brassens. However, he always felt that his own efforts were as nothing compared to the writing of 'Tonton Georges', and realised the impossibility of conveying fully to anyone who didn't understand French what made him so special. 'You can't export him,' he would say. 'I think he's just there. All you can do is stand under the great oak tree and watch the acorns fall.'[15]

With Jake, Brassens's acorns landed on very fertile ground.

A Good Skive

'Before I became a "performing dick" I used to be a "teaching dick"... and I wasn't awfully good at that either...'
— **Jake Thackray, 1983** [1]

In the summer of 1963, at the age of 25, Jake returned to live in Leeds with his mother at 8 Old Oak Close, the small council house in West Park to which they had moved following Ernest's death. Built on a new estate in the 1950s, it had a garden and the surrounding area was a good deal more pleasant than Burley Lodge Road and Kirkstall. For Jake, the next five years here would be a happy and prolific time, during which he would write many of his most famous songs.

Whilst in many respects he was picking up his life where he had left off, there was one obvious difference: he had gone to France as John, but returned as Jake. The reason for the change of name is unclear. His friend Ian Watson, who first met him in 1966, believes that he adopted the name 'when a French friend, or relative, addressed a letter to him as Jacques (though it's hard to understand why)'. It may have been a nickname he picked up. Perhaps it was linked in some way to his admiration of Jacques Brel, or it could be that he adopted the name to avoid any confusion caused by the pronunciation of 'John', hearing which, French people would have written as

'Jean'. Whatever the reason, from now on he was Jake to everyone except his mother, to whom he remained John Philip. Having given her son a perfectly good saint's name, she saw no reason to stop using it.

Now that he was back in Leeds, he needed to find a job. After three years out of the country and with no teaching qualification, he couldn't be choosy, and so he applied to Leeds education authority for work as a supply teacher. In September 1963 he was sent to Intake County Secondary School, where the headteacher, Charles Gardiner, had a short-term vacancy.

Intake was a secondary modern in Bramley, a working-class district of Leeds where the Victorian terraced slums were being demolished to make way for new council estates. It was a tough area in which to grow up and a tough area in which to teach.

As Jake would tell his audiences, 'life was rough to the children, so they were rough back'.

His initial appointment made his job harder still: he was covering for a Home Economics teacher, something for which he was completely unqualified. 'It was a baby-sitting job really,' says Trevor Thewlis, who taught with him at Intake. 'But that wasn't good enough for Jake. He thought, "I've got to do something." So he got the girls to make tea, and you would be sitting or standing in your classroom, the door would open and in would come two girls with a tray and a cup and a little pot, and they would pour you a cup of tea. We thought this was fabulous – what a wonderful idea! But, of course, with health and safety, the headteacher found out and stopped it immediately because Jake wasn't qualified. So from then on he became known as the man who wasn't qualified to boil a kettle.'

Although Jake wasn't a good match for this temporary post, Charles Gardiner could see he was someone who had much to offer and after a term, when a position teaching English became available, he was offered the job. Jake had landed on his feet.

Intake was in many ways a remarkably progressive school

which offered him many opportunities to develop his creative talents. Much of this was down its extraordinary head, as Jake's colleague Graham Stanley recalls: 'Gardiner was very supportive of people if he liked them, and Jake was someone he really supported and wanted to see develop.'

Charles Gardiner was truly a force of nature. He was tall, charismatic, inspirational and, in the words of one colleague, 'frighteningly uninhibited'. During the war he had been a grenadier guard and tank commander, and he left the army as a major and decorated D-Day veteran. Although he trained as a teacher, he had always wanted to be an actor, and he brought his passion to Intake. This was evident from his office, which often looked more like a dressing room, strewn with can-can skirts, feather boas and Edwardian shawls.[2] He made the performing arts, including compulsory dance, a central part of Intake's curriculum,[3] but his primary aim wasn't to turn out professional actors: he saw dance and drama as an educational medium, which could be used to tap into what he called the 'natural spring of talent' of his pupils. He believed passionately that the performing arts could empower and improve lives, and was convinced that there was little beyond the children's capabilities, despite their disadvantageous start in life.

Theatre was at the heart of Intake's innovative 'Festival Fortnight', a highlight of the school year. The timetable stopped and all the teachers put on an activity they enjoyed doing that was outside the usual curriculum. Some of these activities contributed to a major theatrical production, which was the focal point of the fortnight.

The plays, directed by Gardiner, involved pupils in all aspects, and were usually Shakespearean. 'They were substantial and remarkable productions, and not just for the quality of the performances from the children,' says Gardiner's son, Andy. 'The Head of Woodwork would oversee the set building. There was an Elizabethan house in one play, and a fabulous ship on stage for *The Tempest*. The costumes made at the school were of such high standard that Yorkshire TV would frequently hire them.' Art teacher Ian Gliddon recalls that the results of this ambition were remarkable: 'The standard of professionalism achieved in those shows was quite astonishing, especially when you consider the background the children were coming from.'

Recognition for what was being achieved came when *Coronation Street* actor Bryan Mosley helped to arrange the fight scenes for one production. 'He came to a performance, was impressed by one of the boys and got him some TV work. That got the ball rolling,' Charles Gardiner later explained.[4] Many pupils went on to become professional actors, including two in Jake's form, Terry Gilligan and Ian Shaw.[5]

Whilst Intake's creative ethos was highly progressive, the same wasn't true of the approach to discipline. Even in an era where corporal punishment was common, the headteacher was old-fashioned and unusually strict, insisting that this was the only sanction his teachers could use, and that a central record was kept. 'It is the only form of punishment here,' he said. 'One has got to have order. I don't use the cane as the ultimate deterrent, I use it for breaking school rules. For the girls as well.'[6] So strongly did he believe this that he allowed Intake to feature in a television documentary wherein he sought to justify his approach: 'Other forms of punishment, lines for example, can lead to bullying, and I will not give detentions, as I try to encourage pupils to stay behind for other activities. I do not want to make school a punishment.' He came to regret the adverse publicity the programme generated.

How did Jake react to this regime? 'He wasn't keen on caning, perhaps because of his own experiences as a schoolboy,' recalls Trevor Thewlis. 'Neither were several other teachers, but we went along with it because it was how the Head insisted on imposing discipline.' Gardiner was meticulous in his implementation of this harsh regime, he says: 'Everyone had their own cane and their technique had to be correct. Charles would offer training to new teachers by having them use the cane on him while he wore wicketkeeper gloves to be sure they could hit the palm of the hand and not the wrist.' Jake followed the school's policy of only ever giving one blow on the hand, but he went about things in his own way. He used a metre ruler rather than a cane, and the blow, which would not be hard, was largely for show. He was also known to lob a blackboard rubber at anyone who spoke out of line while he had his back turned, writing on the board: 'He had such a great ear and always hit his target. He was a good cricketer, I believe,' recalls his pupil, Derek Sharp.[7]

Jake quickly earned the respect of other staff. 'He was well-liked,' says Graham Stanley. 'As a colleague, he was extremely pleasant and friendly, but quiet, and not at all extrovert. When he became a performer I was really surprised at how very different his personality was on stage.' Bryan Smith, who joined the staff in 1967, found him rather introverted but says that, despite being self-effacing and apologising for himself all the time, he never kowtowed: 'He seemed to be a free spirit and went his own way really, doing what he thought was right, rather than what he was told to do, which I admired.' Charles Gardiner was well aware of this: 'He always was an unorthodox character. I once went into one of his classes in which he was supposed to be teaching *Julius Caesar* – a set text. When I got in, however, I found he was doing *Romeo and Juliet* – because he preferred it! That was typical of his teaching methods.'[8]

Jake was a charismatic teacher who was interested in his pupils and refused to write them off as failures, which is how they might easily have seen themselves, given that they had failed the eleven-plus and might leave school at 15 with no qualifications. They responded well to his approach. 'Jake was very popular with pupils. He built a rapport and was trusted,' says his colleague, Rod Whitely. One group of pupils showed their appreciation by presenting him with a sign, made in metalwork classes, bearing the legend 'El Thack', which he kept on his desk. 'Jake was different to other teachers,' says his pupil,

Terry Gilligan. 'You went into other people's classes and it was all straight: "Sit down, get your books out". You could have a laugh with Jake.'

He could certainly be unorthodox in his approach, and Ian Gliddon thinks that he deliberately made himself into a bit of a character: 'When he broke a lens in his glasses by sitting on them, he didn't get them fixed. He would wear the broken glasses in class, and his pupils were hypnotised by this behaviour.' Bryan Smith remembers him sometimes whistling from the staff room window to get a pupil to go and buy a packet of cigarettes for him.

When Bryan first joined Intake, he was advised to observe Jake teaching and was impressed by what he saw: 'He had a great rapport with the pupils. He really interacted with them, and he moved around the room, he wasn't stuck behind the desk. The kids were young adults, and they were treated in a special way. They were listened to.' He got his pupils really engaged in English. 'He would tell great stories and put on voices,' recalls Allan Hunter, who was in his form. 'He was such a fabulous storyteller.' He would also regularly send pupils off to the library to look things up mid-lesson, and was creative in his approach. For one class, he worked with Ian Gliddon: the pupils made papier maché puppets in Ian's Art lessons, whilst Jake got them to write scripts that were then performed in class using the puppets on an improvised Punch and Judy stand.

After his stifling experiences in French schools ('a funny sort of academic atmosphere', he called it), Jake relished the freedom of his life at Intake: 'Coming home and teaching lots of boys and girls was like going to heaven.'[9] He did a lot outside the classroom. On Saturdays, sometimes accompanied by a girlfriend, he took his form of 43 pupils on nature rambles to places such as Grassington and Bolton Abbey, organising a free bus pass for the entire party. 'I think he realised that these were a great way to educate children,' says Ian Shaw, who joined his form in 1964.

Jake also supported the P.E. department, helping to coach rugby league and going to Saturday fixtures. Admittedly, he surprised everyone by turning up for his first training session smartly turned out in a jacket and tie rather than rugby kit, but he impressed his fellow coach, Ron Miller, with his expertise: 'He definitely understood the game. He knew positions, had ideas and knew how to bring people on.' In the third form Ian Shaw found himself playing against Jake in Intake's annual staff v pupils match; he thought Jake was a good player, and his long legs certainly made him difficult to tackle.

Unsurprisingly, given his love of French culture and proficiency in the language, Jake was keen to teach in the modern languages department as well but, lacking a formal qualification in the subject, he was never allowed to do more than take cover lessons. Whenever he did so, he ploughed his own furrow and did something which interested him, and the teachers he was covering would find their pupils excitedly reporting what Mr Thackray had done with them.

Jake wrote and produced a staff pantomime, *Babes in the Wood*, playing the part of Little John. He also helped out at Intake's mammoth fundraising jumble sales. which Bryan Smith is convinced provided the inspiration for the song 'Jumble Sale'. Charles Gardiner roped in everyone, and would offer to do a forfeit if the pupils reached their fundraising target. This resulted in him leading one assembly memorably dressed only in his swimming trunks.

Jake enjoyed staff social activities. He joined the Leeds schoolmasters' cricket team but his enthusiasm clearly outstripped his ability: he batted at number 11. He also joined a staff fishing trip on the River Swale, for which he brought along two crates of beer rather than a rod. The empty bottles were subsequently seen floating downstream.

Two teachers with whom he particularly connected were Ian Gliddon and Geoff Burton. 'They were like live wires, all together,' says Geoff's wife, Anne. 'Ian, Jake and Geoff would trade word games with each other without thinking twice about it, without even realising that they were doing it. They could cap each other's remarks more or less in conversation, in passing. There weren't many people who could do that and could keep it up without really thinking about it.'

Jake and Ian spent a lot of time together. They shared a strong interest in the creative arts, the focus of many of their activities. They talked about literature and the nature of creativity. When Ian designed sets for school productions, he drew upon their discussions for ideas. Jake was keen to develop himself, and seemed to Ian to regard himself as unfinished. He went to evening classes on novel writing and, at his suggestion, they both attended an extra-mural course on Tragedy at Leeds University.

Jake was particularly keen on the poetry of Robert Graves. 'He liked the fact that Graves wrote in ordinary words, using language that referred to his own experience,' says Ian. '*The White Goddess*, Graves's book-length essay on the nature of poetic myth-making, was of great interest to him, bringing together poetry from different times, with thoughts on how poets get their inspiration.'

At home, Jake spent much of his time writing poetry. 'He would never have called himself a poet, but at that time that is where his whole focus was,' says Ian. 'He would regularly send poems off to publishers, including *The Listener*, only to have them rejected, time after time.' However, he doesn't believe Jake was disheartened by this: 'I think he felt he was busy making himself. He also felt, as a socialist, that some things would be stacked against him, in the way that society organises itself. It didn't mean that he was happy about it, but he just understood that that's how it was, and he wasn't going to let it ruin his life.' Years later, when Jake was famous, he laughed with Ian at the fact that, after all the rejections, publishers were suddenly interested in his poetry and anything else he had written.

He wrote short stories as well, one such being inspired by a painting Ian had made of a woman in a doorway. Ian gave it to him, and shortly afterwards received in return a story, titled 'Its Sweetness on the Desert Air...'[10] Jake attached a covering note, inviting his friend to use it as a stimulus to produce a new piece of art. The note reveals how self-critical he was: he didn't know how he wanted Ian to respond to '...writing so glib and posturing and "knowing" as this (decadent, as well, or pretty)... Should I not write something harder and more honest?'

It is the curious tale of a poor French nobleman's daughter, Veronique, who becomes invisible when she blushes, with disastrous consequences for her lovers. Her sudden, startling disappearances initially cause their accidental deaths. In time, however, she becomes bitter and cynically marries a succession of wealthy elderly men with the intention of killing them off. Eventually the cycle is broken when she marries a rough and ready mill owner from Cleckheaton, Samuel Ackroyd.[11] Faced on their wedding night with the prospect of this uncouth man, she suddenly feels pity and cannot blush. Consequently he survives the night and the marriage is consummated. Following this, she never blushes again, and over time her compassion turns to love.

Writer Neil Gaiman finds 'Its Sweetness on the Desert Air...' fascinating: 'It's a song, in structure, not a story. It would have been an excellent song – we'd meet the young lady, learn that she vanished when she blushed, watch her get richer as old billionaires died around her, then follow her into a real marriage with a Thackray stand-in. As a prose story, it's overwritten and clunky, but interesting to anyone interested in Jake's work.'

Its combination of French and Yorkshire settings is indeed clumsy, but the idea at the heart of the story is clever and original, and the approach taken to the construction of the plot is a sign of things to come, comparable to what Jake does with greater skill and success in his music. For example, in 'Bantam Cock', he has a lusty farmyard fowl 'tup' its way through a series of birds of ever higher status, before keeling over, apparently dead, setting up the punchline.

Ian Gliddon remembers Jake's love of storytelling being an unusual feature of their weekend hitch-hiking trips: 'On Friday, we would agree to meet up at a pub on Saturday. It was Jake's view that we had a responsibility to entertain whoever it was who gave the pair of us a lift back. So while we had a drink, he would come up with a plan A, B and C as to what characters we should play, depending upon the age of the driver. So if it was a young driver who liked pop music, Jake would say that he was a performer and I was his manager. He took the lead in all this, deciding what characters we would be and the reason for our journey. However, I would often forget the details, so I would leave him to do the talking.' In the years ahead this love of fantasy and storytelling would be distinctive features, not only of Jake's songwriting, but also his approach to life.

This creativity with language and character led him to invent an amusing pub game for his colleagues. 'A group of us would regularly go to the Wine Lodge in Leeds,' recalls Ian. 'We would sit in the big room upstairs and watch people as they came out of the toilets. Jake had each of us describe the person using a single adjective, going round the group in turn, and we were not allowed to repeat a word used previously.'

Another activity Jake initiated with his friends was a poetry reading group, the core of which included Ian and Geoff Burton, along with their girlfriends, Maggie and Anne. They took it in turns to lead the meetings at a different house or pub each time. At the first session, Jake distributed anonymised passages of poetry that were read out and discussed, before inviting everyone to guess the identity of the authors. They would then learn to their amusement that they had sometimes disparaged writing by the likes of Shakespeare or Swift.

Not everything Jake did was intellectual, however, as Ian revealed at his funeral: 'Being close to Jake could be great fun and dangerous. He could be like one of his characters... D.H.

Lawrence said we could avoid risks and live like cabbages, or we could take risks and live life to the full. Jake lived life to the full.' To illustrate the point, Ian told the story of an incident which took place after one of their poetry meetings, when they were driving back from a pub in Ilkley with Geoff and Anne. It was a hot night, and when they reached the River Aire, Jake and Ian decided they wanted to have a swim to cool off:

> We both went swimming in the nude, or would Jake say 'naked'? When we reached the other side a car stopped with its lights on us. A firm voice demanded we swim back. As we neared the bank we could make out the shape of a policeman.
>
> It is difficult naked – or is it nude? – to exit a river with dignity. In the dark and over stones and slippery grass it's even harder. On approaching the policeman I was preparing to grovel. Jake strode past me, walked close to a policeman and, putting his wet arm around his neck, he pulled the policeman against his wet body, and in a *Dixon of Dock Green* voice said, 'Evening, Officer.'

'That was Jake,' says Ian. 'I think that used to frighten people a little bit, so that they would be a bit careful where they got to with him.' Thankfully, the police let them both off with a stern talking-to.

Jake started to learn the guitar soon after his arrival at Intake, and from the outset a desire to write songs was his motivation. 'Jake was a writer, and he told me that he thought playing the guitar might help him with the things he was trying to do,' says Graham Stanley. Ian thinks that Jake's lack of success at getting his poetry published prompted him to head in this new direction, but his chief source of inspiration was undoubtedly Georges Brassens, who had made exactly the same change.

Jake followed Brassens in opting to play a warm-toned, nylon-strung guitar, rather than the more widely used steel-stringed version of the instrument. He colourfully suggested in an early interview that he took lessons from a bankrupt businessman from Bradford, '...a marvellous guitar player. His method was, he'd drink whisky out of a jug and play bits for me to imitate.'[12] In reality, he was self-taught. Lin Pass, who joined the staff at Intake in 1966 and played guitar in the School's jazz band, remembers occasions when he and Jake would sit in the staff room with a guitar: 'He used various chords but didn't know what they were called. He would place his fingers on the fretboard and pluck strings, changing the fingering until he achieved the chord sound he wanted. He would turn the fretboard towards me, fingers still in position, and ask, "What do they call that one?"'

Initially, Jake's playing was functional but unorthodox: he employed a mixture of picking and strumming, rarely using full chord shapes. In time, he would develop into a skilled (and under-rated) guitarist who had his own, highly original style, using complex fingerpicking with great subtlety to support the performance of his songs.

From early on he made writing part of the process of learning how to play, as he explained to Graham Stanley: 'His original practice was boring for him, so he said, "I'm just going to write some little ditties to go with the exercises I'm doing."'

Jake said nothing to his closest friends about his new hobby. When, therefore, he asked Ian whether he might perform some of his songs for the poetry reading group, the request came completely out of the blue. Given that it was Jake's turn to lead the session, Ian told him there was no reason why he shouldn't, although he was privately anxious as to how it would go.

At the meeting Jake sang a number of his songs, including several which would later appear on his records. His friends were astonished. 'We had never heard him sing or play the guitar before, and we were amazed when he started performing,' says Ian. When Graham Stanley got to hear the 'practice ditties', his reaction was the same: 'I was utterly

amazed, both at how much Jake had progressed in such a short
space of time, and the brilliance of his way with words.'

It seems strange that Jake should have kept from his closest
friends what he had been doing. However, with hindsight, Ian
thinks it typical. Jake certainly talked a lot with him about
creativity, but it was always in general terms. He never sought
advice on songwriting and he didn't share work in progress; he
only shared his writing when he regarded it as finished.

He had undoubtedly chosen the right audience on which
to try out his material – friends who shared his love of language
and were warmly supportive of him. 'Jake, Ian and Geoff just
worked as a threesome together in the very early stages,' says
Anne Burton. 'Ian and Geoff supplied Jake with the confidence
to continue learning the guitar and they appreciated what he
was doing in a way that he understood – the internal rhyming,
the sideways movements in his texts which you wouldn't see
coming when you saw the title. I think they helped to give Jake
an appreciation of what he could do.'

Jake's friends began to look forward to him testing new
songs out on them. 'All of us, very early on, were charmed
because the songs always made you laugh,' says Anne. 'It was
always a delight to have Jake say, "I've written this one this
week. What do you think of it?" And after we had picked
ourselves up off the floor, we would say, "Yes, that's not bad!"'
She thinks the earliest songs included 'The Shepherdess',
'Country Bus', '(I'm Just A) Dog' and 'The Little Black Foal'.

Anne remembers the songs being more impressive than the
guitar-playing initially: 'Jake was very much a three-chord man
to start with. He wouldn't always have either the fluency to
play the chords to complete a whole song in one go, or
sufficient variation to make an interesting background, but
being Jake, intelligent and musical, he cracked it fairly soon.
My memory is that in three months he progressed massively,
and had become a competent guitarist. He was so interested
and, possibly, amused himself by what he could do with the

words and the music. He worked hard at it and, once he got the music, he came on, hand over fist.'

He began to play more and more for friends, taking his guitar to social gatherings. 'Many's the time we persuaded Jake to get out his guitar at parties and sing some of his newly-fledged songs in a fug of Capstan Full Strength,' says Trevor Thewlis. 'There were lots of parties, and at virtually every one, Jake would sing,' recalls Graham Stanley. 'However, he was always genuinely reluctant to play, and it was no false modesty. Jake would only perform because of the encouragement of others.' When he failed to bring his guitar along to one party, he was sent home in Graham's car to collect it.

Ian recalls discussing with Jake how to create characters using words and art: 'We were both searching for ways to create or define characters concisely, without them being clichés.' In their conversations, Jake was focused on how to achieve this in a song, where the space to create characters is necessarily limited. In time, one of the most distinctive features of his songwriting would be the originality of the characters created, and the deftness with which he brought them to life.

As early as his second year at Intake, Jake began to take his guitar into the classroom. He later explained his thinking in an interview: 'I started playing the guitar because textbooks weren't getting me anywhere in class. One afternoon I got a bit pigged-off. All this keeping up an academic appearance with kids who were far better at other types of work. "Come on," I said to them, "you are all supposed to be learning stuff. Let's just see at how I get on at learning something. You say what you want me to learn and we'll see how I get on." The class told 'sir' to learn the guitar. 'Mister Fackry' strummed some chords then began putting words to them, out of boredom.'[13]

Graham Stanley's classroom was below Jake's and he can remember hearing pupils singing to guitar accompaniment. Generally, these weren't songs Jake would later record, although Graham recalls one class singing 'Remember Bethlehem' (known as The Intake School Carol). Jake came up with lots of little songs for his classes. Some gave an eye-witness view of an historical event, others were written from the perspective of historical figures; another carol, 'Joseph', took that approach. Whether the songs were always related to the content of the lesson is debatable. 'If he'd had enough of the class he used to get his guitar and we used to sing,' says Terry Gilligan.

Jake started an after-school guitar club, working with a group of pupils to write songs around a story and put on a show: 'Sometimes I'd write, but I preferred them to do the writing, and they used to come up with some funny little tunes. I encouraged unusual layouts a bit and in fact discovered that a child would whistle a tune or they'd devise a little phrase, say in four-four, then add the words which would turn it into seven-four, which was unusual and often worked. It didn't matter about notation, we worked with a tape recorder... I was teaching them shapes, but my own shapes, very rudimentary, because I was never taught myself. I remember there was one kid who showed me minor 7ths, just using a finger barre and not playing the fifth string.'[14]

'He was writing his own songs,' says Terry Gilligan, 'and he used to write mini-musicals which he got the class involved in. We used to perform them in the school hall, and we also used to go around some church halls doing them as well.'[15] These musicals consisted of comic songs interspersed with short pieces of dialogue. The first was *The Harmonious Omnibus*, staged in late 1965 or early 1966, when Terry was in the second form. It was about the passengers on a bus, and opened with 'The Bus Conductor's Song', which had something of the spirit of Flanders and Swann's *A Transport of Delight*:

> At going slow we pride ourselves, we really do excel,
> But if you're sprinting after us we drive like merry...[16]

The musical featured a turban-wearing Ian Shaw playing the

role of a lonely Sikh. Using a melody Jake borrowed from Brassens's 'La Complainte des Filles de Joie', he sang:

> If I ever found a wife, if I ever found a wife,
> Who'd wash my socks the rest of my life, wash my socks
>   the rest of my life,
> I'd smother my missus in kisses, in kisses, in kisses,
> I'd smother my missus in kisses.
>
> If I found a wife who could, if I found a wife who could,
> Make a steak and kidney pud, make a steak and kidney pud,
> I'd buy her a fridge and a bingo hall, a bingo hall, a bingo
>   hall,
> I'd buy her a fridge and a bingo hall.

Another song was about a lost property shop:

> If you've left your luggage on the train,
> Come around to us and claim it back again.
> There's some things that defy belief:
> Grand pianos and old false teeth.
> It's quite amazing just what some people lose:
> Billiard balls and snooker cues.
> So... if.... you...
> Lost a Cheshire cheese,
> Please come right away:
> It's starting to walk
> And it gets bigger every day.

The next musical, staged in 1966, featured Terry Gilligan singing about a prince who had been turned into a dog. There was also a princess, guarded by a chorus of soldiers who sang:

> We are the royal knockers-up,
> We are always hail and hearty.
> If she is snoring,

We have to break the door in:
We are the royal waking party.

The songs are joyful in their innocent silliness, and full of Jake's idiosyncratic humour and love of wordplay. He would look back on these activities fondly: 'I used to enjoy playing the guitar and making up songs and the buggers enjoyed doing it. It was a good skive... musicals were a good skive.'[17]

Jake's next musical, however, ran into trouble because of its subject matter. Lin Pass, who had been enlisted to help him, remembers Charles Gardiner cancelling the show after seeing the dress rehearsal: 'The show contained a song about a Mrs Murphy[18] in which it was suggested that she had become pregnant but couldn't work out what her "illness" was. The problem, however, was that the parent of one of the pupils, a real Mrs Murphy, was something of a battleaxe, and Gardiner didn't want to upset her and have to deal with the consequences.' Everyone involved was understandably very disappointed with the decision.

When Jake's performing career started to take off, Charles Gardiner highlighted to him the importance of ensuring that none of his colleagues would be left thinking any of his songs were about them. He took this advice on board and, whilst he undoubtedly drew inspiration from the people and events in his life, he was at pains to emphasise that his characters were entirely fictional. He would later offer an ironic explanation of this in the introduction to his book of lyrics and stories, *Jake's Progress*:

About all the people in this book, the names, and places and dates and animals I am telling lies. I am even telling lies about me. In this book not even 'I' am real.

Nothing is real here, everything is a pack of lies. And to tell you the truth I could be lying about that. I have only once written a song about one real person.

I do not write about anybody real. I have a much better

system than that and I can recommend it, if you need a system. What I do is make people up and then write songs about them. They're much more interesting like that and also you meet a better class of person.

Jake gave a lot to Intake creatively, and it gave him an outlet for his talents. As well as his musicals, his songs featured regularly in school concerts and, whilst his role was initially confined to accompanying his pupils on guitar, as time went by he was given his own regular performance slot.

Some of what he wrote for Intake eventually appeared on record. These included those beautiful carols, 'Remember Bethlehem' and 'Joseph', which Jake said 'were never intended for adults to sing because they were very childlike songs. They were written for two children to sing in a Christmas play and they sprang to fame. We did them at Radio Leeds. And they were also on the *Today* programme and on *Pick Of The Week*.'[19]

With typical generosity, Jake split his performance fee of five guineas with his pupils.

Another song which first saw the light of day at Intake is 'The Cactus', in which a sickly pot plant has a devastating impact on the marital bliss of a couple of newly-weds. Having been commissioned to write something for 'Festival Fortnight', Jake asked Charles Gardiner to pick a subject. With more pressing business in hand, the headteacher glanced around his office and suggested the cactus on his window sill. When Jake later sang it on BBC regional television in April 1966, he asked that his performance fee be paid to Intake.

Jake's pupils were amazed when they realised his talent, and he says they urged him to write a song for them – something they could understand, and with a gruesome ending. 'Ulysses' achieved both, and they loved it: a pet dog comically drives his owner to distraction, to the point where he decides that one of them has to go, and prepares poison. It is typically idiosyncratic, and certainly not a 'soppy little songy-wongy', as Jake would disdainfully characterise children's tunes. He would always associate 'Ulysses' with his pupils and sang it for them at his farewell assembly when he left Intake in 1968.

Although some of his writing was for Intake, much of it was for his own amusement. 'Jake was always asking his mum for ideas,' says Sheila Thackray. 'It was a happy time because it was his hobby. He was coming home from school, going upstairs to his bedroom, his mum downstairs cooking his tea. It was his pleasure.'

He was prolific, and within two or three years had built up a substantial catalogue of highly original songs of real quality, many destined to appear on his albums. However, the humility which the Jesuits had instilled in him persisted. Sheila remembers that at the top of every page of lyrics he wrote 'A.M.D.G.' ('to the greater glory of God'), 'so he hadn't to take any personal pride in his gift'. And if he forgot to do that, his mother wrote it for him.

Jake met the woman who would become his wife during his third year at Intake. Sheila Clarke-Irons, as she was then, was originally from London, although her family had moved to Coleford in the Forest of Dean when she was in her mid-teens. In October 1965 she went up to Leeds University to study English and, in early 1966, became great friends with another student, Carol Hawkins. For the rest of their time there the two shared a flat, and even clothes. Sheila was bright and extrovert, and Carol recalls she was keen to enjoy all that university and life had to offer now she had escaped sleepy Coleford; she was undergoing that growth in confidence which Jake described so well in his song 'Those Are The Days'.

Early in 1966, Sheila met Jake at the Swan with Two Necks in Leeds. 'The Poetry Society, the English Society, had its A.G.M. [there],' recalled Sheila, 'and Jake walked in, in a big, flappy greatcoat and a pair of teacher's specs... his chat-up line would have been something like, "What do they call you, then?"'[20] She was immediately taken with him: 'I was really impressed. What a character.' In the packed pub they could scarcely hear each other speak, so spent most of the evening calling each other Jock and Shirley.

Carol remembers the night well: 'Sheila came home and said, "I've met this man, but he's so much older than us.[21] He's really tall and he has a long black coat."' For the two students, it was a standing joke that a man in a long black coat was the epitome of cool. When she met her friend's new boyfriend, Carol approved, finding him funny and kind. As for Jake, it is easy to see what drew him to Sheila: she was not only attractive, but bright, sparky and interested in literature. She soon joined him at his poetry reading group.

If Jake and Sheila's initial encounter was somewhat comical, their first proper date was little different. They went to the cinema, where he bowed to Sheila's desire to see the romantic *Dr Zhivago* in preference to his suggestion of a Monsieur Hulot comedy.[22] 'We sat right down the front because Jake said he couldn't see the world from the back,' recalled Sheila, 'and when he put his glasses on, they were totally shattered from when the children had put them under Mr Thackray's seat. He had made an attempt, before he came out, at mending them with a bit of Sellotape, and he would grin at me through these. I'm absolutely convinced that he was putting me through a test. He fell asleep anyway. He was bored out of his tree by the film.'

Evidently Sheila passed the test, and the relationship blossomed. Like Jake's mother, Sheila was soon providing him with ideas. 'When we were courting,' she said, 'I showed Jake the back page of the *Yorkshire Evening Post* and what made me giggle – the personal column. We spent an evening chuckling over this and devising dafter adverts.'[23] The song 'Personal Column' came directly from that. It contains private jokes,[24] including one alluding to Sheila's new-found freedom, living away from home: in a personal notice 'mummy and daddy' send birthday greetings to 'darling Sheila', wherever she may be.

In their second year, Sheila and Carol moved into a dingy, mouse-infested flat at 6 Ridge Mount. It had two things in its favour: it was close to the university and Jake's favourite pub, the Packhorse on Woodhouse Lane. It had a private entrance, so visitors could come and go without disturbing the neighbours unduly. Jake regularly drank there with other teachers, and because the pub was opposite the university, he socialised with students there as well. On Friday nights, after closing time, he would go to the flat on Ridge Mount with 20 or more drinking companions and they would party until the early hours. Games would be played, fun would be had, but Jake never got his guitar out – perhaps wisely, given the volume of drink taken.

Rather as with his moonlight swim in the river with Ian Gliddon, Jake sometimes got into scrapes on these nights out in Leeds. After one session at the Packhorse, he and two students (who shall remain nameless) decided to gatecrash a party. Although they got in, they were soon identified as interlopers and ejected, whereupon one of Jake's companions, angry at being thrown out, decided to kick in a cellar window and steal some beer. At this point a policeman arrived. As one of those present recalls, Jake, well-oiled, then launched into 'an extraordinary speech in the most elevated language, along these lines: "We are three young men, full of the vigour of life, and if we are to be absolutely honest, we have to admit to having had the odd libation, alcoholic in nature. We've done many things this evening. We've sung too much, we've possibly made too much noise, and done one or two other things which might be on the very edge of the law. But the one thing, officer, that I can absolutely guarantee you is that none of us has been guilty of wanton damage..." He went on like this, deadpan. It was all delivered very professionally. Eventually the policeman told him in very colourful language to shut up, and told us all to get out of his sight, with the warning that if he saw the three of us again that evening, he would have us. It was Jake's silver tongue which saved us.'

As Anne Burton put it, 'Jake had a way with his imagination and a great confidence that things would work out for him.'

An early publicity shot.   *Noel Gay*

Woodhouse Pamela

'A voice adequate enough for interpreting his lyrics which are excellent in a Noël Coward sort of way, if a little too sophisticated for Light Entertainment. Guitar accompaniment adequate. Unsuitable for Pop Music Department but up to broadcasting standard.'
– BBC Talent Selection Group, 1966

Jake's years in Leeds in the mid-1960s were undoubtedly happy. He was courting Sheila, enjoyed a lively social life with a stimulating and supportive group of friends, and worked in a school where he was valued and had the freedom to be creative. He also had the certainty that his mother was there to look after him at Old Oak Close, and that together every week they would go to Mass.[1]

Then, of course, there was his songwriting. Immensely productive, writing for Intake, friends and his own amusement seems to have been its own reward. There was no hint that he expected the pattern of his life to change, or that he planned to develop his music into a professional career. 'He wasn't the type of person to have a masterplan,' says Ian Gliddon, 'but he was the type of person who realised he was developing himself.'

Nevertheless, in late 1965, a few months before he met Sheila and barely two years after starting to learn the guitar, the first in a series of events occurred that would ultimately lead to him becoming a professional entertainer: someone at the BBC in Leeds picked up on his talent.

Details are sketchy. According to the *Daily Mirror* in March 1968, a BBC scout heard him entertaining friends, but one of his early concert programmes suggests he was performing in the tap room of a pub on Kirkstall Road, possibly the Cardigan Arms, where Jake is known to have played. The 'scout' was Pamela Howe, a producer for BBC regional radio in Leeds, then part of the North of England Home Service (N.E.H.S.). Perhaps she came across Jake by chance, but it is possible she was tipped off by Charles Gardiner; the frustrated actor had excellent media contacts and when Jake's chance came he encouraged him to take it.

Howe, meanwhile, was a colourful character who had a long BBC career producing spoken-word programmes, including many involving literature.[2] In an obituary, *The Guardian* described her in these terms:

> The most reticent newcomers to the studio and microphone were coaxed into giving performances of which they would never have believed themselves capable...
>
> Pamela was great fun, often irreverent, sitting with her pug in the office, unwilling to give up smoking and impatient with demands for political correctness.[3]

Given her character, attitude and literary interests, it is hardly surprising that Pamela immediately took to Jake. Furthermore, her ability to coax performances out of newcomers would stand her in good stead with him, given that he was a nervous performer. 'Woodhouse Pamela', as Jake would later refer to her,[4] would become both a personal friend and his champion at the BBC, and provide a new stimulus for his writing.

Recognising Jake's talent, Pamela decided to feature him on her weekly radio programme, *Northcountryman*. On Friday 5th

November 1965 therefore, after work, he went to the BBC studios on Woodhouse Lane, Leeds, and in a 30-minute session recorded 'The Little Black Foal' for the princely sum of five guineas.[5] This charming bucolic ballad served as a good introduction to his writing for Pamela's radio audience: it is, by turns, sentimental and wittily irreverent, while showcasing his love of pictorial detail and the sound of language.

The song's love-lorn protagonist is caught between hope and despair, wondering who is clip-clopping down the lane on a pretty foal: the beautiful girl he has just fallen for, or one of the ghastly members of her family? Jake uses poetic, alluring descriptions of this dream girl to build a mood of expectation, before breaking it with amusing pen portraits of her pompous father, gossiping mother and bastard of a brother.

'The Little Black Foal' was broadcast on 21ˢᵗ November and again a week later. It was well-received, and Jake returned to Woodhouse Lane to record more songs, starting in December with 'Ulysses' and 'Greasy Joan', broadcast in early 1966.[6] Thanks to Pamela, he now had a regular outlet for his songwriting that earned him good money to supplement his teacher's salary. All the songs featured on her programmes would later be released on record, apart from the intriguingly titled 'Walter and His Pig', which is lost without trace.[7]

Pamela also commissioned Jake to write and perform his two spoken-word pieces about university life, 'What is a Prof?' and 'What is a Student?', broadcast on *Talkabout* in March 1966. Along with allowing him to show his versatility as a writer, this gave her an opportunity to hear how his lugubrious speaking voice worked on radio.

A ball had begun rolling, and within three months of his first radio recording Jake was appearing on regional television. He had Pamela to thank for this too: convinced of his talent, she contacted BBC staff in Manchester to draw him to their attention. He was approached by James Entwistle, who produced the evening news programme *Look North*, and was booked initially to sing three songs: 'The Shepherdess', 'The Drunks' and '(I'm Just a) Dog', for a fee of 15 guineas each.

'The Shepherdess', broadcast on 2nd February, was a strange song with which to introduce Jake to a tea-time television audience. It tells the story of a young man's encounter with a shepherdess bathing naked in a stream. She threatens to punch him when he propositions her, but he refuses to return her clothes. Afterwards they marry.

It is one of Jake's earliest songs, and this shows. The contrast between the archaic politeness of the youth ('prithee, pretty shepherdess...') and her calling him a 'bum' and threatening to hit him is amusing but rather clumsy, and when he vows suggestively that he will never let the naked shepherdess be covered by anything except him, his words lacks the sharpness of the double entendres in Jake's best songs. Furthermore, it all ends with a weak punchline.

'The Shepherdess' is chiefly interesting because the inspiration for it clearly came from Georges Brassens's exquisite 'Dans L'Eau de la Claire Fontaine', in which a man likewise finds a young woman bathing naked. When a gust of wind blows her clothes away, he fetches flowers so that she can cover her modesty. Full of gratitude, she embraces him, and he responds with such passion that her substitute fig leaf falls. When he next sees her in the pool, she is again bathing, and praying for gusts of wind.[8] Jake's song is a somewhat gauche homage and he evidently remained dissatisfied with it: he would go on to rewrite the lyric and record two different versions, but never felt it was good enough to be released.

'The Drunks' is likely to be an early title for the song later known as 'The Statues', which describes a late-night encounter between two drunks and some statues in a park. It was broadcast on *Look North* the day after 'The Shepherdess'. As for the third song, '(I'm Just a) Dog', viewers never got to see Jake perform it. Perhaps this was because its witty, pun-filled comparison of the courtship rituals of humans and hounds, including a reference to a canine being put in 'the family way', was judged inappropriate for a tea-time audience.

Despite this, Jake's first performances on *Look North* were judged a success, and he was booked to sing eight times on the programme during March and April 1966.[9] Whether he recorded the songs or had to travel to Manchester after work to perform them live (which would have been both nerve-wracking and cutting things fine), it was a busy few months, and the money was very good.

Pamela Howe had been successful in raising Jake's profile with the BBC in the north, but London was her ultimate goal. Conscious, perhaps, that she might lack credibility because her expertise was in spoken-word programmes, not music, she sent a memo and tape of Jake's songs to William Relton in the BBC's music department in Manchester, who made a pitch on her behalf. On 4th January 1966, he forwarded both items to Andrew Gold, the Chief Assistant of the Light Music Department, along with his own observations: 'For our part in North Region, we are not aware of the market on Light Programme for this material, but I personally find his songs interesting, both rhythmically and in subject matter(!)'

Gold was unimpressed, and it would be 14th March before he sent a brief, dispiriting response: 'I have listened to this tape and, frankly, didn't find it very interesting at all. We have lots of people who play and sing a lot better. I am sorry to pour such cold water on this.'

Pamela did not give up. A couple of months after the knock-back from Light Music, she approached Popular Music. On 6th May, she sent Donald Maclean (Chief Asst, Prods), a tape containing seven songs. She also summarised Jake's career to date on local radio and television, and pre-emptively made a virtue of his 'lack of professional gloss':

We feel he has got a certain unusual quality, despite (or perhaps because of) a lack of professional gloss (self-taught on the guitar). I suppose one could say that he came into the more sophisticated end of whatever category you would put the 'singing postman' in! He himself says he has been influenced by Georges Brassens.

Maclean passed the tape on to the department's Talent Selection Group which, ominously perhaps, met on Friday the 13ᵗʰ and did not listen to it all. The responses were mixed, underlining an issue that was to characterise much of Jake's career: what do you do with an artist who does not fit into standard categories, such as light entertainment and pop?

The group's report gives a fascinating insight into the BBC's approach to music in the 1960s:

REPORTS ON: JAKE THACKRAY
TAPE FROM LEEDS

HEARD BY TALENT SELECTION GROUP:
FRIDAY, 13ᵗʰ May, 1966

Items: 'Little Black Foal'; 'The Blacksmith'; 'Greasy Joan'

This sounds like a bass voiced Noël Coward. Not Popular music at all. Pass to Light Entertainment in case they could find something for him, because he is quite entertaining.
NOT FOR US

Quite entertaining but not suitable for this department. I find this very entertaining and I think it would prove entertaining during interludes between programmes as and when they occur (shipping forecasts etc.).
NOT FOR POP MUSIC

A singer of satirical songs accompanying himself on guitar. Not for Popular Music Department but I suggest that he is heard by Light Entertainment.
PASS TO L.E.

A voice adequate enough for interpreting his lyrics which are excellent in a Noël Coward sort of way, if a little too sophisticated for Light. Guitar accompaniment adequate. Unsuitable for Pop Music Department but up to broadcasting standard.
YES

A monotonous voice with an unattractive style. He puts his songs over in stilted phrases with no variations of tone or expression. The guitar accompaniment is primitive and unvaried and frequently the voice and guitar don't match in pitch. A good amateur at best, and certainly not up to broadcasting standard.

Clearly, while some members of the panel liked what they had heard, Jake and his songs weren't seen as Popular Music material, and the view set out in the final paragraph seems to have been decisive. The tape was not forwarded to Light Entertainment.

In sending a tape of seven songs, Pamela Howe had obviously hoped to indicate the quality and range of Jake's writing. It is a pity that the Talent Selection Group only listened to three, and that their selection included the dark and downbeat murder ballad 'Greasy Joan', which was untypical.

'The Blacksmith and the Toffeemaker', which Jake later said was taken 'wholemeal... as opposed to piecemeal' from a short story in Laurie Lee's novel, *Cider with Rosie*, is a magnificent piece of writing. He gives life to Lee's characters in a way that is both amusing and moving, telling the tale of a shy blacksmith and an old spinster who find love in the most unlikely of ways. For years, the blacksmith loves the lonely toffeemaker but is too shy to tell her, until in desperation she goes into the church and begs God for a man. Unbeknown to her, the blacksmith is in the tower, mending the clock. He hears her prayer, seizes his moment and, in the tones of the Almighty, asks whether she would consider a blacksmith. Utterly astonished, she declares that any man will do, and so he gets dressed up and proposes. The happy ending comes with a teasing and suggestive picture of their marital harmony, as his fires are put to use, boiling up her sweets.

The song is an exquisitely crafted piece of storytelling, full of feeling and wry observation, and abounding in the skilful use of internal rhyme. However, it is long and requires concentration, particularly as Jake's deadpan musical delivery makes no concession to any lapse in the listener's attention. Given this, and the fact that none of the songs bore any resemblance to what was being played on the BBC's Light Programme (forerunner to Radio 1 and Radio 2), the Talent Selection Group's verdict is hardly a surprise.

None of this was revealed to Pamela Howe until 14 weeks later when, in August, she sent a memo to Maclean, explaining that she would shortly be moving to work for the BBC in Bristol and would like to receive feedback before she left Leeds. She made clear that she was realistic in her expectations, and 'would be very glad to pass on some professional opinions to him [Jake] before I go. He is still writing and recording songs for our local programmes, but would naturally like to extend his market if possible. Some of his latest songs are really excellent.'

A few days later, she got a phone call from Maclean, who made a note of their conversation:

> Spoke to Pamela Howe. She said that she was not interested in an actual audition for the above artist. She had simply submitted his tape so that she could learn the views of more experienced producers, and so advise this artist where he could improve, and whether it would be worth his while giving up his job as a teacher and moving to London. He is a personal friend of Miss Howe.

I gave her gist of reports – and explained that not all producers had been able to hear the tape due to leave etc. And this was the reason for the delay in advising her. I told her that whilst the reports were semi-favourable no-one had shown unlimited enthusiasm and, to be realistic, the number of such artists available to us in London was considerable and it would thus seem advisable that he stayed at teaching and supplemented his income by the occasional broadcast from Leeds, which, according to Miss Howe, were forthcoming.

I told her that we'd put the tape in our 'Library' as she didn't want it back, so that if future interest was shown here it could be referred to.

Clearly, he agreed with the Talent Selection Group that Jake should not give up the day job.

On the same day Maclean called, Pamela received more bad news. Reading the autumn programme schedules, she noticed that her *Northcountryman* programme was going to be rested. She wrote immediately to John Ecclestone, Head of Northern Radio Programming, to lobby him on Jake's behalf:

I am a little concerned that there will be no outlet for Jake Thackray's songs during this quarter. He is writing new songs regularly, and I think they are keeping well up to standard. I wonder if it would be possible to include them occasionally in 'Talkabout' during the autumn? Their usual duration is between two and four minutes, and from listeners' letters we've received, he does seem to be popular.

She also explained that she had asked Jake to write two or three new songs, to build up a stockpile, so she would need to tell him if these songs would not be required.

Her appeal fell on deaf ears. Ecclestone rejected her suggestion regarding *Talkabout* and admitted that he was 'not too keen personally' on using Jake's songs beyond the *Northcountryman* context.

So, despite Pamela's best efforts, Jake's radio work was drying up. As for television, he had not appeared on *Look North* since April. In July he wrote to the programme's producer enquiring whether he would like more songs and offering to write some to order. His offer was politely declined: he was assured that he had not been forgotten, but that the programme was not currently featuring musical items. For the time-being, at least, the *Look North* boat had sailed.

Jake's career is highly unusual in that he started appearing on radio and television whilst having very little experience of performing on stage. During 1965 his performances seem to have been limited mostly to informal, private gatherings of friends and playing at Intake. Pamela Howe told Donald Maclean in May 1966 that 'his performances have been confined to singing occasionally at a pub or student folksong club', and in that year *Yorkshire Folksy*, a Leeds-based folk magazine, included him in its directory of singers, indicating that he was looking for paid bookings on Leeds' vibrant folk-club circuit. However, none of Jake's friends at Intake know of any public performances before September 1966. During the mid-1960s he went regularly to singers' nights at the Grove, Leeds's oldest folk club, and occasionally took his turn and sang a song. As his reputation grew, one night, probably in 1967, he was given a push by the club's organiser to do more: 'Geoff Woods, God love him, encouraged Jake to do a few numbers with the aid of a few pints and a friend's guitar and he played the whole of the second half.'[10]

Lin Pass, who joined Intake in September 1966, believes that Jake started playing regularly in public during the course of that academic year, and knows he was travelling to gigs because he sold him a guitar case. He thinks he was singing in working men's clubs, but was never given any details. One of Jake's student drinking companions remembers him playing at the Cardigan Arms on Kirkstall Road (not far from Burley Lodge Road) and at rugby club dinners, where he would sing for his supper. The atmosphere at these gigs would doubtless have been raucous, and he would have adapted his set-list to suit his audience.

Jake's earliest dateable performances were on 15th, 16th and 17th September 1966, in an amateur Old Time Music Hall show staged by Whitkirk Arts Guild in east Leeds. The master of ceremonies, Don Jackson, taught with Jake, and invited him to perform a couple of songs as a guest artist. Jake initially declined the invitation, declaring, 'No, no, no. I don't do that sort of thing,' but was eventually persuaded. Guild legend has it this was his debut performance, and the Jackson family remembers the evening well. Having tea with them before the show, Jake was obviously very nervous, recalls Don's daughter, Chris Ingram: 'By then, I'd met him a few times and knew he was a "jumpy" person. He fretted all through the meal about whether he would be good enough and how he was going to go down. We went across to the church hall where the show was being performed, and I was given one job – to get Jake on stage, come hell or high water.' Chris was successful and Jake was well-received. His short set included one of his newest songs, 'The Last Will and Testament of Jake Thackray'.[11]

A month later, on October 19th, he gave a lunchtime concert in the University Theatre in Manchester. He got the booking through Pamela Howe,[12] and it was probably his most high-profile concert appearance to date, as he took a group of friends along. It was certainly the first time he received a review in a national newspaper. *The Guardian*'s Benedict Nightingale[13] wrote with remarkable insight:

> Jake Thackray, a young teacher from Leeds, gave a lunchtime recital at the University Theatre yesterday and proved an unexpected, original talent. He sings in neat, almost delicate phrases of lusty subjects. His manner is French, light, unemphatic, a little melancholy, facially unexpressive; his matter, behind the scampering guitar, unmistakably British.

His hero is the 'scallwag', the likeable rogue who drinks all the booze, spits on the magistrate, and visits eager women after dark. His message is iconoclastic, antiromantic, hedonistic: Arthur Seaton's philosophy set to music. He takes pains to remind us that we are all creatures of instinct. The first song is about a dog's courtship; most of those that follow are cynical, without being vulgar or tasteless, about human bitches.

'There was Julie: she was truly well-proportioned, but her caution brought exhaustion to my arteries.' The rhymes, frequent and usually unpredictable, are sustained from the dogs of the beginning to 'Jake Thackray's Last Will and Testament' at the end. Characteristically, this advises friends and relations to treat his funeral as a gigantic beano: if the women must heave their bosoms, he says, let them do so in the direction of men. His audience – students mostly, postponers of the age of responsibility – laughed at this and everything else a good deal.

Jake would always enjoy playing to university audiences, and it is easy to understand why: they were well-equipped to appreciate the skill and subtleties of his writing. Given the assuredness of his performance in Manchester, it is hard to believe that he had only made his stage debut a month earlier.

It had been a year of significant achievements. Jake had built a catalogue of highly original, increasingly accomplished work, appeared numerous times on local radio and television and had an excellent review in a national paper. But despite all this, and Pamela Howe's lobbying, London had not come a-calling. By the time she moved to Bristol in October, a fledgling television career had long since ground to a halt and Jake's radio work was dropping off; with 'Woodhouse Pamela' now hundreds of miles from Woodhouse Lane, her capacity to help was limited.

He would need a huge stroke of luck – and a more powerful champion at the BBC – to get his big break.

That moment was about to come.

Akker

A Very Valuable Property

*'I think this young man is a very valuable property, and I
like to think that we could do the most towards promoting
him here in this Department.'*

– Roy Rich, BBC, 1967

Pamela Howe's belief in Jake's talent remained undiminished. Although based in Bristol, in December 1966 she arranged for him to make a new recording of 'The Little Black Foal' in Leeds, to be broadcast on her West Country programme on 11th January 1967. Neither one of them could have foreseen the importance this would hold for Jake's career.

By chance, one of the BBC's most senior staff was listening. Roy Rich, a veteran broadcaster and the BBC's Head of Light Entertainment (Sound), was immediately struck by its original quality, and he wrote to Pamela asking for a copy on tape. Seizing the opportunity, she sent him not only 'The Little Black Foal', but also 'Lah-Di-Dah' and 'The Last Will and Testament of Jake Thackray'. This was a stronger selection than the three songs heard by the Talent Steering Group the previous year, and Roy was immensely impressed.

Over the next few weeks he played the tape so often to other BBC staff that he wore it out and had to request a replacement. At the end of February, he wrote to Pamela, explaining that he was unsure how best to exploit Jake's talent: did she recommend 'throwing him in at the deep end' or introducing him gently via Light Entertainment shows such as *I'm Sorry I'll Read That Again*?

To help him make a decision, he wanted to meet Jake: 'I would know so much more what to do with him if I knew what he looked like and what his personality is.'

Pamela moved straight into action, on the telephone and via a follow-up memo, explaining that she had called Jake at school and asked him to write to Roy. She also gave the BBC man Jake's address and Intake's phone number.[1] Finally, she revealed that her 'cherished baby', as she called Jake, had been given his own 20-minute radio pilot in Leeds, to be broadcast on 12th March.[2] Titled *My Family Tree*, the programme would consist of him singing five songs and introducing them with his own self-scripted spoken links.[3] Keen to hear Jake's speaking voice, Rich immediately ordered a tape of the show.

He also now decided that the time was right to introduce the Chief of the Home Service to Jake's songs. The excitement in his memo about 'the brilliant young Yorkshire folk-singer' is palpable: 'I am now informed by Pamela Howe that he is 28, tall, dark and extremely good-looking (which doesn't fundamentally affect broadcasting, but is a colossal help from a presentation and P.R. point of view). I think this young man is a very valuable property.' He was given permission to invite Jake to make an expenses-paid trip to London.

Roy Rich and Pamela had both worked rapidly to get the wheels moving at the BBC, but Jake was slower to respond to the opportunity. It would be a full ten days after Pamela's call before he would write to Roy, explaining that he couldn't meet him on a weekday until the Easter holidays. He finally travelled to London on 6th April, almost three months after Roy first heard 'The Little Black Foal'. There he met the BBC executive over lunch and was introduced to some of his producers. The meeting was clearly a success and things now started to move quickly. On 20th April, Roy wrote to Pamela explaining what was in prospect for her 'cherished baby': an 'almost certain' pilot programme on the Home Service, a music publishing deal and a single, to be made with top record producer Norman Newell.

Roy was championing Jake's cause in London and, with things developing apace, he asked him to let him know the outcome of the meeting he'd arranged with Newell. However, Jake went silent. Eventually, after hearing nothing for three weeks, Roy wrote to him on 27th April, expressing his concern. Jake's lack of communication was something of a character trait, but perhaps he had other things on his mind at this point. On 16th April he had written to the BBC's northern region, apologising for taking two months to return signed contracts, and pleading the excuse that he had recently been burgled. In the same letter he asked for a summary of his BBC earnings: 'The taxmen are after me, and I want to be prepared.'

In his letter, Roy explained the importance of Jake having someone to act on his behalf in London and generously offered to do so until he had an agent. He also had some good news: a representative of Liberty Records, a US label, was interested in signing him, and David Toff, one of London's most respected music publishers, wanted to do a publishing deal. Roy pointed out that, as Jake now had two record companies chasing him, he could play this to his advantage to get the best contract. This was excellent advice, but it came too late: on the very day he was writing the letter, Jake was in a recording session with Norman Newell at Abbey Road studios.

Newell was one of Britain's most respected and successful producers. After starting out in music publishing, he had moved into production and talent development in the 1950s, becoming Head of A&R (Artists and Repertoire) at Philips Records and then EMI's Columbia label. A lyricist as well as a producer, during his career he amassed hundreds of writing and production credits and won numerous Grammys and Ivor Novello awards. The artists he worked with included Shirley

Bassey, Judy Garland, Matt Monro and Petula Clark. His musical instincts, however, were conservative, and during the 1960s he was eclipsed by other producers whose ears were more tuned to rock 'n' roll and pop. Nevertheless, he still had hits: in 1964 he achieved a number one in the US and UK with Peter and Gordon's 'A World Without Love', and in 1967 he recorded Bassey's legendary version of 'Big Spender'. By this point, like other top producers, he was working freelance.

Newell said he had been encouraged to seek out Jake by an old associate: 'One of the best musicians and orchestrators in the country, Brian Fahey, telephoned me one day and said he had heard Jake Thackray on the radio and said I should go after him, which I did.' A lyricist himself, he was immediately bowled over by Jake's talent: 'I brought him into the studio and was amazed by his lyrics. His lyrics are sensational... I was so impressed by his ideas and the magic rhyming.'[4]

He was lucky to sign Jake before a rival record company had the chance to make him an offer, and the singer's inexperience in the music business probably helped. However, the prospect of having a contract to record with a highly-respected producer for a major record label was obviously very attractive. In the view of Beatles producer George Martin, Newell's greatest talent lay in 'his ability to handle big showbiz entertainers'. Jake hardly fell into that category but, for all his politeness and humility, he was a complex man who knew his own mind and it is testimony, both to Newell's skill and his faith in Jake's talent, that they enjoyed an excellent working relationship throughout the singer's nine years with EMI. The producer oversaw all his recordings and, as time went on, adjusted his approach to take account of the singer's musical preferences.

'Jake enjoyed making the early albums with Norman Newell,' recalls Alex Armitage,[5] who knew both men well. 'He loved Norman, and they were great friends, but it was a very odd friendship, because there was this bluff Yorkshireman and this rather flamboyant homosexual, in the days when to be a flamboyant homosexual was very, very unusual indeed. And they just got on really well. They went out and drank together, but they wound each other up by being as separate as they possibly could. Jake would have a pint. Jake sometimes drank other things – he liked and appreciated his wine – but with Norman he always had a pint, and Norman always had a little dry sherry. And I knew Norman very well, and he never, ever drank little dry sherries except when he was with Jake. The pair of them had this wonderful way of winding each other up by being extreme cartoon versions of their own personality.'

Through Newell, Jake met the man who would be his first agent. Richard Armitage was head of Noel Gay Artists, one of the country's most powerful agencies.[6] At a time when the show-business world centred on London, his company enjoyed particularly strong relationships with television and radio executives, aided by regular social contact at drinks parties and business lunches. Jake would benefit, therefore, from the professional expertise of two well-established, well-connected men who knew each other and the requirements of show business very well.

His first recording sessions, at EMI studios, Abbey Road, were booked for 26th, 27th and 28th April. That was during term-time, so he was presumably given special leave of absence. Part of Jake was always suspicious of the music industry, but he was undoubtedly proud to be recording there. 'He loved the fact that most of the albums were made in studio two, the Beatles' studio,' Alex Armitage says. 'Jake loved all that. Slightly *malgré lui* ['despite himself'], but he loved it.'

He would soon find himself rubbing shoulders with the Fab Four, and may well have done so on this first visit: they often looked in on the sessions of other artists and were at Abbey Road that week, working on the *Magical Mystery Tour* album. John Lennon was impressed by Jake's dress sense, telling him, 'I like your gear, man'. More importantly, The Beatles liked his songs and guitar-playing. Paul McCartney later acknowledged Jake's influence on the 'White Album', recorded in 1968: 'A lot of it was written in India, where we were working with acoustic guitars. That affected the kind of music that was made... John had somehow sneaked in a cassette player, battery-operated. He was listening to a lot of folkie stuff – he had about half a dozen cassettes with him – a Buddy Holly, an Incredible String Band tape, some Dylan and a tape the singer Jake Thackray had done for him... He was one of the people we bumped into at Abbey Road. John liked his stuff, which he'd heard on television. Lots of wordplay and very suggestive, so very much up John's alley. I was fascinated by his unusual guitar style. John did "Happiness Is A Warm Gun" as a Jake Thackray thing at one point, as I recall.'[7] If Lennon was listening to Jake's songs whilst meditating in India for three months, it is hardly surprising he apparently knew 'The Statues' word for word.[8]

After three prolific years, Jake had amassed an impressive catalogue of songs, and his first task in the studio was to make demo recordings so his producer could pick the best. No other musicians were present, and he accompanied himself on guitar.[9] Twenty-five of these demos were eventually released in 2006,[10] and they reveal that Norman was spoilt for choice: Jake's first two albums would largely be made up of the songs Newell first heard at these sessions. All he had to do was decide which material to release first and how best to record it.[11]

Jake's performances on the demos are brisk and assured. He sounds as relaxed as could be expected under the circumstances. Listening to these intimate recordings, it is fascinating to hear his explanations as he introduces the songs to his producer. He describes 'Nurse' as 'another public house one' and offers an apology before 'Remember Bethlehem': 'I can't really attempt to avoid mistakes in these because I've never sung them through properly... you know about the children...' (i.e. they were written for his pupils to sing).

Twelve of the recordings were initially identified for release as a mono LP, with the working title *Last Will and Testament of Jake Thackray*.[12] With Jake's guitar the only instrumentation, this would have introduced him to the record-buying public with a sound that replicated his live performances, and Bob Dylan's career showed that this strategy could be successful.

However, such simplicity was at odds with the nature of much of the veteran producer's previous work and he had second thoughts. A different approach would be taken, but the demos still served a useful purpose: copies were made so that arrangements could be produced, in preparation for future recording sessions.

Jake would have to wait until the summer holidays before he could return to the studio. In the meantime, other opportunities came along, as Roy Rich's promotion of him in London bore fruit. In June, he returned to Woodhouse Lane to record his first songs for national radio, broadcast on the Home Service's *People Singing* on 28th August.

More surprisingly, in July he was approached with a view to becoming a presenter on *Play School*, the BBC's long-running television series for the under-fives. The programme needed people who could 'sing, tell stories and talk to young children'. Jake agreed to meet a producer in Manchester but, for whatever reason, things went no further. However, it would not be the last approach from children's television.

There was much he needed to do to prepare for his new life as a recording artist, and he spent most of the summer holidays in London, where he sought out university friend Ivan Mansley, with whom he had lost touch after leaving Durham. To Ivan's complete surprise, Jake landed on his doorstep one evening, guitar in hand, and revealed he was about to record an album. Ivan sensed that he was somewhat apprehensive about his new life, and perhaps suffering from the stereotypical northerner's sense of inferiority. Jake explained that he wanted company when he signed a contract the following day, declaring, 'I don't want to go down and meet these people on my own'.

Ivan agreed to join him after work and, after Jake had spent the day getting measured up for his expensive new stage suits, they went together to a flat in Montagu Mansions, near Baker Street, the London home and office of Norman Newell. Ivan remembers that Norman was 'outrageously camp' and insisted on showing them his teddy bear collection in his bedroom. After the contract was signed, the producer sent them off with a pair of tickets for the West End's latest hit show, *Fiddler on the Roof*. It was a bizarre experience. Travelling in this strange new world, Jake would often stay with Ivan, seeking the reassurance of a familiar face.

The exciting developments in his career as a performer were matched by what was happening in his personal life.

In the summer he went with Sheila to the Forest of Dean, to meet her family and announce their engagement. The visit didn't go well, as her brother Rick vividly recalls. Her parents had liked her previous boyfriend, the local doctor's son, and were disappointed when she ended the relationship. They really didn't know what to make of Jake, and his decision to sing to them 'Lah-Di-Dah' didn't help: his amusing love song describes everything a bridegroom is prepared to endure for love, including his tedious in-laws. The song wasn't auto-biographical, but the reaction of Sheila's parents was predictable. 'It went down like a lead balloon', says Rick.

Meanwhile, plans for Jake's first records had crystallised. Newell had decided they would make a single and, alongside it, an eleven-track album, *The Last Will and Testament of Jake Thackray*.[13] Both would be recorded in August and released in early November, just in time for Christmas.

He had reached another decision, too: Jake's music needed more professional gloss. Newell therefore hired Roger Webb to lead an orchestra on some songs, and Geoff Love to write arrangements for guitar, bass, piano and percussion for the rest. The producer regularly worked with both men, and Geoff had arranged one of his biggest hits, 'A World Without Love'.

Newell trusted him totally: 'He was so reliable and he could record so many different types of things. He could do "Cowboy Jimmy Joe" for Alma Cogan one minute and conduct beautiful music for Manuel and his Music of the Mountains the next.'[14] Along with his musical skill, Geoff's warm, down-to-earth personality was an asset in the studio.

With the personnel now in place and studio time booked in August, the scene was set for Jake's first proper recordings.[15] EMI was making a big investment in its new recording artist, which was testimony to the company's confidence in Newell's musical judgement and Jake's commercial potential.

For these recordings he had to overdub his vocals onto backing tracks, which took him into strange new territory. 'The whole process of recording amused Jake enormously,' says Alex Armitage. 'He saw sitting in a dubbing booth, without a guitar in his hand, laying down a track, as bizarre, and he just laughed at it. He understood that it's what he had to do, it's one of the hoops as a "performing dick" he had to jump through, but he found it all very bizarre, very false.'

Jake wasn't only in new territory in the recording studio. For the duration of the sessions, which lasted several weeks, he stayed at Monterey, Newell's plush country house in Crowthorne, Berkshire. Soon afterwards he wrote to his friend, Carol Hawkins, and gave her a colourful description of his summer spent 'sponging off Norm':

> I spent weeks in Norm's fairy-castle (and I think that's accurate enough) in Berks. Fighting my way through the carpet pile to get at the drinks cupboard and the technicolour telly, lounging on the patio throwing cake at the gardener, snapping my fingers at the maid.[16]

Jake always had a way of sharing his good fortune, and he would be joined at Newell's home by Bob Haverly, a drinking buddy from the Packhorse in Leeds:

Bob Haverly and his girl met up with me in London once, and since we were off to a posh dinner Norm invited them along – Norm got drunk and said he wanted to adopt Haverly, but anyway for time being should spend a few days in my fairy palace with Thackray. So we had nearly a week – we did our best to make a hole in the store of booze in the drink shed but it seemed to make no difference at all. Even the gardener joined in.[17]

Jake was enjoying the luxury of his surroundings, but feeling somewhat out of place. His songs were having a similar experience.

The Holy and the Horrid

'We did a single, two children's carols... all dressed up fancy with orchestra and ladies' choirs going "Oooaah! Oooooooo! Oo!" every now and then. And then the L.P. – some of those with your orchestras and trumpets and harmonickers and even a string quartteters. No kid.'

– Jake Thackray, letter, 1967 [1]

'The Holy and the Horrid.' In 1967, this was how Jake bizarrely and memorably characterised the types of songs he wrote. Simplistic and misleading though it was, this amusing, eye-catching phrase was gladly taken up by EMI's marketing department, and that was the whole point. It neatly addressed a problem caused by Norman Newell's decision to launch his career with two completely different records.

'The Holy' referred to 'Remember Bethlehem' and 'Joseph', the two carols Norman had chosen for Jake's debut single in November, with the intention of capitalising on the festive season. Anyone hearing them would be forgiven for thinking he was a conventional light entertainer. However, if they then bought his album on this basis, they were in for a shock. Whilst Jake's songwriting never fitted into conventional musical categories, promoting these two records would require him to be positively schizophrenic.[2]

As for 'The Horrid', this represented a humorous and typically self-deprecating warning that the more prudish (including his mother, perhaps?) might find some of the album's content surprising, shocking and inappropriate. Yet the tracks on *The Last Will and Testament of Jake Thackray* do not merit the description. They are highly original creations in which cynicism, comedy and pathos rub shoulders – often within a single song – and Jake's talent as a storyteller and poet is everywhere.

The LP starts with the beautiful 'Lah-Di-Dah', surely one of the most honest love songs ever written, certainly among his most popular.[3] A bridegroom-to-be contemplates marriage, and all the 'fancy pantomime' that goes with it: for the sake of love, he is willing to tolerate his bride's appalling aunts and uncles, a knitting, wittering mother-in-law and her mangy cat, a father-in-law who could bore for his country, and the ordeal of the wedding breakfast. He will put up with all this because, as he keeps assuring his bride, he loves her very much, and this refrain is given an amusing twist at the end when he promises that, once they are married, they won't have time for any more such nonsense: he'll be loving her far too much.

'Country Bus' is a wry, poetic and sentimental love song to a 'lumbering, cumbersome' old vehicle. Using a sweet melody set to an appropriately swaying waltz, Jake paints an evocative picture of life on board: the sheepmen and chickens, the lovers who manage to make do on the backseat, the closing-time drunks who stagger as much as the bus. His genius is not only to make the bus the central character, as full of life as its motley passengers, but also to win our sympathy for it, battling its way through the cruel winter weather, getting snow up its nose.

'The Cactus', written at the suggestion of Charles Gardiner at Intake, is a ludicrous tale of two newly-weds whose love life falters due to the wife's obsession with a potted plant. In his frustration the husband resorts to hurling comic insults at this rival for his wife's affections, and the situation is only recovered when he realises that, like him, the cactus is pining for female company. Once this issue is addressed, everything looks up, and he proudly boasts of the size of his family and cacti collection: the contrived rhyme of 'in fact I' and 'cacti' makes the punchline all the more satisfying.

'Scallywag' deals with a character-type and theme of which Jake was fond: the disreputable rogue who is looked down upon by society, but whose free-wheeling lifestyle and appeal to women are a cause of quiet envy.[4] The song paints a colourful picture of a scoundrel who smokes foul-smelling tobacco, gets drunk, spits on the magistrate's car and steals clothes from washing lines. But despite the public disapproval his behaviour incurs, a succession of women, ranging from the shy green-grocer's daughter to a countess, quietly give him the eye, knowing full well that at night he will tip-toe along to tap at their windows.

Haunting, pathos-laden 'The Black Swan' deals with the age-old theme of the lover drowning his sorrows in his cups. He is drinking hard and strong, 'now that she's gone', and urges his former lover not to attempt to find him, but to go to bed early and take a book with her, now she is free of him. Wearing its *chanson* heart on its sleeve, it is one of Jake's most melodic and overtly emotional songs. When he landed on his friend Ivan Mansley's door in the summer of 1967, he declared that he had modelled some of his work on that of Jacques Brel, and 'The Black Swan' could well be one example: it is reminiscent of 'L'Ivrogne' ('The Drunkard'), which deals with similar themes in an equally heartfelt way. The influence of Brel would be shown on the album's closing track, too.

Jake had a real gift for finding gold in the most unlikely of subjects, as with 'Jumble Sale', a tale of love at first sight. Here his keen observational eye is cast over this most English of settings, the song's narrator finding himself ambushed by the vicar outside a parish hall. After painting a colourful picture of women squabbling over bric-a-brac (compared to Visigoths fighting for pillage, no less), Jake brings us his protagonist's moment of epiphany: he spots, at one of the stalls, what he most wants to take home – a beautiful, wild-eyed girl – to whom he makes his tongue-tied pitch.

'Jumble Sale' is a bravura display of Jake's brilliance with words. He fills it with internal rhyme and also uses unexpected pauses to great comic effect. His language is rich and sometimes recherché ('bibelots', 'Junoesque') and there are playful double entendres. At the point when his hero takes the plunge and approaches the girl, he even presses into service some schoolboy Latin, with a witty allusion to Julius Caesar's declaration 'alea iacta est' ('the die was cast').[5]

Two songs involving animals follow. First, the sweet, onomatopoeic clip-clopping of 'The Little Black Foal', and then the darker 'Ulysses', in which an irrepressible dog comically ruins its master's television viewing, social ambitions and love life. The humorously lugubrious mood of the master is skilfully created through a combination of melody and assonance: 'it's *use*less to purs*ue* my *view*ing...'. However, nothing prepares the listener for the pathos of the song's dark and poignant twist: the master's thoughts turn to poison, but not, it transpires, for Ulysses – the dog is too loveable to kill. Suicide is the only way out. It ends with the heartbreaking image of Ulysses weeping for his dead master.

This technique of serving up amid the comedy a moment of pathos, prompting the listener to consider everything afresh, is something Jake also uses in 'Personal Column'. In among the fanciful adverts for 'artistic' photographs in plain envelopes and hair removal treatments, Sidney posts a notice asking Molly to forgive him and return home, leading Jake to speculate amusingly on whether dodgy photos or superfluous hair played a part in their falling out. An advert for anti-nuclear shelters (free trial offered) is followed by a wittily ambigious description of debutantes coming out with the usual 'Belgrave balls'. But after such diverse and entertaining flights of fancy, he delivers the sucker-punch: a 'mummy and daddy' send birthday greetings to their darling daughter, *wherever she may be*.

'The Statues' describes the misadventures of two drunks, flat out on their backs in the flower beds of the corporation park, late one Saturday night, who attempt to stop a statue of Sir Robert Walpole from ravishing a naked bronze nymph,[6] but end up soundly beaten. There is an amusing progression as the drunks recount their fanciful tale with absolute conviction to three representatives of the law: first a constable, then an inspector, and finally a judge. The punchline is that the drunks are surprised at how changed the nymph is after the encounter with Sir Robert: she is smiling, having evidently enjoyed the sex which is coyly passed over.

The record closes with joyful, defiant 'The Last Will and Testament of Jake Thackray', in which Jake gives instructions for his funeral and wake: once the priest has been summoned, bring out the booze. He wants the party to be riotous, and if the police turn up, his friends should pin the blame on him. He has no desire to be remembered, life is for the living. All his possessions, including his songs and debts, are for others to do with as they wish. He's even happy for his friends to kiss his wife, if she wants. The message is clear: no regrets.

This last song contains echoes of the writing of both Jacques Brel and Georges Brassens. Brel has exactly the same ideas and attitude to death in the defiant chorus of 'Le Moribond' – laugh, dance and party like madmen when they bung me in the hole – and in 'Le Testament', Brassens, like Jake, declares he is happy for his wife's new husband to use his possessions. Despite these similarities, though, Jake would say that his inspiration came from the poem 'Adrian Henri's Last Will and Testament': 'I was inspired by Adrian Henri, as he had done a poem like that. Other poets have done them too, and so I thought, "I'll hop onto this genre."'[7] Although he was writing within a tradition, 'The Last Will and Testament of Jake Thackray' remains a very personal song which expresses his irreverent attitude to life and death. Unsurprisingly, it was played at his funeral.

The two carols which appeared on Jake's first single show a completely different side to his writing. There is a directness to them, reflecting the fact that they were originally written for his pupils to sing, and they focus movingly on the unassuming people at the centre of the Christmas story.

The hauntingly beautiful 'Remember Bethlehem' considers all that Mary, a humble country girl, endured: the cold, the long journey, the painful labour in the darkness. Jesus's birth is presented as a moment of importance for the whole of creation, to be remembered even by 'the sulky old sun'. The song ends with a reference to Christ's sacrifice and Holy Communion.

'Joseph' reflects simply but movingly on the loyalty and simple, steadfast faith shown by the lowly carpenter, asking why he isn't surprised at the events unfolding in the Christmas story. The singer bemoans the lack of songs about Joseph, but promises to remember him at Christmas. Perhaps Jake felt this all the more keenly, given that Joseph was his chosen saint.

Norman Newell's understanding of the quality of Jake's writing was excellent, even if his decision regarding the two record releases presented a marketing challenge. But what of his judgement regarding the musical arrangements?

The producer's dilemma was how best to present these idiosyncratic songs with their unusual subject matter and mixture of comedy and pathos. Having abandoned the idea of recording Jake performing them solo, he decided to make them commercial in conventional terms. The results were mixed.

Where Geoff Love's small ensemble is used, such as on 'Country Bus' and 'The Little Black Foal', the simplicity and intimacy of the arrangements largely work, but the tempo is rigid, robbing Jake of the flexibility he enjoyed when playing solo, where he could change speed at will for dramatic effect to enhance his performance. (This is exactly what he does on 'The Cactus', the only track on the album to be performed solo.)[8]

The songs which use an orchestra enjoy mixed fortunes. On 'Ulysses' and 'The Statues' the restrained orchestrations complement the storytelling by adding touches of colour and drama. On 'The Black Swan' the orchestra is much more prominent, but the arrangement still works because it suits the inherent emotion, and the strings heighten the pathos, much as in the romantic balladry of Jacques Brel. However, the lush orchestration works much less well on 'Lah-Di-Dah' which, musically, is dressed up as a conventional love song, but is not, and this jars with the humorous lyrics. However, 'Jumble Sale' fares least well. It is turned into a brash and busy rumba, a world away from the charming intimacy of Jake's demo.

Sadly, the commercial gloss applied to Jake's delicate carols is also heavy-handed. Norman Newell hired John McCarthy, one of London's top chorus masters, to lead the backing singers, and as Geoff Love's ensemble chugs out a rhythm reminiscent of Peter and Gordon or The Seekers, massed voices warble dramatically; the effect tips the music towards bathos, rather than pathos.[9]

From the outset, Jake had mixed feelings about the arrangements, but when he wrote to Carol Hawkins, he took a pragmatic view: 'Some of the songs just can't take the strain of so much finery but others bear up quite well. Anyhow, I don't care. Norm said I'll be rich.' Privately, he would later declare that he hated the orchestrations, but publicly he was always diplomatic, doubtless out of loyalty to Norman. Perhaps because of his inexperience, he put his trust in the professionals and went along with everything.

At this early stage in his career, he may also have liked the fact that his songs were having such attention paid to them. 'I think Jake was enormously flattered that there was this orchestra, and there was the great Geoff Love, the great Norman Newell,' says Alex Armitage. His friend, the singer-songwriter Ralph McTell, understands the attraction of an orchestra for a new recording artist: 'I'm sure Jake was seduced by that. Whenever you hear your own songs arranged and produced, it's kind of grown up, it's "Well, they think enough of me to do this."' But recording with such extravagant backing was a challenge for Jake, as a solo performer. In Ralph's view it showed: 'The vocals are not quite right, they're not quite relaxed. I can see that he's had to overdub those vocals, and a lot of us from this acoustic tradition are not very good at dubbing vocals.'

The arrangements on these records have long divided fans. Some find them overblown and dated and believe that this has limited Jake's audience. However, they were part of a learning process. 'I think most of those involved felt that, on the early albums, people were only just learning what Jake Thackray was about,' says Alex Armitage. 'Personally, I think the album with the orchestra is lovely, but not really all that Jakey. It almost tries to make him into something that he wasn't. That is no criticism of Geoff Love or Roger Webb, who did the job that EMI and Norman Newell asked them to do. But, as Jake evolved, and as people understood him better, then the brief changed.' By the time he made his next album, there would be neither sight nor sound of an orchestra.

Whilst Jake put his faith in Norman's musical instincts, he was keen to entrust the design of the album's artwork to his friend at Intake, Ian Gliddon. He arranged for him to submit samples of his work to EMI's design department, who were suitably impressed and gave him the go-ahead to present a design. Consequently, Ian did a photo shoot with Jake in Leeds, with the intention of showing his urban roots, with shots of run-down pubs and demolished terraces. The photo they chose for the cover showed him wearing a dark donkey jacket and looking up at a church black with pollution. Something Jake particularly liked about this strong image is that it put the focus on the soot-encrusted church, not him. It was well-received by the designers at EMI, but when it went to Management for approval ('the accountants', as Jake would disparagingly call them), the idea was dropped and replaced with an in-house design that represented the album's title directly: a parchment mock-up of a will, with a wax seal attached, featuring an unflattering photograph of Jake's face peering out of it.

He was angry that his preferred design had been rejected, and was determined to take the matter up with EMI. However, Ian talked him out of it, explaining that the professionals had only done what they thought best, and that he shouldn't make trouble so early in his career. His view prevailed, even though Jake remained convinced that EMI was making a mistake. The episode is testimony not only to his strong sense of loyalty and desire not to compromise, but also, perhaps, his naivety.

After a productive summer, EMI's new recording artist was ready to be introduced to the world. With Norman Newell and Richard Armitage at the helm, Jake's career would receive a high-profile and well-coordinated launch, and they set about making him a star. In the press pack accompanying the record Norman gushed: 'The word "genius" is completely warranted as far as Jake is concerned. I believe his first single is the most beautiful recording ever made. I urge you to listen to it again and again. He is a brilliant composer, but one is so intrigued by his lyrics that not until you hear his songs a second or third time do you realise his great strength as a composer.'[10]

The single and album came out in early November. The week before, Jake returned to London during the school holidays for EMI's launch event (or 'Exploitation Party', as he called it) on 26th October.[11] Flanked by promotional displays and accompanied by a small ensemble, he performed his songs wearing one of the expensive new stage suits made for him that summer. 'Honest, two suits, eighty quid each – semi-shiny', he told Carol Hawkins. It was a far cry from *Look North*, where he performed in what he wore when he was teaching.

He was entering a new world.

From the Exploitation Party, Jake went straight to the BBC to record songs for Radio 1 and Radio 2's *Late Night Extra* and

Roundabout, but with a day job in Leeds, opportunities for further appearances were limited. Nevertheless, an interview was booked for 19th December with Reverend Roy Trevivian of the BBC's Religious Broadcasting Department, to be broadcast on Radio 4's *Home This Afternoon*. The *Radio Times* listing described Jake as 'schoolteacher, songwriter, pub singer', and the interview's strapline was 'The Holy and the Horrid'.

The album got good reviews. *Record Mirror* gave it four stars: 'Jake sounds like a kind of sick Noël Coward. His folk-tinged songs and his unusual songs made me laugh spontaneously.'[12] The *Melody Maker* reviewer thought he had 'a talent for off-beat doggerel that is at times hilarious and at others, obscure', and suggested that 'a bitter-sweet sense of humour and lyrical talent could bring him to a wider audience'.[13] As for the single, 'Remember Bethlehem' received a respectful, if somewhat cautious, response: 'With chorus backing, this is a religious slice of philosophy and is unusual enough to attract a lot of attention.'[14] Although the album sold well, neither record troubled the charts.

After all the excitement and promotional work which accompanied his record releases, Jake's teaching had to take priority until the end of the autumn term, but one booking Richard Armitage secured for him was too good to turn down: an appearance on the bill of a prestigious gala performance at London's Playhouse Theatre on Sunday 10th December, to be broadcast on BBC radio.[15] Jake dashed down to London to appear alongside stars including Jackie Trent, Vince Hill, The New Faces and Kenneth Horne (of *Round the Horne*). He was moving in new circles. He was also burning the candle at both ends: singing in London on Sunday night hardly sat easily with teaching English in Leeds on Monday morning.

Something would have to give.

Becoming a 'Performing Dick'

'And then I turned into a performing dick. As if I'd been fairy waned and ting! There I was, a full time performing dick. I know the Wednesday when it happened. In the morning I was a mediocre teacher, chucking the blackboard at forty people every forty minutes. In the evening, a mediocre singer, coming on after Vi Tye (housewife and stripper) at the music hall in Leeds.'

– Jake Thackray, 1977 [1]

From the moment Roy Rich first heard 'The Little Black Foal' in January 1967, Jake's performing career had been gathering momentum. This would move to a completely new level in 1968, when he walked through the doors of BBC Television Centre in London. But success came at a price, and he would soon be forced to make a difficult choice about his future.

His national television breakthrough came in March 1968 on *Beryl Reid Says 'Good Evening'*. Reid, a highly-respected actress, had recently won a Tony award on Broadway, and the six-programme series was designed to showcase her versatility in sketches by writers like Harold Pinter and John Mortimer. It would be broadcast on BBC1 in a prime Monday evening slot, going head to head with ITV's *Coronation Street*.

Richard Armitage had done well to secure the booking for

Jake, for whom it represented a tremendous opportunity: he would be seen by an audience of millions.

Publicity for the series emphasised that he was a school-teacher from Leeds making his national TV debut. Erring on the side of caution, the producer initially only contracted him for the first two programmes, but with an option to extend if Jake came across well. He did. As soon as the first programme was recorded, he was booked for the rest of the run.

From the start of February, therefore, Jake's weekly routine involved catching the train to London to rehearse a show on Saturday and record it on Sunday. He performed one song in each programme, always seated in an armchair with his guitar, fresh-faced and wearing a jacket and roll-neck jumper.[2] He sang live and, with a full orchestra accompanying him, there was no pressure on his playing. He performed the comic songs with a wry expression, no sign of the deadpan, lugubrious look that later became his hallmark. In one show, he also had a brief walk-on part in a sketch, playing a bailiff. Tall and good-looking, he was perfect for its punchline.

The first *Beryl Reid Says 'Good Evening'* was broadcast on 4th March, and EMI capitalised by releasing 'Lah-Di-Dah' as a single.[3] Trade newspaper *The Stage* gave the show a lukewarm review, but warmed to Jake and his idiosyncracies: 'Guest singer Jake Thackray has sung some weird songs in an even weirder voice that grows on you by the end of the song. I am not sure that contrived comic subjects like "my wife's in love with a cactus" are ever excusable, but his amiable presentation gets him by.'[4]

Jake was paid handsomely for his contribution to the six programmes: almost £300, plus expenses. It would take him three months to earn this much as a teacher.

He was now in his fifth year at Intake and, much as he enjoyed the job, balancing teaching with his burgeoning career as a performer was proving increasingly difficult. Popping into the BBC studios in Leeds for half an hour to record a song was one thing; the slog down to London another, and the strain began to show. His colleague, Lin Pass, remembers him arriving at school in the morning, having had no breakfast and looking the worse for wear. Although he had a supportive headteacher and sought to minimise the impact of his performing activities on Intake, the situation was not sustainable.

The obvious solution, as far as Jake's agent and record company were concerned, was for him to give up teaching and concentrate on performing, and he shared with Ian Gliddon the argument they put to him. To capitalise on his success and increase his earnings, he needed to make more time for concert appearances because these, along with his television and radio work, would drive up record sales. Remaining a teacher would only hamper his ability to self-promote and limit his earnings. 'They saw a package of recording and performing which wouldn't fit with teaching,' says Ian. 'Jake said he wasn't sure he wanted that, because he'd got nothing against teaching and was earning a living. And they told him, "You'll earn a lot more with us," or words to that effect.'

Jake was reluctant to leave Intake and initially saw no reason why he couldn't continue to combine two careers. Furthermore, exchanging the steady financial security of education for the uncertainties of life as an entertainer was a big decision, particularly given his working-class background. He revealed that Molly was anxious too: 'My mother was very worried about me giving up teaching. After eight years of it I had got to the £1,200 a year level, which wasn't bad.'[5] He discussed his dilemma with his headteacher. Given Charles Gardiner's own frustated ambition to act and his recognition of Jake's talent, it is not surprising that he encouraged him to seize the chance.

Contractually, he had to give Intake half a term's notice. As his friend Trevor Thewlis recalls, 'It wasn't until he saw his potential, or other people saw his potential, that he took the decision to go.' The BBC's offer of an extension to his run on Beryl Reid's show seems to have been pivotal and gave him the confidence to take this leap of faith. Jake handed in his notice and left Intake at the end of the spring term.

This decision to quit teaching provided an opportunity for publicity, and the *Daily Mirror* ran the story in early March: 'After the Singing Postman comes the Singing Schoolteacher. His name is Jake Thackray and he's beginning to make quite an impression.'[6] Jake explained that his decision was pragmatic: '...the two [jobs] started to clash and I thought that it would be better for everybody if I made a choice'.

For all that the future might hold, he was undoubtedly sad to leave Intake. He'd made many friends there, loved working with his pupils and knew the job had enabled him to develop his creativity. 'The school was very sad that he was moving on,' recalls Graham Stanley, 'but I am sure people saw his talent, saw that he was a unique talent, and felt he must move on.' Jake would later admit that leaving had been a big wrench: 'For two days it felt as bad as leaving a woman.'[7]

His new-found celebrity did provide Intake with a useful media opportunity, and an interview and photo shoot were arranged. One pupil, Anne Medlock, recalls it vividly: 'We all crowded into the classroom, excited by the commotion, a few of the boys hurling definition jokes around... the whole room erupting with giddy laughter, Mr Thackray almost but not quite! And at the end, after a touching rendition of 'Ulysses' (wag wag, woof woof), he said that if we ever passed him on the street, or came upon him anywhere, we should never be afraid to say hello – in fact he demanded we speak to him, that we'd always be a part of his life...' His colleague Bryan Smith remembers the final assembly, in which Jake sat on the steps of the stage and sang 'Ulysses'. Some of the older girls wept.

Those last words to the pupils were true enough. Jake would always speak warmly of Intake, declaring it was 'God's own school – marvellous place.'[8] He would also draw inspiration from his time there for some wonderful flights of fancy in his storytelling at concerts and in his newspaper columns.

The farewell at Intake was inevitably followed by a leaving 'do' in a pub, the Rodley Barge in this instance. Bryan Smith remembers with amusement Jake generously ordered more and more drinks for everyone, and then, handed the bill, enquiring confidently of the bar staff, 'You'll take a cheque, won't you?'

He kept in touch with his friends and returned to Intake occasionally. He also still cared about his former pupils, even taking the time on one visit to seek out the religiously-minded pupil who had provided the inspiration for his song, 'Salvation Army Girl'. It was full of wry sexual undertones and, sensitive to the girl's feelings, Jake wanted to be sure she understood that it wasn't about her.

He had a similar caring attitude towards children who were fans. In April, the mother of nine-year-old Kate Booth alerted him to her daughter's distress over the fate of his fictional dog, Ulysses, following its master's threatened suicide. He wrote Kate a charming handwritten letter, reassuring her all was well with them both, as they each now had a lady-friend, '…and we are waiting for the chestnut trees to blossom when we shall all be reunited'.

As well as leaving teaching, Jake left Leeds and moved south. This made perfect sense, given that the show-business world centred on London, and many other northern entertainers had taken this step before him. Keen to develop himself, he also recognised that the move would give him more access to people from whom he could learn.[9]

Nevertheless, he was a Yorkshireman through and through, and in interviews did not hide his antipathy towards the 'fat lands of the South': 'I hope I don't get softened up. I see a lot of things I feel I am right to dislike. All this opulence – I mean they don't know what hard times are like down here… It's all like another country to me… I try hard not to have a Northerner's inferiority complex.'[10] In the same interview he declared that he would like one day to return to live in Leeds, but he never did.

At the start of April he packed his bags, said farewell to his mother in Old Oak Close and headed for the capital.

He had brief spells living in Blackheath and St Margaret's in South London, where he stayed with Bob Haverly, who had moved there from Leeds. However, he couldn't bring himself to settle in the city,[11] and by May had moved to the village of Whitchurch-on-Thames, five miles from Reading. Here he could enjoy country living whilst still being able to reach London easily, catching the train from Pangbourne, just across the river.

He enthused about the place to a local reporter: 'Here the land is worked. I love it. Besides, there's the Thames a couple of hundred yards away. And I'm mad about fishing.'[12]

Initially, he got digs in a pub, The Ferryboat, whose landlord and landlady he liked so much that he sang their praises in the local press and invited them to his wedding. He would even write and perform on television in 1969 a tribute to the pub's legendarily relaxed opening hours:

If you ever seek to find us
And you don't know where to search,
You could try the local prison
Or the back row of the church.
But 10 to 1 we're in the Ferryboat with cronies of our ilk,
Men of our kidney who've been boozing ever since they
Came off mother's milk.
Big Frank, Sailor George, Sidney and me,
Drinking at the Ferryboat never-endingly.
We won't be in the Duchess's Arms,
Nor in the Prince of Wales,
We'll all be in the Ferryboat
Unless we're all in jail.

In the final verse he declares that when it's time for them to meet their maker, they'll still be in the taproom 'singing hymns and clinging to the pumps'.[13] Hopefully, his performance didn't lead to the police raiding the premises.

Down south, Jake was far better placed to capitalise on the offers coming in following his small-screen appearances and to reap the rewards of having a well-connected agent keen to develop his career.[14] He was upbeat about his prospects when speaking to the *Sunday Mirror* in late April: 'Until recently I wondered if I was doing the right thing in giving up a regular job in favour of a risky livelihood in show business. Especially as I was thinking of marriage. But now my own TV series is being negotiated, I've been offered stage dates, a TV commercial and other lucrative work and at present I'm working on my new LP. So I don't regret a thing.'[15] Not all of this would come in to land, but a lot would happen in the next few months, and by the late summer he was back on television. Meanwhile, Richard Armitage secured him a steady supply of bookings on BBC radio's *Roundabout* and *People Singing*.

A small but significant milestone came on 13th May when Jake returned to his hometown as one of the headline acts on a variety bill at the legendary Leeds City Varieties.[16] He spoke of his appearance in the glamorously titled *Parisienne Scandals* as being the start of his professional career, and saw it as a valuable experience. However, with the venue specialising in burlesque and strip shows, *Parisienne Scandals* hardly lived up to its glamorous title.[17] The week-long run was a treadmill, two shows a night, plus matinees on Tuesday and Saturday, and Jake was competing for audience attention with the likes of comic mime artist Roger L'Idiot and Vi Tye, Leeds's own 'Strip Star'. While Sheila and her friend Carol Hawkins turned out to support him, he knew full well that most people weren't there to see him, and his spot was after Vi's.[18] He told his friend Trevor Thewlis that his act was received in total silence, and that the seedy-looking men in the front row, with raincoats folded over their laps, threw coins at him (and not as a sign of appreciation). Years later, he was scathing about his

performance, declaring that he 'died': 'At the Varieties, I was
very, very bad because I didn't know how to do it.'[19] It was not
an auspicious beginning to his professional career, but there
would be better things to come in the years ahead, and it taught
him which bookings to reject.

The BBC in Leeds had been very good to Jake, but much
had changed since Pamela Howe first booked him onto her
radio show in 1965. By 1968, she had long since moved on,
and now there were other changes afoot, with the launch on
24th June of Radio Leeds, the BBC's new local station. To
celebrate, Jake was invited to write a song. He came up with a
jingle that had a strong tune (soon to be re-used) and quirky
lyrics containing a mix of public information and colourful
description:

> If you can't get a sound out of Radio Leeds,
> Well, it's not that your set is decrepit;
> And you're not going deaf,
> It's on VHF,
> And there's not many radios can get it.
> But come down to Radio Leeds,
> Just walk in, you're welcome to enter.
> They've a radio car and a budgerigar
> In a fish tank in the radio centre.

It was an ephemeral piece, but his ability to write quickly and
amusingly to order would stand him in good stead.

In April, Jake had spoken of plans for his second LP, for
which he had no shortage of excellent material, but after a day's
recording at Abbey Road in mid-July no further sessions took
place for nine months. The reasons would soon become clear.
He received, in quick succession, two very different offers of
TV work and these would take priority for the rest of the year.

The first was an invitation to appear in *Tickertape*, London
Weekend Television's new Sunday afternoon children's series,

broadcast from August to November. Each week, viewers were to be invited to see what came out of the 'tickertape machine', and were treated to a mixture of music, poetry, animation, sketches and information items, along with a 'Star Spot' featuring a well-known actor or performer.

Jake was booked to appear in all 16 episodes, working closely with *Tickertape's* other two mainstays, warm-mannered lead presenter and *Carry On* star Bernard Bresslaw, and actress Janet Henfrey, who joined Bernard in performing sketches.[20] Jake's role was to provide the songs, which he sang perched with his guitar on a high stool, often with Bernard and Janet accompanying him on banjo and percussion and singing on the choruses. To reinforce the idea that they were a company, the trio dressed identically in bowler hats and striped jumpers.

Working to tight deadlines on a new show inevitably meant that there was a lot of pressure. Nevertheless, Janet remembers *Tickertape* as a very enjoyable experience: 'I have very happy memories of the programme because of working with Bernie and Jake. They were both so lovely and supportive.'

Jake provided songs for every show, along with a theme tune that got steadily faster as it went along: 'Tick-tickertape, tick-tickertape, a most peculiar machine. Tick-tickertape, tick-tickertape, the strangest one I've ever seen.'

Janet recalls that the other songs were all more or less related to the content of the programmes 'in Jake's idiosyncratic way'. The final episode, for example, included an item about body-building, for which he possibly wrote 'Flex Your Do-Dahs'.[21] Another featured a poignant thing that began 'Sophie is shy, she's ever so shy', and ended 'Sophie and Timothy, they're two of a kind'.[22] Perhaps Jake recycled some of the material written for Intake.[23] Alas, no footage of the programmes has survived and, as far as is known, Jake never took any of the songs written for the series into the recording studio.

On 3rd August 1968, just a week before the first episode of *Tickertape*, Jake had pressing business at St Margaret Mary's

Catholic Church in the Forest of Dean: at the age of 30, he was getting married. Sheila, who had graduated that summer, had just turned 22. Among the friends celebrating the day with them were Carol Hawkins, Bob Haverly, the landlord and landlady of The Ferryboat and best man Ian Gliddon, along with various people from Jake's new show-business life, like Norman Newell and the owner of London's Duke of York's Theatre. Apart from a last-minute panic caused by Jake's trousers only returning from the cleaners in the nick of time, everything went off well, and the reception was held nearby at the vicarage of All Saints Church, Newland.[24]

Jake and Sheila spent their wedding night at a local pub, and later told friends and family that the combination of nylon sheets and pyjamas literally led to sparks flying. With work on *Tickertape* imminent, they had only the briefest honeymoon, during which they went to London with Carol and Bob to see John Osborne's latest play, *Time Present*, at the Duke of York's Theatre, where they had the best seats. Carol found being invited along on her friends' honeymoon and entertained so lavishly highly amusing, but it was typical of Jake and Sheila's generosity and desire to share good experiences.

They set up home in a rented riverside flat in a grand period property on Shooter's Hill in Pangbourne, an area Jake dubbed 'the Tío Pepe – Hush Puppy belt'. However, their time in this idyllic spot would end early, in 1969, after they apparently incurred the displeasure of their 'Knightsbridge landlady', as Jake called her: it seems that they had lowered the tone of the area unacceptably by hanging out washing on a line.[25] It is not hard to imagine his reaction to such snobbery, and they moved back across the river to Whitchurch-upon-Thames.

For four months following the wedding, much of Jake's time was taken up with writing, rehearsing and performing on *Tickertape*. The series received a glowing review from *The Stage*, which declared that it 'treated youngsters as rational beings and put before them a variety of items appealing to a wide range of tastes'. The reviewer also liked Jake's 'eccentric vowels'.[26] Despite such praise, a second series wasn't commissioned.

Jake almost immediately saw his involvement in *Tickertape* as an embarrassing mistake and soon spoke candidly about this in an interview: 'I'm a terrible performer. That children's programme I was in, I just want to forget about it. You see they made me move about and do things. I can't act or anything like that.'[27] It would not be the last time he would be dismissive of a programme in which he was involved and critical of his own performance. However, Janet Henfrey has a very different view of his contribution to *Tickertape*: her memory is that Jake always did a very professional job.

If Jake took a lesson away from *Tickertape*, it was that he hadn't turned professional in order to be a children's entertainer, and for the rest of his career he usually kept children's TV at arm's length: it could not provide him with opportunities to perform the sort of songs he wanted to write.

Despite his misgivings, *Tickertape* had given Jake steady work and raised his profile. He was now a celebrity, as is evident from how, in November 1968, he was invited to open a shop. Or, more accurately, a shop extension. Collins, an ironmonger's in Pangbourne, was expanding, and the *Reading Evening Post* gave this lavish coverage, announcing that 'Jake Thackray, star of ITV's Tickertape show will declare the newly extended store open today.' Clearly, Jake had arrived, in Pangbourne, at least. It was hardly the sort of celebrity game that he would have enjoyed playing, but there was a local connection, and at this early stage in his career he played along.

Far more exciting than any of this was that during the autumn of 1968 Sheila became pregnant with their first child. Sam would be born the following summer and during the pregnancy Jake was an attentive husband, cooking (competently, but spectacularly messily), reading up on pregnancy and fussing over what Sheila ate. In interviews, he could not hide his excitement about the prospect of fatherhood.

Since turning professional, Jake's life and career had swiftly moved on. Financially, predictions made by his record company had proved accurate: in November 1968 he told the *Sunday Mirror* that in six months he had earned £1,600 from record sales and radio and television appearances – far more than he had earned as a schoolteacher. And this was just the start. The anxieties he and his mother had felt were misplaced.

Nevertheless, he remained ambivalent about his decision to quit teaching. In that same interview he dismissed himself as 'a lousy guitar player' and expressed a very jaundiced view of his new profession: 'I'm just a performing man now, but I don't want my children to grow up identifying their father with seedy dressing rooms and stale make-up. I don't want them to see me sweating, nervous, and say to themselves – well that's his trade!'[28]

For all his success, Jake would never be comfortable with the choice he made, nor the pedestal upon which people would place him. And even as he gave that interview – with *Tickertape* yet to finish – he had just started work on the programme that would do more than any other to put him there.

Above: Jake's mother, Ivy May 'Molly' Armitage (*seated, second from left*), with the rest of her family, c. 1915.   *Thackray family*

Left: Molly Thackray in her 20s and 70s.
Above right: Jake's father, Ernest, in his West Riding Constabulary uniform.

Thackray family

Above: 'We were procession crazy.' Jake (*third from left*), age 7, hands held in prayer, heading to his first communion, 31ˢᵗ May 1945.

Right: Jake as a baby, outside 2 Park View Terrace, Rawdon.

Below: Jake, age 12, with brothers Richard (*left*) and Michael (*right*), in December 1950. *Thackray family*

A caring lad: Jake with a young friend outside his home, 90 Burley Lodge Road, *above left*, and, *right*, standing on the doorstep, behind his mother, with friends.

Thackray family

Having fun: Jake, *above left*, with friends in the mid-1950s and, *right*, as a shy and studious pupil.

Thackray family

College days: 'Fine work at left half.' Jake (*back row, third from left, above*) and the St Michael's College 2nd XI, 1956.

Right: A gangling, awkward youth no more. Passport photo.

Below: Jake (*standing far left*) in his Scholarship year at St Michael's College, 1957. Don Stoker, who hitch-hiked with him to Rome, is pictured front row, fourth from left.

Thackray family

Jake (*nearest camera*) rowing
with Tom Wingate at Durham
University. The pair would win
a regatta together.
Below: A blurred Jake on
graduation day, July 1960.

Thackray family

Above: 'God's own school – marvellous place!' Jake the teacher at Intake, Leeds, with his form 3B in 1967. *Below*: Jake and future wife, Sheila; alone in the back garden of 8 Old Oak Close; playing with a canine friend, c. 1966-67.

Thackray family; Carol Hawkins

Snap happy:
Jake, *left*,
pictured
at Ridge
Mount,
with Carol
Hawkins,
c. 1967.
Carol Hawkins

Above: Sheila in her
flat – and flat-mate
Carol's dress.

Left: Jake, Sheila
and friend in her
student flat, c. 1967.
Carol Hawkins

All the lah-di-bloody-dah: The shy, beaming bridegroom, August 1968.

Below: Sheila's brother Rick, *right*, pint in hand, at the reception. Norman Newell, in glasses, can be spotted in the background.

Carol Hawkins

Above: The newly-weds outside the church in Coleford.

Thackray family

Right: Sheila, the beautiful bride, vists the buffet and poses for the camera.

Carol Hawkins

Braden's Week

THE STAGE

JAKE THACKRAY — BRADEN'S WEEK

'*THE SUN*' — *27th October 1969*

. . . Just one point. There was grief in my household when JAKE THACKRAY failed to materialise. Have you mislaid him? If so, please put an ad. in the Times or something . . .'

NEVER FEAR, HE WILL APPEAR

on

8th and 29th November, 20th December and 17th January

– **Noel Gay notice,** *1969*

When Jake performed in the pilot episode of *Braden's Week* in July 1968, he can little have imagined where it would lead. This would be a pivotal moment in his career. Four years of work on late-night television followed and, for millions of viewers, his name would forever be synonymous with the programme.

Braden's Week was broadcast on BBC1 on Saturday nights, straight after *Match of the Day*, to a large audience. It was a new show, but had much in common with its highly successful ITV predecessor, *On the Braden Beat*, capitalising on the popularity of its star, Canadian actor Bernard Braden. The programme took a wry look at the week's events and, alongside consumer affairs investigations, interviews with children, sketches and other humorous items, included a topical song of the week.

In his proposal for the show in May 1968, producer
Desmond Wilcox said he wanted a song from 'Jake Thackeray
[sic] or someone like that'. Jake's name had been put forward
by Esther Rantzen, a BBC researcher who would appear in the
programme.[1] 'They wanted music and I had heard Jake on the
radio,' Esther recalls. 'I thought he was amazing. I talked about
him to John Lloyd, the producer of *Braden's Week*, and he
probably met him, and then booked him.'

Before the Corporation would commit to a full series, a
pilot was commissioned, recorded on Saturday 27th July, a week
before Jake's wedding. He performed two songs, 'Personal
Column' and 'Salvation Army Girl', but the latter was cut from
the final edit due to lack of time. When he saw the programme,
the BBC1 controller was critical of much of its content, but
noted that 'Thackeray [sic] was interesting'.[2] Evidently he was
so interesting that when the first series was commissioned, he
performed in all 26 programmes. The *Braden's Week* producer
clearly shared Roy Rich's view that Jake was 'a very valuable
property': his fee was a hefty 75 guineas for each of the first
six programmes, rising to 85 guineas for the rest.[3]

For six months, starting in November 1968, Jake was on the
nation's television screens every week.[4] It was an extraordinary
and unrivalled opportunity, and the producer's confidence in
him wasn't misplaced. Such was his success that he would be
invited back to appear in three further series.

Jake's brief to write topical 'point numbers' wasn't new. Cy
Grant's satirical calypsos had featured on BBC's *Tonight* in the
1950s, Lance Percival and Millicent Martin had sung topical
songs on the ground-breaking *That Was The Week That Was* in
the early 1960s, and Tom Lehrer's acerbic, satirical writing had
occasionally graced *The Frost Report*. However, never before
had a songwriter of Jake's quality and originality been secured
for a six-month run.

Braden's Week placed enormous pressure on him as a writer.
In an interview he suggested that he had a well-oiled routine,

scouring the national papers for ideas on Monday and Tuesday, before phoning Braden or one of his team to agree the song's focus and then start the writing. 'I just keep going until I come up with something,' he said. 'Then I put [i.e. send] the words in... I usually have my work back in the studio by Thursday, well in advance of the show.'[5] Although he wasn't required at Television Centre until Saturday to rehearse and record the programme, his lyrics needed to be approved in advance and inserted into the shooting script.

Whilst he made the process sound straightforward, finding inspiration every week to order wasn't. He had high standards, and knowing that what he sang would be heard by millions only increased the pressure. So there were often last-minute changes. 'Point numbers were quite hard,' recalled Sheila Thackray. 'You'd [Jake] just come down from the Saturday night [performance]... Tuesday, you'd start to panic... "Got to think of something!"...Wednesday [nothing]...It was really, really scary.' As a result, there could be a gap between what the production team was expecting Jake to sing and what was delivered. 'He used to have to phone the lyrics through to the Beeb to make sure that they were suitable,' says Sheila's brother, Rick. 'Jake would get to Thursday and think, "I don't like this song," scrap it and put another in. And so [the song would] get introduced, and he'd say, "No, I'm not singing that one. I'm singing another one." And so he'd sing another one which bore no relation to the titles as they went up.'

Bernard Braden himself acknowledged all this humorously in the sleeve notes for Jake's second album: 'Writing a new song each week isn't easy, and Jake usually selects a subject by Tuesday. Our set designer, Don Giles, spends several days arranging a suitable set for a song about an old lady who lived in a room above a rural post-office. On Saturday afternoon Jake wanders in with a look of abject apology. The song hasn't worked out to his satisfaction, so he's written instead a number about a trendy girl who lives in sin in Swiss Cottage. It's a mark of the quality of Jake Thackray that Don Giles happily goes to work improvising a new set which will be seen on the air in a matter of hours.'

The transcripts of the lyrics in the shooting scripts show the pressure under which Jake was working, containing many last-minute alterations. In December 1969, he performed 'Leopold Alcocks', his celebration of a fictional, accident-prone relative. The draft lyrics he phoned through to the production team included:

> Leopold Alcocks cracked all my crockery,
> My kitchen's a battlefield, my lounge is a rockery.
> I'd much rather harbour a love-sick gorilla,
> Robespierre and Hitler and also Attilla.

By the time he arrived at BBC Television Centre on Saturday, the contrived catalogue of villains and allusion to Georges Brassens's 'Le Gorille' had disappeared, replaced by sharper lines that established the song's premise much more amusingly.

Sometimes he went even closer to the wire, phoning no lyrics through at all, and on these occasions the scripts contain a simple, hopeful statement: 'Jake's song'. This must have caused frustration and anxiety, but he always delivered on the day, and so everyone was prepared to live with it.

Jake came up with some brilliant point numbers for *Braden's Week*. For the first episode the production team suggested that he write about the Miss World competition being staged the following week. Reusing the tune from his Radio Leeds jingle, 'Miss World' marries a brash, saucy chorus with sharp political satire. It contains good jokes about Miss USA not caring about Miss Vietnam and alleging Miss Russia is a man, but the best is about Miss South Rhodesia's skin tone: Jake advertises UDI[6] as a soap which 'washes whiter'. The song was a terrific opening shot.

Another stand-out point number was 'Pass Milord the

Rooster Juice', which was prompted by news that Barbara Cartland had held a high-society launch party for a book proclaiming honey's virtues as an aphrodisiac.[7] Jake turned the subject into a satire on the decline of the ruling classes, making the joke that 'nobs' don't do what they used to. Witty double entendres abound, as he links crumbling architectural features to declining libido, and no one could be in any doubt about his politics: these 'cocky thorough-breeders' are only getting what they deserve.

'The Ladies Basic Freedoms Polka', inspired by news reports of members of the Women's Liberation Movement pinching men's bottoms, was another strong point number containing bizarre images and clever puns, the best of which involve a cook being goosed and a priest turning the other cheek.[8]

Whilst Jake's writing was almost invariably rooted in Yorkshire and Britain, in one USA-themed programme he looked across the pond.[9] The deeply ironic 'God Bless America' is more akin to the writing of Tom Lehrer or Randy Newman than Jake Thackray and never appeared on record. The song's protagonist is a bigoted, home-sick American who lists everything he misses while stationed abroad. Amid the cultural trivia, Jake makes satirical points about racism, America's sense of identity and its diverse contributions to the world:

Carry me back to the land of the tranquillizer,
Home of the free and the cut-price gun,
Cradle of democracy and roll-on deodorant,
The land of the Flying Nun.
I miss tomato ketchup and sody-pop,
Black-eyed peas and blueberry pie,
I miss the clubs of the coppers in Chicago,
I am a regular guy.
God bless, God bless America, God bless Uncle Sam.
God save, God save America, Vietnam Goddam.

This verse, with its references to the Vietnam War and police brutality in Chicago (where riots had followed the murder of Martin Luther King Jr.), was cut before broadcast, presumably because it was considered too political, even though Jake had referenced Vietnam similarly in 'Miss World'.

The racist protagonist uses the 'n' word, and the song has a chilling ending which would no doubt resonate with the far-right in Trump's America:

> God bless, God bless America,
> God bless the Klu Klux Klan.
> God save, God save America,
> He's the only one who can.

Jake enjoyed considerable freedom on *Braden's Week*, but 'God Bless America' shows that there were limits as to what he could sing. Requirements to compromise irritated him: ever the anarchist, he did not like others controlling his creativity, an enduring theme in his career. In later years, as a newspaper columnist, he could become irritated when the paper didn't publish *exactly* what he had written.

This frustration led him to accept a bet to see what he could smuggle past the censor during the second series of *Braden's Week*: 'I... was really irritated by a producer in *Braden's Week* who said I'd never get away with "Bugger" – change it to something else. Well, I got so mucked about with it; anyway there was another bloke in the programme, a right swine he was, a lovely bloke, but very coarse. He bet me that I couldn't submerge certain unspeakable expressions into a song and get it passed. You know the various rhymes for wanking – Jodrell Banking – well, I got eight of them all into a song, and they read it over and said it sounded very picturesque.'[10]

The song in question, written in February 1970, was the jaunty, filthy 'The Policeman's Jig'. The debate around censorship, pornography and obscenity was a live one at this time, with the police raiding shops, theatres and cinemas. Aside from the bet, Jake probably took inspiration from events on 16th January, when the police raided a London art gallery and confiscated lithographs by John Lennon which were allegedly obscene. The song presents the police raids in comically obsessive and covertly sexual terms, while also making serious points about the reactionary nature of censorship. In it, Jake claims that the 'inflammatory pap' of dirty bookshops gets ignored, and that the police only confiscate material that is artistic and which they don't understand: masterpieces are 'right handy'. Of course, the joke was on the *Braden's Week* censors for passing this as fit for broadcast: clearly they did not understand what *they* were looking at. Even more amusingly, Jake performed the song twice in the series.

Through *Braden's Week* he gained an enduring reputation for his ability to write topical material. However, quality always mattered more to him than topicality, and many of the songs weren't point numbers at all. If he couldn't produce something topical which was good enough, he abandoned it and turned to his stockpile of material, carefully avoiding songs available on record, meaning viewers still heard something 'new'.[11] When Jake's second album was released in 1969, it would include 12 songs previously heard on *Braden's Week*, but few were point numbers, which he always regarded as a financial means to an end. His finest work was rarely inspired by what was in the headlines.

Despite much of his publicity presenting Jake as the 'Leeds schoolmaster', he almost never mentioned his hometown in his lyrics. However, 'The Kirkstall Road Girl' places the listener virtually on the doorstep of his childhood home and he performed it early in the first series of *Braden's Week*.[12] Full of memorable contrasts and images, it tells the tale of a young woman who was once on the game in Kirkstall, but who now moves in altogether different circles as the darling of the glossy magazines. The days of deals under lamp-posts are far behind her: she has swapped Leeds's boozers for cocktail bars and reinvented herself, with a new wardrobe and nose. Jake underlines how far she has travelled, with clever puns about her now having a 'Rolls Royce voice' and 'E-type smile'.

The song finishes with the distinctly unpalatable suggestion that she was better off when being true to herself, working the streets of Kirkstall. It is hard to believe Jake actually believed this, and the clumsy and ill-judged ending is indicative of the fact that this was an early song. However, it does show his deep-seated antipathy not only towards wealth, but any form of pretence or lack of authenticity. It chimed with the private misgivings he shared in a letter to his friend Carol Hawkins, following his first encounter with the glitzy world of show business in London: 'It's good to get back to Leeds after the dolce vita bit. I presume that all the golden boys and girls are in touch with some kind of reality besides their own lovely faces because they make their money and they know what's what about making it – but most of them baffle me. I find it hard to believe that some of them actually crap – or do they have a system of polythene disposable units that somebody calls for every now and then. Norman [Newell] craps OK. Norman's good. But not the rest. That's my new criterion – Homo Cacans. The Thackray Crap Factor.'[13] As Jake would put it later in one of his greatest songs, 'beware of the bull!' It was a theme to which he would return repeatedly.

Despite his high-quality output on *Braden's Week*, Jake was highly critical of his writing for the programme, declaring: 'Unfortunately, when I've had deadlines I've done a lot of rubbish and some of it's on record and I feel ashamed of that.'[14] His low regard for some of these songs is evident in how he never considered them for release on vinyl, and they never seem to have featured in his live set either. Consequently, 'Lady Penelope', 'Fifi Golightly', 'Old Age Pensioner' and 'When I Get Filthy Rich' now exist only as titles.

However, an examination of other unrecorded songs whose

lyrics survive in the *Braden's Week* scripts reveals that Jake's
verdict on his writing could be unduly harsh. 'When Lucy
Comes', for example, is a wonderful story of a ne'er-do-well in
hiding from the law and his creditors. It could sit comfortably
in the Georges Brassens songbook:

> If the grocer comes trotting round wagging his bill,
> Tell him I'm ill,
> Say how much I miss his smile.
> If the baker complains I have borrowed his bread,
> Tell him I'm dead,
> But tell him I'll willingly crawl out of hell
> To kick his backside,
> If he can prove that he's got one.
>
> Open the door when Lucy comes,
> Say where I've gone and she'll follow.
> Look how her eyes are tortoise shell,
> See how her hair is yellow.

It is a pity that no recording of Jake's performance survives.[15]

Writing for *Braden's Week* brought one form of pressure,
performance brought another.

Jake always found the experience traumatic. The
programme was rehearsed and recorded in front of a studio
audience every Saturday. 'It was never actually broadcast live,
but it always went out as if live,' says Esther Rantzen. 'The
lawyers said, "There's a chance you'll say something libellous
[being a consumer affairs programme], and we may need to be
able to do something about that at the very last minute." So
we would record it, but only just before the show was broadcast,
and we would never edit it, so all the mistakes stayed in.' In
effect, therefore, Jake was singing live.

During the first series he told a journalist candidly why he
disliked the process: 'I'm always very nervous before my spot,

and then I can't always remember the words... sometimes I think there's a small Jake Thackray inside trying to get me, producing such complicated words I can't learn them!'[16] There was a further practical problem: he was short-sighted, but wasn't allowed to wear his glasses, and so had to read the words written in huge letters on prompt boards.

Jake's songs are cruel, unforgiving things to sing: beautifully -constructed, but often with difficult phrasing, little or no repetition and always a precise trajectory. They are hard songs to master in any circumstances. On *Braden's Week*, performing for a huge audience, he might find himself singing something only written that week, with lyrics finalised a day or two before the broadcast. Given he was a nervous performer at the best of times, it is hardly surprising that he found this purgatory.

Much of his dislike of television work was down to nerves: 'I never enjoyed it... Staring at the red light and shaking with fear!'[17] This was literally true: he told his friend Ian Gliddon that awaiting his turn to perform, he had to keep his hand on his leg to stop it from shaking. Sometimes his nerves would overwhelm him, as was the case when he performed 'Bantam Cock' in 1972. After introducing it as 'a mucky song', he fluffed his guitar intro twice, then stated bluntly: '...and that is a cock-up...' The audience roared with laughter. Eventually he regained control of the situation: 'So, in order to lower the tension, not necessarily in your sitting rooms, but in my own trembling bowels, may I please start again?' Making no attempt to hide his mistake, he stole the show, and Bernard Braden congratulated him ironically on having managed to get seven minutes out of a two-minute slot. Nevertheless, Jake must have found it a terrifying experience.

The weekly jitters were followed by relief, and the ritual of drinks at BBC expense. He loved to share his good fortune and would invite friends and family along; indeed, Bernard Braden would joke about how much advantage Jake took of BBC hospitality.[18] Sheila Thackray wrote to Carol Hawkins about the experience: 'We all had a real good night. After the show there's drinks and snacks in a big room, for all the cast, production team and friends. You'll have to come with us. I don't go every time cos I don't like to push it. Looks like J's going to be doing this for a good few weeks yet. Desmond Wilcox, big shot of the *Man Alive* team, is pretty impressed with J.'[19]

In fact, Jake impressed everyone with whom he came into contact on the programme. 'We loved him,' recalls Esther Rantzen. 'We thought he was amazing. The studio audience loved him, and Bernie loved him.' Despite the tremendous impression he made, however, he remained an enigma to Esther: 'He was incredibly talented, musical, gorgeous to look at, but shy to the point of torture. I don't think I ever had a conversation with him. I used to ring him up and talk about ideas for the song of the week, but it was barely a conversation, and I felt it was my fault. I felt that I was gushing and unattractively enthusiastic, and I felt very intimidated.'

This shyness was very evident to his friend Ivan Mansley when Jake took him to a *Braden's Week* party: 'He insisted that I come with him, and I didn't really want to go. But Jake was so modest, saying, "No, Ivan, you come with me. You can look after me." And he added, "It's free booze!" I remember we were standing in the foyer of the building, and he said, "Look! There's Eric Morecambe!" He was so thrilled and excited being there. But at the party, instead of mixing with Bernard Braden and the other people from the show, he spent the whole evening with me. He was just overcome by the sudden ascent to fame, and he was embarrassed by it.'

Jake's appearances had a big impact on viewers, as Bernard Braden himself noted: 'We know for a fact that Jake is an acquired taste. When our series commenced late in 1968 letters poured in demanding his instant dismissal. Now most of them ask for an autograph, a photograph and, occasionally, an assignation. Perhaps the greatest tribute to Jake's staying power is that a number of the people who first wrote in to complain about him wrote again to say they'd changed their minds.'[20] His six-month run on the programme had made him a household name, and for years to come gig adverts would call him the 'star of *Braden's Week*'.

From the outset, Jake rejected the idea of stardom and disliked its impact upon his privacy, as he explained in January 1969, when a journalist asked whether it frightened him: 'Well, for a start, I'm not a star. The idea of it does frighten me a bit, but I think I could control it. I don't think I'd like to feel I belong to a public. Even now I can go in only one pub out of eight in Pangbourne because I'm recognised. Sometimes when they come up with "Aren't you Jake Thackray?" I say "No, I'm not. I just look like him." Of course I like people to know who I am, we all do, but it would be nice if they all reacted in the same way. Sometimes I can't think of a damn thing to say.'[21]

Such was Jake's success that he was retained for all four series of *Braden's Week* although, after the first, didn't perform every week. Doubtless he was relieved to have the pressure reduced. When he failed to appear in the first two programmes of the second series, an anxious viewer wrote to *The Sun*, suggesting that an advert be placed in *The Times* to track him down. Jake's agent picked up on this and placed a notice in the press: 'Never fear, he will appear'.

In the second series, Jake alternated performing duties with a man who was a kindred spirit, politically and artistically. Alex Glasgow, a staunchly socialist songwriter from Gateshead, shared his dislike of show business and love of Brassens. The two became great friends, staying at each other's homes; Jake and Sheila even joined the Glasgows on their honeymoon. Playwright Alan Plater, who knew both men well, recalled that Alex revered Jake, and saw at first hand how quickly he could write: 'As Alex told the story, they would go to bed Friday night, and he knew that Jake had to write a couple of songs by the next day, and these songs would emerge.' The two songwriters once spent an entire evening trying to work out the joke in a key verse of one of Brassens's songs: 'It turned out the joke was that the last line was sung in French but with a Belgian accent, and that's what made it funny. And this was the kind of pedantry that they devoted to their art of the song.'[22]

By the time the fourth series of *Braden's Week* started in 1971, there was a carousel of singers. Jake only appeared monthly and, firmly installed as the programme's veteran performer, he was no longer under pressure to write point numbers. Instead, he sang some old favourites, alongside songs which would be released on his next album. Some of these were comic, but his songwriting was developing and becoming darker. This was most powerfully illustrated in 1972 when he sang 'The Prisoner', in which he addresses a 'poor bastard soldier' occupying a foreign land. He appeals to him to think of what home and family mean to him (does he ever weep for them?), and to consider what they mean to his prisoner. He creates harrowing images of dead children and the rage and grief caused by their deaths, before predicting that the prisoner will kill the soldier. Both have his pity. Both are poor bastards. His debate with the producer about whether he could sing 'bugger' had been left far behind.

Introducing the song, Jake implied it was a point number, claiming to have calculated how many countries around the world were living under occupation. He then made light of the subject with a joke: 'There's a famous lavatory wall slogan which proclaims – it's a middle class lavatory, by the way – which proclaims "fighting for peace is like fornicating for virginity"...' But 'The Prisoner' was a world away from 'Miss World', the point number with which he had started his run on *Braden's Week* four years earlier. And Jake was a world away from the caricature of him as the strange-looking bloke who sang funny songs.

Braden's Week never saw a fifth series: the BBC cancelled both the show and Braden's contract when he appeared in a

margarine commercial. *That's Life!* soon replaced it, with
Esther Rantzen at the helm, but no Jake – for the moment
anyway. Doubtless he was ready to move on. His songwriting
had outgrown the format and the audience's expectations.

As with *Tickertape*, once *Braden's Week* was gone, he didn't
mourn its passing, and in an interview in 1973 he was keen to
distance himself from the show: 'I didn't associate myself with
it at all. I've got commitments to the Leicester Permanent
Building Society; I needed the money.' He didn't have a single
good word to say for it: 'Even the jokes they have on are
crummy – I've seen better in the Packhorse lavatory.'[23]

Jake's Progress

"I've concluded that the time it takes you to appreciate Jake Thackray is not a measure of him, but of you. In fact, he's a satirist with both bite and compassion. There aren't very many of them around.'

– Bernard Braden, 1969 [1]

The pressure of being on *Braden's Week* might have been a nightmare, but the programme provided Jake with a level of exposure of which many artists could only dream.

By 1969, his star was in the ascendency, and to develop his career he needed to capitalise upon his new status as a household name, drawing upon the expertise and guidance of his agent and record producer. He would need to make the most of opportunities in the recording studio, as well as on radio and television, and get used to life on the road as a live performer. He would also need to keep writing. Talented as he undoubtedly was, he was pursuing a career in which success could never be taken for granted.

His top priority, after the first series of *Braden's Week* finished in May 1969, was to release a new record. In the 1960s, artists regularly made an album a year, and it was 18 months since his debut release. Work on its aptly titled follow-up, *Jake's Progress*,[2] had been postponed due to his commitments

to *Tickertape* and *Braden's Week*, but there was an advantage to
this: by the time it was released, his television work had
significantly increased his audience.

Once again, Norman Newell and Geoff Love oversaw the
sessions and, whilst their musical instincts remained
conservative, the sound and arrangements on this album would
be different. Most importantly, no orchestra was used, which
would not only have pleased Jake but also EMI's accountants.
Instead, the album featured the jazz trio that had been
accompanying him on *Braden's Week*.[3] These outstanding
session musicians not only already knew his songs, but also had
the skill to contribute to the arrangements.

In the show, Bernard Braden once commented that the trio
obviously enjoyed playing with him; for his part, Jake was in
awe of what he called 'proper bloody musicians'. When
journalist Ann Purser sat in on a *Braden's Week* rehearsal, he
told her they had taught him a lot, and she enjoyed watching
them interact: 'It was fascinating to hear the thin, repetitive
line of Jake's composition developed and strengthened by
professional men who were enthusiastic about the song and
pleased to answer his earnest questions about technique.'[4] The
collaboration worked well, with the trio embellishing Jake's
tunes with appropriate jazz colourings.[5]

The album was recorded at Abbey Road in three days.[6] Rick
Irons, Sheila's brother, accompanied Jake to one session and
was fascinated by what he saw: 'We walked past Yoko Ono in
the studio foyer – she was instantly recognisable. In the studio
there was great camaraderie among the musicians. Someone
asked for a cigarette, and when he was thrown one, a drummer,
with perfect timing, did a drum roll as he caught it.[7] I remember
that the guitarist, Ike Isaacs, kept getting electric shocks off his
guitar. At one point one of the musicians quietly nodded to me
to look up at the control room window, where one of the
Beatles – John or Paul – was looking in on the session.'

Many of the songs on *Jake's Progress* were already several

years old and they were selected from a rich stockpile of material. The tracklisting is interesting because, although the album includes some wonderful comic material, its overall mood is distinctly more melancholy than its predecessor. Whether or not this was deliberate, the album would declare emphatically to listeners that there was much more to Jake than comic songs.[8]

'Country Girl' signals immediately that he is entering new territory. Humour is a secondary consideration and the primary focus is on creating an evocative picture of a woman who does as she pleases. She goes about her work on the farm, whilst all the while looking forward to the Saturday night dance, where she'll find a good-looking lad for sex. Sundays she cycles along the hedgerows to Mass, singing hymns as she goes. It is a sentimental picture of a life of simple, idealised pleasures, timeless in its rural setting, and yet suggesting the sexual liberation brought by the arrival of the pill. The woman's carefree approach to life is matched by Jake's use of metre and rhyme, which are markedly more relaxed than usual.

In 'Family Tree' he takes the listener on a glorious, fanciful tour of the fictional Thackrays, in which their only monument is a cousin's enormous cleavage and his boy-scout brother offers the Queen a cigarette. Throughout, he revels in the fact that their sheep are black and cheques bounce. Some of the humour, however, now shows its age: the prospect of the wittily-named Uncle Will and Auntie May dressing their children in white at their wedding is quaint rather than scandalous, and the inclusion of a joke involving rape completely unacceptable. (As his career went on and attitudes changed, Jake would change the offending lyric in live performance.)

'Sophie' paints a wistful picture of an inscrutable woman, and Sheila Thackray believed that it was inspired by the Sofia to whom Jake was engaged in France. Her lover knows that she likes Liquorice Allsorts and having her back stroked, and enjoys intimate knowledge of 'her deep, dark navel', but he yearns to know what she is really thinking. As they lie together in the dark, she remains a mystery to him. The song's melody neatly matches the ambivalence of the lyric.

'Worried Brown Eyes' is overtly comic and mines a similar seam of inspiration to 'Personal Column'. It tells the story of a 17-year-old regular of the problem pages who airs in print her anxieties about her tummy bulges, moles and relationship with boyfriend Dicky, who is becoming just a little too demanding. The song combines sympathy and wry amusement at her preoccupations with advice that belongs to a pre-feminist age, as she is urged to give Dicky a treat and show him the never-before-seen mole.

For anyone accusing Jake of misogyny, 'Worried Brown Eyes' is one of the songs which might be cited in evidence, but to label him in such a way is too simplistic. 'Country Girl' portrayed a woman who is sexually liberated and in control of her own destiny, and many of his songs show great compassion for women. 'On the Shelf' is a case in point.[9] This beautiful piece of English melancholia paints a moving picture of a spinster who is pragmatically getting on with her life. She seems happy enough, in her own way, and yet sighs from time to time and longs for company. As so often with Jake, he poignantly brings her existence to life through the inclusion of small details: the solitary chair at the table, the paper bag kept for feeding ducks in the park. Her life is one of lonely routines, and yet she has no time for tears.

'Salvation Army Girl' is another in which Jake deftly and quickly creates a vivid sketch. Here the protagonist describes a 'do-gooding Judy' with bony hands and woollen stockings, who sells *The War Cry* in the pubs. However, appearances can be deceptive, and he reveals that when this street angel is out of uniform, she is ready for some earthly pleasure with him. Jake irreverently repurposes the titles of 'All Things Bright and Beautiful' and other hymns to suggest the sexual pleasure they will enjoy, although his adaptation of the children's hymn 'Jesus

Wants Me for a Sunbeam' is somewhat unsettling. Indeed, the song treads an ambivalent path, both musically and lyrically. Doubtless the song would have horrified Molly Thackray, and no wonder Jake felt he needed to talk to the former pupil who had inspired it.

Having been passed over for his debut album, 'The Blacksmith and the Toffeemaker' at last made the cut and is one of the record's highlights: embellished with double bass and Ike Isaacs's beautiful guitar lines, it shines.

'The Hole' is the absurd tale of a man who gets his finger stuck in a hole in a door. His life spirals farcically out of control, as he attracts the unwanted attention of a policeman, a crowd of on-lookers, the media and a doctor. Eventually he, the door and the hole are carted off to court. The song contains some delightfully contrived rhymes, including the wonderful 'fidgeting... digit in'. Throughout, Jake mocks the reaction of every figure of authority, and this lack of deference reaches a glorious climax when the judge is advised to shove his 'Worshipful finger' up a hole.

'Caroline Diggeby-Pratte', one of the few point numbers on the album, was doubtless inspired by the sorts of reports and announcements regularly published in the 'society pages' of newspapers at this time. With his antipathy towards any form of privilege, Jake creates an unloveable character and uses the song to mock not only the attitudes and behaviour of high-society débutantes, but also deferential reporting.[10] Caroline, from a line of 'aristocratic Prattes', is a snooty, superficial girl who is into all the 'horsey balls' and has romantic thoughts of walking alone on beaches, but can't be without her gossip columns and cocktails. He concedes that some day someone will fall in love with her, and Heaven alone knows what *he* will be like.

'Grandad' is an old song which Jake had performed on radio and television back in 1966. As in 'Family Tree', he takes as his theme the scandalous behaviour of his fictional family. But here, with the focus on a single character, he develops the idea in glorious and ludicrous detail. The song owes something, perhaps, to Georges Brassens's 'Le Testament', in which the singer declares that, when his time comes to die, he will take the long road to the grave, so that he can enjoy some last earthly pleasures. Jake's character makes full use of his final hours; indeed, although this uproarious, drunken old scallywag is supposed to be dead, in truth he isn't actually dead enough. The hell-raiser spends his 90th birthday boozing till his friends drop, making sexual advances to the Ladies' Union and sticking two fingers up to the doctor who pronounces him dead. Heaven should brace itself: Grandad will be trouble.

'Mrs Murphy', like 'On the Shelf', paints a picture of a lonely, repressed woman, a middle-aged widow who lives with her budgerigar. Her life is stuck in a routine and her hopes are pinned on a gentleman friend who takes her for afternoon drives in his 'magical' motor and spends evenings on the sofa with her. However, she doesn't know his intentions and cannot bring herself to reveal the depth of her feelings for him. He smiles as he drives off, and Mrs Murphy is left weeping. So the weeks pass, and there is no fairytale ending to the melancholy tale.

The murder ballad 'One-Eyed Isaac' was one of the first songs Jake recorded for radio in December 1965, and is one of his darkest pieces of writing. Its protagonist, a brutal killer who boasts of his gleaming knife, finds love with a prostitute called Greasy Joan. However, she still has a living to earn, and when he catches her with one of her punters he cannot contain his jealousy: he kills them both, before tearing out his own hard, black heart. With a melody that owes much to Charles Trenet's 'La Java du Diable', the lugubrious music is well matched with such a sombre story.

'Nurse', one of Jake's 'public house' songs,[11] is a bawdy but elegantly worked joke, cast as a conversation between a nurse and her patient. The amorous patient begs the nurse to kiss him, citing the ever more extreme and ridiculous symptoms caused by his desperation, culminating in the suggestion that his war-wound is jumping. She seeks to maintain her professional distance, offering a variety of excuses, as well as some medical advice: closing his eyes and breathing through his nose might help. The song reaches its climax with a punchline which is obvious, but no less funny for that.

The final song on the album is 'The Castleford Ladies Magic Circle', which may well be a point number.[12] It is one of Jake's most memorable comic creations, painting ludicrous, outlandish pictures of the clandestine behaviour of the most unlikely cabal of witches. These ordinary middle-aged women engage in weekly pagan rites with the aid of their tabby cats and broomsticks from Woolworths. While their husbands play snooker, they dance naked for Satan, cavort with bogeymen and play 'hysterical leapfrog'.

At the heart of the humour is the ordinariness of these women who are behaving so extraordinarily, as Neil Gaiman observes: 'One of the things I love most in the song is the incredible approval of these Women's Institute types going off and consorting with Satan, and it's beautiful and it's hilarious, but it's also human, because it's not about beautiful young women in the forests, having sex, it's about lovely retired ladies, going off to be the Castleford Ladies Magic Circle.'

The album's cover design, featuring a portrait photo of Jake, was unimaginative but at least ensured that he was immediately recognisable to his *Braden's Week* fans.[13] Bernard Braden's amusing sleeve notes emphasised his connection with the programme. Doubtless Jake would have been pleased that the 'proper bloody musicians' all received prominent credits.

Jake's Progress was released in July 1969 and received less attention in the music press than its more heavily-promoted predecessor; no doubt reflecting the fact that his music was so off-beat and difficult to categorise. *Melody Maker* was struck by the record's melancholic mood and offered some insightful praise, while still managing to sound unenthusiastic: 'No one in their right mind would call Jake Thackray a singer – what he is is a droll troubadour, singing little satirical songs with bite and wit and a sort of understanding of our foibles. A bit of a lot to take in for three-quarters of an hour, but a sadly pleasant little selection of ditties.'[14]

The *Newcastle Evening Chronicle* was altogether more positive: '14 superb tracks by this latter-day Northcountry Noël Coward'. However, Jake would have been irritated at the comparison, which had been made before: the BBC's Talent Selection Group had made the same point three years earlier.

There are some superficial similarities between the two singer-songwriters – the sharpness of wit, the well-enunciated, clipped vocal delivery – but the differences are more significant. Jake's turn of phrase and much of his subject matter are inescapably northern, and his songs show a real interest in, and compassion for, the lives of working people. He combines lyrical sophistication with a perspective that is working-class through and through. Coward's outlook, despite his humble origins, was markedly different; indeed, he actively courted the limelight and 'tried to climb the social scale' (to borrow a line from Jake). His songs, which were often written for other people – and characters in shows – to sing, are much more concerned with the preoccupations of the fashionable society circles in which he moved. To characterise Jake as a Yorkshire Noël Coward, therefore, is misleading, and does a huge disservice to his distinctive genius. Jake would share his views about Coward in a radio series in 1987.

Jake's Progress received a delayed release in the USA, as did its predecessor. Both records were given a make-over for the American market, with new artwork and sleeve notes. The cover showed the singer leaning forward lugubriously on a tombstone, with the strapline: 'Jake Thackray is his own man. He sings his own songs. He sings them with a unique, sophisticated sensitivity.' This was all true, but less pithy than the somewhat bizarre 'sophisticated songs by Britain's jet-age troubador' which adorned its predecessor.[15] The records were well publicised and, despite Jake's writing being embedded in the language and culture of England, surprisingly well received. *Billboard*, America's leading music paper, gave them four stars, and the reviewer for *The Miami News* rated *Jake's Progress* 'one of the greatest disks of the year', comparing him not only with Tom Lehrer and Noël Coward, but even Charlie Chaplin: 'Few folk singers can evoke pathos – and then, in a flash, humor. In Thackray's world, everything is slightly off-center, like the unsynchronized color in a comic strip... What Chaplin did visually in treading constantly on life's banana skins, the marvellous Jake Thackray does verbally.'[16] It was an interesting comparison.

Having completed *Jake's Progress* in April, Jake spent the summer giving priority to his live work. However, he returned to Abbey Road on 4th August to record new vocals for his most unusual release.

In the 1960s, it was common for artists to record translations of their hit songs for overseas markets[17] and, given how much Jake had been influenced by *chanson*, it made sense to test out the French market with a single. However, rather than present Jake as an English Georges Brassens, Norman Newell selected songs with lush orchestral arrangements which placed him closer in style to the more flamboyant and romantic Jacques Brel: 'Lah-di-Dah' ('Tra La La') and 'The Black Swan' ('Le Cygne Noir').

To translate the lyrics the producer recruited Boris Bergman, a young, London-based French songwriter who did a serviceable job of adapting the cultural references. However, Jake brought along to the recording session his own translation for 'Le Cygne Noir'. His version is highly competent and retains more of the emotional impact of the English lyrics than Bergman's, while using slightly simpler French. Both were recorded, but Bergman's was selected for release.[18]

By chance, some friends of Jake's were at the session. John Grace and Eric Blackburn were Pangbourne-based folk musicians whom he had met singing in a pub. With typical generosity, he invited them to meet Newell at Abbey Road and sit in on the recording. From the control room they watched Jake overdubbing his vocal, singing in an excellent French accent to the orchestral backing track. 'I remember this vast, dark studio with Jake, on a stool, screens round him,' recalls John. 'He performed so confidently.'[19]

Afterwards, the producer let them record a short demo tape, which was doubtless what Jake had been hoping when he had invited them along. They capped a memorable day by meeting Ringo Starr and John Lennon, who were working on the *Abbey Road* album.

The single was released in France in November 1969 but didn't attract enough interest to make the exercise worth repeating. Nevertheless, it was an intriguing experiment which gave Jake the chance to sing his songs in a language he loved. Decades later, he would sing in French at concerts and on the radio, but when he did so, it was always in homage to Georges Brassens. Forever Brassens.

Show-business dress code in a folk club setting.

Stuart Allison 1971/Colchester Express Archives

Signing autographs at the Big Window Hotel, Burnley, April 1969.

Burnley Civic Heritage Trust

Tetheradick

Stepping Out of the Big Window

'He had this incredible skill of making the biggest, coldest, most impersonal hall feel like the Hare and Hounds in Birmingham.'

– Alex Armitage, agent

A few days after recording *Jake's Progress* in April 1969, Jake was on a week-long tour of pubs and community venues in the mill towns of Lancashire. On 22nd April he performed at the Big Window Hotel in Burnley, and the occasion was captured for posterity in an evocative photograph.

In the picture, seen on the back of this book, he is in his element and at his most informal, singing in a packed bar. With no stage or microphone, he is perched on a couple of stacked stools, his shiny suit the only concession to show business. This is how he most liked it, on the level, eye to eye with the punters. The audience is packed in around him; some sit, others stand, beer glasses in hand, eyes and ears on Jake. The night was apparently a triumph: 'His appearance at the hotel was such a draw that many had to be turned away from the door, and those fortunate to attend were left calling for more when the singer guitarist ended his two hour spot at ten p.m....'

Jake had been singing for several years in pubs like the Big Window. While teaching and arranging his own bookings, these performances had inevitably been irregular, mostly at weekends and confined to Leeds; the lunchtime concert he gave at Manchester University's theatre in October 1966 would have been a rare exception. However, everything changed following his record releases and TV appearances. Whether he liked it or not, television had made him a star, and if his career was to thrive he needed to capitalise on this. Six months on *Braden's Week* had provided rich rewards and financial certainty, but such work could never be guaranteed. To capitalise on his celebrity and make a good living, he needed to spend time on the road. His horizons also had to change: he must take the step up into bigger venues.

Jake would come to speak of live work as his 'bread and butter' and it would dominate his working life for the next three decades. He was fortunate to be represented by one of the country's best agents. Richard Armitage was not only well-placed to secure bookings and maximise earnings, but also keen to develop Jake's career and help him make the move into large concert halls. There was one problem, though. Jake was a sensitive performer, with the thinnest of skins and, as his friend, singer-songwriter Harvey Andrews observes, 'He didn't cope with performing too well. He was happiest in a small club with an intimate audience, as he was immensely nervous when he performed.'[1] Jake disliked being in the spotlight and needed conditions to be right for him to feel even remotely comfortable on stage. This would present a formidable challenge for his agent.

If Richard Armitage was to get Jake into the large theatres and concert halls his reputation could now fill, he needed to build up his client's confidence and move him far beyond his comfort zone. To achieve this, he took a strategic approach to bookings, as his son Alex explains: 'Obviously, when you have someone who is relatively unknown, unless they have a massive hit single, they don't go straight into doing the big halls. So what my father will have done with Jake is give him a mix of the smaller rooms Jake really enjoyed – folk clubs, and so on – and mix that in with the odd television or radio appearance, and on the back of that persuade the larger halls to take him.'

Richard waited and allowed *Braden's Week* time to grow Jake's audience. Then, in 1969, he began to increase live bookings and experiment by putting him on at different types of venue. Whilst this led to some chastening experiences, it was a valuable learning curve.

One early experiment was to try Jake out in after-dinner cabaret. In February 1969, he performed at the Mid Pennine Arts Ball at Accrington Conservative Club, and in May at Change Is, a nightclub in Newcastle-upon-Tyne, where he strode on stage in his suit and declared, 'Hello, my name is Jake Thackray and I sing songs about the human condition.'[2] With these gigs, the risk was that they were primarily social events; an audience was not necessarily there to listen to him. However, the performance in Accrington was well received and led to him being booked for his tour of Lancashire in April.[3]

By July, Richard's confidence in Jake was clearly growing, as he secured residencies at two of London's most prestigious cabaret venues, the Allegro and Quaglino's, where he shared the bill with the memorably-named Freddie Ballerini and his orchestra. His cabaret set would have been no more than 40 minutes, which was just as well, as he was performing at the two venues concurrently.

Quaglino's had some pedigree: four months earlier it had hosted Judy Garland's fifth wedding reception, and for many decades had been a popular haunt of 'the great and the good', including royalty.[4] It is hard to believe that Jake, a staunch socialist, could have felt comfortable in so exclusive a setting, but Alex Armitage understands his father's logic: 'My dad was a great believer in trying out everything. So Jake wouldn't have been a natural fit in a sophisticated cabaret venue like Quaglino's, but my dad would have tried him out in things like that to see, firstly, if Jake would enjoy it, and then to see if the venue would enjoy Jake.' *The Stage* was enthusiastic about these appearances, observing that his work 'has a rare individuality, enhanced by the coolly dominating way in which he puts it across...'[5] It declared that Jake was 'maintaining the superbly high standards of cabaret in these rooms', and predicted that 'from the reception he is obtaining it seems certain that he will be asked to return, and quickly'. The journalist clearly understood Jake's work, but not the man. Quaglino's and the Allegro would not see him again.

Whilst being served up as after-dinner entertainment for fashionable London society might have made Jake feel queasy, he found performing in large working men's clubs positively harrowing. 'Working men's clubs were a huge thing in those days,' says Alex, 'and had Jake been a natural fit in them, it could have been a good and steady source of income for him. Some performers do really well, whereas others think, "Never again in a month of Sundays!"'

Jake fell into the latter category. He told his friend Trevor Thewlis that he had deliberately been given such challenging gigs to help him get used to potentially hostile audiences. This was certainly his experience when he performed at Seacroft Working Men's Club in Leeds. 'The club was a vast cavern,' Trevor says, 'with hundreds of people in serried ranks of tables. Jake said nobody took the slightest notice of him throughout the performance, they just carried on talking and supping. When he came off he was very shaken. The Concert Secretary tried to console him, saying, "Eh lad, tha' did alreight – we 'ad Bob Monkhouse last week and they threw glasses at 'im!"'

If Jake's Seacroft booking had been meant to toughen him up, it didn't succeed. The only thing that was learned from the experience was that working men's clubs weren't right for him: he needed an audience that had come to listen to his carefully crafted words.

Fortunately, Richard Armitage secured a steady stream of venues like the Big Window, where people came to listen. Across the country, Jake's success in such intimate settings led

to countless re-bookings in the decades ahead. The Stanford
Arms in Brighton is typical: two performances in 1969 were
followed by six more in the 1970s. Quite simply, they adored
him. However, whilst he found playing in such places less
intimidating and therefore more enjoyable, comfort came at a
price: making small venues his bread and butter meant that the
jam was spread more thinly, and he received a smaller fee.[6] He
therefore had to spend more time on the road, to guarantee a
living. In time, this would have consequences.

The small venues included countless folk clubs. Although
Jake's songs bore little relation to traditional folk music, he took
to the folk music community and it took to him. Doubtless his
politics and lack of pretension had a part to play in this, as
would become very evident to his fellow performer Jasper
Carrott. Jasper would go on to have a hugely successful career
on television, primarily as a comedian, but in the summer of
1969 he was part of the Birmingham folk scene, where he
booked Jake to perform in July at his new club, the Boggery
Folk Factory. He immediately took to him: 'I liked his morals.
I liked his integrity. Basically, he was a true socialist, he wasn't
a weekend socialist, he wasn't a *faux* socialist. He was genuinely
a socialist with socialist ideas and carried it out in his life. He
had a respect for everybody, no matter who they were or where
they were from.'

Jasper was particularly impressed by Jake's response to the
poor turn-out for his show, a consequence of the wrong date
being advertised. The mistake could have been financially
ruinous for the club, given the size of his contracted fee.
'Instead of 200 people, we had about 30,' says Jasper. 'I said to
Jake that unfortunately the paper had got the date wrong, and
he wouldn't accept any money. At the end of the evening he
just said, "No, I don't want any money. When the club is up
and running, give me a call and pay me a bit extra next time."
That made a big impression on me, a big, big impression. I
thought, "You are for real."' Jake would go on to play many

times at Jasper's clubs; they became good friends, and Jasper even named his son after him.

In the midst of all this work, Jake's life underwent a huge change in June 1969, with the birth of his first son, Sam. He would proudly mention him in concerts, introducing 'Country Bus' as 'a song of which I am fond, and which I associate with my first-born son, Samuel. Why I connect the two, it would be difficult and unnecessary to explain. Both of them have similar qualities... which I like... Both of them were composed in similar bursts of enthusiasm.'[7] There would be more such bursts of enthusiasm, and within two years Sam would have a couple of brothers, Bill and Tom.

A growing family only underlined the need for Jake to keep performing and, given the unpredictable and anti-social demands of his work, it was decided that it made sense for Sheila to remain at home to look after their children. Whilst his work often took him away, family mattered enormously to Jake. He wanted to be the loving and engaged father he'd never had. After interviewing him in May 1969, one journalist concluded that he would 'never allow success to threaten the family life he values above all else. A career as an entertainer will be geared to the Thackrays and not t'other way about.'[8] While his children were young, he would manage to strike a good balance between family life and work.

By the autumn of 1969, Jake was playing residencies at arts festivals in Newcastle-upon-Tyne and Belfast. Although these took him away for a week at a time, they at least gave him the experience of a settled run in a venue and a break from endless hours on public transport. (Jake had yet to learn to drive.) A letter written to Sheila from Newcastle offers a window on his world. He misses her, and 'it's not that I'm short of friends here, or the possibility of drinking sessions, or good times or cultural times'. He complains about the cost of digs and eating out, and reports that there is a hole in the trousers of his stage suit, which he is convinced was spotted by a grim-faced woman in the front row. He is full of gloom about his performance and the venue, where he feels that everything is conspiring to prevent the audience laughing:

> I've done two nights, 2 hours a time, and I've not been very good. I don't know what it is about the hall (over the YMCA; also used for Methodist thrashes at dinner-time) but I feel most uneasy in it. The stage is high, and the lights are all on. Also the audience can't have a drink.[9] They haven't laughed much – yesterday I did five songs without any reaction, except the clap at the finish. When it happened I was all set to do something destructive like stop and say the alphabet – or run up the gangway. As for remembering words in that situation, well it's a toss-up.

Things would pick up. At the end of the letter, which was written over several days, there is a P.S., with a mixture of news, some good ('Last night was a lot better'), some bad ('There is another hole in my trousers'). Such was the world of Jake, the 'performing dick'.

Whatever his own doubts about his performances, he won excellent reviews in Belfast: 'Jake – who plays expert, and haunting, guitar – was lapped up by his audience last night. And no wonder. He's marvellous. Don't miss him.'[10] Peter Hepple of *The Stage* was equally complimentary about a cabaret performance in London, and made an interesting observation about his approach: 'As a performer he is quite fascinating, adopting as he does an attitude of complete detachment from his audience. This is about the last thing I would advise any other artist to do, but in Jake's case it seems to work, for his songs have a habit of insinuating themselves into the brain. He writes not as an attacker but as an observer and for my money he is about the best reporter in song we have got.'[11]

By 1970, Richard Armitage had decided that Jake was ready for the big stage and the nature of the bookings changed.

Cabarets, like working men's clubs, were a thing of the past. Alongside folk clubs, pubs and community venues, *An Evening with Jake Thackray* was now presented at large regional theatres, including the Playhouses in Oxford and Liverpool, and the Theatre Royal in Bath. These prestigious and lucrative bookings, which included some two-night residencies, were a clear indication of Jake's rising profile and popularity.

Working as a solo performer can be a lonely experience, with no-one to share the highs and lows. As we have heard, Jake felt particularly keenly the pressure of being on a large stage, far removed from the audience and blinded by the lights. The complexity and wordiness of the songs themselves added to the ordeal, not allowing for the slightest lapse in concentration. In a two-hour show he might sing as many as 30, an exhausting task. His spoken introductions were witty, if somewhat nervous, but they were brief, allowing him little time to relax.

Early on, it seems, not everyone thought that Jake was ready for the challenge. One reviewer who saw his concert at Oxford Playhouse in June 1970 was positively dismissive: 'In a theatre the size of the Playhouse, which is not exactly of band-box proportions, Mr Thackray's entertainment was rather too pint-size. Close on thirty numbers, of very varying inspirational quality, dwelling too frequently on the most obvious physical aspect of sex, sung with calculated off-beat lugubrity to rather similar tunes strummed on the guitar, proved to be too much of a not very good thing.'[12]

But another reviewer had a very different view of the same performance, praising the 'musicianly skill' of Jake's guitar work and his stage presence: 'Perched on a high stool, intent and self-contained, he held his audience with the authority that comes from working in social clubs and tap-rooms.' This reviewer contrasted Jake's songs with those of Noël Coward: 'Thackray takes an irreverent swig at Coward's vintage whine, but his lyrics, uncondescending and detached, are more akin to Eleanor Rigby than Mary Make-Believe. His people carry out their lives as best they can; the way they go about it is meticulously observed in these songs; only when he finds pretension, as with the parents of a girl-friend, is there a vicious twist to his lines.'[13]

Perhaps the clearest evidence of his agent's confidence in Jake's ability to draw and command an audience is that in 1970 he appeared at no fewer than four of London's largest and most prestigious concert venues. In April, he performed at Fairfield Halls and the Roundhouse, and in late October featured in a royal gala charity show at the 3,000-seat Astoria Theatre, with Princess Alexandra in attendance and Tony Bennett and Louis Armstrong topping the bill.[14] Three days later, on 1st November, he gave a concert at the 900-seat Queen Elizabeth Hall on the South Bank. It was a world away from the Big Window.

This would be a landmark moment in Jake's career. It was London's newest and most prestigious auditorium. Benjamin Britten had conducted at its inaugural concert. Jake would never have seen it in such terms, but performing there amounted to a statement of his stature as an artist. The working-class lad from Leeds standing tall in the home of London's cultural élite.

'The Queen Elizabeth Hall concert would have been booked on the back of some fairly successful record sales, and also a relatively steady diet of television and radio,' says Alex Armitage. In the first half of 1970, Jake had been appearing regularly on *Braden's Week*, and also performed on ITV's *The Golden Shot* in May and BBC's *Nationwide* in October. Richard Armitage's planning and hard work on Jake's behalf were bearing fruit.

As if to confirm the importance of the occasion, Norman Newell arranged to record the sell-out concert with a view to releasing a live album. Backstage, Jake apparently got cold feet about going on, declaring that he had no right to entertain people,[15] and had to be persuaded otherwise by Norman. It would not be the last time he experienced such a crisis.

Having got on stage, Jake gave a superb performance. His songs come to life in a concert setting, and when the album

Live Performance was released in March 1971, it rightly received excellent reviews: 'One can see how the sardonic Mr Thackray is not everybody's cuppa, but this live recording... really does underline his swift, special, straightforward style of writing... and his languid, but punchy way of putting lyrics across. It's his third album, probably his best, and there is often evidence of sheer genius.'[16]

Jake's performance reveals not only his skill as a musician, but also his ability to build a rapport with an audience. He starts by apologising for the fact that he is surrounded by recording equipment, which he promises to kick over, and expressing his doubts about whether the concert should be recorded. He then works his way through 29 songs with scarcely a slip.[17] His guitar playing is fluent and, when needed, subtle; his singing is assured and diction impeccable, and his wry spoken introductions, though brief and displaying an audible nervous edge, enhance the entertainment.

Whilst the setlist includes plenty of material from his studio albums, he also sings the best point numbers from *Braden's Week*. 'Pass Milord the Rooster Juice', 'Miss World' and 'Ladies Basic Freedoms Polka' all work well, helped by spoken intros that wittily put them into context. Jake amusingly wrong-foots everyone with a false ending on 'Leopold Alcocks', inducing premature applause. He also sings 'Isabella', his wonderful adaptation of Brassens's 'Marinette', before acknowledging his musical debt.

One of the concert's many highlights is 'The Lodger', in which Jake takes a well-worn bawdy joke and turns it into something timeless and genuinely hilarious. It tells the tale of a young man who, to his surprise and delight one night, finds his landlady's three daughters taking it in turns to climb into bed with him; each one scolding and sending her predecessor away before seizing the opportunity to have her own sexual desires satisfied. By the time the third sister enters the bedroom he is flagging but, being British, can still call upon a stiff upper lip. When her mother then joins the queue, all is set for a show-stopping denouement. Jake builds momentum through the verses so skilfully; 'The Lodger' is packed with fine jokes and double entendres en route to its irresistible climax. And when the coup de grâce finally comes it is impeccably delivered, with a level of comic timing guaranteed to bring any house down. It's hard to believe that in his final years he would dismiss this comedic masterpiece as 'rubbish'.

The applause at the end of the show is thunderous. Jake performs two encores,[18] genuinely demanded and deserved, but this was a show-business ritual he hated and would, in time, abandon. His amusing question to the audience ('Haven't you got any homes to go to?') is underpinned by genuine modesty and embarrassment. He didn't like the fuss.

Jake had triumphed on the big stage, and would do so on many further occasions. But whilst he would return to the Queen Elizabeth Hall several times in the 1970s and receive glowing reviews, he never felt remotely comfortable with the experience. It was a cause of great regret for his agent.

'His performances on television and radio meant that the whole world of the concert hall, the larger venue, was opening up, but that world took to him a lot more easily than he took to it,' observes Alex Armitage. 'He was a very reluctant player of the huge halls, which was a great shame because they loved him.' Jake liked the financial rewards the big venues offered, but this was not enough to overcome all the things he hated: the high stage, the lights, the distance, the sickening fear. For him, the Big Window, Burnley, would always be big enough, whereas for his London agent it would always be too small.

Over the years, it would become increasingly difficult to persuade him to step out of the world of the Big Window.

And one day he would refuse to do so.

start looking like this ——————————

Expressive
performer –
some early
concert
programme
photos.
Noel Gay

—————— it will pass

Metheradick

Jake's Scene

'It wasn't pressure, it was work, and it taught me to write quickly to a deadline. Some of the songs were duff – absolutely bloody duff – and I blush to think about having sung them.'
– Jake Thackray[1]

Jake's songwriting had been prolific when it was his hobby; he was writing primarily for his own pleasure. However, once he turned professional, he had to take a more utilitarian approach.

The stockpile of songs from his days in Leeds had served him well for several years, but it was not inexhaustible, and he needed to keep coming up with new material for television and radio commissions. Inevitably, with broadcast deadlines to meet, not every song was written to the same high standard. He was candid with audiences about his motivation: 'Point numbers are songs which I write quickly, and principally for money, and they are songs which are concerned with the weekly headlines. As soon as the news is forgotten, the song loses its value, my mortgage begins to look sick.'[2]

His success on *Braden's Week* had established him as a go-to writer for point numbers, and he was soon receiving one-off commissions for other programmes. These brought added pressure: he had to meet a specific brief, without the latitude he enjoyed on *Braden's Week*, where he could choose the topic and always substitute another song if he was unhappy with what he wrote. Whilst he didn't like the pressure of deadlines and was dismissive of these commissioned works, the best of them contained some fine writing.[3]

On 1st July 1969, Prince Charles was invested with the title 'Prince of Wales' at a ceremony at Caernarfon Castle, and the BBC broadcast the pomp and pageantry live to the nation, with suitably respectful commentary. Jake was invited by Radio 1's *Late Night Extra* to mark the occasion by writing his own tribute.[4] Sadly, no recording survives, but it was clearly less than deferential: its title was 'Oh Charlie Windsor'.

In October, coinciding with his week-long residency at the Newcastle Festival, Tyne Tees Television commissioned Jake to write a song for a documentary, *Close Up: Newcastle Festival*.[5] 'God Bless Newcastle Fest' celebrates the festival programme and, above all, the joys of Geordie beers:

> God bless the Newcastle Festival,
> All the cultural titbits you may choose.
> God will bless the Newcastle Festival
> Because Newcastle makes God's own booze.

Amid the song's references to Yehudi Menuhin, Ray Charles, *Così Fan Tutte* and T.S. Eliot's verse drama *Sweeney Agonistes*, Jake makes his priorities amusingly clear:

> Don't get me wrong,
> I like my bit of classical –
> Mister Menuhin is sublime!
> And my ears and my eyes
> Will be glued upon Yehudi,
> But only till it's opening time.

In the programme, it was accompanied by footage of a bespectacled Jake wandering around the festival locations and pubs of Newcastle ('dressed in my best shirt and suit and wearing spectacles, to prove that I am no Philistine'). With this song we get a rare insight into the joys and frustrations of the creative process from a letter he wrote to Sheila:

> 'The ITV song was "orl rite reely". I finished it off and it had quite a catchy chorus – naming local brands of beer (I'd rung up and asked if this was OK and a bloke said yes) but when I turned up they said no, don't mention God please or Newcastle Exhibition. So I had to rewrite the chorus and virtually every verse, because every verse's punch-line was a rhyming proprietary brand of beer.'

He was working at speed and the song was finished and recorded during the week. Sadly, the first draft doesn't survive, but it's interesting to see where compromises were and weren't made: whilst Jake was ultimately allowed to keep references to the Almighty, advertising beer was evidently deemed sacrilege. Nevertheless, Tyne Tees were obviously impressed and would soon offer him more work.

In March 1970, Jake received a very different commission from Yorkshire Television, to write a song for *Grown up World*, an educational series about child psychology and development. Whilst it sits oddly in such an earnest context, 'You and Your Child' amusingly matches the content of the programme, which looked at the impact upon children of their upbringing. It has a neat chorus:

> You and your child,
> You and your child,
> You watch everything they do.
> But don't be surprised
> When you realise
> That they may be watching you.

Some of the verses contain memorable comic images:

> Rodney St John-Cholmondeley
> Is going to be a brigadier, of course.
> His little sister, the Honourable Caroline,
> Is trying very hard to be a horse.
>
> Valerie would like to be a dancer,
> She pirouettes and strikes a pose.
> But where did she learn to finish off her act by
> Stepping out of her clothes?

Neither of these songs had any life beyond the programmes for which they were written.[6]

In the spring of 1970, as the second series of *Braden's Week* drew to a close, Jake returned to the studio to record an album showcasing unreleased songs performed on the show. Sessions were booked at Abbey Road between April and August and, once again, Norman Newell and Geoff Love took charge. However, despite considerable time and money being invested,[7] the project was abandoned. The recordings eventually saw the light of day in 2006.[8]

Listening to them now, it is not hard to see why the record was shelved. Jake is backed once more by a small jazz ensemble, augmented by percussion and woodwind, but the musical arrangements feel somewhat dated, and much of the album sounds like a less successful re-run of *Jake's Progress*. More problematic than this, however, is the use of an orchestra, which does not suit the material. Newell and Love had reverted to the easy-listening route they knew best, and any reservations Jake may have had were initially ignored.

Admittedly, some arrangements are jaunty, and the orchestration is never as heavy-handed as it was on 'Jumble Sale'. However, 'Leopold Alcocks' is bizarrely adorned with an instrumental interlude reminiscent of The Carpenters' 'Close to You'. Worse still, with its funereal pace it suffers the slowest of deaths, and 'Pass Milord the Rooster Juice' experiences a similar fate. Jake was a master of comic timing, but on the evidence of these two songs, his producer and arranger weren't.

Equally oddly, the arrangements take some of the songs off in the direction of music hall. 'The Kirkstall Road Girl' fares most badly: with its honky-tonk piano and washboard percussion, it is comically brash. It sounds as though Jake's music is suffering an identity crisis.

Even more problematic than the arrangements, however, is the song selection. Had the album been released, it would undoubtedly have been regarded as weaker than either of its predecessors. There are some fine pieces of writing, but it is telling that seven of the eleven songs had already been passed over for *Jake's Progress* and would never be released in Jake's lifetime. Whilst his wit, sophisticated use of language and eye for unusual subject matter are all in evidence, some songs do not compare well with his best work.

This is certainly the case with 'The Vicar's Missus', a song about a man obsessed with kissing the wives of priests. Jake works hard to make the most of this limited theme, but the humour is broad and the jokes generally weak. The best pun involves some violence: the protagonist is put on crutches after being 'converted' by an angry clergyman's crucifix.

Jake's love song to a cook, 'My Roly Poly Girl', likewise explores a scenario with limited scope. Whilst he serves up a rich menu of double entendres, the humour is again broad, in the tradition of saucy seaside postcards and *Carry On* films: suggestively, at the sight of her tasty tidbits, the narrator feels his juices begin to rise.

'My Pipe My Boots and My Lord' is more successful, if still somewhat contrived. It is the bizarre tale of a man's relationship with his smoking habit, his wife and his landlord, against whom he uses his pipe as a subversive form of chemical warfare. The song may have been inspired by Jake's own smoking habit and the unhappy experience he and Sheila apparently had with the owner of their flat in Pangbourne.[9] It contains some amusing and outlandish images: the wife finds it difficult to kiss her husband with his pipe still in his mouth, and complains that his smoking in bed leaves rather too many burn marks on his chest, and hers.

The melancholy 'Freda' tells the story of a man's troubled relationship and infatuation with his lost cat. Her owner feeds her gin and takes her to the cinema, but the inscrutable creature proves hard to please, and when she disappears he speculates as to who might have taken his 'honey child': could it be the milkman with the smile he has never liked, or the flirtatious dustbin man? And what are the implications if the butcher has taken her? The song's language is playful and it is packed with internal rhymes, but the lugubrious mood of the music weighs everything down.

'The Shepherdess' was given a lyrical reworking, which removes most of its clumsy humour. The end-result is slower, gentler and rather immemorable. Only 'The Lodger', featuring just guitar and bass, truly shines.

This collection of material is overwhelmingly comic, and for the most part *merely* comic. There is nothing here to match the honesty of 'Lah-Di-Dah', the storytelling of 'The Blacksmith and the Toffeemaker' or the bittersweet poignancy of 'Personal Column'. As for the point numbers, only 'Pass Milord the Rooster Juice' rises above the ephemeral, and they require contextualisation; had the album ever been released, explanatory sleeve notes would have been essential.

The production team must have recognised these problems because they cut their losses and abandoned the project in August 1970. Jake surely had a hand in the decision, given his ambivalence about its content. A radical change of strategy swiftly followed, with the inspired decision to record the Queen Elizabeth Hall concert and release a live album. This delivered an excellent new record quickly, with minimal additional expense, and provided the perfect platform for the best of the point numbers.

Just a month before the concert, Jake received a commission from *Nationwide*, the BBC's early evening news and current affairs programme. 'The Municipal Workers' Strike'[10] is a neatly crafted point number which delivers up some wonderful images:

> No supple public bath attendants guard us while we bathe;
> Many a sinking pensioner awaits to be saved.
> Your corporation muscles used to loom so large:
> Many a female cleavage heaves for your massage.
> Lowly sewer men shovelling sewage, take no notice of sniffs
>   and jeers;
> We all know that, down at the town hall, they have all been
> Shovelling it for years.

By the summer of 1969, Jake's career had taken off, and he was earning more than he could ever have imagined when he was a teacher. As a result, shortly after Sam was born, Jake and Sheila could afford to buy a house. A journalist reported that he 'has set his heart on a dream cottage near Wales where he can retire on the royalties of his present success and write his "funny odd novel" and bits of "this and that".'[11]

Retirement and writing a novel were a pipe dream, but the Welsh cottage wasn't. They bought a house in the hamlet of Mitchel Troy Common, a few miles from the Welsh market town of Monmouth.[12] Their new home, Hillside, was a small cottage, but there was plenty of space and it came with a field. It was in a beautiful spot and its position, up a steep road, gave fine views of the Welsh hills. They would remain here for the next two decades, putting down roots and developing strong friendships with many neighbours.

In some ways, hearts ruled heads when they bought Hillside. The attraction of the location was obvious: Jake loved the countryside and here he had the privacy he craved. It would be a good place for children to grow up. 'Bringing up the family, they had all the space and the land, and the kids ran and roamed,' says family friend Don Burton.[13] Hillside also had the benefit of being near the home of Sheila's parents in Coleford. However, life in the hamlet was totally reliant on having a car, and Jake and Sheila didn't own one. More importantly, neither of them could drive.

The practical implications for his career were not trivial: he worked regularly in London and had concerts to give around the country, and yet the house he had bought was a 30-minute drive from the nearest train station, which wasn't even on the main line to London.

If this made Jake's travel arrangements more complicated, Don Burton was also struck by how hard it made life for Sheila, bringing up her young family, when he was away: 'She didn't drive in those days, she didn't have a car, she couldn't get anywhere, and there was just a mobile shop which came twice a week and parked at the end of the lane.'

In urgent need of wheels, Jake purchased an old blue Morris Oxford estate, which he immediately put to use, driving, unlicensed and unsupervised, down to his new local, the Somerset Arms. During the course of 1970 and 1971, his brother-in-law Rick, who had just left school, was pressed into service as his driving instructor and chauffeur, accompanying him to local gigs and delivering him to the train station when he was travelling further afield. Rick found teaching Jake a chastening experience: 'He was one of the worst drivers ever. He would drive fast into a corner, in third gear, but then apply the clutch rather than the brake, and the car would career round the bend.'

In life, Jake often took things close to the edge, and this was the case on the day of his driving test, as Sheila Thackray recalled: 'Jake had a gig booked in Edinburgh, 400 miles away, but had nobody to take him. So when he went for his driving test, he had to pass. And the moment he passed, he pulled the L plates off, got in the car and drove off to Edinburgh.' He later managed to drown the family's blue Volvo Estate by driving it into a flood, with everyone onboard; it gained the nickname 'the blue whale'. Inspiration for the accident-prone Leopold Alcocks came from very close to home.

The Thackrays threw open the door of their new home to friends. Two early visitors were Bob and Sue Haverly, who decided to move from London to the Forest of Dean after spending many happy weekends with them. Jake and Sheila were delighted, suggesting they move in with them while looking for a house. It was a generous and selfless offer, particularly given the state of play in the Thackray household. 'That was a big thing,' says Sue, 'because they had a toddler and an almost-toddler and, by then, another baby, Tom. And their house was in various states of being done, depending upon what project Jake was invested in at the time. I think they'd got a goat as well – Rosie – who used to stand on top of the car, eating the washing. Sheila was there, with Sam on the floor somewhere, Billy in a high chair and with Tom on her hip, stirring away at the stove.'

Bob and Sue accepted the invitation, moving into Hillside in October 1971. During three months there, they saw at first hand the pressures on Jake. 'When we turned up, Jake and Sheila were so delighted to see us, irrespective of what was happening to them,' recalls Sue. 'But Jake, of course, was working on *Braden's Week*, and so he was either working, doing something to do with the house, or with the children, or he was in this little room that he had, writing his weekly song, which, of course, he had to do. So, whatever was going on in the house, there would always be Jake twanging away in the background, singing away... a backdrop to what was going on in family life. Sometimes he was up against the eleventh hour, and sometimes he was a little bit before the eleventh hour. And then, of course, he would disappear off to perform.'

Despite their close relationship, he never performed his new
songs for his friends.

Jake was full of enthusiasm and keen to embrace country
living, even though he possessed none of the necessary practical
skills. He loved animals and soon acquired a menagerie which
neither he nor Sheila knew how to manage. Rosie the goat –
so named because she ate all the roses – was joined by an
assortment of equally wilful farmyard fowl. 'Mum and Dad
used to go down together to the Somerset Arms in the
evening,' says Sam Thackray. 'It had an old-style, small front
bar, and there was a lot of good craic going round, with
everyone pulling each other's legs. Dad had decided that he
wanted to run a smallholding because we had a field. We had
a goat and rabbits, and he wanted chickens. And so one of the
old farmers – lovely blokes – said, "Oh yeah, Jake," nudging his
mates, "We'll sell you some chickens. Yes, some lovely hens,
lovely layers." And Dad came back with half a dozen of what
he thought were hen chicks. Six months later, they were
growing up and getting feathers, and not laying any eggs. And
Reg Moulton, the farmer next door, was looking on, chuckling
– I think it was one of these slow-burning jokes – because they
had sold him some bantam cocks, and he was never going to
get any eggs out of them.'

One of the cockerels, christened Gregory because he pecked
everyone, entered family legend because of an incident worthy
of one of Jake's songs, which Don Burton witnessed: 'One
Easter weekend, Jake said, "I've had enough of that frigging
cockerel. I'm going to kill it. Give us a hand." I said, "I've never
killed a cockerel before." He said, "Neither have I. We've got
to learn how to do these things." And it sounds bizarre, but
between us we tried to put to death Gregory, with much neck-
pulling. At the end of the experience, with the bird appearing
to be dead, and the two of us feeling emotionally shattered,
having killed one of God's creatures, Jake threw it in the
woodshed and we went off for a pint, full of remorse and guilt,

thinking, "We've just killed Gregory, and what the hell are we going to do next?" And this is a true story. This was on Good Friday, and on Easter Sunday, Jake went to the woodshed, opened the door, and guess what? Out came bloody Gregory. So Gregory rose from the dead on the Sunday.' After its miraculous resurrection, Jake didn't have the heart to make a second attempt to do away with the bird, and Gregory would live on, forever recognisable by the distinctive kink in his neck.

Jake's attempts at DIY were equally inept, says Rick Irons: 'You couldn't even trust him to bang a nail in a wall.' Soon after the move to Hillside, he was keen to build a rockery, and so he bought the stones from an old pigsty. While moving it, he managed to drop a large stone on his foot, and by the time Don Burton paid a visit, a week later, he was still in pain and the foot looked horrible. Don ferried him off to hospital, a fracture was diagnosed, and Jake spent the next eight weeks limping around in a plaster cast. 'For a week he had wandered around, performing with a broken foot,' said Don.[14] 'But it was sort of semi-typical of the man. He was a bit cack-handed. If anybody is going to buy a pigsty and drop a bit on their foot, it was Jake.'

Evidence of the Leopold Alcocks moment with the pigsty is preserved for posterity in *Jake's Scene*, a two-programme series he made for Tyne Tees Television, broadcast in 1971. Viewers would see a plaster-booted Jake hobbling around Swaledale, prompting one reviewer to observe wryly, 'Of course he has to be different'.[15]

Jake's Scene was an experiment that not only drew upon his songwriting talent, but also tested Jake's potential as a TV personality.[16] In each programme, filmed on location in the north east, he explored a theme by visiting places and talking to people. His conversations were interspersed with recordings of specially commissioned songs, illustrated by film footage.

In the first programme Jake looked at the fashion industry, visiting a boutique, modeling classes, a photo shoot and a fashion show. Throughout, he exhibited a sense of curiosity, bemusement and awkwardness reminiscent of Louis Theroux. His blunt and unexpected line of questioning bemused some interviewees: 'When my mum wanted to buy my sister Pauline a pully, she used to go to the Co-op, and there they were, all in a row. Now a similar mum will go to a boutique. How does this affect mums, pullies and Co-ops?' Unsurprisingly, given the theme, the programme now looks extraordinarily dated, and this extends to some of the attitudes. Jake started a conversation with a beer-swigging male model by observing, 'A male model is supposed to be as queer as a 5-legged camel!'

The songs about fashion vary in approach and quality. The programme's theme tune is short, jaunty and lightweight, with Jake joking that the sight of grandma wearing only a spangle would leave grandad only wearing a smile.

'Uncle Arthur' is an incongruously fashion-conscious older relative of The Kinks' 'Dedicated Follower of Fashion'. Jake paints a colourful and bizarre picture of him, with his primrose balaclava, lace shirts 'daringly' left unbuttoned to the waistline, and large stomach on display. It is an amusing if lightweight piece of writing which is done no favours visually in the programme, being accompanied by excruciatingly literal footage of an actor, dressed up as Jake's fashion victim, wandering around a boutique.

It is hard to believe that Jake had any interest in a subject as superficial as fashion, which may account for his awkwardness in the programme and the slightness of these two songs.[17] 'The Girl in the Window', however, which considers poignantly the plight of a shop-window mannequin, is in a different league. It is full of empathy for this pitiable figure, unable to talk, and forever waving and smiling to no-one. There is some humour amid the melancholy but, above all, Jake's genius for seeing something from an unexpected perspective is displayed. His masterstroke is in the final verse, turning the tables on his audience: the girl is staring out at all the dummies staring in.

Whilst the first programme was something of a curate's egg,

the second, in which Jake explored the changing nature of life in Swaledale, was far more successful in every respect. Footage of him riding in a pony and trap makes the dale seem an idyllic place, frozen in time, but he discusses the realities of life with its residents, including John Squire, a young idealist intent on protecting the area from change. Jake is much more comfortable in this programme, showing a genuine interest in the people and subject; his manner is natural and empathetic, his questions thoughtful but unsentimental.

Filming provided challenges, particularly when it came to getting the plaster-booted singer up to John's hillside house. It was obvious to him that Jake was enjoying what he was doing: 'He took sheer delight in arguing, much to the amusement of all the crew. He stopped the filming at one point and said [to one of the crew], "Steve, you're getting right up my nose. You ask us to talk about a subject, and then what do you say? You say 'Cut!'." And, of course, everybody was just rolling with laughter.' John vividly remembered what happened when the director decided they needed a close-up shot of him: 'They said to Jake, "Speak to John and say anything serious." So Jake said, "John, can you tell me where the nearest brothel is?" We didn't film for another five minutes. Everybody was just rolling.'

Whilst Jake was seen in an interesting new light in front of camera, the programme's beautiful, poetic music is its greatest gift. Here were the first in a series of fine serious songs about rural life that moved his writing beyond the lightly comic romanticism of 'The Little Black Foal' and 'Country Girl'.

'Go Little Swale' is a love song to a landscape and vanishing way of life. Employing an abundance of personification and a beautiful melody which gently rises and falls, it paints an evocative picture of the river's descent through the dale, past the 'scowling hills' and 'crouching towns'. Jake sings of the farmers' timeless way of life and relishes the music in the names of the villages: Gunnerside, Grinton, Booze and Crackpot. However, there is sadness as well as beauty in the song: the children have horizons beyond the dale, leaving the old men with nothing to do but spend their afternoons sitting and staring.

A centuries-old way of life is dying.

'Fine Bay Pony' is a highly original love song, full of hope and longing. In its brisk, onomatopoeic chorus Jake paints an evocative picture of a pony and trap, briskly rattling along through the dale. In the verses, however, the focus switches to a weeping onlooker who is watching and waiting, her head against the window, hoping for a glimpse of the driver. Whilst the sense of anticipation is reminiscent of 'The Little Black Foal', here the object of desire remains out of sight and undescribed: the focus is all on the beauty of the pony and trap. A happy ending is hinted at, but much is left to the listener's imagination.

The haunting 'Old Molly Metcalfe' takes Jake's writing into completely new territory, sounding for all the world like a traditional folk song. Using as his refrain a Swaledale sheep-counting system (yan, tan, tether, mether, pip...), he sings of the short, hard life of a young shepherdess on the moors. Through wind and rain she minds her sheep, so that others wealthier than her can live in the luxury she will never enjoy. She ends her days a mad woman, singing to herself on the moorside, lying frozen in the bracken. This is an extraordinary poetic creation, moving and beautiful in its bleakness.

Jake's Scene was broadcast in August 1971 and, if the results of the experiment were mixed, the tour of Swaledale made for interesting TV and provided inspiration for some outstanding songs. It is a pity that the exercise was never repeated, but Jake was a shy man and reluctant presenter, so the biggest surprise is that he agreed to do the series in the first place. However, it demonstrated that his material could work outside the confines of a television studio, he was capable of outstanding writing in response to commissions and, more importantly, was a song-writer of genuine substance.

Jake's experiments weren't limited to television. He rounded off the year with his most unusual radio commission, writing music to accompany a play.

Hit and Run, broadcast on BBC Radio 4, was a serious piece by the German writer Alfred Andersch in which a shop girl is killed in a hit and run accident by a terminally-ill businessman, his escape assisted by a petrol pump attendant. Through a series of monologues the lives of the characters are explored, along with events before and after. Jake's seven short songs were clearly conceived as a thematic whole. He deftly creates atmosphere and sets the scene:

In the Café Bristol
On the Kurfürstendamm,
September and five o'clock
On a cool afternoon.
All around about tea-cups
Tinkle discreetly.
Sitting at the next table to Mary-Lou.
Her eyes flicker and phosphorise,
Grey-blue, viable.
Sitting in the Café Bristol
On a cool afternoon.

He gives insight into their inner lives; the shop girl was on her way to visit some stables when she was killed, having just met a jockey, who plants in her mind dreams of horses in America:

Kentucky grassland,
Where the big red barns
Await tornadoes,
Where the winner of the Saratoga Derby stands
Behind a
White stockade.

The businessman had been sitting by a hotel pool, drinking and eyeing up the women:

> White ice and red Campari,
> I'd make more of it
> If I had the time.
> Oh, white ice and red Campari,
> Underneath the pitch-black forest pine.
> She climbs from the water in a shower of silver,
> Daddy is a banker,
> She's a sweet little piece.
> Rich, seventeen,
> Exclusively bikini-ed,
> 'I got people to meet.'

Whilst some of the songs are upbeat, the mood of most is melancholic. One has a melody which *Braden's Week* audiences would soon hear re-used for 'The Prisoner'.

Hit and Run was an interesting departure for Jake and his music served the needs of the play well. However, these songs make little sense out of context, so unsurprisingly they enjoyed no life beyond the radio broadcast. Nevertheless, it is a real pity he didn't do more work of this sort, as he had an aptitude for it.

Although the songs in *Hit and Run* would vanish without trace, those written for *Jake's Scene* fared much better: they would soon be heard on *Braden's Week* and Jake's next album.

His scene was about to undergo a significant change.

Bumfit

Bantam Cock

'I was finding songs everywhere. I'm a Catholic and I remember being in church and thinking, "What's funny about being a Catholic?", and realising it was everything. That led to "Sister Josephine".'

– Jake Thackray[1]

In early 1972, Jake recorded his third studio album, *Bantam Cock*.

He had been working with Norman Newell for almost five years, and as their understanding of each other had developed, so too had the approach the producer had taken to his music. *Jake's Progress*, recorded with a jazz trio, had been far removed from the orchestra-laden *The Last Will and Testament of Jake Thackray*. No doubt Jake welcomed the progression, but – as we've seen – Newell's musical instincts remained conservative and *Jake's Progress* still felt a little old-fashioned. However, now the winds of change were blowing and, although Jake would have one last encounter with an orchestra, *Bantam Cock* took his music in a new direction.

Before making the album, he recorded a single. In May 1971, he had performed 'Country Boy' on *Braden's Week*. This overtly religious piece focuses on the compassion and humanity at the heart of Jesus's ministry and crucifixion, and Jake's faith.

He sings of Christ reaching out to society's outcasts, sharing the shame of the prostitute who lives a life caught between scandalised fists and beckoning fingers, and the pain of the thieves crucified beside him. It is a moving and highly melodic piece of writing.[2]

In September 1971, Jake recorded an intimate, jazz-tinged version of the song with a small acoustic ensemble. However, this wasn't considered suitable for release and it was re-recorded in December, with an altogether grander arrangement, courtesy of Geoff Love. With a choir and full orchestra, including a harpsichord, the scale of the production dwarfed all Jake's previous work, and the recording seemed designed to appeal to those who enjoyed the easy-listening music of TV variety shows and Love's orchestral albums. Intimacy and feeling were being sacrificed on the altar of commercialism. The single was released in February 1972, in the run-up to Easter but, perhaps predictably, failed to chart.

By the time 'Country Boy' was released, Jake had started work on *Bantam Cock*. If the tracklisting for his abandoned studio album in 1970 suggested that he was running out of high-quality material, the situation was only temporary, and by the end of the year he had hit a new purple patch in his writing. This may reflect the reduced demands of *Braden's Week*: he was now only on the show once every three or four weeks, giving him more time to hone his contributions. Viewers were treated to a series of exceptional new songs, all of which would be recorded for *Bantam Cock*.

As usual, Newell and Love took charge of the sessions, but while the faces were familiar, the sound was different.[3] The tone was warm, and Jake's guitar playing far more prominent than on his previous studio albums, as was the double-bass. In addition, electric guitar was used, and there were even some guitar solos.[4] With a mixture of styles, including jazz and folk, the aim seems to have been to bring Jake closer to the musical mainstream, with a more modern and commercial sound.

The new musical direction chimes with a conversation Jake had with his friend Ian Gliddon: 'I think EMI suggested to him that he ought to do some voice training, and at the same time they were suggesting to him that he might make his songs a bit more in the tradition of Ella Fitzgerald and jazz, because they thought the market was bigger, and he said to me that they didn't understand what he was doing.'

If the record company was making such suggestions, they were clearly well-intentioned, but Jake had reservations. 'He had in his head a fairly strong, clear idea of where he wanted to go and what he wanted to do,' says Ian. 'He didn't think that he had a good voice, but he didn't think his songs were about having a good voice.[5] And he liked jazz and music of that kind, but knew the music he wanted to produce was not in that tradition.' No doubt his desire to preserve the authenticity of his approach was rooted in knowledge that Georges Brassens had scarcely changed any aspect of his sound in 20 years.[6] So, whilst *Bantam Cock* would see some musical changes, Jake remained true to himself.

The album's title song is one of Jake's most famous comic creations. It tells the story of a strutting, over-sexed bantam cock which 'tups' all the farmyard poultry, before forcing itself upon a catalogue of ever more exotic victims, including columbines, a budgerigar, and even a parrot, perched upon its owner's shoulder.[7] Eventually it keels over, the vultures begin to circle, and the song's punchline is set up. Just as with 'The Lodger', Jake had taken an old, bawdy joke and created something which is not only much funnier, but also beautifully written, rich in alliteration and internal rhyme, and full of character. With its inclusion, like 'Family Tree', of a now unacceptable joke about rape, the song is of its time, as he later realised: in concerts, he changed the offending word. However, it is no surprise that 'Bantam Cock' became a perennial live favourite and was covered by other singers.[8]

Jazz-flavoured 'The Singer' is one of his most unusual songs, not least because it is obliquely autobiographical. Singing at the upper end of his register, he celebrates what his lover means to him, using a series of beautiful metaphors: she is a dancer, a Jenny Wren and a juniper bush. She brings inspiration, pleasure and a sense of freedom. He contrasts this with the pressures he feels from show business, and of having to deal with mohair-coated men 'with Aqua Velva smiles',[9] who have maggots in their ears and crocodiles in their pockets. His jaundiced view of these men is clear: they don't understand his music and he doesn't trust them.

In 'The Girl with the Fragile Eyes', which was probably written with *Jake's Scene* in mind, his focus is on the inner life of an inscrutable model. This fragile, beautiful creature cuts a melancholy figure, parading herself in front of a succession of men, and she dances, smiles and sleeps alone. Away from the superficial world of her work, Jake wonders when she is ever real. It is a poignant song which throws up many questions, but no answers.

Like 'Bantam Cock', 'The Jolly Captain' is a brilliant musical reworking of an old joke, and one of Jake's finest pieces of storytelling.[10] On the death of his shrewish wife, an old sea captain ignores her warning not to remarry but takes shrewd precautions to ensure she cannot return to haunt him. The song contains some wonderful poetry and a moment of real tenderness when the old man, seeking to console her bitter heart, brings his dying wife small, comforting gifts of peppermint and violet. But it is full of humour as well, notably in its use of unexpected vocabulary and deliberate abandonment of rhyme: Jake ambushes the listener with 'apoplexy' and 'vexatiously'. The wife's dramatic deathbed warning to her husband, and manner of her death, as she spits out her peppermint and heads off to torment her maker, are the stuff of folk tales. It is a delicious story, deliciously told, and leads to a perfectly delivered pay-off.

With typical self-deprecation Jake often suggested that his

songs had no tunes, but he does himself an immense disservice. 'The Jolly Captain', like so many of the songs on *Bantam Cock*, has a wonderful melody, and is enhanced by his inventive and accomplished guitar lines.

'Isabel Makes Love Upon National Monuments' is the last *Braden's Week* point number Jake recorded, and one of the best. His inspiration was a news story about a woman who was prosecuted for having sex in public; upon investigation it emerged that it was not the first occasion, and that she kept a diary of her exploits. In the song he has Isabel take this idea to its preposterous limits, as she cavorts at landmarks ranging from Balmoral to the British Museum; with many cathedrals on her list, no sacred place is sacred.

Jake presents several rollicking images of her scandalous behaviour, but his masterstroke is to make the Albert Hall a character in the story, frustrated and forlornly aware that he alone has been denied Isabel's favours. The song reaches a suitably satisfying and hilarious climax at the Last Night of the Proms.[11]

After years spent acknowledging his debt to Georges Brassens on stage, on *Bantam Cock* Jake finally paid tribute to him on record with 'Brother Gorilla', his superb adaptation of 'Le Gorille'. Jake added some of his own jokes and reworked the tale for his British audience, as he later explained: 'I found that I couldn't do a straight translation as there are all sorts of things in it which don't exist in our culture. For example, at the end of "Le Gorille", there is a reference to the guillotine. We would have to have hanging. Also, I wanted the song to feel English – I wanted to adapt the feeling of the song and make it English.'[12] Like the gorilla, it romps vigorously along, until the foolish judge, who complacently stands his ground, gets his comeuppance.

'It Was Only a Gypsy' is a beautifully told story of a self-important policeman being cuckolded. The lampooning of the representatives of law and order was one of Brassens's favourite

themes, and it appears regularly in Jake's songs as well.[13]
Returning home from work, the policeman is full of ardour for
his beautiful wife, but he's also complacent, and blind to the
mockery in her words when she asks her 'big blue hero' what
he did at work. After explaining that he had to get a little
physical in an encounter with a gypsy, it emerges that his wife
has had a similar, but altogether more pleasurable, brush with
the fellow. The twist in the tale is wittily done, and its poetic
and amusing postscript lays out the trail of evidence the
policeman has missed in his own home: the hedgerow flowers
in her breasts, the whiskers stuck in her teeth and the
abundance of clothes-pegs.

'Sister Josephine', in which a burglar disguises himself
incongruously as a nun and hides from the police in a convent,
is one of Jake's most loved and celebrated creations. As well as
being covered by other singers, it may have inspired the plot
of a film, *Nuns on the Run*. He apparently wrote it fast: 'I'm a
Catholic and I had to write that song very quickly. I had to be
singing something new on Saturday night on TV and I had
got back home on the Friday morning. I went to church and
when I came home, I thought, "Quick, let's get a song on the
wheels," and I thought, "I'll take the mickey out of being a
Catholic. What's funny in the Catholic church? Why,
everything is!" So I picked up a nun.'[14]

The idea of a burglar dressing as a nun came from 'Sœur
Marie-Louise', a song by Francis Blanche, a popular French
comedian. However, beyond this central premise, the songs have
little in common. The French lyrics are not particularly funny:
the humour lies primarily in how it is performed on stage.[15]
'Sister Josephine', by contrast, is packed with good jokes.

Jake explores all the comic possibilities of the scenario, with
ever increasing absurdity. The nuns find it hard to believe that
Josephine could be a man, even if there are clues: the body hair,
the tattoo, the deep voice, the fact that 'she' leaves the toilet
seat up. The song is full of comic imagery: the convent pontoon

team, the 'rare magazines' in Josephine's cell, 'her' flight from the convent, wearing only a rosary and wimple. The jaunty, jazzy melody is one of Jake's best.

The album ends quietly with the jazz-inflected 'Lullaby', one of his most intimate and personal songs. Jake sings softly at the upper end of his vocal range and two guitars follow him gently, cascading down through a series of diminished chords. The effect is perfectly matched to the tranquillity of the scene painted in the lyrics as, in exquisite poetry, he describes a weary mother sitting in the evening in the kitchen, breastfeeding. He dwells upon every detail: the lulling effect of the suckling, her falling eyelids, the infant riding on her breasts as though sailing on an 'endless sea'. In the final line a nickname, 'titmouse', alludes to the source of his inspiration: his youngest son, Tom, born in August 1971.

The collection was completed by four outstanding tracks, all written for *Jake's Scene*: 'Go Little Swale', 'Old Molly Metcalfe', 'Girl in the Window' and 'Fine Bay Pony'. 'The Prisoner', which Jake performed on *Braden's Week*, was also recorded, but ultimately rejected. A fine piece of writing, but exceptionally dark, it would have sat oddly in the company of the other songs on the record.[16]

As for artwork, a photo of a bantam cock was used for the album cover, and Jake was nowhere to be seen. His distinctive presence was felt in the self-penned sleeve notes, however. Declaring his dislike of the requirement to provide a biography, he indulged his love of fantasy, telling a delicious, fanciful tale of the behaviour of his hens. He ended with this:

> I tell you this to avoid telling you anything else. It is the songs that count and not the singer. Listen to the songs. If you don't like them much talk to members of the opposite sex. Or go to bed early.
>
> Or both.

Record Mirror's reviewer was in agreement: the songs were the thing. When the album came out in September 1972, the paper gave it glowing praise: 'Quite simply, and not to put too fine a point on it, Jake Thackray is a genius. It's not so much his actual singing as the songs he sings. Even his own brand of sleeve notes stands out. There are some tremendous songs on this.'[17] The *Reading Evening Post* agreed: 'Yet another brilliant record from the Yorkshire tyke.'[18]

With *Bantam Cock*, Jake's music had undoubtedly moved on. Where *The Last Will and Testament of Jake Thackray* had channelled the 1960's sound of Jacques Brel and the jazz-tinged *Jake's Progress* had harked back to the 1950s, *Bantam Cock* sounded like a record made in the 1970s. Moreover, it was a strong and diverse collection which showed how Jake was experimenting and developing as a writer. And the Brassens-Thackray writing credit on 'Brother Gorilla' underlined his connection with his musical hero.

That connection would be reinforced in a remarkable way a year later.

Jake at the Recreation Hotel Folk Club, Colchester, March 1971.

Stuart Allison 1971/Colchester Express Archives

Jake and Georges Brassens at Hillside, October 1973.   *Colin Evans*

Rachmaninov and Charley Farley

'Can you imagine? Me, a two-bit, unknown singer from Leeds, appearing with such a great star? I had a bar of chocolate in the dressing room, and Georges came in. He was nervous. He said, "Oh, you have chocolate... can I have a piece of your chocolate?" Can you imagine? It's like a great pianist like Rachmaninov was sharing a dressing room with Charley Farley[1] and he asks, "Can I have a bit of your chocolate?"'

— Jake Thackray, 2000 [2]

A year after Jake released *Bantam Cock* came the high point in his career, at least in his eyes. It had nothing to do with the conventional measures of success – sales, television appearances or celebrity. When asked about it in an interview three decades later, his sense of joy and wonder were still palpable.[3] It had been a dream-like experience. He had appeared in concert with Georges Brassens. He, Jake 'Charley Farley' Thackray, had actually shared a stage, dressing room and bar of chocolate with Georges 'Rachmaninov' Brassens.

'Can you imagine?', he repeats.

The concert at the Sherman Theatre in Cardiff on 28th October 1973 was a special occasion for anyone lucky enough to be there, because it was the only time Georges ever sang in

217

Britain. Performing on the same stage as his idol was a huge honour for Jake, and (though he would never have seen it in this way) amounted to a very public endorsement from Georges.

Ever since his love affair with Brassens's songs had started, the impact upon Jake had been profound, and he took every opportunity to laud him publicly: 'I think Georges Brassens is easy, *easy* the greatest songwriter in the world, bar none... he's chest and knees, and shoulders, above anybody else that I can think of.'[4]

Most artists might view playing support for a bigger star as a stepping stone to greater things. Not Jake. In Britain, he was hardly the 'little-known Charley Farley' of his self-deprecating description. He had been a household name for five years, with a reputation that could fill venues far larger than the Sherman Theatre. But in Cardiff he was happy to play second fiddle to someone who, for all his fame in France, was little known across the Channel. Jake did so, and felt such humble pride in it, because Brassens was so special: 'Professionally speaking, being a player, and playing with a great virtuoso, was unforgettable.'

It is remarkable that Brassens ever came to Wales, given that he hadn't performed outside the French-speaking world in 15 years. Colin Evans, the concert organiser, put his appearance down to one thing: 'Friendship brought Brassens to Cardiff.' But a certain amount of luck was also involved, and a postal workers' strike.

Colin was a French lecturer at Cardiff University. In 1970, he'd been in Paris, working on a doctoral thesis, and every week posted a draft to Cardiff, to be typed up and then returned to him for checking. A postal strike brought the process to a shuddering halt and, finding himself at a loose end, he began working on a book about *chanson*. Never a man to back away from a challenge, he decided to start by trying to secure an interview with the master of the genre, Georges Brassens.

'With the carefree confidence of the 30 year-old,' Colin recalled, 'I found the phone number of Pierre Onteniente

[Brassens's private secretary] and spoke to him on the phone and explained my project. He said he would speak to Georges and call me back. Next day he called me and said yes, Georges would like to speak to the young English teacher; we could go to Rue Santos-Dumont [Brassens's home] in the afternoon.'[5]

When Colin met Brassens, he was awe-struck. 'The effect which reality has on the media image is astonishing,' he wrote later. 'You know the voice, the face – and yet the man whose hand you shake is no longer the star; he exists in another dimension – as we exist in another dimension for him. We are no longer one of those who clap and cheer and whom he never sees because he arranges the lights deliberately at eye-level to prevent him seeing. There are two of you; and there's a gulf between you and you need to build a bridge.'[6]

It was never clear to Colin why Brassens agreed to meet him: 'Pierre told me later that he got hundreds of similar requests from people much more deserving (it seems to me) than I was. I think it was Georges's human curiosity – to see an Englishman close-up interested him, amused him.'[7] And then – as ever – sheer luck; he had just got back from a holiday, he was available; chance and my phonecall worked together. And we hit it off.'[8] The interview was a great success, more meetings followed and a friendship developed. In October 1970, Brassens even made a rare trip outside France to visit Colin and his wife, Carol, in Wales.[9]

An important connection was made the following year, when Colin and Carol went to see Jake in concert at the Casson Theatre in Cardiff. 'Jake was marvellous,' Colin recalled. 'He prefaced one song with a story about Brassens, calling him the greatest singer-songwriter in the world. He said he had made a "very poor translation" of a Brassens song, and sang "Brother Gorilla" – probably one of the greatest translations of a poem or song ever made.'

They were so impressed by Jake's performance and struck by his admiration for Brassens that after the concert they went backstage to meet him. 'Jake was exhausted,' recalled Colin, 'and when I told him that we knew Brassens he went weak at the knees!' A friendship developed, and Colin and Carol visited Jake in Mitchel Troy, where they saw at first hand the challenges he faced, balancing the demands of writing and performing with making time for his young family.

After years spent idolising Brassens from afar, Colin encouraged Jake to seek him out, much as he had done in 1970. 'Jake wasn't the sort of person to have the gumption and the push to dream that something like that would ever be possible,' says Carol. 'He was intimidated by the grandeur of Brassens.' Nevertheless, Colin gave him the confidence to take this step. 'I went round to Paris,' recalled Jake. 'Colin hadn't given me the address, but I knew the name of Georges's manager... So I looked it up in the French telephone directory, I went round, I knocked on the door and said, "Listen, I'm besotted with Monsieur Brassens." He said, "Come in, have a pint and sit down and chat." He took me round to see Georges that night.' Jake went with Sheila to see him in his modest flat and, like Colin before him, was clearly in awe at this first meeting: 'Imagine! A young bloke who loves this [man's work]... there he [Brassens] is, in person, saying, "Oh, you're an Englishman? Oh, you know Colin? Sit down, have a *pastis* [aperitif]..." And it went on like that. I told him that I was a singer and I sang some of my songs for him.'

Sheila was struck by Brassens's regard for Jake, and thought he was intrigued that an Englishman could translate his work: 'He was such an intense man, but so generous to his kind – he recognised Jake as a fellow artist and encouraged him in his own talent... Jake's particular fine-tuning between the two languages, his linguistic gift, and his genius for matching lyric to rhythm and music (in songs of his own imaginative creation and in translation of Georges's songs) was instantly recognisable to Brassens, even though Brassens couldn't speak English.'[10]

Jake paraphrased Brassens's reaction with typical bluntness:

'I really don't frigging understand any of this, but it sounds nice.' A friendship developed, and Jake visited Brassens several times in Paris. 'I kept on seeing him,' he said. 'You know, [it was amazing] for a young, unknown in France, hardly known in Britain... a young singer... We became buddies. He almost took a kind of glee in being surrounded by mates, "les copains".'

In 1973, when the Sherman Theatre was about to open, Colin came up with the idea of inviting Brassens to perform. 'I thought, wouldn't it be fantastic,' he said, 'if I could get Georges Brassens, the greatest troubadour, the greatest singer-songwriter in the world, who never sets foot outside France, to come and sing at this theatre on its opening night?'[11]

The chances of getting Brassens to accept such an invitation appeared remote. 'Georges never wanted to play abroad,' explained Jake. 'He had an unhappy experience in Italy. He was invited to sing in Rome, and he said yes reluctantly, and he found himself faced with an audience of élite people, who didn't know who he was at all, didn't really like his songs, but knew that he was "the thing" to be known to have gone and seen.'[12]

Nevertheless, to Colin's amazement, Brassens again said yes – proof not only of the strength of their friendship, but also the trust he placed in him that there'd be a receptive audience. A week before the show, Brassens explained his decision in an interview: 'I have never sung in Britain because I assumed no-one except the French could make head or tail of my complicated texts. But this is a very special audience – they are all French experts, and Colin is my friend, so I come.'[13]

Having secured Brassens's agreement, Colin was keen to involve Jake, deciding to ask him to perform as the support act. Jake was flabbergasted: 'Colin said, "Georges is a bit interested in coming over to sing in the Sherman in Cardiff." "Goodness me," I thought, "Why? What? Wonderful!"... "He would like you to do the first half." Great Scott! Jake Thackray, actually appearing with a great star! Bless my soul!' While the idea was

Colin's, suggesting the invitation came from Brassens was both
flattering and persuasive.[14] And it resulted in the perfect pairing.
As Sheila Thackray put it: 'No one else in this land could
match or pay homage to Brassens as Jake could.'[15]

The concert wasn't widely advertised, but it sold out quickly
by word of mouth. 'People called me and asked, "Is this a joke...
is Brassens *really* playing?"' recalled Colin. Whilst the publicity
was low-key, the importance of the occasion was not lost on
everyone. Colin secured Brassens's agreement for the concert
to be recorded,[16] and his record company released it as his only
live album, *Georges Brassens in Great Britain*, clearly aimed at
the British market.[17] The BBC also gained permission to film
the concert for a documentary that would involve both Colin
and Jake, but on the strict proviso that the cameras were
unobtrusive: nothing must disturb the connection between the
audience and performers.

Jake and Colin were keen to give their honoured guest the
red-carpet treatment. Richard Armitage was amazed that the
legendary singer was visiting and lent his chauffeur-driven Rolls
Royce so they could meet him in style at Heathrow. For Brassens,
who lived modestly, it was his first ride in such a vehicle.

Jake was again awe-struck at welcoming his idol: 'I picked
him up from the airport. I mean... imagine! He'd got this
small, shabby suitcase, and he had his lady friend, Püpchen,
with him. They just came out of the terminal and there he
was... just in ordinary clothes. We stayed in London for two
days, and he said, "Show me London."' They toured the sites,
with Brassens enjoying an anonymity he rarely experienced in
France. Years later, Colin wrote about that time: 'It was in a
Rolls that night that Georges and Püpchen discovered
London, amazed at everything, happy as children. We stayed
in an old, traditional hotel in Mayfair, Browns, and, in the
evening, Jake invited us to Ronnie Scott's [London's legendary
jazz club]. The star that evening was Stéphane Grappelli.
Grappelli was told during the interval that Georges was in the

audience and, thinking someone was pulling his leg, came out to see. He fell into Georges's arms, tears in his eyes. They had known hard times together.'[18]

From London, Jake drove them to Cardiff, and on the day of the concert Brassens spent the afternoon with the Thackrays at Mitchel Troy. Sheila had fond memories of the visit: 'He drank bottled water, because of his kidney problem. But he was on form and made us all laugh. He sat in an old armchair and chatted for ages. Goodness knows what we talked about, I was so nervous... It was all about poetry and music and literature. Georges and Jake played together, and he relaxed in our family home.'[19]

Jake and Georges then headed to the Sherman to prepare. The set-up on stage was simplicity itself – a chair, to serve as a foot rest, and a couple of microphones. Pierre Nicolas, Brassens's usual bassist, was there to accompany him, but he was reluctant to lug his hefty double bass all the way from Paris, so it was left to Colin to supply one. This would not prove easy, but eventually a young Welsh musician called Alan Williams agreed to lend his instrument. Little could he have guessed where his generosity would lead.

Brassens's fans flocked to the Sherman from across Britain. Ian Watson was there and remembers the sense of anticipation: 'I had driven over to Cardiff from Exeter and it was like driving drunk, really, I was so excited...'[20] The atmosphere in the theatre was electric.

Sue and Bob Haverly also went, and found Jake even more nervous than usual. 'He was obviously overcome with nerves and pride,' says Sue. 'When he was excited about things he used to jiggle about, and he did an awful lot of jiggling that night. And he also had a mannerism where he would go "Hum... Er... Right!" He was obviously preoccupied and very, very anxious.'

Jake remembered the mood of anticipation: 'I was standing behind the curtains waiting for the lights to go down. You hear the sound of people excited, settling down.'

Jake's performance was brisk and strong, and he adopted Brassens's approach, dispensing almost entirely with his usual patter between songs. No doubt he was conscious that this was not his audience, and he had no desire to upstage his hero. He did a very professional job, getting through 16 songs in 50 minutes and cutting short the applause, aware he was paving the way for the evening's star. 'Jake was visibly nervous, but he didn't forget any lines,' recalls Carol Evans. 'He did his songs beautifully.'

In a brave and self-confident display of his admiration, his set included 'Isabella' and 'Brother Gorilla', his two adaptations of Brassens's songs. The Frenchman watched from the wings and, although he could not understand a word, the quality of Jake's achievement was not lost on him. 'I remember Georges in the wings of the Sherman, when Jake was singing "Brother Gorilla"', recalled Colin, 'and Georges recognised that the audience was laughing, and they didn't laugh in the song when he, Georges, was singing it, and that's because there are jokes in Jake's version which actually weren't in Georges's version.'

Jake proudly recalled the strong bond between them that night: '[Brassens] was stood in the wings all the time... I could see him, and he stood there and nodded, and [gave me the] thumbs up. When I went off, it wasn't a shaking hands job, he didn't embrace me, but he did the French way of holding a man, one cheek, then another. "Bien fait!" ['Well done!']' However, Jake was typically self-deprecating about the audience's reaction to his performance: 'They were polite and nice to me, and I did well... and they gave lots of claps, but it was almost like... theatrical foreplay.'

Now it was Brassens's turn. 'There was just this sense of expectation in the theatre... it was palpable,' said Ian Watson. 'Something quite amazing was about to happen.'[21] Jake could sense it in the dressing room: 'You could hear the excitement of people talking through the speaker. "Yes, he [Jake] was okay, but next time we go in, it's Georges!"'

Jake went to the wings with Brassens, who had the nervous energy of a performer about to step on stage, pacing about, adjusting his tie, checking his fly. Then, for Jake, came a priceless, intimate moment: 'This man – this seems so childish, but I will treasure it – he said "Hé! Tiens ça!" ['Hey! Hold that!'], and gave me his guitar to hold while he did something. Wow!'

Brassens took the stage to resounding applause. He was on top form and sang 16 songs, including 'Le Gorille' and many other favourites, along with one encore. The applause was thunderous and sustained. Colin Evans felt 'in a state of amazement, of triumphant delight – delighted at everything that had happened; we were very happy'. Jake was equally effusive. 'I was overawed by the sense of occasion,' he said. 'He sang so well. When he finished, the place explodes... He puts his hand up... and shambles off... He said to me, "I'll do an encore. What encore was I going to do?" And I told him... He waited for a moment, then went back on. It was a stupendous theatrical experience for the people who were there on that famous night. And for me, I shall never forget it... that experience... not just as a sort of two-bit singer, but, I suppose, as a man, seeing this theatrical phenomenon happen on that little night in Cardiff... it was like a big bomb, a big, magic explosion, something very valuable.'

Jake was clearly star-struck. 'I think he must have been in a bit of a dream to be actually performing with his hero,' says Carol Evans. But despite sharing the bill, the two men never actually shared the stage. This certainly wasn't Brassens's doing. In fact, before the concert he had invited Jake to join him for the encore: 'He said, "I tell you what, you are going to do the first half and I am going to do the second... For the encore, would you like to join in with the encore?"... Really? Really! I've got to do a double-act with Big Georges! [*laughs*]' Brassens proposed that they sing 'Le Roi des Cons', in which he declares that all the great dynasties of the world will crumble, but no one will ever unseat the king of *les cons* (a very colourful French expression for 'prats' or 'fools'). It was a call and response song with a chorus, and Jake already knew it. It was the perfect vehicle for a duet.

Jake was thrilled, but after the euphoria had worn off, he turned the invitation down: 'Fortunately I came to my senses and said no, I couldn't do that. I mustn't do that. But it still dances among my fantasies, does that, doing a double-act with Georges. Fortunately I didn't, and I'm glad I didn't.'

This revelation was astonishing. Most performers would jump at the chance to appear on stage with their idol. But then, Jake was not 'most performers'. Asked in the interview to explain his decision, he offered this: 'It would have looked like a Morecambe and Wise, a theatrical turn, and the singing of Georges is not about buddies. I mean, I hate to say this, but the Americans tend to do this. Frank Sinatra meets, say, Charles De Gaulle, and they do a song together. Georges thought it would be a good idea... "Perhaps it will show that my songs are loved in this country." But it wouldn't have been right, it really wouldn't. It would have been too bloody show-bizzy. Georges isn't show-bizzy. Georges is just Georges.'

Jake's reasoning is strange and doesn't stand up to scrutiny. Although he might have viewed a duet as too 'show-bizzy' for Brassens, the Frenchman was perfectly comfortable with such an idea. Indeed, on other occasions he used 'Le Roi des Cons' to share his stage in exactly this way.

Jake's act of self-denial shows his huge respect for Brassens, but also an attitude which borders on the puritanical. Was there perhaps a sense of Catholic guilt at play here? Did he refuse to indulge this 'fantasy', as he called it, because he thought it would not have been 'to the greater glory of God' (A.M.D.G.), but a self-indulgent act? Or did he see himself as not good enough, or not worthy enough, to be allowed this moment of pleasure? How difficult was the decision for Jake, and did his self-denial torment him later? If accepting the invitation might have led to a feeling of guilt, did not doing so leave him with a life-long sense of regret, despite all his protestations to the contrary? Hearing him in the interview with Ray Brown in 2000, it is hard not to feel that he 'protests too much'.

Jake never shared with Carol Evans that he had turned down his chance to sing with Brassens, but she believes that it was a missed opportunity for everyone: 'It would have been much more in the spirit of the evening for Jake to have dropped his inhibitions and his self-deprecation and just joined in with the joy of the occasion by singing with Georges. It would have been the *clou de la soirée* ['the high point of the evening']. I very much think it would have done Jake good to drop all that... I can't call it false modesty, because I think that self-doubt was inherent in his personality... but if the joy and the spirit of the thing could have overcome that self-doubt, just for that one evening, the evening would have been even more wonderful. Whilst Jake was unaware of his own stature, the audience that night had no doubts about it, and it would have been good if, for once, he had let others' view of his great gift prevail over his own modesty. However, afterwards I think that possibly it would have been too painful for him to admit that turning down the chance to sing with Georges had been a mistake. In a way, he had to have his version of why sharing the encore would have been wrong, and that was the version that he could reassure himself with.'

While the audience likewise never knew Jake had declined the invitation to sing with his friend, his determination not to share the limelight showed itself when Brassens beckoned to him to join him on stage for a final bow. Jake never moved from the wings.

After the concert they returned in triumph to the dressing room to open a bottle and celebrate privately, before heading to the Sherman's bar, where a group of friends and admirers had assembled. Brassens remained relaxed and polite in the face of all the adulation.

The following day, still in a state of elation, they returned to Mitchel Troy for a celebratory party with Jake's friends and neighbours. Photographs, taken in the garden, capture the spirit of the moment: in one, he towers over Brassens, beaming; in another, the Frenchman places an avuncular hand on his shoulder, and Jake's eyes are closed, as though in a dream. Carol believes that this is the essence of what had happened: 'It all had a kind of dream-like quality, really. It wasn't something that was *meant* to happen. There was such a series of odd coincidences which led to it.'

The concert had been a huge success, and Jake was disappointed at how little attention it received in the media: 'I think Melvyn Bragg did a short thing on him...[22] It wasn't written about in the papers, it was neglected, it was totally neglected and he [Brassens] knew this.' This wasn't quite true. Maurice Rosenbaum's review of Brassens's performance for the *Daily Telegraph* was glowing, and he wrote approvingly of Jake's appearance on the bill: '...there could not have been a better choice to share the programme'.[23] But he was the only London journalist to go, and the piece the *Sunday Times* ran on the day was very short, with no mention of Jake and only a brief quote from Brassens.[24] Jake had a point: the media in London paid very little attention to the French star.

In fact, he believed that Brassens's parting shot at the end of his visit suggested this lack of recognition had contributed to his decision to perform in Wales: 'I think he went to Cardiff, especially Cardiff, because it wasn't London. When I was waving bye-bye to him at Heathrow... he had a sly way of talking to you, like buddies, you know, really wicked... he said, "Je suis allé chanter aux Gallois pour emmerder les Anglais." ['I went to sing to the Welsh to piss off the English.']'

Tanabum

Jake on Georges

*'Any impressario worth his fat hands would smile and pat
your cheek if you suggested that this sort of thing could
succeed, that such a performer could last for five minutes,
never mind a quarter of a century.'*
– Jake Thackray on Georges Brassens, 1973

In 1973, prior to the concert at the Sherman, Jake wrote an
essay about Brassens, probably intended for a newspaper or
magazine, but which was never published. In it, he explains
Brassens's importance in French culture, and the reasons for
his own admiration. He writes about the attitudes, themes,
poetry and melodies of Brassens, and is enthusiastic about his
capacity for vulgarity. He illustrates his views through a
detailed analysis of two songs.

The essay reveals a great deal about Jake himself, including
his knowledge of French poetry and contempt for the money-
men in show business. He clearly admires Brassens for being
his own man, and possibly overstates his reluctance to give
interviews and refusal to appear on TV. Is he, perhaps, projecting
onto Brassens his own attitudes and producing an idealised
version of his hero, a hero he sees as being almost completely
detached from show business? Certainly, what he writes here
is consistent with the reason he later gave for not joining

Brassens for the encore at the Sherman. What does it suggest about Jake's aspirations for his own career?

The essay is printed below. Sadly, the final page is lost but, apart from the removal of one repeated passage, this is the unedited text of Jake's original manuscript.

See what you think, as Jake would have said.

***

On Sunday 28th of October, Georges Brassens is going to sing at the Sherman Theatre in Cardiff. He'll be there for one night only and it is unlikely that he will ever sing in Britain again. If you know the songs of Brassens and his way of singing them and you think, reading this, that you've got a hope of seeing him there, well best forget it because the place has been booked up as soon as the word got out. You'll have to wait for two, three, maybe four years and try to catch him when he is next singing in Paris or during his short tour of French provinces. His appearances are rare and brief.

Every few years or so Georges Brassens emerges from his private life with a dozen or so new songs. Then, for six nights a week, and four months on the trot, he sings these plus around twenty of his old songs at a relatively small music hall in Montparnasse, the Bobinot. A couple of months of one nighters round France and maybe Belgium, and that's it for a few more years. Half a million people see him – eight million would like to but can't get a place. Within days, hours, of the announcement in say the preceding March all seats are taken for the November–February. Despite his apparently suicidal way of treating his public, the French are always faithful to him because they know for certain, and I'm sure for once they are right, that Georges Brassens is easily the greatest songwriter and singer that there is, bar none.

On the face of it what show biz would term his 'stage act' is absolutely nil. He shambles on, puts a foot up on a chair, and sings to his own scratchy guitar. Song finished, he waits for the crash of applause to die down and then he sings another one. More pandemonium. He paces around the stage waiting for things to settle, sips water, has a word with his only accompanist, a string bass player, and then off again. No antics, no gesticulations, his voice is warm and gruff but with no flourishing in it. A smile every now and then, never, never a single word to his audience. Just the songs. After an hour and a half or more, he simply goes off and does not come back. That's it.

Any impressario worth his fat hands would smile and pat your cheek if you suggested that this sort of thing could succeed, that such a performer could last for five minutes never mind a quarter of a century. Mention to the poor bugger what Brassens has achieved however and the cigar will drop from his jaws in gasping disbelief and greed. More sheet music of his songs sold than any other French music, and sales on the increase; the book of his lyrics, four hundred thousand copies and still going; each new LP sells 300,000 copies first year, and every LP is still being re-issued; the 'complete works' album, containing ten discs and costing about thirty five quid, sold 20,000 in the first month; Brassens has sold altogether the equivalent of over 20 million singles. And yet he is rarely seen on television, is never seen at the first nights, and parties and receptions, hardly ever gives press interviews, is scarcely ever interviewed, refuses to give the story of his life.

French audiences are hard to please – not by nature warm and acquiescent; they want their money's worth. In the early sixties nobody else in the world listened so stonily as the Bobinot did to the Beatles who, elsewhere, had got baseball stadiumsful fainting away with pleasure. When Brassens finishes an evening, it is very difficult to make them go away. The curtain is brought noisily down and all the lights turned on. The doors are banged open, windows (!) as well and nobody moves. Ten minutes pass and he comes back and sings another one – no elaborate leave taking and thank you so muches – he just sings a last song. Bedlam again. And unlike those polite marathons at the end of most symphony and most pop concerts the people clap, cheer, shout stamp every night because Brassens always moves them and they love him for it.

Brassens's songs are, every one, and every bit of every one, stupendous. Of the hundred and forty that he has published there is not a dud, not a potboiler, not a lapse in taste or a lack of muscle in any of them. He is always better than you expect him to be.

This is because Brassens is his own man and because his songs are pure gold. The melodies are immediately haunting and unlike any other melodies I know of. They are not based upon American jazz and blues as most of our songs now are. Not derived from Western classical music. There are some strains of the lovely lilting French traditional songs, and some echoes of the French music hall which has been batting along ever since their main revolution and which unlike ours is alive and never felt better. Brassens has made up his own tradition; as if he found a complete new melodic seam which is inexhaustible and full of beautiful things and only he knows the way to it. His tunes take often startling turns and progressions, finishing at unexpected places, or changing into odd rhythms. And in them there is never any dead wood, no busking structure, no throwaway middle eight (that place where the usual popular song fills in time, getting the wordy bits over and done with so you can sweep on into the catchy chorus again) no fussy openings or finishes, no frilly effects to brighten things up.

His tunes are stirring or shocking or melting or passionate or rowdy. And always infectious. Most English people who know them will agree that the first time they were immediately seduced by the melody. Third or fourth hearing you get used to the Setois accent, the gruff voice the unostentatious delivery the fast tricky jokes, the unusual words, the classical references, the outrageous slang. The words are then so strong and riveting you're tempted to forget what took you in the first place: Brassens's enormous muscular musical strength. He has set to music fifteen or sixteen French poets, and infused them with a life that they may well have had before, but which I for one could never make out. Reading the poems afterwards it's impossible to keep the tune out of mind. He had the nerve to make a song out of Francois

Villon's Ballade (with the refrain Mais ou sont les neiges d'antan), and I'm afraid I've got the nerve to think the poem is better for it. The poems of Victor Hugo, Lamartine, Verlaine, Aragon, James T. de Banville, Paul Fort, and, especially, Jean Richepin are now heard and known and sung by people who are not usually accessible to poets.

One of his songs, Les Copains d'Abord, a best seller in its time, is by now a standard in France. After the first four or so notes most people immediately identify it. Once at a Christmas dance I heard a couple of dozen carousing Frenchman joining in as the band started it up, and they sang it through, pretty beefily as drinking dancers do, but still they went through every verse. Now in that song, written in racy and compressed, punning French there is a Latin tag (*Fluctuat nec mergitur*), allusions to Castor and Pollux, Montaigne, Boethius, Gericault's picture the *Raft of the Medusa*, the New Testament and the battle of Trafalgar. I don't say it's a virtue that all these things are bunged in, but it's at least astonishing that a popular song can use all the resources of language and culture intelligently and still be so well-known and so unaffectedly and rousingly sung, by singsonging boozers.

One of his earliest songs 'Le Gorille' passed straightaway into legend. First heard in 1952 it tells of a lovesick gorilla escaping from a travelling zoo and shagging a judge. 'Gorille' means also a tough nut, a strongarm, a heavy, as does the English gorilla. But it's also specifically one of De Gaulle's policemen, later the barbouzes, those state chopmerchants often let out of prison for 'special' political policework. The song ends with the judge shrieking for mercy just like the poor sods he daily condemns to death. It is a ravishing assault on the state and is just as wincingly relevant nowadays. And it is, into the bargain, a lovely, mucky song with a bellowing chorus; it is also complex passionate, delicately worked and an integrated work of art. Moreover, it's a work of art that is on the lips of the people because millions of Frenchmen know it and sing it.

There is every reason why they shouldn't sing his songs, however funny. For a start he assaults the sense of decency over and over and over again, with the persistence of a maniac. The songs abound with every possible four letter word for every possible bodily function, and a few variations as well. Not just slipped in, daringly – there's nothing so coy as being daring. He is outright about it and very thorough, repeating them, hammering at them bawling them in your ear until dizziness and moral shellshock set in. And what is even more offensive is that he does this bawling in tunes that are so appealing, so bloody unforgettable, and so unostentatiously, almost shyly, sung. He should be stopped – they've been saying it for years somebody stop him. He is a subvert.

Not only that, but he is a perpetual affront to the society that loves him so much. Absolutely nothing is sacred to him – or more exactly, anything that is considered to be sacred he will brutally dismantle. The villains in his stories are invariably the decent, self respecting citizens, les croquants, les gens bien, the well to do, the OK people the bourgeois, the incrowd – the very people he sings to. All the people who maintain the social order firmly in place. His heroes are the lowly, the distressed, despised, the humble the poor: prostitutes, the hunted thief, the village murderess (who, repenting her grisly crime, is hung and goes straight to paradise – not a few church going folk were quite upset about that) the old woman gathering wood so that her dying husband can have a fire in the room, the erstwhile royal mistress hounded, and head shaven by the mob. Even in his tenderest love songs he refuses to accept what everybody says you should accept. 'I have the honour,' he sings, 'of not asking you for your hand in marriage. Let's not engrave our names at the bottom of some parchment'. To idealists he sings 'to die for your ideas is a great idea; I very nearly got myself killed not...'

[Jake's manuscript ends there. The full quote, from Brassens's 'Mourir pour des Idées' is 'to die for your ideas is a great idea; I very nearly got myself killed for not having had one'.]

The Camera and the Song

'I know that a lot of people said, "Who is that po-faced bugger who dominates Saturday nights? We don't want any more of that. Why can't he smile? And what's he on about? I can't understand the words.'

– Jake Thackray, 1981[1]

As time went by, Jake would become increasingly outspoken about his dislike for television and show business. Bowing out of *Braden's Week* in 1972, after almost 60 appearances, he performed 'The Singer', in which he voiced his distrust of the smooth-talking, mohair-coated, maggot-eared men who ran the entertainment industry. It was a telling choice.

After four years of the programme, he was ready for a change: 'I did a lot of television... at the end of the 1960s, early 1970s, I did enough television for the whole of the folk scene. I did far more than my share, and I never enjoyed it.'[2]

'Jake was never a natural television performer,' observes Alex Armitage. 'He didn't enjoy the rehearsal and what he called the "frigging about", the make-up and so on.' A television studio was a sterile place in which to perform and, if there was an audience present, it was tightly managed, with cue boards telling people when to clap. Jake never felt at ease in such an artificial environment and a three-minute performance allowed him little opportunity to build any sort of a rapport with his audience. In a concert, he would declare: 'If TV people were here, you would not be enjoying the singing at all... between the singer and audience there would be no connection.'[3]

For the next five years viewers rarely saw him. In 1973 he popped up singing 'Sister Josephine' on *A Degree of Frost*[4] and appeared in a variety show compèred by country singer George Hamilton IV (hardly an obvious musical match). If the reduction in appearances reflected changing tastes and the desire of television executives for something new, Jake had no problem with this: his reputation was sufficient for him to make a good living from concerts and record sales for the next few years. But whilst he may have had enough, for the time-being, of doing three-minute turns, he remained open to other television offers, which led to some interesting work and outstanding music.

Jake's Scene had been somewhat hit and miss, but had shown the range and depth of his writing, and that his songs could make an effective soundtrack. In 1973, the BBC developed this idea further in a new series, *The Camera and the Song*. In each programme a different singer-songwriter was commissioned to write on a theme, which was then illustrated visually, with no spoken commentary.[5] Jake's episode was about life in the Yorkshire countryside – an obvious choice, given his excellent material about Swaledale. The programme served as a showcase for some fine, serious new writing, while also allowing him to revisit two songs from his back catalogue.

His contributions were paired with the camera of Philip Bonham-Carter, who was delighted to get the job, given the calibre of the other cameramen involved in the series.[6] Filming took place in Wharfedale, in the Yorkshire Dales, mixing real-life action with staged footage involving actors. Jake, however, never attended filming, and Philip wonders if this stemmed from his reluctance to appear on screen.[7] Indeed, to his surprise and disappointment, the cameraman never got to meet the singer: the production team was simply given a tape of the songs and left to get on with it.

Although Jake had no interest in what viewers saw, rural life again proved genuinely inspirational for him, and the songs he wrote, recorded with musical arranger William Southgate,[8] were excellent. Most featured a quintet comprising piano, woodwind and brass, giving them a texture akin to chamber music, which worked well.

Set to a beautiful piano accompaniment, the melodic and wistful 'The Rain on the Mountainside' surely ranks as one of the finest things ever written about life in the dales. Jake sings movingly of the harsh weather's indifference to the suffering of the landscape and its inhabitants – the shivering lapwing, the 'agonised' trees and 'tormented' river – and expresses his admiration for the determination and unbreakable spirit of the poor shepherd and hill-farmer who, however wild the weather, go stoically about their work. Perhaps seeds of inspiration had been sown on a grey day during the filming of *Jake's Scene* when, standing on the moors above Swaledale, he discussed with a shepherd the realities of rural life.

By contrast, 'The Brigadier' celebrates the lives of rural scallywags and rants about the local bigwig who lords it over them. Jake's cheeky rogues laugh at everyone: the gullible day-trippers they tap for cash and beer, the outsiders who move into their community, and even the programme's film crew and 'po-faced pillock' who thinks he can sing.[9] But the chief target of their contempt is the 'frigging' brigadier whose influence is ubiquitous, whether sitting in judgement on their drunkenness on the magistrates' bench, or reading the lesson in church with a self-satisfied smile. 'The Brigadier' is full of Jake's familiar hostility to deference, pomposity and privilege, but here the mocking portrait is more developed than in his earlier songs and painted with masterly skill. The rage with which the song is infused is colourful, amusing and memorable.

The inspiration for 'The Brigadier' came from close to

home: a neighbour, a former services man, known to everyone, including even his wife, as 'The Commander'. 'He lived near Jake and was always complaining about the Thackrays, because their kids would be making noise and leaving their bikes in the drive,' recalls Rick Irons. 'He was on the local council, and Jake was always at war with him.' As so often, he had drawn upon the mundane to create something memorable and magical.

'The Poor Sod' is a short, moving portrait of the life of a farm labourer who lives in utter poverty, and for whom any pleasure is fleeting and in the past. Even the natural world seems to have something against this luckless man. The song's lack of rhyme only adds to its bleak simplicity, and the mood of the lyrics is matched by its melancholy melody.

'The Cenotaph' is a powerful but peculiar song about heroism and fading memory. When he sang it later on the radio, Jake explained: 'I am haunted by the First World War. In the village where I lived my mother used to take me to the bus stop which was by the Cenotaph, which was filled with names of men, and my mother used to say, "Why don't they put the names of wives on it? Those poor buggers are dead."'

'The Cenotaph' starts poignantly with a musical roll call of women who have lost their men, followed by 'The Last Post'. Then, to a marching rhythm, Jake sings of the lack of respect shown to the memorial upon which old men blasphemously spit, the village youths lounge and couples have sex. In the face of these indignities the voice of the fallen heroes is stoical: they have all endured much worse. The song ends with a roll call of the men. There can be few more powerful or unusual songs on the subject, and it is a shame that Jake never released it on record.[10] He would revisit the theme of war a few years later in one of his late masterpieces, 'The Remembrance'.

The two older songs used in the programme were given new arrangements. He sang the haunting 'Old Molly Metcalfe' *a cappella* over an eery electronic soundscape, which conjured up a bleakness worthy of Emily Brontë's *Wuthering Heights*.

'Country Bus' received very different treatment, and was remodelled to become a nostalgia trip. Alongside poignant film of a derelict bus rusting away, it had a wistful new introduction, in which Jake declared that the happy days spent riding 'bumbily' along were gone. Musically, the bus sways along as cheerfully as ever, with woodwind and brass adding colour, and even some honking. However, Jake replaces all the present tenses of the original lyric with the past tense, which changes his celebration of the bus and its motley passengers into a bittersweet lament for a way of life (and bus service) now gone. It is a simple but affecting transformation which brings the mood closer to that of the other songs.

The programme ends with 'Little Thomas Haverly', which celebrates the birth of a child and brings welcome light. It is a sweet, simple piece, full of love, hope and promise for the future: the boy's parents will plant a cherry tree, which will one day bear fruit for him. This was a very personal song, written for Bob and Sue Haverly, after the birth of their son in 1973. Excited at the news, Jake phoned to tell them he had written it, but what happened next is revealing.

'He didn't play it to us,' recalls Sue. 'He told us that he had written a song for Tom, and I think we saw it in print, but I can't remember a grand presentation – that wasn't Jake's style. He totally underplayed it. He was so self-effacing, and his attitude was along the lines of: "I've written a song for Tom, it means a lot to me, but it's not so good, you won't want to hear it…".' Jake never told them that it featured in *The Camera and the Song*.

Just as the song never reached them, nor did the cherry tree, which was meant as a gift from the Thackrays. Unfortunately (and predictably), while awaiting delivery at Hillside, it was eaten by their goat. It was one more Leopold Alcocks incident to add to Jake's catalogue of mishaps.

His songs for *The Camera and the Song* demonstrated conclusively that Jake was a writer to be taken seriously, and led some to revise their view of his work. In his review for *The Guardian*, Peter Fiddick, who had never been a fan ('it's a style that strains the ears'), declared 'it was a half hour of great charm' and 'the pictures and the songs were neatly worked together'.[11] The *Birmingham Daily Post* called it 'an enchanting and entertaining marriage which caught exactly the flavour of that part of Yorkshire'.[12] For Peter Lennon of the *Sunday Times*, Jake's songs had enhanced his reputation.[13] Given all this, it's a pity he never undertook a TV project of this sort again.

Other television commissions came along which didn't require Jake to perform on camera. In 1975, this led to 'Those are the Days', his song about university life, and the following year he wrote the theme tune for *A Ripe Old Age*, an Anglia TV series aimed at enabling pensioners to get the most out of retirement. His own performance doesn't survive, but in one programme a hall of pensioners sing it lustily. Its message is simple and hopeful: even at a ripe old age, there is much to look forward to, with wines yet to be tasted and songs yet to be sung. It is a simple piece which is tuneful enough and effectively met the brief.

In the same year, viewers would finally see Jake again in two revealing programmes. *Thackray and Loudermilk* paired him up with John D. Loudermilk, the American singer-songwriter whose songs had been hits for Eddie Cochrane and the Everly Brothers, among others. For the programmes, Jake and Loudermilk were filmed in a recording studio, chatting and singing for each other, and informality was the order of the day: the crew is seen and heard laughing, and Jake smokes and drinks between songs, a crate of stout at his feet. From the outset, he makes clear that he doesn't want any show-business pretence: 'Don't let's bugger about with elaborate introductions... there's enough frigging about as it is.'

Whilst they both play nylon-strung guitar, their styles are very different, the American coming from a country and blues tradition, which makes for an interesting musical conversation.

Jake mostly performs comic favourites that have everyone roaring with laughter.[14]

The between-songs chat is revealing. Jake explains to Loudermilk how English music has changed: 'We had a music hall tradition, people used to get up and sing funny songs and dirty songs, you know, and this tradition of ours goes back, certainly in England, it goes back ever such a long time... People have always been singing mucky songs, and it's disappeared.' He also speaks of what motivated and influenced his own writing: 'Now, instead of singing something frivolous like that ['Brother Gorilla'], you're on a hot shot if you sing something a bit serious and mainly something about the little, flickering, sacred flame that you've got inside, if you sing about your own personal feelings. I prefer not to. You can tell a joke to somebody three or four times, and if you tell it, their eyes will go glassy, but if you formalise it, if you put it into verse, or make it up into a song, they will listen to it over and over again because the form is there, the structure, and they love the structure, and I do, you know. And also, the French tradition is very strong in wordy, comical songs, a bit bawdy, preferably a bit bawdy, you know, and this is a tradition I feel right rooted in.'

Loudermilk seems to be in awe, contrasting the simplicity of his own writing with the sophistication and wit of Jake's, but this prompts an interesting and somewhat contradictory response: 'I've just sung a comical song. Why should that make you feel uncomfortable, you know? I am pretty sure that I can never do anything else except to make up comical songs like that... Generally, I can't see myself rising above my raising, you know? I can actually, because I'm a Catholic... [*laughter*] I turn up for training every Sunday morning... [*laughter*] I'm hoping for better things, of course I'm hoping for better things. I want to be a better bloke, but mainly I want to write better songs.'

Jake also voices his strong views on the impact of American culture on music in Europe: 'I've not got a tradition behind me like you have, and like a lot of singers in this country have. Your American music came across and ours disappeared... your social songs, the songs that were made up by the poor black and the poor white, the strength of those, the muscle of those, is still with us now. That sort of musical thrust has never stopped thrusting... and you're a part of it. What irks me is that this should be taken to be, as it has been, generally in Europe, and certainly in this country, as the only possible way to go about singing about your experience... to take the blues.'

Most revealing of all, however, is his response when the American suggests that this change is no-one's fault. Jake disagrees and is forthright about whom he holds responsible: 'You can blame the way that the popular music industry drowns this country, it just came over. It's like dropping bombs, the record industry, so that nowadays English singers tend to immediately think in terms of rock and blues... You've taken over, it's been a take-over job, and there are people to blame for it. The music industry's done it... for money.'

Loudermilk listens politely, before quietly slipping into an amusing version of his song 'Abilene', which breaks the tension and forces Jake to laugh.

The second programme finishes with Jake singing 'The Poor Sod', introducing it with an assertion: 'Nobody likes it, you know. And it's a peculiar little song, and when I think about it, I'm still fond of it. But the public, you know, they look at it with a more or less objective eye and that doesn't please them, so they withdraw.' Having sung crowd-pleasers, he seems determined to break the mood and share something which pleases him. It is a small indication of a wilfulness and frustration with his audience's expectations which would grow in the years ahead.

Admittedly, the intimacy of *Thackray and Loudermilk* was contrived, but it worked. When the programmes were broadcast on BBC2 in July 1976, they were well-received, with the *Sunday Times* reviewer declaring them 'a very agreeable record of the work of two interesting singers'.[15] *The Camera and the Song* and *Thackray and Loudermilk* both showed that television could provide Jake with a platform, without the constraints and pressures of the three-minute slot.

But he never revisited either format, and when viewers next saw him, in 1977, there would be a strong sense of *déjà vu*, as he became a resident singer on *That's Life!*, the successor to *Braden's Week*. It would be a triumph for his agent, but also a last hurrah: the days when Jake would willingly step into a TV studio and stare into the red light would soon draw to a close.

Jake on stage in Caerphilly, October 1977.

A Singer's Place

'A singer's place is on his feet on public floorboards, taking risks in front of paying punters and not ducking and weaving and smirking on the flickering rectangle.'
– Jake Thackray, 1981[1]

'Jake Thackray is at the stage in his career where it is sufficient merely to put his name on a poster for the public to know what he does and how well he does it.'[2] So declared an advert for a concert at Canterbury's Marlowe Theatre in March 1973, and it was true enough. The profile which television had given him ensured that throughout the 1970s he played to packed houses. He was at the height of his fame and the height of his powers, and the reviews were glowing:

> Jake's last Bromley concert was a smash sell-out and the wildly enthusiastic audience could be heard applauding in the High Street.[3]

> Mr Thackray, alone on stage with his guitar, has a tremendous personality, reminding one on occasion of a gauche garçon, and yet capable of bringing this most sophisticated audience to its feet clamouring for encore after encore.[4]

Undoubtedly live performance gives him the scope which a television programme never could (unless it were his own) and he proved conclusively on Thursday night that he does not need a cosy intimate atmosphere to communicate his warmth and personality to an audience.[5]

To say that Jake Thackray is Britain's answer to Georges Brassens is high praise indeed, but it is a comment fully justified by last night's enthralling and highly amusing solo performance.[6]

Mr Thackray has a way with offensive songs which can almost render them drawing room material.[7]

Theatres, folk clubs, universities and arts festivals were his bread and butter and, wherever possible, he kept to venues where he was sure the audience was there to listen to him. His appearance, in June 1972, supporting American proto-punk rock band MC5 at Bedford College's all-night *Midsummer Madness* festival, was an outlier.[8] His agent was always keen to put Jake on in the large concert halls and theatres which he knew he could fill, but was mindful that he was dealing with a reluctant performer. And so every lucrative concert at a Theatre Royal, Philharmonic Hall or Playhouse had to compete for space in Jake's diary alongside folk clubs such as the Bell and Pump, the Boggery and the Stanford Arms.

In 1972, this preference for small venues struck Ronald Faux of *The Times* as remarkable: 'Jake Thackray is a difficult man to catch. His popularity, boosted now by television, would surely allow him a steadier run of appearances, but he insistently threads his way around folk clubs, working men's clubs and universities throughout Britain, only occasionally perching for a couple of hours before a theatre audience with a fresh batch of well-polished songs.'[9]

For Jake, much of the appeal of performing at folk clubs stemmed from a sense of connection, as he explained in 1977:

'Folk clubs... are unbeatable, because you're sitting on top of the people, you can feel the human warmth blasting out. When I've been to folk clubs to sit and listen, it's not only that you can see that the human warmth goes out to the bloke who's singing and it bounces back, and you come out of a folk club and people say, "We had a right good night down there." What they mean is that they were... they were cured of various things. Sounds corny to say that, but it's true. Happens to me regular. I've come for the cure.'[10] He was also drawn to folk clubs because he saw them as being part of an authentic cultural tradition: 'Folk clubs is [*sic*] the life and soul of a folk singer... Folk clubs is English music hall, it's proper English entertainment, and as a singer-songwriter person I couldn't do without them.'[11]

This need for connection was not the only thing that kept Jake in the folk clubs: his humility, self-doubt and refusal to be put on a pedestal also played a part, as seen in a bizarre encounter he had with a reluctant audience member in December 1973. He was performing at the Bay Horse in Doncaster and 17-year-old Gerald Sables was in attendance, nursing a terrible hangover. He wasn't a fan, and by the interval he had had enough of the music:

At the break I decided I needed somewhere quiet to just sit and relax and try to ease my headache. I bought a pint at the bar and looked for a suitable spot, but everywhere was busy. Then I remembered there was a small room downstairs, so I opened the door and went in. It was pitch black, but I wasn't bothered, as the light was hurting my eyes anyway. I sat down alone with my pint, just relaxing. Well, I thought I was alone. After several minutes I heard a muted cough, so I said hello. A voice said hello back, and then asked how I was enjoying the evening. 'Well, not much,' I replied. 'Not with a head that feels like it's about to explode.' 'Sorry about that,' came the reply. 'What do you think of the act?' 'What, Jake Thackray, you mean?' 'Yeh.' 'Well, to be honest, I'm not a big fan of his.

I like a few songs, like "Sister Josephine", but that's it.' 'Have you seen him on TV?' the voice said. 'Yes,' I replied, 'but I think he's the most boring part of the show.' 'I agree. I'm not a big fan of his either.' I said, 'I'm hoping he's going to be a lot better in the second half.' 'So do I, but I wouldn't bet on it.' I asked, 'Have you ever seen him live before?' 'Oh yes, many times.' I replied: 'You must be a glutton for punishment then.' 'Yes, I must be.' 'Well,' I said, 'I had better get back upstairs – don't want to miss the beginning. Are you coming or staying?' 'I think I'll come as well.' As you will have guessed, when I opened the door and he followed me out, I discovered it was Jake who I had been sharing the room with. I apologised, and I must have been bright red with embarrassment, but he said I shouldn't apologise – he was grateful to hear an honest opinion from somebody.

Life on the road was hardly glamorous. Whenever possible, Jake went home after concerts, but this meant long drives in the early hours of the morning in unreliable cars. Often, however, he was away from home for days and weeks at a time, staying in boarding houses or cheap hotels. Where he could, he stayed with friends. Alan Plater remembered him turning up at his house once with a witty pair of gifts for his host: 'Only Jake would turn up with an Andy Capp book and bottle of Bell's whisky, i.e. cap 'n' bells [a type of fool's hat] – that was a very Jake thing to do.'

During down-time on tour it was easy to lapse into listlessness and to brood. Jake's gig diary gives a strong sense of this, as a week of entries from the mid-1970s shows:

Sat night. Off to Boscombe Down. Unfindable. When I found it, unspeakable. Sergeant's Mess, 1 hour cabaret. The West Indian disco-compère got my name tortuously wrong. Drank Guinness and watched Kojak and Match of the Day but very nervous in my white ducks [canvas trousers] and navy cardigan. Staggered through an hour, feeling more and more weary, wise-cracking quite nicely but very bored and tired with the job. Home, home, diddly ding, diddly ding. Slept on the couch with Sheila.

Monday. Reading. Big audience. Me mechanical and v. nervous (after pre-performance visit to bog, I find I have peed down my white ducks – put this down to intervention of Holy Ghost as ducks so sparkling would have been too posh for students). Promise to write for their Rag Mag. Home v. late.

Wednesday. Off to L'pool. Slept in with Sheila till 12. Bought bottle of whisky at Ross for after-gig drinking. Straight to Bromborough.[12] Big breasted bird brings me bottle of Guinness on stage, my thoughts, even during following songs, are unworthy. Later at Radio City broadcast she rings me up, nice big vowel sounds to match. An assignation? Nobly, I don't.

Thursday. Early up, crossword, droop all morning in New Stanley Lounge. Drink whisky all afternoon. Sleep. One day dead. Then I am galvanized to terror by ad in paper which indicates that my venue, the Huyton Suite, Huyton, is not the quiet, Thackray worshipping, village hall I think, but a great, big jolly POPULAR working class club. Oh Christ, not the PEOPLE! Just like an Arts Ass [association] to try me out with the masses. They've done it before. Terror compounded by inability to find the fucking place. Oh God, Liverpool, I breathe, you scare me. Blow me if it isn't the quiet J.T. worshipping mob I hoped for. Candlelit, quiet, worshipful. So, frenetically, I perform as if I was really used to doing the Masses and this artistic sort of gig was not really my sort of scene. Brother two-face.

Friday. Up early again and after crossword I really do settle down to write a bit. But it comes out duff. Theme – I am a man, I think nothing human is indifferent to me: caught *in flagrante* – could have been my ankles the trousers were round, there but for the Grace of God (and the bus fare) go I. To

Woodchurch Comm. Centre Complex, with Community Gym + Swimming Baths. Very fearful because this is Birkenhead and these people live on an estate but I do well – and there are lots of them.

Elsewhere the diary is punctuated with references to football scores ('Oh Leeds United 0-1 Oh!'), church services ('Mass at St. Cedd's. Lovely.'), and the misery and mishaps of late-night driving:

Came home, meeting folk singer 3 a.m. at Aust, hitch-hiking to Hereford.

Out of petrol, walked 6 miles over bridge in cutting wind.

Long, long drive home, plus breakdown at Berry Hill.

A recurrent theme is how hard Jake found his life as a 'performing dick':

First day back [after Christmas holidays], and scared, scared, scared.

It was a variety hall – bluegrass music – cowboys in the front. My hour was agonising, before, during and after. Never again.

Forgot 'Cactus' and apologised winningly. Forgot 'Fine Bay Pony' and apologised defeatingly.

His anxieties and feelings of isolation must have been exacerbated by the fact that, ever since he had first started singing in the pubs and folk clubs of Leeds, Jake had been a solo performer.[13] This changed in 1973, and the impact upon his touring life would be very positive.

The catalyst was the concert at the Sherman Theatre, where he watched Brassens perform with his bassist, Pierre Nicolas, and decided that he should do the same. In the theatre bar after the concert he sought out Alan Williams, whose double-bass Nicolas had borrowed. Years later, Jake recalled the moment fondly: 'I went up to Alan Williams at this "do" and said, "Can you recommend a bass player? I'd like to do what Georges Brassens has done this evening, and have a bass in the background to go against the guitar. Do you know anybody?" And Alan said, "Yeah!" I said, "Who?" He said, "Me!" [*laughs*] And after that we played together and it went like good pudding. We both clicked in, and I am eternally grateful to Georges and to Pierre Nicolas that I met this ace musician at Georges's "do".'[14]

There were clear advantages to Jake having company on the road, particularly given his dread of large venues. Alex Armitage, who became his agent in 1976, observes: 'Jake liked the money, but he felt the space between him and the audience, the lack of intimacy, didn't really suit him, so he began taking Alan around, which helped enormously. It wasn't just the space between the mic stand and the front row of the stalls, it was the sitting in the dressing room in the interval and beforehand, on his own. I think he got lonely. Also, it gave me as his agent a certain amount of comfort, too, that there was someone travelling around with Jake, because he could be somewhat less than reliable.'

Williams was a gifted musician who entered the profession late, having worked in a bank, and had no formal musical training until he went to college in Cardiff. He could play by ear, and took up the bass simply because players were in short supply, which meant more work. Equally adept at classical and jazz, he enjoyed a flourishing freelance career and played with the BBC Orchestra, Welsh Opera and Welsh Jazz Orchestra.

It quickly became clear that this new musical partnership had clicked, as Alan's widow, Gaynor, remembers: 'They got together for a few sessions, and Jake thought it worked, to have a more prominent bass line. They started with a few gigs, and it went from there.' Lacking formal musical training himself, Jake only provided the bassist with the song chords, but this was not a problem. 'Alan had always played by ear, he'd never been glued to a manuscript,' says Gaynor. 'I think Jake kept him on his toes because he probably didn't play the same thing twice. Alan really had to listen very hard, but that added to the spontaneity of it all.'

His background in jazz enabled Alan to improvise inventive, sympathetic accompaniments, and Jake appreciated the new dimension his playing brought to his songs. Early in any concert, he would introduce Alan jokingly as his 'backing group', and apologise when he was absent: 'It's a shame that he's not here, because he's a stupendous musician and it does make the evening a lot more musical!'[15]

Alan was a 'proper bloody musician', and Jake used this to disparage his own musicianship. But the bassist recognised the effectiveness of the singer's guitar playing. 'He realised that it worked,' says Gaynor, 'and that the response of the audience proved that it worked beautifully, so who was he to question it? It spoke for itself, really, and he loved it.'

The two men not only enjoyed a musical partnership, but also an enduring friendship. On stage, Williams was the model of professionalism and never said a word, but appearances were deceptive. He was a huge *Monty Python* fan, with a wicked sense of humour.[16] 'There was terrific banter between Jake and Alan,' recalls Gaynor, 'they were a great double-act and shared a lot of fun.'

They also wound each other up. 'It was always competitive,' recalled Sheila Thackray. 'The driving, the getting there, the coming back. Everything. They scored points off each other all the time. They argued like a married couple as well.' Arguments would centre on where the gig was, and which Newport they should be driving to, but the accident-prone singer was in good hands. 'Alan looked after him. He was wonderful,' said Sheila. 'Jake on his own wasn't safe. Alan used to try and get them to the right town, get him set up, make sure that he had got all that he needed, and pick up his shoes and his guitar on the way out, as they were leaving, not to leave stuff behind.' Increasingly Jake came to rely upon him to do the driving, particularly after gigs.

The two men had some great adventures on the road, where hotel stays could be eventful. Once, when checking out, Jake queried the big drinks bill, and Alan was forced to admit that he had raided the mini-bar each day and filled his suitcase with miniatures, thinking this would go unnoticed. The items were duly returned. Sometimes, Sheila recalled, they even had to share a bed: 'They might go to a Holiday Inn or a motel, only to be told, "We're sorry, we don't have two rooms, just the one." And Alan used to go [*rolls eyes to Heaven*], "Please! Please! Twin beds." A few times it was a double bed. Alan said he used to cling to his side and hold on like to a cliff edge, trying to shove the pillow down between them before Thackray, in the middle of the night, would come put his arm around him. Jake was hopeless. He never used to know where he was.'

On other occasions they got themselves into riskier situations. In 1982, they went to perform for the British forces in Germany.[17] Driving through East Germany on the autobahn from West Germany to Berlin, their curiosity about life behind the Iron Curtain got the better of them and, ignoring strict instructions not to deviate from their route, went exploring. Driving among the Trabants in a car which proclaimed that they were western capitalists, they attracted a good deal of attention, including from the East German police. They duly got their marching orders, but not before Jake had managed to off-load to the inquisitive locals some of his decadent western chocolate, whisky and clothes, and even a pair of shoes.

Their experiences provided Jake with the inspiration for a fanciful *Yorkshire Post* piece about life on the road, in which Alan appeared, thinly-disguised, under a pseudonym:

At the end of a week when many luminaries (George Best, Oliver Reed, Joan Collins, Elton John, Paul McCartney, to name but a many) exposed the magnitude of what they are worth, Alan Parry and I were climbing onto the early Sunday morning southbound train from Darlington.

'You musicians?' said a man as we lugged our instrument cases. 'What a fulfilling life that must be!' He was from Maidenhead. 'It must be fascinating!'

'Where are we staying tonight?' said Alan. I showed him the card.

'Seaview Guest House, 5, Canal Avenue, North Salford, is a small friendly establashment,, with comfortable rooms and home-cocking. Hot and cold television. Famly atmosphere. All welcome. No children, anamals, DHSS, or ethnicks. NO smoking in room. NO alcohol in room. NO food in room. No radios, no visitors. Bath £2 extra. No entry after 11pm. Breakfast 7 am – 7.15 am. Vacate room by 9 am. Payment in advance!'

'How fulfilling!' said Alan. 'Spelling lessons extra and in-house self-service scaffold facility available for cases of despair.'

'Fascinating!' says Maidenhead man.

****

From the working diary of Alan Parry, Bass Player, Sunday, Salford

7.30. Leave Gateshead (JT has trots. I told him he shouldn't eat the breakfast.) Change York and Leeds and Ashton Under Lyne. Manchester Victoria. Lent JT a tenner because not paid last night: - 'Sorry, the manager went home early. Cheque is in the post.'

2.30. Arrive Salford North. Raining. No taxi. We walk to Town Hall. Cafe shut because Sunday. JT begins swearing. Words I have never heard before – well, he went to university, didn't he?

3.00. Town Hall shut because it's Sunday.

3.30. Still raining. JT decides to go in through a small window in building at side of Town Hall. Gets there but is swearing.

4.15. Two policemen come round corner: 'Mr Parry, is it? Ah, well. A middle-aged Yorkshireman using very foul language has just broken into our police station through the side window. He claims you will vouch for him. Accompany us to the cells, now, please.'

5.15. Sgt Metcalfe gives us tea and sandwiches. JT goes again to station toilets. Then apologises for bad language, we hand out photos of ourselves and give the station a song.

6.15. Sound check and lighting; tune up instruments and rehearse; no hot water because Sunday; put on best suits and posh shoes. Get nervous. JT has lost spare socks and no! he may not borrow mine!

7.00. We go on stage. Good gig, full house. Wonder if punters can smell the JT feet as strong as I can? Makes me giddy and if wind changes he could empty Salford Town Hall. He says he is wearing his odour-eaters. Well, they're not very hungry tonight.

10.45. Come off the stage.

10.50. Packed up and waiting to be paid. 'Sorry, the manager went home early. Cheque is in the post.' Raining. We walk to Sea View. How does JT find these flea pits?

11.30. No doorknocker, no bell, so JT on knees hallooing through letterbox. Madam Sea View appears with some big dogs and a fag in her face. She is wearing - (I suppose it started life out as a) – nightie, but it frightens me. 'Room 18, fourth floor,' says fag and nightie. Stair carpet sucks at your feet.

12.05. Bed. We tossed a coin. JT got the M61 window and I got the shunting yards.

6.30am. Early morning call, i.e. the Madam opens door of room 18 and lets in the dogs. Raining. Walk to station...

                                        ****

'You musicians then?' says man as we lug the instruments. 'What an exciting life you must lead! Fulfilling, eh?' JT is going to swear again but Alan Parry, who is a fine bass player indeed, says: 'Yes, actually, it is.'

Because he is a proper musician, he knows it and he knows what he's really worth.[18]

While Jake's career was riding high in the late 1970s and early 1980s, the two men performed together most weeks, and without doubt the singer gained a great deal from the partnership, both musically and personally. However, Alan still needed his orchestral work, and so his gigs with Jake had to fit in around this.

His company also came at a price, which Jake had to pay out of his own fee. This wasn't a significant additional cost when the theatres and ticket receipts were large, but it made playing at the smaller venues on the folk club circuit far less profitable. Jake's thinking, however, was ruled by his heart, not his head, and he was no businessman. Eventually, though, as his audiences declined in the late 1980s, he couldn't afford the luxury of a bassist. Meanwhile, Alan's orchestral work had grown, and he moved to London, although he always remained available to perform with his friend.

At about the same time as he recruited Alan, Jake was starting to change his stage act. Early in his career, in the course of a two-hour concert he would sing almost 30 songs, prefaced by short introductions, as exemplified wonderfully on his *Live Performance* album. His audiences lapped it up, but it was an exhausting nightly feat of memory and concentration. Furthermore, he disliked the predictable, formulaic approach, which he felt smacked of show-biz contrivance. He was ready for a change which would take some of the pressure off him as a singer and reveal another remarkable side to his creativity and skill as a performer.

On stage, his ironic explanation of his rationale became, in its own right, a memorable part of the act:

> I like the job, I like being a singer. You know, when I grow up, I want to be a singer. But, perversely enough, you can't be a singer without having to talk... you've got to talk. What I prefer to do, given the chance, just facing you like this, I'd just prefer to sing the songs, you know, pell-mell, one after another: I sing, you go clap, I sing, you go clap... or not, as the case may be. And for me, in any case, the evening would be pleasant. It would trot away nice and briskly.
>
> But you can't do that. You can do it if you're an acrobat. I mean, if you're an acrobat, all you've got to do... You're billed as an acrobat, so what do you do? You check that your flies are done up, and you come on and you acrobat, you just acrobat all night. Hooray! And if you're a conjurer, you come on and conj [*sic*], and people would be disappointed if you sat down and gave them a few Helen Shapiro numbers at the piano. But, perversely enough, if you're a singer... and it's something I'm trying to get used to, and I can't... it might sound a bit disingenuous, but I can't get used to it, the fact that you've got to talk. Because if you don't, if you don't talk, after a few songs... in my case people... I can see 'em... I can look down,

and after song number 3, without saying anything, I can see them, and they're going, 'Say, can't the bugger talk?'

Going home afterwards in the motor car, I used to think, 'How did you sing the songs? Well, that was a bit duff.' I used to think about the songs, and then I thought, 'Christ! What did you say in between?' And I remembered, and then I started blushing... and there's nothing worse than blushing to yourself in the dark... So, listen, I stopped doing it, I've stopped doing it. Sometimes I just won't stop, sometimes I'll finish a song and just lumber on into the next one. And then, when I feel that I ought to do a talking bit, I'll stop, and do a talking bit.[19]

This was classic Jake. Far from talking less, he would now be talking much more, putting more space between the songs. He wasn't the first singer to do this: both Jasper Carrott and Billy Connolly had developed as comedians from such beginnings. For Jake, this new approach was a declaration that he was no longer going to play the show-biz game, that he wanted to be more spontaneous; it was an assertion of his authenticity which went hand in glove with his rejection of stardom. It was also an inspired change of direction which only increased his sense of connection with audiences. As one reviewer put it: 'It's almost as if he's holding a private party in his own house and just by chance offered to sing a few numbers by way of entertainment. In between songs he talks about how he writes them, the people roundabout, what it was like when he was a kid, offers some good solid advice on the subject of love and romance, until you really feel he should be sitting in the seat next to you, he's so approachable.'[20]

Jake always maintained that he couldn't tell jokes, and so his 'talking bits' took the form of extended anecdotes and musings. The inspiration for subject matter came from a variety of sources, including his days at St Michael's College and Intake, his children and his Catholicism. Particularly memorable were his glorious, colourful accounts of the doom-laden existence of his alter ego, Reggie Sedgewick, a fictional, accident-prone teacher whom he made out to be the inspiration for 'Leopold Alcocks'. In the midst of all the well-observed humour, Jake's values shone through, as he used his anecdotes to call out bigotry whilst mocking celebrity culture and deference to the royal family.

What he had to say was hilarious and beautifully-constructed, and yet his skilful delivery gave the impression that these were off-the-cuff reflections. 'Jake had astonishing comic timing,' says Alex Armitage. 'The technique he had of picking up his guitar, making the audience think he was going to sing a song, and then he would begin a couple of bars of one of his extraordinarily complicated introductions, and then he suddenly would stop and say, "And another thing...", and continue an anecdote, or go off on a tangent to another story. And the audience enjoyed that, because they thought the anecdotes were great.'

Jake would likewise play mistakes to his advantage. During concerts he would often cut a song short, unable to remember the words. He would immediately follow this with a profuse apology, and assure the audience that he knew the first half of a lot of other songs. 'He forgot the words at the beginning,' recalled Sheila Thackray, 'and then realised that that got as big a laugh as continuing, so he contrived to forget then.'

With their mix of songs and talk, no two concerts were the same: the balance and sequence varied, depending upon Jake's mood and the audience's response. Over time, as his skill and confidence as a raconteur developed, the balance shifted towards talk, and he would regularly sing as few as 15 songs in an evening. It was a winning mix. 'Audiences really felt they were getting part of his heart, part of Jake, which they absolutely loved,' says Alex Armitage. 'They really, really loved him as a bloke. They loved his anecdotes, loved the stories about his life in the north, loved how the truth and fiction were interwoven, and the edges were frayed.' Few would disagree, although at a concert Jake once had to deal with a heckler shouting, 'You're talking too much!' His response was typical of him: he growled back a put-down ('So are you, pal!'), then promptly apologised for his rudeness.[21]

This abandonment of a traditional approach to the structure of his performance went hand in glove with his rejection of another show-biz ritual – the encore. Jake's thoughts on the subject became an entertaining routine with which he ended every concert:

> You know this business about the plastic encore? You know the plastic encore, it's *de rigueur*, it is mandatory, statutory business... You know, you all go laugh, laugh, clap, clap, and the three of us stand here looking all shy and modest... Because that is the funny thing, it's a funny thing... If you're a singing man, if you're a singer, if people are clapping you, you're supposed to look humble! You know, you've got to look modest and winsome. You mustn't go 'Hooray!' or any of that sort of thing.
>
> So we stand here, looking sort of shifty, you know, and goody-goody, and then you've only just clapped, and we've disappeared... we've disappeared! This is the standard business. We've marched off, and the way we march off, you're supposed to think to yourselves, 'Well, good God! Those three lads, by now, they're out to the bus stop and... [*gesture*] home!' So, in a spirit of politeness, you carry on clapping for a bit... you know... Well, the clapping is just dithering down, there's the last few claps left in you, and suddenly we come swerving back on here... and you've got to start all over again...
>
> We've been nowhere near the bus stop.
>
> Anyhow, none of us minds marching backwards and forwards, that seems to be part of the evening, to see grown men marching backwards and forwards, you know... Now I'm willing to do that, I don't begrudge the leg work... you know... Think of him [Alan Williams with his bass] and the furniture! I don't mind that part about it, but the part that I really can't stand about it is that when we reappear, we've got to have a look of total astonishment on our faces! You know, as if we

just made it down to the bus stop and we're all stood there
with our cases... [thinking] 'When's that bus coming...?' And
suddenly the manager of the place, no less, comes running
down the road and says, 'Hey, lads! You'll never guess! They
want another one!' And we're all supposed to go, 'Oh? Really?!'
That sort of look of astonishment... you know...Well, to tell
you the truth, I can't manage that sort of look, you know... It
is a bit preposterous, so... so... listen, I've stopped doing that,
I've stopped doing that for a long time... you know, pretending
to go home and then reappearing...

That was the last song, goodnight, and we're going to sing
another one.[22]

Jake was true to his word. Audiences no longer saw him
marching back and forth across the stage. They laughed, and
they loved him for the peculiar honesty of his stance. But amid
the humour he was making an important statement: he could
not abide pretence. As time went on, his impatience with the
conventional expectations of his career would grow, and his
rejection of show business would become an ever more
destructive driving force.

Before then, however, his determination to do things his
way would lead him to make the album that would be his
masterpiece.

Nerves and a final drag on a cigarette before facing the audience.

On Again! On Again!

'Lots of the stuff of life we shared turned up again in his songs. I'd hear him reconstructing and putting another voice to another rhythm to a tune in his head. In fact, he turned everything into song, even what the chickens were doing!'
– Sheila Thackray[1]

When Jake returned to the recording studio in October 1976, more than four years had passed since he'd last made an album – an eternity in music business terms. This reflected the fact that, without the pressure of regular television deadlines, he was writing far less: in the three years since *The Camera and the Song* he had completed barely a dozen new songs.

This declining productivity seems not only to have been down to a lack of discipline, but also a growing perfectionism. So, whilst the quantity of material was modest, the quality was superb. *On Again! On Again!* would be full of poetic, finely-polished beauty.[2] It would be his finest, and last, studio album.

The similarities between Jake's music and Brassens's are at their greatest on this record. With only two guitars and a double-bass, the album has the Frenchman's signature sound and includes two adaptations of his songs. However, his influence goes beyond this. It is on *On Again! On Again!* that Jake comes closest to his hero in his approach to writing.

Always his own fiercest critic, as time went on Jake was increasingly inclined to dismiss as trivial songs that were purely comic. The popularity of 'Bantam Cock', 'Sister Josephine' and 'The Lodger' embarrassed him, and he felt trapped by the demand to sing them.[3]

His writing had long mixed light and shade, but during the 1970s, as *The Camera and the Song* amply demonstrated, the balance shifted towards the latter. Jake had no desire to be pigeon-holed as a comic and was moving away from writing songs whose only purpose was laughter; he wanted listeners to think as well, and sometimes not to laugh at all.

This change may have been a natural development as he matured creatively. However, it coincided with his blossoming friendship with Brassens. From the early 1970s onwards they socialised together, and their conversations ranged over poetry, literature and music. Jake, of course, had long been influenced by Brassens's writing, but their interaction may have served to heighten further the ambition of his own work. Many of Brassens's songs are amusing, but they are rarely *simply* comic: more often than not, the humour goes hand in hand with a serious underlying point. The same is true of much of the writing on *On Again! On Again!*. The album abounds with magnificently told stories that are peppered with humour but also have something to say. For this reason it not only serves as Jake's greatest homage to Brassens, but also confirms that he had developed into a chansonnier of equal stature in his own right. Jake, of course, would never have accepted this.[4]

As always, the album was produced by Norman Newell, but its sparse acoustic sound meant Geoff Love's services were not required. Whilst the new approach might look like a victory for Jake's musical instincts, in reality, much had changed since *Bantam Cock*, and Newell probably required little persuading. 'I would imagine, knowing all the characters as I do, that it was a fairly easy decision to make,' says Alex Armitage, 'because with the albums Geoff Love worked on, it was generally felt that, although the arrangements were obviously clever, sometimes they got in the way of what we wanted, which was Jake and his guitar.'

Jake's musicianship had by this time developed greatly; his guitar work was both inventive and subtle, immaculate in its execution, and ready to take centre stage in a studio recording.[5] A session musician, Dick Abell, was booked to play second guitar, but Jake naturally wanted Alan Williams on bass. 'Alan on stage became increasingly important to Jake as a fellow musician, performer and friend,' says Alex, 'so it was absolutely obvious that Jake would be most at ease having him there.'

The modest scale of the recordings meant that the album could be made on a smaller budget than previous records, and there was no need to use the palatial and expensive facilities at Abbey Road. Instead, three days were booked in a small studio at EMI's Manchester Square headquarters.[6]

The album opens with the title track, one of Jake's most brilliant creations. It is also his most controversial. The song's protagonist, a self-confessed misogynist, complains about the propensity of some women to talk incessantly, before proceeding to describe at length, and in hilarious detail, the behaviour of his wife. The problem reveals itself at their wedding where, instead of just saying 'I do', she sounds forth expansively, and continues in the same vein in every possible situation – whether her husband is asleep, saying his prayers, on the roof, or making love. Eventually her husband appeals to the Virgin Mary to silence her, and gets more than he bargained for as the Mother of God answers his prayer.

From the opening lines using Latin ('a posteriori') to make a superb pun,[7] the song is utterly dazzling in its use of language and packed with ridiculous images and great jokes. Jake explores all the comic possibilities of the theme, and the listener is taken through a beautifully orchestrated series of ever more preposterous scenarios, culminating in a tremendous punchline.

Truly a *tour de force*, its writing was a high-point of creativity for Jake. Indeed, Sheila Thackray remembered the laughter coming from his office as he worked on it – a good sign when he was writing. She always maintained that it was inspired by her, which perhaps explains why he was nervous when he first played it to her in their kitchen. He needn't have worried: she loved it. In interview, however, perhaps out of loyalty, Jake explained his inspiration differently: 'My wife didn't inspire it, but she persuaded me to write it. Sheila and I were sitting in somebody's front room and this woman was talking so much that our brains were bloody reeling. You are trying to keep a polite smile on your face all the time. On the way home, Sheila said, "That could be a fun song."'[8]

Brilliant as it was, it took Jake into dangerous territory at a time when the Women's Liberation Movement was growing ever more vocal. It mattered little that the protagonist calls himself a misogynist, nor that some of the other songs on the album were distinctly feminist in outlook: those women who wished to take offence did so and protested by heckling or walking out at concerts. Following one such incident which left him visibly shaken, Jake defended himself in an interview: 'The song is about the folly of incontinence in conversation... about the folly of people talking too much and how destructive it can be. Now, I would cheerfully have done it about a bloke. But I'm not married to a bloke. You know, I can only do it about women... The protesters in the audience weren't listening, for it's not a generalisation about women, it's specifically about SOME women and it says that five times in the song. But of course women are equal and should be equal. Nevertheless, I reserve the right to take the mickey out of women, vicars, the Pope, the Virgin Mary. I tell you what, I've even had a Catholic who's got up and walked out. Hard chuff, hard chuff. Why shouldn't I take the mickey out of anybody? Anybody can take it out of me. Anybody can stand up in a theatre and shout sexist, or blasphemer or communist, and all of those have happened.'⁹ Sadly, the 'misogynist' label would stick and damage his reputation, despite evidence to the contrary in his other writing.

Whatever the origins of 'On Again! On Again!', Sheila was surely Jake's muse when he wrote 'To Do With You', which feels remarkably personal and heartfelt. He sings of the realities of married life, in which love can be 'racked and pinioned', and acknowledges that his wife isn't perfect – other women may be better cooks, better in bed and better read. But none of this changes the depth of his love for her. It is a sentiment which is reminiscent of Shakespeare's 'Sonnet 130' ('My mistress' eyes are nothing like the sun; coral is far more red, than her lips red...'). The song is lightened by wordplay – Jake sings of 'tongue and grooving' women – and he makes a wry joke at his own expense: he will have to make do with his wife because other women have better taste in men. However, the humour he employs cannot disguise his true depth of feeling, emotions accentuated by a sombre rhythm and jazz-flavoured musical setting.

Jake acknowledged that it was not in his nature to express personal feelings in his songs: 'I would be uneasy singing a straight-faced serious song, all very earnest and full of meaning, as I find it works best when you take the piss out of things and then when people are laughing you can lob in a little hand grenade. I like a song to have a bit of cutting edge. That's probably why I've never written a good love song. With me, any song about love has to have an ironic side to it.'¹⁰ As so often, he does himself a disservice. 'To Do With You' is unorthodox, but it is, nonetheless, deeply moving and romantic, and bears comparison with the equally unorthodox 'La Non-Demande en Mariage', in which Brassens promises never to ruin his relationship with his long-term partner by proposing marriage.

Several songs on the album were inspired by people in Jake's life. The origins of 'The Ballad of Billy Kershaw' can be traced

to the bar of his local, the Somerset Arms. 'There was a bloke
who used to come into the pub who was famous for shagging
anything on two legs,' says Rick Irons. 'That's where Billy
Kershaw came from.' In Jake's hands this tawdry topic is
transformed into something extraordinary. Billy is a small, shy
ploughman who, despite his unremarkable appearance, is
irresistibly attractive. However, he charitably shares the life-
enhancing pleasure of sex with only the most neglected and
unattractive of women: the ugly, the hunchbacked, the lame.
His healing powers surpass those of Lourdes, earning him the
gratitude of many Catholic husbands, and Jake conjures up
hilarious images of his sexual activities with women on the
colonel's tiger skin and the potter's rotating clay wheel.
Eventually, however, as his fame spreads, Billy becomes a victim
of his own success: when coach-loads of women start turning
up in the village, capitalism kicks in and tourism begins to
boom, he becomes disillusioned and disappears.

Jake's songs are full of sex. His friend Colin Evans believed
that this aspect of his writing represents more than the physical
act: 'They're all about sex and potency... I think that what he's
actually celebrating is not really sex; sex is just a metaphor for
the creative impulse – it's the life-force... That's what Jake is
doing, he's saying "There's the life force."'[11]

Journalist Benedict Nightingale sees it differently: 'Thackray
is a moralist as well as a poet. The point is to celebrate love,
sex, freedom, indeed to insist on them as basic human rights
belonging equally to women and men, old and young, ugly and
handsome.'[12]

'The Ballad of Billy Kershaw' certainly presents sex as life-
enhancing and something to which all have a right, but Jake
ends this memorable tale by lobbing in one of his disconcerting
hand grenades. He turns the spotlight on the listener and offers
a moral: it takes one to know one. We all stand accused of being
less compassionate and, indeed, more brutal than Billy. With a
final cry of 'mea culpa' (a Latin reference to the Catholic

practice of confession), Jake suggests that we all need to atone for our selfishness.

'Isabella', his adaptation of Brassens's 'Marinette', was more than a decade old. Its hapless protagonist is in love with a woman forever out of his league: he wants to sing her his songs, but she is listening to Bach; he buys her fish and chips, but she is eating caviar. Even when he eventually snaps, he is made to look a complete idiot: he goes round to kill her, only to find she is already dead.

Jake said his aim when adapting Brassens was 'not so much to translate the songs, as to make them again, in England',[13] and his skill as a translator and flair as a poet meant he did so with extraordinary success. Indeed, his confidence in his own ability shows itself in two ways here. Firstly, he abandons Brassens's final verse, in which the protagonist goes to pay his respects at Marinette's grave, only to discover she has risen from the dead. Secondly, and even more boldly, he adds an entirely new lyrical and musical introduction. This sets the scene by painting a tantalising picture of Isabella, with her enticing hips and thighs, her 'Hello lips' and 'Goodbye eyes'. It is an inspired enhancement.

'I Stayed Off Work Today' is a story in which love is tested by the cynical, deceitful ways of the world. Its protagonist finds himself the victim of a series of deceptions taking him further and further away from the woman he loves. He is swindled, in turn, by a butcher, soldier, magistrate, bishop and angel, and ultimately is booted off to Hell. The song trips along lightly, its tale exquisitely told with rich, musical language, as Jake delivers up tasty, tongue-tripping phrases, such as 'tricky old juridical' and 'rascally Episcopal'. Its message is that there are swindlers in every walk of life, and even in death, but at least there is the consolation of love.

'The Kiss' gives delicious lie to the idea that Jake Thackray was a misogynist. The song's hero is a young lad who describes a brief, flirtatious encounter with a girl who is '17-ish as the

month of May'. For a dare, he kisses her in public and finds, to
his surprise, she rather likes it. However, this brief skirmish is
witnessed by the ladies of the village and word soon reaches
the girl's father, the butcher. He arrives, intent upon protecting
what is his and, following King Solomon's example, splitting
the lad in two. But just as he is about to bring the cleaver down,
his daughter throws her arms and legs around the lad, declaring
she will be the one to decide what she does with her body, not
her father. Both men are astonished. The 'jealous cleaver' never
falls and the father leaves in tears, knowing that his relationship
with his daughter has changed forever.

Once again, the attention to detail and use of language are
superb. There are moments of great humour, as when the lad,
with his nose pressed in the girl's breastbone and the cleaver
about to fall, admits, with wonderful understatement, that there
was a lot to take in. However, the humour is secondary to the
storytelling and the vividly-drawn characters.

Jake claimed that 'The Kiss' was based on a true event in
the village where he grew up, but this is in all likelihood one
of his many fantasies. In fact it has many of the features of a
folk tale, and its structure is similar to traditional ballads such
as 'Gypsy Rover' and 'Matty Groves'. All three songs feature a
liaison between an independently-minded woman and a male
viewed as socially inferior by the head of her household, with
whom she defiantly stands her ground once the relationship is
discovered.

In 'The Hair of the Widow of Bridlington', humour and
poignancy are again beautifully and skilfully interwoven. Once
her children have flown the nest, the widow realises that life is
for living, and decides to please herself. She takes up the violin,
plays in bars, buys a motorbike and, in a neat feminist inversion
of the old cliché about sailors having a girl in every port, has
dalliances with a string of fishermen. However, such free-
spirited behaviour scandalises her envious neighbours who, in
their fury, attack her house and shave her head. But her spirit

is unbroken: she picks up the pieces and heads off to make waves in Scarborough.

The song is laced with humour but, as with much of the writing on the album, the story is the thing, and it is a story with a point. Jake puts himself on the side of those whose lifestyles don't conform to society's expectations and conventional morality: if no harm is being done, live and let live.

One of the song's most inspired features is the repeated use of a simile that likens the widow of Brid to a blackbird. When she decides to let her hair down, this statement of intent is like the bird's 'cocky' song; when she refuses to settle down with any one fisherman, it is because blackbirds don't sing from the same bush each day; when her shame-faced neighbours beg her to stay, Jake states simply that startled blackbirds fly away. Throughout, the image is used to suggest the freedom the widow enjoys: unlike others, she is not stuck in a cage.

He later explained the song's origins and his approach to writing: 'I wouldn't want you to think that I'm a keen observer on life, oh Christ no. I've got to sit down with a pot of tea and a sheet of paper, though I sometimes think about words in cars. The only example I could give which would be convincing is the song I wrote about the Widow of Bridlington. There was this knockout bird who was a widow with five kids, all left home, and I asked her what she did and she had a job as a Guinness rep, and she said, "I've just discovered that I can do anything – I've bought a motor bike, 750cc". A little later up came the words Widow and Brid which sounded pleasing; after that bit of enthusiasm it was hard, hard work.'[14]

'Over to Isobel', adapted from 'Je Rejoindrai Ma Belle', is his final tribute to Brassens. As with 'Isabella' and 'Brother Gorilla', he makes the song his own, changing cultural references and modifying the music. The end result arguably surpasses the original, which is no mean feat.

This curious piece is effectively structured as a conversation between an ever-hopeful lover and a doom-laden answering voice. The lover is determined that no obstacle will stop him reaching his beloved: he will cross to her on stepping stones, and if they are flooded, he will sail across; if pirates scupper that plan, he will grow wings and fly. At every stage the voice of doom warns that his plans will fail: if he takes wing, he will be shot by a hunter. Finally, the lover shows amusing fatalism and realism: if he must die, he asks only that Isobel be told of his love, and leave it a few days before taking a new lover. As with so much of the writing on the album, the poetry is exquisite.

The record includes fine versions of 'The Poor Sod', 'The Rain on the Mountainside' and 'The Brigadier' (all written for *The Camera and the Song*), and ends with a new recording of 'Joseph'. Jake had always hated the choir-laden version of 1967 and, although he didn't like other adults singing his carols ('They were never intended for adults to sing 'cause they were very childlike songs.'),[15] he was fond of the song and performed it regularly. This gentle rendition does it full justice, conjuring up a sense of wonder and empathy.

Also recorded at the sessions were 'Little Thomas Haverly' (from *The Camera and the Song*) and three new songs: 'Famous People', 'The Gravedigger' and 'Family Grave'. Sadly, none would make the final cut.

The lugubrious, plodding beat of 'The Gravedigger' is well matched to the melancholy perspective of its protagonist, as he reflects on the dismal nature of his work. Shaking his shovel at the sky in impotent rage, he bemoans the things he has witnessed: the lonely burial of a prisoner, attended only by a priest and a policeman; two-faced mourners whispering in the chapel; a mother screaming hysterically over a pitiably small coffin. The pathos alternates with dark cynicism as Jake pictures a family who can hardly wait for the funeral to end so they can get their hands on the grub, the cash and the widow.

'Family Grave' is musically and lyrically almost the same song, but the gravedigger narrator is removed. The effect is more darkly comic, not least because there is a different final verse in which the mourners are 'studying form' at the wake, calculating who will be next to die, and who next to foot the funeral bill.

Of these two songs, 'The Gravedigger', with its second guitar, is the more developed musically, but 'Family Grave' was recorded later in the sessions. They give us an interesting insight into Jake's creative process and the choices he made, suggesting he was undecided as to what balance he wanted to strike between light and shade. Perhaps that is why neither made it onto the album. It is a pity, because 'The Gravedigger' could have come straight out of the Brassens songbook; indeed, it invites comparison with 'Le Fossoyeur', sung from the same perspective.[16]

'Famous People'[17] likewise has an air of Brassens about it. It takes a highly jaundiced view of celebrity, removing the scales from the eyes of anyone foolish enough to think their fame means anything. The famous shouldn't suppose that they are loved by the people they look down on; their statues have no value, except when passers-by need something on which to strike a match. Jake pities the poor children who will have to learn about the great and the good at school, but predicts they will get their own back in startling fashion: they will swing on their statues, skip on their plaques and, most shockingly, piss joyfully on their monuments. This remarkable piece of writing seems never to have featured in his live set, but Jake would have more to say on the subject of fame and its futility.

The album was released in January 1977, followed soon after by 'On Again! On Again!' as a single, to rave reviews: 'The lyrics of his songs have the added appeal of depth, for Thackray rarely cracks a joke that doesn't have a deeper meaning... Marvellous new album.'[18] Unsurprisingly, the title track attracted most attention. The *New Musical Express* was complimentary: 'Traditional music hall sentiments disguised as up-market, drawing room folk, and very neatly written with it.' *Sounds* erroneously declared 'WEST COUNTRY RACONTEUR'S ANSWER TO FRANK ZAPPA TURNS MALE CHAUVINIST PIG... Nice goin' Jake, but will the Beeb play it?'[19]

Jake's work had always existed outside the mainstream. With *On Again! On Again!*, he had turned his back on it completely. When 'Anarchy in the UK' was the sound of the moment, he was offering listeners the sound of Brassens in the 1950s. He was producing magnificent work, but was out of step with the times and with popular culture. This was neatly summed up by *Melody Maker*: 'With a face like a surprised blood-hound and a certain off-beat charm, Mr Thackray is one of those well-known personalities – a club performer, a "TV Spot" artist – who it is difficult to place. He is unlikely to move out of the well-trodden path he's determined for himself. For him, a hit single would be about as unlikely as the sight of Johnny Rotten with waist-length hair.'[20]

The album benefitted from a well-coordinated marketing campaign and, courtesy of Noel Gay, Jake's five-month residency on *That's Life!*.[21] It is hard to imagine that he would have relished being in a television studio again, but at least this time he had the comfort of knowing Alan Williams would be accompanying him, alongside guitarist Ike Isaacs, whom he revered.

Jake's discomfort won't have been helped by the way his songs were presented, with photographs, cartoons, film clips and, for 'Leopold Alcocks', a collapsing set. Such unsubtle and contrived touches scarcely did his writing justice: his lyrics did not need visual reinforcement.

Other compromises had to be made, too. With *That's Life!* going out on Sunday evenings, 'On Again! On Again!' was inevitably censored: its language was toned down and the final verse, containing the epiphany of the garrulous Virgin Mary, was cut completely. Nevertheless, the television exposure served its purpose, boosting his record and ticket sales.

Capitalising on his raised profile, a book was published.

Jake's Progress contained song lyrics and some of the anecdotes used in concerts. Esther Rantzen wrote the introduction and cartoonist Bill Tidy did illustrations. 'A book of Jake's lyrics is a very obvious thing to have done, because the lyrics are so fantastic,' says Alex Armitage. 'It sold reasonably well because people really enjoyed his songs. Sometimes people didn't entirely understand his accent, so a book of lyrics was an obvious thing to do and it turned out to be extremely popular.' He has one overriding memory of it, however: 'Jake absolutely hated the cover.'

While its image of an anxious-looking Jake was hardly flattering, the garish design was ghastly: brash lettering declared 'ROLLICKING, FROLICKING, UPROARIOUS VERSE' and, in a blazing yellow sun, 'INTRODUCTION: ESTHER RANTZEN. ILLUSTRATIONS: BILL TIDY.' It was completely devoid of the wit, subtlety and poetry of its content. No wonder Jake loathed it.

On Again! On Again! showed that Jake had moved on and reached a new high-point artistically, as Benedict Nightingale recognised: 'Thackray has developed. He has become more unpredictable, discursive, imaginative, metaphorically ambitious, syntactically unconventional and demanding. He has developed, and, as anyone listening to his record will surely agree, he has improved. And there is a lot of future before him.'[22]

Nightingale's analysis was impeccable. He was only wrong in one respect: there was to be less future than he thought.

Getting busy in the shed. Jake and his sons get to work at Hillside.
Tish Murtha
© Ella Murtha.

Jake fostering an interest.
Tish Murtha
© Ella Murtha.

Lots of Beans, No Songs

'I know when things are down, if I stare at the paper long
enough, ideas will come, they'll pick up. I've gone through arid
periods before and came out with the goods by trying hard.'
                                                – Jake Thackray, 1979[1]

By the time *On Again! On Again!* was released, Jake was
entering his tenth year as a professional entertainer and, with
six albums and a book to his name, along with countless TV,
radio and concert appearances, he had become a wealthy man.
Sam Thackray puts it simply: 'Money was phenomenal for a
period in the 1970s.'

Money, however, like fame, did not change him. 'Jake and
Sheila were always generous with their time and their
affections, in real terms,' says Sue Haverly. 'As they became
more affluent, there was definitely a feeling that they wanted
to share it; it wasn't something to aggrandise themselves.
Although they had a lot more and did a lot more, there was a
real sense of generosity towards other people.'

Jake was always keen to share with friends the passing
happiness his career offered, such as invitations to recording
sessions and show-business parties, and he took the same
approach to money. Indeed, he was generous to a fault. He
bought his brother-in-law Rick his first car, no doubt in

recompense for the purgatory of teaching him to drive. When a clapped-out car jeopardised the Haverlys' plans to join the Thackrays on a trip, Jake found them a replacement. He also once offered to pay for a holiday for them in France.[2] But not everyone was comfortable with his new-found wealth. 'As they became more affluent,' recalls Sue, 'I saw Jake's mother a couple of times at their home, and you just got the feeling that, like many of her generation and working-class background, she found the new affluence of her son a bit bewildering and didn't know what to make of it.'

Jake was equally generous with his time and was carried away by his enthusiasm to help others, despite having lots of unfinished DIY projects awaiting him at home. When the Haverlys decided to relocate to the Forest of Dean, he threw himself into house-hunting with them and, once they had bought their cottage, helped to dig up floors.

With his friends, he was tremendous company, full of fun and enthusiasm. Invariably, he took the lead in creating and organising games: at Colin Evans's 40th birthday party this resulted in him spending the evening running around in a Native American head-dress. Mealtimes in the Thackray household provided no let-up. 'We endlessly played games: teatimes, mealtimes, we thought it was normal,' said Sheila Thackray. 'Jake was brilliant at inventing things.' His word games – 'Ghosts', 'Superghosts', 'Nuns Across the Border' and 'When I Go to My Desert Island' – were as legendary as they were bewildering.

He enjoyed being part of the Mitchel Troy community. 'He loved ordinary people,' says Sue Haverly. 'He never went out of his way to surround himself with stardom at all. He was at home with Reg and Margaret Moulton on the farm next door, and Dan and Gladys Sullivan who ran the Somerset Arms. But equally, because he had this amazing, appealing nature to him, he had others in his social circle whom I was quite surprised were in there, because I knew that their attitudes to politics would be very different to Jake's. But he embraced them as warmly as anybody else, metaphorically. He was interested in their humanity, as opposed to other aspects of them.' The tension between his strong left-wing views and friendships was amply demonstrated during the miners' strike of 1984. He attended a Conservative Association barbecue because so many friends were going, but first leafleted the assorted Land Rovers, Volvos and Saabs in the car park with 'Coal, not dole' flyers, declaring that this was to 'atone for the sin of hobnobbing' at a Tory 'do'. However, when the local MP stood up and made a speech attacking the miners, it was too much for him: Jake walked out in fury.

He loved contributing to community activities, and in the 1970s got heavily involved with an exchange partnership with Carbonne, fundraising and joining visits to the French town. On one such trip he and Sheila memorably broke the bed at their hosts' house – not the first time they had managed this feat, apparently. Back in Monmouth they enjoyed acting as interpreters for visitors from Carbonne; Jake loved using his French to promote cultural understanding, and mucking in at social events with the sherry-pouring and glass-washing.

Despite his limited skill, he enjoyed playing cricket for the nearby village of Penallt, doing much to support club activities, including doing the mowing. When a 'Thackray' (no initials) was listed as a patron and enquiries were made as to who this might be, Jake revealed that he was supporting the club financially under the name of his dog. However, his most remarkable and generous contribution came in the early 1980s, when he organised a fundraiser involving a celebrity cricket match, supper and concert, covering all the expenses personally. 'It was extraordinary, and all provided for by him. It was very, very generous,' says his friend, Peter Carpenter.[3] 'He didn't do it for any reason, except that he liked the neighbourhood and liked the people.' With his infectious enthusiasm triumphing over his poor organisation, Jake fielded a celebrity team which included singers Mike Harding, Ralph McTell and Roy Harper, along with Robert Plant, his rock-god neighbour and front man of Led Zeppelin.[4] Hundreds of people attended the concert and the camaraderie of the day is remembered almost as fondly as a streak performed during the match by a beautiful, dark-haired young woman: when she ran across the pitch, wearing only black gloves and black socks, Jake declared, 'I think I've just seen the five of spades!'

Life at Hillside in the 1970s was very good for the young Thackray boys. As a dad, he couldn't have been more different from his own father, and Sam Thackray has fond memories of these years: 'Dad was very good with us kids. He would do loads of stuff with us, going to castles, taking us swimming. He would get involved, and he would explain everything to us. He was a great dad in many, many ways, and he was ideal for those early, formative years.' Jake was also keen to take his sons to church with him – in accordance with the promise made when he had married, that he would bring them up in the Catholic faith – but apparently Sheila would not agree to this. He would have to attend Mass alone.

Sam remembers his father being great fun: 'He used to pretend to be Leopold Alcocks in the car, speaking in a funny accent, driving the car. We would be laughing our heads off in the back because he was weaving around the roads, and on the country lanes he'd bump up onto the verges and he'd say [assumes funny voice], "Tell me how to drive in your country." I remember coming home from cubs and there was one kid who lived on a farm track, and the track used to go up through the fields, but there was no hedge. Dad had us laughing, pretending to be Leopold Alcocks, and he veered completely off this track and we ended up right in the middle of this field, skidding around.'

The family enjoyed the fruits of his success. Low-budget camping holidays made way for trips to France, and when he was booked to perform in Nairobi in June 1974, Sheila and the boys went too. Although he was deeply angered by the poverty he saw and the attitude of many ex-pats to the native Kenyans, the four-week trip provided happy memories for his young sons, with days spent playing in the hotel pool, taking a boat trip on Lake Navashu and going on safari, where Jake managed to run over an impala in their hired camper van. To cap it off, on Sam's fifth birthday, the children were allowed into the aircraft cockpit on the flight home.

Jake missed his young family when he was away on tour, as is abundantly clear from his letters home. Here he is writing from Scotland in the 1970s:

> Hello my darling Sheila, and chaps,
>
> It was very dreary having to leave you this afternoon, what with you looking so sad and having looked so happy before. In between Pnycraig [*sic*] and Ross I was very desperate thinking of the boring miles to go and lovely you just behind, also no doubt feeling lost.

However, he writes primarily to entertain, and in the rest of the letter he shows his keen observational eye and flair for amusing storytelling:

> Well, Fatty is a good old car and I started doing calculations about time/miles/weather/meals and began to settle into the dullness of getting there. Said the rosary and shouted at travellers (Hail Mary, full of grace, bleedin' idiot!) and got to Carlisle just before dark and ate something.
>
> After that, over the border and it did feel foreign. And it was foreign because just by Glasgow I stopped for another sandwich at what was like a Little Chef. I go in and there's bunch of little chunky waitresses like little horses shifting and whinnying up at the counter. One of them trots over, with a fringe she keeps tossing back. 'Eye?' Can I have this beef burger in a bap please? Then she says this: 'Awumpa' I say pardon she says it again 'Awumpa' So I point to the picture of

it on the menu. 'Wumpa' Honestly. So then I go, can I have a cup of tea please. And tossing the fringe she goes 'Tee wumpa' I didn't think everything was right, I mean she might have been telling me the place was closed or beefburgers were off so I started again can I please have a... and then she lost patience and leaned on the table with her hand and in between the thumb and first finger there was a tattooed bluebird and she looked back at the other horses and then back at me and said it again 'tee wumpa' Honestly boys and Sheila it could have been East Germany. So the rest of the talking went like this. 'Yes please then' 'Wit?' 'Well, tee wumpa' and then she did her lean again and said this: 'Oorban fanny?' (Urban fanny?) God, I don't know, I thought the best was to start all over again and defuse everything, more horses with the bluebird brand were trotting over, so I said all placating, look miss I come from Wales and I don't really understand may I have one of these and a... and then she said 'Uut fannyman' and of course I went. Uut. Because that bit was clear and she obviously wanted a fight. Well I know what it all meant now, because I asked a stage manager in Kirkcaldy just now and he said, oh yes two wimpeys.[5]

Then on to Kirkcaldy via Glasgow and Edinburgh, even in the dark it looks dreadful. The hotel is a 3 star AA and is very basic, brown painted skirting boards, thin carpet and gasmeters in rooms but the stage manager (who is a cockney and knows me from when I was at Welwyn Garden City) says in rooms in other hotels there's no carpet or fire, just an aerosol paint spray and a bicycle chain in every room to make all Scotsmen feel comfy. So depressing. I rang you half an hour ago from the hotel 'luunge' and everybody had elbows on the bar and were glaring at me over their shoulders when I was saying things like Hello darling, and all my love. God knows what'll happen tomorrow; especially when I want to eat. I look for a Chinese restaurant where they'll understand. Goodnight darling.

While Jake was enjoying family life (and perhaps because of it), he was finding it harder and harder to write songs. At

Hillside, his ground-floor office was equipped with all the tools of his trade: a piano, guitars, his typewriter and desk (inevitably piled high with papers), and his cherished collection of books. A dart board – a reminder of his student days – hung on the wall, along with a huge framed poster of Georges Brassens, while a stern-faced bust of Nelson Mandela looked down from the shelf above. He would spend many hours here but, by the late 1970s, little was emerging, other than clouds of cigarette smoke and the strains of Django Reinhardt or Radio 4, and he would readily abandon writing in favour of spending time with his sons.

There were other distractions too, says Sam: 'Dad enjoyed watching (or sleeping through) test matches with the curtains closed, mowing and building garden patios and walls.' Building projects, embarked upon with more enthusiasm than skill, provided endless days of diversion as, with the help of his neighbour Reg, he extended the house and built a workshop. Through it all the distracted spirit of Leopold Alcocks reigned supreme: Jake destroyed Reg's cement mixer by leaving concrete to set in it, and once left his friend Don Burton stranded for hours, holding up a ceiling panel, while he raced off for Mass and a pint.

The freewheeling life he enjoyed as a performer was in marked contrast to his earlier career as a teacher, and he seems to have been ill-equipped to deal with it. The lack of structure to his days presented a problem only made worse by his poor organisation, insomnia and anti-social working hours. After returning from concerts he often slept in until late-morning, leaving his days out of sync with those of his family.

In 1979, he spoke bluntly about his growing lethargy: 'Now I'm writing hardly anything at all – I'm such an idle bastard.'[6] Sheila Thackray believed this drop in creativity was a result of having to perform so often: 'It's quite punishing, that sort of lifestyle, especially if you're doing one night after the other, and very often they would be at different sides of the country, with no sort of geographical sense about the progress.' Indeed, Jake once half-jokingly asked his agent to use an atlas rather than a dictionary ('Aberdeen, Brighton, Carlisle, Dover...') when scheduling his gigs. 'It was exhausting,' recalled Sheila. 'He didn't come home every night, but if it was within striking distance, he'd drive an awful long way. And he'd get a very uneven cycle: even if he'd got two or three days not performing, that didn't mean to say he'd come round and was ready to get his mind into writing... it's enough to unwind, but it's not long enough to get your head into another frame of mind to settle down to writing.'

Sheila knew how much Jake loved to write, and could see that his struggle to come up with new songs was a source of great frustration. It also had serious long-term implications for his career and finances, and they both realised it was an issue he needed to address. 'I can remember Mum and Dad talking about it,' recalls Sam. 'He was trying to keep the writing going and trying different ways of doing that – getting a break away from home or away from kids or distractions.'

Various solutions were attempted. Jake asked Sheila to suggest ideas for songs, much as his mother had done, and 'On Again! On Again!' was one glorious result. Sheila remembered that he would often return to the songs of Brassens when he was struggling for inspiration: 'I know that he began to translate Brassens when he was feeling, "Oh well, if I can't [come up with my own songs]..."' However, no new translations appeared. In fact, he even sought the Frenchman's advice, who suggested that he follow his method. 'Brassens had said to him, "You should take six months off. Perform for six months, take six months off," recalled Sheila. 'But it wasn't possible.' Jake lacked the huge fan base and record sales which enabled Brassens to take such an approach, and his reluctance to perform in large concert halls meant he had to spend much more time on the road. He settled upon a compromise, setting aside every April and May for writing, with perhaps a further month off later in the year, but Sheila didn't think that this was long enough, and she could see that the results were mixed: 'Sometimes he would have an idea and would just get on with it, and you knew he was a-buzz and something was happening. Or we'd have this April and May, and it was supposed to be for writing, and he couldn't think what to write, so he'd dig the garden, and get some cow muck and dig it in really deep. So we had huge beans that year. No songs, lots of beans...'

In 1977, Jake acquired a caravan to use instead of his office, in the hope that, free from distraction, he would be more productive. Initially it was parked in the family's field at Hillside, but other, ever more remote locations were tried over the years. However, despite all this, Jake found that his writer's block persisted. 'Mum and Dad had some discussion about the fact that it wasn't working, and that Dad was maybe spending the time reading and smoking cigarettes, and drinking, possibly,' says Sam.

Early in his career, regular commissions had provided Jake with a stimulus to write, but by the late 1970s this was no longer the case. As 1979 came to a close, however, he wrote a song for a radio documentary on the history of Leeds.[7] In five verses he provided his own take on the programme's themes, including the exploitation of the working classes, packed into slum-housing. Here undoubtedly was a theme that resonated with the boy who had grown up living in the shadow of Kirkstall's tenements:

> And here is the arch mathematician of Leeds,
> Who by cunning and craft made a grand calculation:
> You can square up the mass of the human race
> And its energy, time, its motion, its place,
> If you put twice the number in half of the space.
> Who was it squared up the people of Leeds?

Jake takes a jaundiced view of 'the gritty old city of Leeds',

which is 'gaunt and greedy and grim in the face'. He calls out
the racist language aimed at its migrant communities, but
ultimately concludes that the city's people are its 'one saving
grace'. The song contains well-crafted lines and met its brief,
but had little potential outside the context of the programme,
and there seems to have been a limit as to how much polish
Jake was prepared to apply to it.

In truth, his productivity had dropped off massively, and by
the end of the decade only three new songs would surface in
his live set. However, when inspiration did strike, what he
wrote was of stupendous quality: 'The Remembrance', 'One of
Them' and 'The Bull' all rank among his finest achievements.
All have something important to say.

'The Remembrance' is an anti-war song underpinned by
Jake's deep-seated anarchism. It is remarkable not only for the
quiet sadness of its anger, but also for its unusual perspective.
Its protagonist is a dead soldier recalling the rousing speeches
he heard on his way to his death, first from the King, then a
clergyman, and finally an officer. The song decries their various
appeals to fight for country, God and glory, before bringing the
soldier to the grim moment of reckoning, when he comes face
to face with the enemy. After all the lies, he recognises the
truth: the man who kills him is just another 'poor sod' like him.
The power of the poetry makes 'The Remembrance' one of
Jake's greatest accomplishments and one of the finest anti-war
songs ever written.[8]

'One of Them' is deeply serious, condemning the prejudice-
based humour widely regarded as acceptable in the 1970s. In
casual, highly offensive terms the song's protagonist offers to
tell anti-semitic, racist and homophobic jokes, and suggests
that the targets of his humour don't really object. The horrific
nature of his words is only underlined by the ugly simplicity
of the language, the deliberate lack of rhyme and downbeat
melody.

Yet, as in 'The Remembrance', there is moving recognition

in 'One of Them' that people have a shared humanity: although they may be very different, they show their suffering in the same way. It is a powerful, thoughtful piece of writing on a subject Jake felt strongly about.[9]

He had rarely before assumed such a dislikeable persona to explore a serious subject, and in this regard 'One of Them' may bear the influence of American songwriter Randy Newman, to whose work Jake was introduced in the mid-1970s by Ralph McTell: 'After one of his gigs somewhere, Jake and I sat up late into the small hours and I dug out my Randy Newman albums. Jake sat there with his jaw dropping at each new song. I particularly remember the effect that the album *Good Old Boys* had on him. It was such a buzz to see how instantly the two writers connected.'

Jake liked 'The Remembrance' and 'One of Them', which would both remain staples of his setlist for the rest of his career, despite the fact that they often wrong-footed his audiences who, expecting comic songs, would greet them with soon-to-be-stifled laughter.

'The Bull', a splenetic, hilarious attack on hierarchies, authority and deference is, according to Sheila Thackray, the song of which Jake was most proud. In a series of dazzling verses he calls out false heroes, the hijacking of revolutions and the hypocrisy of organised religion.

His message, that power corrupts, and everyone in authority should be eyed with suspicion, is reminiscent of Orwell's *Animal Farm*, and this is reinforced by his use of a farmyard metaphor:

On my farm the bull is the king of the yard,
He's big and bad and fast, he's strong, he's hard.
All my other animals would readily concur
That he is the one you salute, he's the one you call 'Sir'.
But my hens, a noisy, flighty flock,
Led, of course, by my unsubmissive cock,

Whenever His Majesty the bull importantly goes by,
They dance along behind him and they cry:

'Beware of the bull!
The bull, the bull is the biggest of all.
He is the boss, he is, because he's big and we are small.
But the bigger the bull, bigger the bull, bigger the balls,
The bigger the bull, the bigger and quicker and thicker
     the bullshite falls!'

Jake rarely used choruses in his writing – repetitive make-weight filler was anathema to him – but this musical device is exactly what the song requires: 'Beware of the Bull!' is a rousing call to arms. The point is amusingly reinforced in the final verse where, with typical self-irony, he mocks his own celebrity:

These well-known men, so over-glorified!
There's one of them here, his name's on the poster
     outside.
And he's up here like this, and you are all down there.
Remember his cock and his bull and mutter: 'Beware!'
For when they've done, we clap, we cheer, we roar:
'For he is a jolly good fellow! Encore! More, more!'
How glorious it would be if, before these buggers began,
We all stood up together and solemnly sang...

The song brilliantly encapsulates Jake's world view. Its message is universal and timeless and, had Georges Brassens understood English, he would no doubt have been filled with admiration for the achievement.

It would not be long before a television audience would have its chance to hear Jake's anarchic manifesto.

Jigget • Tan

Jake Thackray and Songs

"I don't know what I'm doing. These people are much better.
Can't I just come and watch them?'
– Jake Thackray, 1980[1]

After gritting his teeth through his *That's Life!* residency in 1977, Jake virtually disappeared from television for three years, only turning up briefly in 1979 to sing 'On Again! On Again!' on Neil Innes's quirky, late-night *The Innes Book of Records*. It was the first time viewers were treated to an uncensored version, complete with its buffalo's balls and irreverent portrayal of the Virgin Mary. This was also the first time Jake was seen on TV performing in a pub, rather than a television studio, and perhaps this sowed a seed in his mind. Then, in 1980, the BBC offered him his own series.

BBC2's *Jake Thackray and Songs* would be his last major piece of television work, and his greatest. The fact it was made at all is testimony to the power of Noel Gay and the persuasiveness of Richard and Alex Armitage. 'In those days there were far fewer channels and the channels always had one person who took responsibility and made decisions, so there were far fewer people for agents to get to know,' says Alex. 'As a result, good agents got to know the channel executives who had their hands on the cheque books pretty well.

'So how would the series have come about? Brian Wenham [Controller of BBC2], my father and I would have met every so often socially, and things like that would have come up pretty organically. Either Brian would have said, "Look, it's about time we had some intimate performance on BBC2," or my dad or I would have said, "It's about time we had Jake back on the box." Those days were much gentler than these days and agency was much simpler.'

The relationship between the Armitages and the Corporation was so strong that BBC controllers sent production staff a list of Noel Gay artists. For Colin Godman, the producer of *Jake Thackray and Songs*, the message BBC Management was sending was obvious: 'You'll be considering these, won't you?'[2] Then he received an even clearer signal from on high: 'They said, "We understand that the Controller would be very pleased if you would have a talk to Mr Armitage about Mr Thackray."'

Getting the BBC to sign up to a series was one thing, persuading Jake to commit was a different matter altogether. 'At that point, Jake didn't really want to have anything to do with this,' recalls Colin. 'He had not had the happiest of times doing the Braden thing.' Given Jake's antipathy, Alex Armitage took things slowly and suggested that Colin see him in concert. He saw him perform in Somerset in May 1980, and the two men shared a few pints afterwards, with Jake declaring at the outset, 'I'll have several because Alan the bass player will get me home.' They got on well, and Jake, always suspicious of television gloss, was pleased to learn that Colin had no background in making music programmes.[3]

A second meeting was arranged at a pub in Monmouth. 'Jake only really wanted to talk about beer and introduce me to the man who wanted to sell us elvers, the elver poacher,' recalls Colin. 'I thought, "This man doesn't want to be on television," and I admire people who don't want to be on television.' He was sceptical about whether Jake would commit to doing anything. It was only when Alex Armitage persuaded the singer to meet Colin for a third time that they started talking seriously about how the series would work.

The project really took off when Jake realised that Colin shared his dislike of the artificiality of musical performances in television studios and was prepared to run with his suggestion that they film his concerts and provide a showcase for other singers. 'It became clear in later meetings,' says Colin, 'that what Jake really wanted to do was a little tour of venues, which we would record as discreetly as possible. Not really to sell himself, but it was the schoolmaster in Jake, I think, saying "I want to give a bit back, I really think there are lots of people who don't get on television, because they don't get pushed."' His determination to provide a platform for less visible artists was typical of his generosity, as was his desire to subvert the show-business system he distrusted, even though he owed it so much.

The guest artists were Richard and Linda Thompson, the Maddy Prior Band, Shusha Guppy, Ralph McTell,[4] Alex Glasgow and Pete Scott.[5] Jake picked singer-songwriters he admired; Ralph and Alex were also personal friends. 'The thing that came out was how supportive they were of Jake,' says Colin. 'He was much beloved by other performers who knew him, as this kind of, obviously not the father of English folk by any means, more as this outsider. They were aware they were in danger of losing him.'

Having secured this line-up, however, Colin had to deal with Jake's self-doubt: 'Dear old Jake. The problem that we had on this was him saying every now and again, "I don't know what I'm doing. These people [the guest artists] are much better, can't I just come and watch them?"' Nerves were also an issue: 'He was much more nervous than he should have been. He did really feel he was giving them a break, and unfortunately, he absorbed their terror.'

Just as at the Sherman in 1973, they sought to ensure that the filming did not intrude upon the experience of the

audiences, and so, unlike TV studio recordings, there was to be
no stopping and reshooting. This was no small technical
challenge, given that filming was taking place with multiple
cameras in intimate venues, but Jake and Colin were working
with common purpose: 'What we kept on thinking,' says Colin,
'the people who were at the concert – and this was Jake's
thought as well as ours – must have a decent night out.'

Even so, Richard Thompson remembers the atmosphere as
being rather odd at the show he and Jake shared: 'I remember
the TV taping. It was in a very small venue – may have held
75 guests at the most. Jake was a bit remote – it was the first
time we had met him – and I remember thinking that the
audience weren't getting his very dry humour at all... it was a
strange night.'[6]

Once all the concerts had been filmed, the programmes
needed editing. In an unusual but generous move, Colin invited
Jake to work with him on this: 'I said, "Look, well, you come
and we'll look at them all together." So he did have a sort of
producer control of his material. He said, "I've never had that
before," and was quite pleased.' Keen to ensure that everything
went out as he wanted it, Jake was totally absorbed, as Colin
remembers vividly from events on 8th December 1980: 'Jake is
sitting in Trelawney Road [the editing booth in Bristol]... and
he's watching the stuff, me playing it on a funny old monitor,
and I've got the news playing on another screen. And I say,
"Blimey, look at that, they've shot John Lennon", and I expect
him to say, "What? Really?" I'm bending down to do the sound,
and he says, "Never mind that, can we get on with Bantam
Cock?"'

Jake Thackray and Songs was broadcast late-night on Tuesday
evenings in early 1981.[7] The programmes provided viewers
with an intimate insight into Jake's skill as a live performer, as
music journalist Ian Anderson observed: 'Filmed in folk clubs,
sweating, hard working, absolutely not compromising anything
to be "safe" for television, he brought the atmosphere of a

packed club into our sitting rooms for the first time that I can remember.'⁸ Alex Armitage understood why the concept worked so well: 'For me, the best television he ever did was *Jake Thackray and Songs* because it was just Jake in his natural milieu of him and a guitar and an audience. It enabled him to build the relationship with the venue audience, and the intimacy transmitted itself to the audience at home, and that worked much better than having the host of a glitzy, Saturday night television show say, "And now, ladies and gentlemen, the wonderful Jake Thackray."'

The programmes featured Jake performing 30 of his greatest songs, including the three newest, along with some of his between-songs chat. Perhaps in anticipation of complaints, 'The Bull' was saved for the final programme. 'In those days you couldn't say "balls" and you couldn't say "shit" [on television],' says Alex. 'I think the mischievous imp in Jake loved the fact that he would all the time be pushing the boundaries, he'd be daring people to go on the journey with him, he'd be daring people to understand him, because he was outrageous. Jake always wanted, not to shock, but to amuse people by how far he and they were prepared to go together.'

In fact, while legend has it that 'The Bull' led to complaints and a ticking off from BBC Management, Colin got into much hotter water for sneaking in, after the credits of one show, Alex Glasgow's brief 'The Song of Margaret Thatcher': 'I'll sing you a song of Maggie Thatcher, and the wonders she's achieved. I'll sing you a song, and it won't take long...' (At which point Alex walked off.) Broadcasting something so politically partisan could get the BBC into real trouble with the Thatcher government. No doubt, Jake totally approved.

Jake Thackray and Songs was his happiest television experience because, for once, he was allowed to do things on his own terms. It is ironic that Colin Godman, a drama producer only available because of a strike, proved to be exactly the right person in the right place at the right time. In fact, as things gathered momentum and Jake's initial wariness was replaced by enthusiasm, he revealed to Colin his dream television project: 'Dear old Jake's cunning plan was, if this worked well, we'd have a lot of leverage to do a Jake and Georges show, possibly two, one in Paris, one in London.' The prospect is a tantalising one, and shows that his desire to promote his musical hero in Britain persisted. The producer proposed the idea to the commissioning editors on his behalf: 'I never told Jake, but it was virtually a thumbs down when I first even mentioned it. "Foreign? No. Singing in French? You've got to be joking." I never told him that, and it's probably just as well I didn't.' His instincts were correct: Jake's antipathy towards the powers-that-be in the television establishment was growing, and it would only have been increased further by news of this rejection.

In a well co-ordinated move (doubtless the work of Noel Gay), the series was accompanied by the release of an album of the same name, featuring a recording of the second half of the concert filmed in Wavendon.[9] Given that the BBC had made the recording, Norman Newell's services were not required and, as Jake's contract with EMI had lapsed, the album was released on Dingle's, a small folk label. The record serves as a fine showcase for his skill as a live performer, and the entertaining 'talking bits' include his wonderful 'plastic encore' routine. Musically, the new songs are the stand-out moments: a magnificent live performance of 'The Bull' and simple, effective studio recordings of 'One of Them' and 'The Remembrance'. The album received an excellent review from *Southern Rag's* Ian Anderson: 'A lot of homes could benefit from owning a copy.'[10]

Jake was never someone to suffer fools gladly, and he used the album's amusing sleeve notes to take a swipe at the normal behaviour of television staff: 'telly people do not listen at all; they stride around in cheesecloth and earphones and frig everybody about... prats!' The jibe can hardly have endeared him to the BBC, but he seems not to have cared whether he was biting the hand that fed him. However, he made a point of thanking Colin and his team 'for the quality and care in everything they did, and for their complete lack of self-importance, cheesecloth and frig'.

With an album and concert tickets to sell on the back of the TV series, Jake agreed to some promotional work, with newspaper interviews and appearances on Radio 1, Radio 2 and *Nationwide*. But he was starting to play the media game by his own bizarre rules. When Radio 2's John Dunn introduced an interview by playing 'Bantam Cock', Jake criticised every aspect of the recording and his performance. Then, when he was invited to plug the title of his new album, he claimed not to know it, and went out of his way to emphasise that it contained very few new songs. Listeners might well have concluded that he didn't want anyone to buy the record. His modesty was endearing, but such eccentric behaviour was self-destructive; it must have been utterly exasperating for anyone seeking to promote his career.

As *Jake Thackray and Songs* came to an end in February 1981, Jake made his most unusual appearance since his days on *Tickertape*, performing on ITV's anarchic Saturday morning children's show, *Tiswas*.

This was hardly a normal promotional appearance: no mention was made of his new album, and it seems that Jake's prime motivator was that his sons loved the programme. Indeed, he took them to the recording, along with Bob and Sue Haverly's children. Accompanied as he sang by Alan Williams on bass – and much laughter – he was bombarded with buckets of green liquid and custard pies by the Phantom Flan Flinger and presenter Chris Tarrant. Covered head to foot in gunk, he just managed to maintain a deadpan expression throughout the raucous silliness. He performed a song written especially for the occasion:

You're no-one, you're nowhere, you're nothing,
And nobody knows who you are, who you are.
But when Tiswas chucks buckets of mucky old yuck on you,
You know you're a star, you are, you know you're a star.

You can go on those shows where they throw the best grot,
It's the grot what did get you to the fame.
Now Parkinson's parties, and Esther's and Bruce's –
It's pretty hot grot,
But it's just not the same...

The song, with its reference to three of the BBC's biggest stars, is a slight, ironic thing which, like 'The Bull', expresses his disdain for celebrity and contempt for what entertainers do in the pursuit of fame. His words would have gone over the heads of most children, if any were actually listening, rather than simply enjoying the slapstick. It says much about Jake's lack of self-regard that he put himself through the experience, and much about his skill that he could say so much in a throwaway song.

His disenchantment with television, and particularly the BBC, was growing, which is baffling given the level of control he had enjoyed on *Jake Thackray and Songs*. This was put into sharp relief following the death of Georges Brassens in October 1981. It was a great loss for Jake, who was visibly moved when he announced the news to audiences.[11]

He wrote the following letter to *The Guardian*, explaining Brassens's cultural importance and bemoaning the lack of obituaries in the British media:

It went pitifully unnoticed here. I counted a mention on the BBC's 6 o'clock news and, from the six quality newspapers of Saturday and Sunday, a total of about 280 words; some inaccurate, some grudging, some – no medals for guessing which paper – from a different story from another page...[12]

> May I reassure your European readers that there are thousands of people here who recognise his stature, cherish his songs and his memory, grieve at his long suffering and disappearance, and wish to join them in their sense of loss.

The BBC in Cardiff was soon persuaded by his friend Colin Evans to make amends for this neglect. It commissioned two programmes paying tribute to the Frenchman, with Jake lined up to play a central role in both. The first was on BBC2's *Tele-Montage* in January 1982, for which he was filmed talking about Brassens's writing and singing 'Brother Gorilla'. The second was a 45-minute Radio 4 special scheduled for broadcast that summer, which Jake was invited to write and present. At last he had an opportunity to introduce Brassens properly to a UK audience.

None of this went as expected. Much to Colin's distress, Jake proved impossible to work with and, in meetings with BBC staff, was full of anger. 'Basically, Jake was so fundamentally hostile to everyone from television,' Colin recalled. 'He was convinced that they would rubbish Georges, that they wouldn't be sufficiently respectful for him.' Astonishingly, little over a week before *Tele-Montage* was broadcast, Jake tried to withdraw his contribution, but it was too late to do so. It was left to his agent to deal with the fall-out.

It is difficult to see why Jake objected to *Tele-Montage*: consisting mainly of footage of Brassens singing and talking, it paid respectful tribute. As for Jake's contribution, he spoke and sang well, albeit he omitted one verse of 'Brother Gorilla'. Did he perhaps feel embarrassed about this? Or, as at the Sherman Theatre, did he feel unworthy of a platform alongside his musical hero? Whatever the reason, his behaviour can't have been good for his reputation at the BBC.

As for the radio programme, Jake's distrust of the BBC trumped his desire to promote Brassens and it was never made. Not for the last time, an opportunity was missed.

Jake Thackray on stage in the 1980s.

The Glowing Red Phone

'I remember feeling, "Oh God, Jake had a gig last night.
I really hope he turned up."'

– Alex Armitage

On the surface, the 1980s would appear to have started brightly for Jake's agent. Alex Armitage had secured a TV series and album deal, which raised his client's profile and provided an excellent platform for concert bookings on the theatre circuit. According to the unwritten laws of show business, they could now expect to reap the financial rewards for several years, until Alex negotiated Jake's next foray into television.

Alas, that was not quite how things played out.

All was not well in Jake's world. As the new decade dawned he was becoming unreliable. Back in 1977, when he attempted to flee the Fairfield Halls, his agent's timely presence and calm reassurance had averted disaster and ensured the show went on. A few years later, however, he now had to deal with the fact that Jake often didn't turn up for gigs at all. It is seared into his memory: 'I remember feeling, "Oh God, Jake had a gig last night. I really hope he turned up." I would get to my desk in the morning and very often the telephone was glowing red from some irate club owner. We used to call them the WTF ("Where the fuck was Jake last night?") calls.' When he failed

299

to turn up, it was Alex's job to find out why: 'You'd ring him up and say, "Jake, you know you had a gig. You knew you had a gig. You signed a contract for a gig. We talked about a gig. Why didn't you turn up?" And then he'd lie. Gloriously, stylishly. He was once delayed by a snowdrift, a freak snowdrift. It must have been a freak snowdrift, it was August. Swans did remarkable things in the lanes around his house. Trees came down. In fact, the same tree came down many times. Jake was obviously a man of infinite compassion and mercy because he spent a lot of time beside the deathbeds of people he loved. The excuses were glorious.' Jake's love of fantasy and storytelling, practised in role play on his hitch-hiking trips with Ian Gliddon and honed in his songwriting, was now used to provide fanciful cover when he failed to fulfil his professional commitments.

More often than not, it was a concert at a large venue and a big payday that Jake missed, the prospect of a remote stage in front of hundreds of people seated in regimented rows proving unbearable. Alex was left with the task of placating the angry promoters: 'I would try and pour oil on troubled waters, and lawyers would be mentioned and curses would be aimed. But actually, people just loved Jake and knew that he lived in his own world. And he would turn up a few weeks later and he'd do the gig for free, which is a thing agents hate, really hate, and he was inevitably fantastic because he knew he'd screwed up, he was really sorry. And so he pulled out the stops and people just forgave him, because people loved Jake. But, as an agent, he aged me prematurely. It was real seat of the trousers stuff.'

As time went on, Alex found that Jake's reputation for unreliability became a barrier to getting him bookings: 'The folk club owners absolutely loved him, but there is a limit to how much you can frig someone around, and I found it more and more difficult to sell him because people were saying, "Is he actually going to turn up?" And I found it more and more difficult to get good money because it became as if I was asking a favour. And, of course, that, for an agent, is enormously difficult. It's part of the job, but a hard sell is a hard sell, and Jake should not have been a hard sell.' Sadly, when his earnings ought to have been growing, he was settling into a financially ruinous pattern of behaviour.

His approach to organisation had always erred towards the 'spontaneous', but this behaviour was something different, and it baffled Ralph McTell: 'That's something I am at a loss to understand, because that doesn't compute with the man I knew... I think it was a sign of things coming to a head. That man would have swum a river on fire to get to a gig before, because he had made a promise to do it... It's indicative of deep turmoil brewing, I thought.'

A central problem was that Jake was no longer enjoying his work, as he told his sons. 'I can remember Dad saying to us that he was getting hacked off with the whole job, and that he would rather be a train driver,' recalls Sam. What had started as an enjoyable hobby had become a grinding routine and he was finding life as a 'performing dick' less and less rewarding. Sheila Thackray could see how draining he found the relentless touring: 'Going around, performing, taking it [your music] with you, on your own, it was hard. He wouldn't say how hard, but you could see the difference when he was travelling with Alan – he got some camaraderie there. I used to go with him as well and think, "How do you do it?" The driving there... you've got to get onto the stage, face lots of people. And the contract says to appear "as known". I used to think what an awful little phrase that is. It was always in quotations. You couldn't just be yourself. Oneself is changeable in normal life, isn't it? You had to keep appearing "as known"; otherwise, the management wouldn't be happy. What a burden.'

His phobia of large theatres meant he spent more time on the road playing small venues. The endless travelling, along with the requirement to meet people's expectations, left him feeling trapped, as he confided to Ian Gliddon: 'On several separate occasions he said to me, "People think that performing your own material in front of a large audience is the most marvellous thing to do, but they don't realise that night after night you have to sing the same songs, and if you miss out one of the songs they want, they feel robbed." He said your life actually becomes quite limited and constrained and, compared to being a teacher, you don't have any more time to do things because you are travelling from one place to another.' Jake was stuck on a treadmill. The days spent working with Alan Williams certainly brought some sunshine, but performing solo was an altogether lonelier business and, as Ralph McTell observes, 'A lot of introspection goes on on the road, and it can be very dark.'

The elephant in the room, however, was alcohol. Jake was always a glass-half-full sort of person and, in Ralph's words, 'He would want to share that with you'. Unfortunately, his glass was emptied and refilled far more frequently than was good for him. Having grown up in a heavy-drinking culture with an alcoholic father, it's hardly surprising that alcohol was part of his life from early on. Throughout adulthood his friends knew he loved to share a drink and, following a memorable evening spent together at Hillside in the early 1980s, his friend Harvey Andrews commemorated this in a song, 'Me and Jake':

Me and Jake and a bottle of whisky, wishing that we were
    French
And living in the Artists' quarter with fires that a drink
    won't quench.
I could be Brel, he could be Brassens, life would be oh so
    fine.
Me and Jake and a bottle of whisky we'd trade for a bottle
    of wine.

'We had a great night,' recalls Harvey. 'We sat up until God knows when, putting the world to rights and talking about our passions. But of course I've never been able to sing it since, because I didn't know at the time what his problem was. It never occurred to me.'[1] He wasn't the only friend blissfully unaware that Jake was suffering from an addiction.

One person who knew the truth much earlier was Sheila Thackray. She had realised that he was an alcoholic before she married him, and for years they both seemed able to cope with his illness. In the 1980s, however, it took control, and the consequences, personally and professionally, were catastrophic. As Sue Haverly sadly puts it: 'In the 1960s and 1970s, there's no doubt about it, there was a lot of fun and there was a lot of alcohol, and it was all fine... and then it was not fine.'

Jake's choice of career was disastrous, given his alcohol dependency. Regularly away, often alone, performing in venues where it was readily available and most probably offered freely to the 'star', the temptation to drink for Dutch courage before going on, and then to help with coming down from the post-performance 'high', would prove irresistible.

Like many alcoholics, Jake sought to hide his addiction and it came as a complete surprise to his friend, Mike Harding, when he told him the truth after a show in the mid-1980s. Perplexed at the revelation, Mike pointed out that they had drunk together many times without any apparent problem, at which point Jake confessed the reason he often volunteered to collect drinks from the bar while drinking socially was so he could discreetly consume a couple of shots from the top shelf. He also explained that he would hide bottles of spirits at home, to consume in secret.

What led Jake to drink? Hereditary and social factors, including a lack of affection from a parent, can play a role in alcoholism. Could much of his illness therefore be ascribed to the influence of his father? Or, as Sue Haverly wonders, could it have its roots in his personality and his conflicted view of himself? 'I think there was a massive disconnect with the person he felt he was and the person he felt he had to project,' says Sue. 'The person he felt he was, obviously, was all tied up with his upbringing, and that included his family life, and I think his religious life, his Catholic upbringing. That massive disconnect was difficult to handle, and one of the ways he handled it was alcohol. You know, whatever pain you're in, if you have a few drinks, it lessens it, doesn't it?' Whatever its origins, he would live with the illness until his death.

The reality of his relationship with alcohol was brought into sharp focus for his agent in 1980 when Jake was arrested for drink-driving. Most worryingly, the incident occurred during the daytime, while travelling to a gig. 'That's when I realised there was a big alcohol problem,' recalls Alex Armitage, 'a serious, grown-up problem.' The practical consequences for Jake's professional life were limited initially: although he lost his licence, he could rely upon Alan Williams to drive for him when they worked together, so only had to use public transport for solo concerts. But the event provided a stark warning that he was not in control of his behaviour. If he didn't address the issue his problems were likely to escalate. Unfortunately, he proved unable or unwilling to get the help that he needed.

Jake's drinking was doubtless fuelled further by unhappiness with his job: he was not only weary of performing, but also increasingly frustrated at his inability to come up with material. Writing had always been his greatest fount of fulfilment, and the well was running dry. He discussed the problem with Mike Harding, who sought to console him, reminding him that he was loved by audiences and could still make a very good living based on what was already written. 'Jake never understood how good he was or how much people loved hearing his songs,' says Mike. 'I told him he could go on doing the same 30 or 40 songs forever, that they were classics.' Sadly, this was not enough: decades spent performing the crowd-pleasers over and over again would leave Jake feeling like 'a real bloody Archie Rice'.[2]

The effect on his mental state of his creative juices drying up was clear to Sheila Thackray, as revealed in a tender letter, written to him on tour in November 1983. Recognising his crisis of confidence, she tried to encourage him: 'I wish you could excuse yourself, no, not excuse, forgive and press on. You have an original mind, you are inventive and observant, and this domestic theatre is not enough for your talent... Please write things when you come home. Anything. Just keep doing it. You can't help being good a lot of the time. Don't bother about what kind of dad, husband you are. You are fine – I love you, boys love you, respect too. Get on with something selfishly. Is it possible?' She expressed the hope that he would be happy when he returned home, or at least that his depression would not get worse.

Given his growing disenchantment with his work, a parting of the ways with his agent became inevitable. Richard and Alex Armitage both appreciated his talent and over the years had skilfully supported him and developed his career, despite the fact that he wasn't the easiest of clients. 'He was stubborn as an ox,' recalls Alex. 'Telling him something a thousand times would not change his mind, because his mind was not something that was available for changing. That was one of the things which made him magnificent.' Ever the anarchist, Jake could react badly to attempts to manage him or tell him what to do. In interviews he would refer begrudgingly to 'the people who run my life, the agents who take the jam off my bread',[3] and he seems to have regarded having an agent as a necessary evil. 'Occasionally, my dad or I would get four or five-page letters,' says Alex, 'with Jake's very neat, schoolmasterish handwriting, where he was tearing a strip off us for some misdemeanour, either real or perceived. They were always beautifully written – of course he used English magnificently – the sort of letters you felt steaming in your hands as his ire, his anger came out, so beautifully expressed.'

Failing to turn up for gigs only served to underline to both parties that their interests were now fundamentally misaligned. Noel Gay Artists were in the business of show business, Jake wasn't. 'Jake was very, very good at being Jake Thackray, and he knew exactly what being Jake Thackray was,' says Alex. 'We were good at the entertainment business, at careers, at television and concerts, and with any artist you have to reach some sort of compromise.'

Compromise, as Alex knew, was never Jake's strong suit: 'Jake knew what he was best at, which actually translated as what he was happiest at, because he was never a great performer when he wasn't at ease. He had strong opinions about what was right for him, which were normally correct, but sometimes clashed with the best advice people could give him. He wasn't enjoying the world of show business enormously, so he understandably blamed Noel Gay for being responsible for his life in show business.'

It is one of the biggest paradoxes of Jake's story that, having embarked upon a career as a performer, with the need to earn a living to support his family, he came to resent, despise and ultimately reject everything that would normally define success: the lucrative engagements in large concert halls and television appearances that would guarantee more bookings, record sales and financial security. In turning his back on Noel Gay, he turned his back on the London-centric world of entertainment, the clearest possible statement that he had no desire whatsoever to be a star.

Jake being Jake, he didn't bother going through the formalities of terminating his relationship with Noel Gay; he simply stopped returning their calls and started getting bookings through a Birmingham-based agency, Acorn Entertainments. Acorn was a natural fit, given the sort of gigs he was now willing to do. Its owner, Jim McPhee, had excellent connections on the folk club circuit and ran two of Birmingham's biggest clubs, the Hare and Hounds and Red Lion; he also had some of Jake's friends on his books. The agent's personality would undoubtedly have appealed to him, as Ralph McTell observes: 'Jim's bluff Yorkshire black-and-white commonality would have been so refreshing to Jake after being surrounded by luvvies in the media and show-biz.' The two men struck up a friendship and their professional partnership would endure for almost a decade.

It was left to Alex Armitage to work out what was going on. 'Jake would sneak off and do little gigs for very little money without telling me,' he recalls. 'I got my ears ripped off by a promoter of a large theatre who had booked him for a huge fee and then found Jake had accepted a gig the week before his show at a pub down the road.' Realising their client had put himself on Acorn's books, Alex and his father graciously decided to cut their losses and accept the *fait accompli*. He was proving to be more trouble than he was worth, and Alex had plenty to do supporting other clients. Richard Armitage wrote to Jake in September 1983, accepting that Acorn would handle all his folk club bookings, and made a magnanimous offer: 'We will continue with theatre and TV recordings should you ever be in the mood to undertake them.' The frustration in his words is palpable. But if the Armitages thought that their problems with Jake were all in the past, they were wrong. Alex would get WTF calls for years to come, and his only consolation was that he now simply redirected them to Jim McPhee.

As Richard Armitage pointedly implied, Jake was now very rarely in the mood to do television work. Six months after the *Jake Thackray and Songs* series, his headline performance at the Cambridge Folk Festival had featured on BBC2, but it would be two more years before he was on TV again. In July 1983, shortly before Richard's letter, he appeared on BBC1's nostalgic *The Time of Your Life*, in which presenter Noel Edmonds looked back at events in 1970 with actress Jenny Agutter.[4] Jake's contribution to the programme underlined how much he had changed, and how unwilling he now was to compromise.

He was asked to revisit an old point number. Viewers initially saw black and white *Braden's Week* footage of him singing 'The Ladies Basic Freedoms Polka', his song about women pinching men's bottoms. Halfway through, this segued into a now greying Jake singing new lyrics which noted how little had changed in a decade, and that there were still the 'same old piercing pains in arse'. The song now expressed his sympathy for the plight of women around the world and support for their pursuit of fundamental dignities, while also declaring that the antics of the 'daft brigades' remained demeaning. With these new lyrics he had stripped the point number of throwaway humour and turned it into a forthright expression of his views. Whether he intended it or not, it was a riposte to those who accused him of misogyny.

Jake was amusing but equally outspoken in the brief interview which followed:

Noel: Are you a male chauvinist pig, sir?

Jake: Of course not, and that's not the point of the song. I'll tell you what I am: erm, I don't like loonies. In most – I dunno, it seems to me to be common wisdom – in most organisations and groupings of people that are underpinned by a value or an ideal in society, they're like bloody flypaper – they attract the loonies! You know: the shriekers on the touchline, the hecklers, the prats... and the prat-esses. And I think that the loonies on the borders have done as much damage to the admirable cause of women's liberation as have, say, the Miss World competition. I think that they are as – I don't like using words like degrading – debasing.

Noel: You think that beauty contests actually do degrade womanhood?

Jake: Oh goodness me, yes! I'd rather look in Dewhurst's window! Well, I wouldn't really but, you know, it's the same sort of display, you know: chops and loins.

Noel: And these comments are coming from a man who wrote a song that started, 'I like a good bum on a woman'?

Jake: But of course! Yes! Oh, listen, I've… I reserve my [right]… I don't mind if people want to be loonies, so long as they don't mind if I take the piss out of them.

'I take the piss out of them.' Jake knew exactly what he was doing: as Sheila Thackray observed, 'He just loved going right to the very limits of things.' While he may have felt that he was remaining true to himself, what he was doing was self-destructive: his language during this prime-time, early evening family entertainment would have horrified BBC Management. It would be his last performance on national television.[5]

Jake was effectively reshaping his job by withdrawing from those aspects of it which made him most unhappy. But happiness (or, at least, a reduction in unhappiness) came at a price: his lower profile meant less income from concerts and fewer record sales. Indeed, come the early 1980s, most of his albums had long since been deleted, and there was insufficient demand to warrant new pressings; only *Jake Thackray and Songs* and an EMI compilation album were still available. He may have had no regrets about becoming yesterday's man, but the implications for his family's financial security were serious.

By the mid-1980s, Jake desperately needed inspiration to write something new, and his creativity experienced a small revival prompted, in part, by the encouragement of Victor Lewis-Smith, a young radio producer.

Victor had first met Jake when conducting an after-show interview in the late-1970s, in the company of Alan Williams and several crates of Guinness. They hit it off and stayed in touch, and when Victor began producing *Midweek* and *Start the Week* on Radio 4, he often booked Jake and invariably encouraged him to perform something different. Usually the singer stuck to familiar material, but sometimes Victor's cajoling was rewarded. Over the course of several years, Radio 4 audiences would hear a clutch of new songs.

They are an interesting mix. Most are comic but slight, and feel like private jokes, lacking the ambition of the writing on *On Again! On Again!*. Some, more serious, were commissioned pieces written in response to a specific brief.

The most poignant is 'Lullaby-My-Daddio'. Set to a beautiful, lulling melody, this dark pastiche is structured as a duet between a father and young son. As the 'little laddio' sits on his dad's knee, he asks innocently whether he will grow up to be like him. When his father assures him of this, he asks whether it means that he, too, will one day come rolling in, singing 'boozy lullabies', and make his child 'maddio'? The song ends amusingly with the son promising to take his revenge, forcing his father to listen to his own dreadful songs, and 'too bloody baddio!'. Jake was always ready to laugh at himself, but for anyone with knowledge of his relationship with alcohol, 'Lullaby-My-Daddio' is uncomfortable listening.[6]

Although Victor was friends with Jake and gave him valuable work, being on the BBC staff meant he wasn't given an easy ride. 'Jake then saw me as the enemy,' he says. 'He was suspicious.' The singer was contrary and constantly sought excuses to bail out of appearances.

In 1985, two minutes before he was meant to be on a live broadcast in London, he phoned Victor to tell him he was at home: he had decided that the hotel the producer had booked for him was embarrassingly posh and refused to stay there. Victor cannily realised that his best tactic was to apologise, rather than tear him off a strip, which is what Jake deserved and was probably hoping for, thus giving him an excuse not to appear again. Victor gave him a cast-iron assurance that he would find him the worst hotel imaginable for his next appearance. It worked.

In May 1986, Jake unveiled two new songs in an episode of Radio 4's *Midweek*. He told a studio audience in Scarborough that 'Tortoise' had been written especially for the occasion. It has a joyous, simple silliness to it: a man who wins prizes at the fair always rejects the teddy bears and goldfish and instead, with 'hunger in his eyes', chooses a tortoise. Or rather, in his words, one of the 'little crunchie pies'. In the second verse Jake bemoans God's failure to provide people with clear distinctions.

Later that year, 'Tortoise' was released on a charity compilation album, *Where Would You Rather Be Tonight?*, with contributions from the likes of Mike Oldfield, Steeleye Span and Fairport Convention.[7] Jake had always readily performed for charity, but it is perhaps telling that the project he supported this time was Broadreach House, a rehabilitation centre for addicts. Jon Benns, the album's producer, recalls that he was the first artist to offer his services.

The second song was one of Jake's most quickly conceived point numbers, and had a very dark subject. At the rehearsal, the night before the broadcast, Jake had learned that one of the other guests was Peter Jacinelli, the Mayor of Scarborough. Victor remembers Jake taking him to one side and explaining Jacinelli's reputation: 'He looked at me sagely and said, "He's a paedophile. I think there's something going on in Scarborough, and he's at the centre of it."'[8] Next morning, the producer had another surprise: 'Jake came in and said, "I have written something original for you".' 'The Dirty Mare' – which was about the Mayor – went completely over Jacinelli's head, but caused a real stir among BBC Management. 'Eyebrows were raised about it because some cleverer people than me realised that there are three or four levels going on with this song,' says Victor, who remembers that Jake was very upset when he learned of their reaction, and clearly felt conflicted about what he had done: 'He wanted to go too far, but he didn't want to go too far.' Unfortunately, 'The Dirty Mare' hasn't survived, so it is impossible to judge how close to the line he had gone.

Another new piece shared with Victor's radio audience was 'Our Dog', a love song to the Thackrays' legendarily stupid English Setter, Elizabeth (nicknamed Thin Lizzie). In mock exasperation ('Oh, Jesus Christ!') Jake bemoans the cluelessness of a dog that is worried by sheep, cannot tell lamp-posts from policemen and farts at parties. But, despite all this, it is so lovely that visitors, including burglars, call on them again. As the song progresses, profane exclamations make way, amusingly and touchingly, for an acknowledgement that Jesus would love to have such a dog in Paradise.

'Our Dog' was well received by the studio audience, but the producer had to field complaints of blasphemy from listeners. After such a long period of writer's block, and with confidence low, criticism of his writing was the last thing Jake needed to hear. He gave Victor a simple instruction: 'Don't tell me. I don't want to know.'

'Our Dog' and 'Tortoise' were welcome additions to his repertoire.[9] Jake recognised their slightness, but loved singing them. He always introduced them as children's songs, but stressed they weren't 'soppy little songy-wongies for the kiddie-widdies... the kind of things you expect Americans to write'.

In September 1986, he received a commission to write something about national service for *Start the Week*. In 'Soon Get The Hang Of It', he adopts the persona of a sergeant addressing rookies on the parade ground:

You will make the bed, clean the kit,
Swear and screw and skive and spit,
And learn to get away with it, and you...
Soon get the hang of it.

You will believe whatever I say to you,
Although whatever I say may not be true.
This is to make a man of you...
And you, you, you, you, and you...
Will soon get the hang of it.

The perspective is particularly bleak and cynical, and in stark contrast to the more positive views of national service expressed

Above and left:
Jake performs
on *Tickertape* in
1968, flanked by
Bernard Bresslaw
and Janet Henfrey.

Below: Happy
times in Wales.
Jake, Sheila and
Sue Haverly, *right*,
at Hillside, 1971.

Bob Haverly

Above: Jake with Georges Brassens and his partner, Püpchen, in London, 1973.   *Colin Evans*

Left: A bespectacled Jake in the company of friends during a visit to Carbonne, France, in 1972.

Below: Jake and family in 1974, on safari in Kenya with their friends, the Bentleys; behind is the van with which he hit an impala. *Thackray family*

Jake, mucking in at Hillside with his sons, in 1978.

Jake lights up a cigarette at home in Monmouthshire.

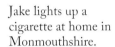

Jake and Sheila outside their 'little Welsh cottage'.

A farewell kiss before it's time to hit the road again.

The not-so-glamorous life: loading up for the next gig.

'Which Newport is the gig at?' Jake and Alan on the road.

Killing time before the show, backstage with his trusted musical partner.

Playing the waiting game with a smile.

'There was terrific banter between Jake and Alan...'

'...it went like good pudding.' Jake and Alan perform together in the late 1970s.

Above: Jake sings on stage in 1985. *Ian Watson*

Right: In Monmouth with Maggie Gliddon, 1993. Like other old friends, the Gliddons were never allowed to see his flat. *Ian Gliddon*

Below: 'Bless thy lambs and make them meat for thy kingdom. Mince them!' Jake as election agent for Peter Carpenter, 1991.

Carpenter family

'I'm not sure I can handle this': Jake pictured here with Roger Stennett, *right*, and Sarah Willans of The Jake Thackray Project, *below*, outside the Punch House, one of his favourite pubs. Taken in October 2002, these are the last known photographs of him.
Ian Watson

Resting place: Jake's simple gravestone in the churchyard at Welsh Newton.
Paul Thompson

The great Jake Thackray, taking a moment backstage in the 1970s.

by the programme's other contributors.[10] Interesting though it is, the song was never performed again.

In the same year, Jake received an approach from a most unexpected direction – a West German TV company. WDR's *Telekolleg*, which produced Open University-style educational programmes, had commissioned an English-language series to help German viewers develop linguistic skills and learn about Britain. It was to be directed by Stuart Marlow, a Leeds-born academic based in Germany, who was an old friend of Bob and Sue Haverly.

The series would explore various geographical, political and cultural borders and divides in Britain and, wherever possible, Stuart wished to involve friends.[11] 'I had an awful lot of freedom over how to shape it,' he says, 'and it obviously needed a theme song, almost like a traditional British series, to give the whole thing a flow, rhythm and identity.' His thoughts returned to an inspirational evening spent at the Haverlys' woodland cottage in 1972, in the company of Jake and Alex Glasgow: 'Bob and Sue had just moved and it was a very impressive evening because the company was impressive. The atmosphere stuck in my mind. It was rustic, genuine and warm, and it was a group of critical, creative minds embracing a different kind of lifestyle, which was anti-pop culture. There was nothing artificial about it. I thought "Wow! This is what we really need to give this programme a kind of identity."'

At Stuart's suggestion, the producer of the series approached Jake, initially asking him to write a song with a different verse for each of the 13 programmes. He accepted the commission, for a fee of £500, but sensibly rejected the idea of having so many verses. The result, 'Borders',[12] is proof of his poetic gift and ability to say a great deal in only a few words. Using simple language to cater for his German audience, Jake deals succinctly and powerfully with tribalism, the 'borders in our bones', in its many forms – social, religious, political, racial and sexual. There is an epigrammatic brilliance to the writing, particularly when he declares, 'We feel the need to keep together, we keep the need to feel apart.'

It is a thoughtful, well-crafted piece of writing which, like 'One of Them', is powerful because of the simplicity of its language. Nevertheless, Jake's confidence by this point was fragile, as is evident from the fact that he was beginning to turn to his sons for feedback. 'He used to really want us to be interested,' says Sam Thackray, recalling the writing of 'Borders'. 'He would ask our opinion, and I see now that he was looking for validation for what he was doing.' Inevitably, however, Sam and his teenage brothers couldn't give the nuances of Jake's writing the attention he craved: 'Our response would be, "Yeah, that's about right. Why don't you just send it off to them? That'll be fine."' Jake was a perfectionist, and 'about right' wasn't good enough.

Stuart Marlow remembers Jake's ambivalence about the song when he brought his film crew to Monmouth: 'He was very witty about it, and almost self-critical, because its themes are very simple and positive, and it contrasted with most of the songs he wrote, which were a lot more critical. But the song created a fantastic atmosphere and made the series unique.'

For Stuart, 'Borders' was an essential ingredient in the series, which culminated in an analysis of its lyrics, both in the programme and the accompanying course book.[13] Initially, Jake was going to sing it on camera, but he rejected the idea in favour of making a studio recording with Alan Williams. 'Because it was such an important song, he wanted to have it recorded professionally with people he knew,' recalls the director. Jake nevertheless agreed to some filming, and the series showed him performing 'The Jolly Captain' and 'Bantam Cock' in a pub, where Stuart saw at first hand his nerves before performance: 'It was an extreme version of what most performing artists go through. Most performers, if they are ambitious, have a fear of failure and of what might go wrong. It's as if they reject what they are about to do. Once he was performing he was very comfortable. His body language really changed in front of a small audience, and his charisma suddenly came out.' Such sharp changes in behaviour weren't confined to performance, though. 'Jake's mood swings at the time were difficult to predict. It was almost like he was bi-polar,' says Stuart. 'He was very enthusiastic and then suddenly it would be, "What the hell am I doing this for?" Sheila had to bear the brunt of this.'

After years of frustration, and despite bouts of self-doubt, in the spring of 1986 Jake seems to have felt that his writing was finally gathering some momentum again and his thoughts turned to making a new album. This would have been welcome news for his fans: it was five years now since the release of *Jake Thackray and Songs*. First, however, he needed to negotiate a record deal, something for which he was ill-equipped: he had no manager and Acorn Entertainments lacked the range of experience and negotiating power of Richard and Alex Armitage. Mindful of how involved Noel Gay had been in his recording career, and perhaps regretting the unprofessional manner of his defection to Acorn, Jake contacted his former agent to ask whether there'd be any contractual implications for Noel Gay if he were to sign a record deal. Alex Armitage wrote back, making clear that Jake was now a free agent: 'We would expect no contractual position either with regard to the Agency side of the recording deal (we would of course consider helping out should you ask) nor from a publishing point of view.' He finished: 'I would love to hear a cassette of the songs when they are ready.'

EMI and Dingle's were ancient history. When it came to making deals to record and publish his new songs, Jake could start afresh, and if he was daunted at the prospect, a generous olive branch had been offered to him by Alex Armitage: Noel Gay would be happy to help.

For reasons known only to him, Jake never took Alex up on his offer. No record deal was done. The new songs weren't recorded. The album was not made.

The strain is showing as Jake sings at a small gig during the 1980s.

It Doesn't Get Any Easier

'With that doleful face he might well have been walking through a minefield. But I can understand why one onlooker came over to say "Please be kind to him."'

— The Stage, 1989[1]

In 1986, Jake's seemingly endless round of concerts included an appearance in August at the Edinburgh Festival, where Stefan Bednarczyk, a young cabaret performer and actor, was delighted to find they were both performing in a live Radio 2 broadcast. Stefan not only admired Jake's work hugely, but also had something in common with him: they had both attended school at St Michael's College. Their paths had briefly crossed off-stage once before, when Jake had made it very obvious that he didn't wish to receive any attention. This time, they chatted in the green room until the time came for the older man to head to the stage. Stefan vividly remembers what happened next: 'Jake was absolutely terrified. His hands were so sweaty that his guitar slipped from his hand as he went on to perform. He turned to me and said, "It doesn't get any easier."'

Life certainly didn't get easier for Jake in the 1980s. The consequences of his actions (and inaction) caught up with him, compounded by bad luck and poor timing, and he was unable or unwilling to take the steps needed to avert disaster.

One event over which he had no control, but which affected him deeply, was the death of his mother in November 1985, at the age of 84. This remarkable woman, who had lived such a tough life, ended her days still attending Mass at the Church of the Assumption in Leeds. Her enduring devotion to her faith and concern for her family had been evident early that year, when she wrote to Sheila about her grandson's impending 'O' Levels: 'It's like my own days as a younger anxious mum – am praying earnestly for Sam's Exams.'[2]

Jake loved and respected his mother and, despite rarely talking about his feelings, would later admit that her death was one of the greatest losses in his life.[3] Molly had been his rock throughout his early years. Role model for his faith and values, she had ensured he got the education she never received, cared for him until he married and provided early inspiration for his songwriting. But she had also been uncompromising in her high standards, her sharp wit matched by a sharp tongue. 'She always tells the truth – it comes out like a laser beam,' Jake once declared. Now the small, strong woman who could control her sons with a look was gone. 'Marvellous woman, much missed', he wrote poignantly on the back of her photograph.

Molly's wake was held, fittingly, in the church hall in Leeds, and Jake and his brothers – including Michael, making a rare trip from France – were all there. As Rick Irons recalls, they gave her a send-off that suited their mother's sense of propriety: 'a tea and crumpets affair with no booze – on display, at least'.

To hold house and home together and raise her family, Molly had had to count the pennies carefully. This was not a quality her youngest son inherited. On his early hitch-hiking trips and at university, Jake had never managed money well, and he would never develop this skill. He was, in Rick's words, 'completely inept' when it came to anything financial.

Teaching in Leeds, this wasn't hugely problematic, and his life in the council house at Old Oak Close had been relatively simple: outgoings were limited, his mother was there to look after him and his responsibilities were few. But when fame and its financial rewards came calling, existence became more complicated and he was ill-equipped to cope. Overnight, he went from the stability and regularity of a teacher's salary, where his employer dealt with his tax, pension and national insurance, to being self-employed and personally responsible for managing all these things. With hindsight, he would have been wise to employ a manager or accountant, but it was not in his nature to go down this road: he was resistant to being managed, instinctively distrustful of anyone who might take that 'jam from his bread'.

'Dad always left things to the last minute, running his life in a chaotic way,' says Sam Thackray. When his career was flourishing in the 1970s and there was plenty of money coming in, his reluctance to engage with financial detail hadn't seemed important. However, during the course of the 1980s, when his income began to fall, his lack of organisation was to catch up with him and eventually sweep away his world.

Sadly, in many ways he set himself up for disaster. Keeping financial records was anathema to him. Wherever possible, he preferred to be paid in cash. 'Mum used to love doing the laundry,' recalls Sam, 'because there would be tenners and scrumpled-up this, that and the other in his trouser pockets!' Travel and hotel expenses were likewise always paid in cash, and Jake kept no receipts. All of which made it impossible to account for his finances when calculating tax bills. 'If Jake and Alan Williams stayed in a hotel, he couldn't claim for two rooms because Alan was always paid in cash,' says Rick Irons. Most damaging of all, he was erratic when completing income tax and VAT returns, ignoring letters from the tax authorities. It would only be a matter of time before the taxman caught up with him, and when the moment came, he was ill-prepared. As Sam remembers bitterly, 'They were right bastards, the VAT and the tax man, absolute bastards, if you weren't on the ball.'

Jake certainly wasn't on the ball. At Hillside, he couldn't face dealing with bills, so didn't. Sam remembers that the telltale brown envelopes remained unopened: 'I would always think, "Dad, there's these letters coming through the front door. What's in them? If I got letters, I would like to open them to find out what was in there." It turns out they're all bills, and even though he's got the money to pay them, he doesn't. Eventually he missed a few VAT returns, so in the end they produced an estimate, a crazy estimate [of the tax he owed]... They took him to the absolute cleaners. They were merciless.' Over time, a series of big bills would wipe him out financially.

Consequently, at the start of the 1980s, Hillside had to be remortgaged. However, interest rates then rocketed (peaking at 18 per cent), just as Jake's income was beginning to decline. Falling behind with repayments, he and Sheila made a decision that would prove disastrous, taking out a second mortgage to help them pay the increased cost of the first. Meanwhile, the bank showed little sympathy and started calling in debts. This perfect storm put a great strain on the family and its finances, and the pressure only mounted as the decade proceeded.

In the face of all this, Sheila tried hard to help Jake with his day-to-day money management, asking him, without success, to give her his receipts so she could at least record his expenses. A letter to friend Carol Hawkins in December 1986 hints at the crisis. By this time, Sheila had got a job as a part-time English teacher to bring in much-needed income. It was her first work in almost two decades and she told Carol she liked the challenge, 'despite Jake's subconscious dislike of it all'.[4] Written on his headed note-paper, the letter prompted a grim joke about their precarious financial position: 'He's got loads of it [headed paper], which shows a lot more confidence in our continuing to live here to use it up than I've got!'

They looked for other solutions, such as obtaining planning permission to build a house on their field, to enable them to sell the land for a high price and clear debts. But at this point their nemesis appeared in the shape of their neighbour, The

Commander: the real-world 'frigging Brigadier' objected and saw to it that their application was turned down.

If The Commander's intransigence added to the stress, so did Jake's own stubbornness, revealing itself in the most extraordinary way. In the midst of his woes, when the family was facing the prospect of losing Hillside, he was thrown a lucrative lifeline: a television commercial. 'Dulux wanted to pay him £15,000 or something for a one-off,' recalls Sam, 'and that would have sorted out the mortgage issues.' However, Jake, with his staunch socialist principles, was determined to look a gift-horse in the mouth and turn the offer down, to the horror and disbelief of his family, who begged him to take the work. 'We said, "Dad, just do it! They only want 30 seconds of you telling people to buy Dulux paint!" He was totally adamant: "No. I do not agree with this capitalist commercialisation," and he wouldn't do it,' recalls Sam. 'I think he ended up saying, with teeth clenched, "Okay." They gave him a chunk of money, just for doing a demo. A few offers came in like that.'[5] Jake's determination to put principle above self-preservation was hard to fathom and put untold strain on the family.

Amid all this, he soldiered on with his life as a 'performing dick'. By the late-1980s he still had some bookings in bigger theatres sprinkled among folk club gigs but, with the days of regular TV appearances now a distant memory, his profile was waning and he was attracting smaller audiences. Despite the warmth of the reception he received, and his real need of the income, he still failed to turn up for concerts. His high no-show rate astonished his agent, Jim McPhee, as did the frequency with which he got himself double-booked when he chose to bypass Jim (and his commission) and arrange gigs directly. Inevitably, this would all take its toll on their relationship.

Just when he least needed it, shortly after his appearance at Edinburgh in 1986, Jake broke his wrist, which led to a couple of months of cancelled bookings and lost income. Even so, he still took it upon himself to travel 150 miles to Stainsby Festival in Derbyshire, where he had been booked as the headline act, to apologise to the audience for being unable to perform. He proceeded to do an impromptu 20-minute stand-up routine for no fee, not the only time he made such a gesture.

Although his income and financial security were declining, his willingness to perform for charity was not. Throughout his career he had regularly and readily given his services for free or expenses only, to support numerous causes. The range was wide: the National Playing Fields Association, Christian Aid, the Scouts, an amateur dramatics society, Monmouth Rugby Club, the Monmouth-Carbonne exchange, an Englishman jailed in South Africa and a campaign against nuclear power in Gloucestershire. When it came to children, communities and justice, Jake was generous with his time. But while his selflessness was utterly laudable, by the mid-1980s it was sometimes flying in the face of his own perilous situation. In July 1986, for example, he followed up a concert for the NSPCC in Solihull with a four-date tour of Lincolnshire in aid of another children's charity. A week without income was something his family could ill-afford. But for Jake, it seems, charity didn't begin at home.

Occasionally in the 1980s he would step off the touring treadmill in the UK to perform overseas, and toured the Gulf States, Cyprus, West Germany, Canada, Bermuda and Hong Kong.[6] The large ex-pat communities in these destinations rarely saw British performers, so such tours were popular and potentially lucrative. But although he sometimes found himself singing for audiences of over 400, most venues were much smaller. Indeed, having flown halfway round the world to Hong Kong in 1984, he spent one night playing to 15 people in a bar, as a favour to the tour promoter, Richard Abrahall. Other audiences there were larger, but his preference for small venues suited the Hong Kong scene. Even so, plagued by nerves, he was physically sick before going on stage for his first concert at the Chinese League Club.

Despite mounting personal problems, he always delivered on stage and even made return trips to Canada and Hong Kong. Richard Abrahall found him refreshingly approachable, neither requiring any showbiz formality, nor a written contract: everything was based on trust and the box office takings were shared between promoter and singer. In fact, Jake showed little interest in maximising earnings: he was unusual in not taking merchandise to sell at concerts and, when it came to payment, seemed almost embarrassed to take the money, asking Richard earnestly, 'Are you sure you're alright [financially]?'

Staying at the promoter's house in Hong Kong, he was an excellent guest. Full of curiosity, he was keen to learn about the culture and people of the former colony and, soon after arrival, went off exploring on his own, only to return three hours later saying he was 'full up' and overwhelmed by all he had seen.

He was likewise overwhelmed – almost literally – on his second trip there in 1989, when he witnessed one of the most traumatic moments in the life of the colony. The tour coincided with the popular demonstrations in China which culminated, on the day he was flying home, in the infamous Tiananmen Square massacre. He had been following the news and was aghast at the unfolding events. On the final day of the trip he drove with Richard to the Happy Valley district for lunch, before heading to the airport. However, the car became surrounded by tens of thousands of distressed Hong Kong residents, gathering to protest at events in China. Both men were suddenly very conscious that they were in the wrong place at the wrong time and intruding upon the grief of the crowd. However, they had to get Jake to the airport, so Richard drove as slowly as possible against the sea of protesters marching the opposite way. They realised the danger of their predicament: theirs was the only car, heading against the flow of thousands of people carrying barriers. 'We were inching our way through this, fearful that if we ran over someone's toe, things could kick off,' recalls Richard. Despite being worried about missing his plane, Jake was reluctant to leave, keen to show his support: 'He was making gestures that he was fully with the people, and that he shared their outrage and grief.' It was a moment neither man would soon forget.

By the late 1980s Jake's working life (and income) revolved almost entirely around concerts. His television career was effectively over – a performance and interview in May 1986 on regional television in Wales was a rare thing – but he still appeared occasionally on radio.

A new opportunity came in March 1987, when he was invited to present a six-part Radio 2 series looking at musical parody. As one of the country's best-known writers of the comic song,[7] he was well-suited to the job. He had considerable input into the eclectic selection of music and, freed of any requirement to sing, used the series to provide a platform for artists he admired who were seldom heard on radio. Listeners were treated to songs by many of his friends: Alex Glasgow, Mike Harding, Jeremy Taylor, Richard Stilgoe and, of course, Georges Brassens.

The series was titled *They Did It Their Way*, and Jake did it *his* way, scripting intelligent, insightful and unpatronising spoken links. He announced his lack of deference at the outset, telling listeners that the series would be 'having a go at songs, knocking them off their pedestals' and laying into 'spurious singers, taking themselves so seriously'. He shared his views on the nature of musical parody and was forthright about what he didn't like, dubbing 'My Way' the 'national anthem of non-entities'.

One revelation was his high regard for a songwriter to whom he had often been compared:

Running not far behind [Brassens] is an Englishman whom I disregarded for a long time. I ignored him. Noël Coward. It was my fault and I regret it. I never took much notice of Noël Coward because I am a pig-ignorant provincial, and he was singing about a group of people who live down south. And also he was called 'The Master'. And, well, somehow this is affected and effête, I thought... Nevertheless, I have learned the error of my ways, and I think that, in English, Noël Coward is 'The Boss'. He is 'The Guv'nor'.

However, his opinions extended beyond songs to show business, capitalism in the music industry, even the press barons Rupert Murdoch and Robert Maxwell. The series gave real insight into the cynicism with which he now regarded the industry that had given him his career. Determinedly biting the hand that fed him, he introduced Brassens's 'La Route Aux Quatre Chansons':

> This Frenchman is examining old folk songs and seeing how they are being diminished and depreciated by what is known as – and this is the rascal of the whole series, the rascal, the villain of the piece – it is the music *business*.

He gave music publishers, in particular, a repeated drubbing:

> A publisher is about as nervous and jealous and vindictive as a virgin's father. They don't like anyone fooling round with what they consider *their* property. It's not because they've got genuine feelings for the song. Oh no! Publishers don't have deep feelings for songs. Publishers have got deep *pockets* for songs. Because if a song becomes a standard... this will keep the publishers in the Porsches to which they are accustomed.
>
> If you are going to chop something up [i.e. by parodying it], you've got to be as good as the thing you're hitting. This is one reason some singers and songwriters – and all publishers, of course, because publishers are rascals – this is one reason why they don't like people playing around with their songs. They want people to *love* their songs, not to question the quality. Because, of course, reverence, unthinking reverence, means *money*! Personally, I think that if it's possible to use mockery, well, use it. I think that if songs and singers are any good, then you can't damage them that way.

Listeners could be in no doubt as to the politics of a presenter who so clearly sided with the People against the Establishment:

> If a song is any good at all, then the People will take it to their hearts. No amount of tampering about with it will spoil it for the People.

Jake was equally forthright in his views on censorship:

> You might have noticed that we had to bleep a word out there [in a song] because the fact that a couple of words are the oldest words in the language, and some of the shortest and the most common, and some of the best words, is neither here nor there. Neither there nor here is the fact that Shakespeare used those words, and Chaucer and Dean [Jonathan] Swift and James Joyce and Pope, and everybody else who was any sort of writer... I've known about censorship all my writing and singing life. Do you know, once I had to write some songs for a television programme. I did the best I could, and I phoned the words through. And the producer rang me back: 'Er, Jake? Jake, it's Rupert here. Rupert. Jake, dear heart, I have your words. Super! We seem to have two pillocks, one bum and a bloody. Now, I'll buy the bloody – that's in. Bloody is in... Yes, Jake. I'll have to confer about the pillocks and I'll come back to you on the bum.' That's how the conversation went!

His language in the spoken links was unbridled: 'bugger', 'toss' and 'piss-taking' all feature, despite the programmes being broadcast at 6.30pm. Doubtless he knew what he was doing – he liked taking things to the edge – but such behaviour on early-evening, easy-listening radio was unlikely to go down well with BBC Management or many Radio 2 listeners.

They Did It Their Way was an interesting departure. Jake, an informative and engaging presenter, sounded comfortable in the role – no doubt because the focus was on the music of others, and people whom he admired. Given his weariness with singing, the series might even have led the way to a new career, had he been prepared to moderate his views and his language. But as his former agent, Alex Armitage, knew only too well, he wasn't interested in playing by the rules of the showbiz game. And so, while he was invited back onto Radio 2 on a few more occasions, it was always to sing, never to present.[8]

This unwillingness to compromise, undoubtedly a limiting factor in his career, stood in contrast to the approach taken by his friend, Richard Stilgoe, who had been a client of Noel Gay as well. Like Jake, he had enjoyed a career writing and singing topical songs on television, but he also accepted more work as a presenter. Offered the opportunity in the early-1980s to write lyrics for Andrew Lloyd Webber, he took it, enjoying huge commercial success and critical acclaim through his work on *Cats*, *Starlight Express* and *The Phantom of the Opera*. Had such an offer ever come Jake's way, it is impossible to believe that he would have accepted it.

Jake and Richard's paths first crossed in 1969, when they both appeared at the Newcastle Festival.[9] Later, they shared the bill a couple of times, albeit inadvertently at the Churchill Theatre, Bromley, in 1977, when they were apparently double-booked.[10] Having both turned up, their solution was to play one half of the evening each, Jake volunteering to take the less prestigious first slot so he could head home earlier. For Richard, it felt strange to have someone he revered taking on the role of his support act. He found Jake's attitude unlike that of any other performer he met: 'He really minded being popular and famous, and I've never known anyone else quite in that position. He was absolutely determined that his talent shouldn't be fully recognised. If there's one thing Jake never wanted to be, it was famous. I've never seen a performer before shout "Stop it!" to an audience who are clapping, because he wanted to get on with the next song.'

By 1987, the trajectories of their careers were very different. Richard's huge success with Andrew Lloyd Webber had enabled him to develop a charitable foundation, and also bring to fruition a cherished personal project – *Bodywork*, a new musical, which the National Youth Music Theatre performed at the Edinburgh Festival that summer. *Bodywork*'s characters are all parts of the body, and the plot centres on what happens physiologically when someone falls in love.

When he made a cast recording, he thought that Jake would be an ideal person to play the Heart: 'I needed a particular voice with that sort of warmth, generosity and humanity.' Jake accepted the invitation, and the night before the recording session stayed at Richard's home, where the family's pet labrador immediately identified the stranger as a fellow creature deserving of its attention. Jake reciprocated and spent the evening in the kitchen, serenading the animal with renditions of 'Our Dog' and 'Ulysses'. 'An absolutely unforgettable moment,' says Richard.

For Jake's admirers, *Bodywork* is a disappointing listening experience.[11] He is, of course, playing a character and singing songs that are not his own, and his contributions are very brief. However, his performance is weak by comparison with his other recorded work: his voice is deeper and sounds tired, and his diction is not as sharp. The deterioration reflects the toll taken by his lifestyle, including his heavy smoking. As a singer, he is a shadow of his former self.

Anyone hearing *Bodywork* might well wonder how realistic the prospects were of Jake making another album, but in November 1989 it came tantalisingly close. Celtic Music, a folk label, offered him a contract for a three-album record deal, with the sweetener of a cash advance of £2,000. To keep his side of the contract, Jake needed to deliver the first album, with a minimum running time of 30 minutes, within six months. However, while he would repeatedly tell friends that he had 20 or so new songs ready to record, no one ever heard them, and the few, such as 'Borders', which had emerged in the mid-1980s, would have filled only one side of the record. Perhaps there was some wishful thinking at play, and he hoped that having a contract and deadline would provide him with the stimulus he needed to write more.

In fact, only one new song appeared in the late-1980s. 'The Berm House' was written for his friend, Peter Carpenter,[12] who in 1988 had built an innovative, eco-friendly, underground 'berm house'. Jake had been fascinated by the project and, upon its completion, Peter suggested that he might write a song about it. Several weeks later, he arrived at the berm house, guitar in hand, in typically self-deprecating mood. 'He said, "I did a song. It's not any good, but I just did it, and I don't know if you want it,"' recalled Peter. He eagerly sat Jake down in his kitchen where, with the words in front of him, 'The Berm House' received its one and only performance. Fortunately, Peter had the presence of mind to make a recording.

It is a wry, eco-friendly love story:

He lived below, she lived above:
They were in love and he wanted to show
The extent and the warmth of his deep, subterranean
    feeling.
'My darling, will you come on down
Into my house? I will show you around.
Feel the heat of my solar panels and gaze at my ceiling.
Oh... Oh, my heart's desire, I am full of an inner fire:
Come and live with me, feel my never-ending therms.
Oh my pretty, oh my sweeting, I'll give you my endless
    heating:
Darling, will you come and live with me at Berm
House?'

Sweetly amusing as it is, 'The Berm House' is a private joke, and it is hard to imagine Jake ever considering it for inclusion on an album. As 1990 rolled on, Celtic Music's deadline came and went. Just as in 1986, no recordings were made, and no record was released.

By this time, Jake's lack of self-confidence, so evident in his dismissal of 'The Berm House', also showed itself at concerts. In February 1989, when he had a short residency at the little King's Head Theatre in Islington, lyricist and broadcaster Don Black took his family along to see him: 'He strolled onto the stage without any introduction, looking more like a stage-hand than the evening's star entertainer. He looked to me a little uncomfortable, as if he'd be more at home on a tractor than in front of a microphone. Many requests were shouted out from a very sparse audience. He paid no attention to us, he played what he wanted to play. All in all, I would say that he is a very reluctant performer.'[13] James Green, who was reviewing the concert for *The Stage*, was astonished by Jake's demeanour:

> He was clearly uncertain and ill at ease and I wonder why he tortures himself with live theatre performances... I felt for him because I have never known an act so modest, truthful and self-deprecating... He talks of his silly and 'old bugger' songs, starts two of them and forgets the words halfway through. 'I might as well own up,' he groans...
>
> [quoting Jake] 'Songs you won't hear elsewhere... good of you to clap duff singing...I am not a very good performer.'... 'Get it right,' he says aloud before each item.
>   With that doleful face he might well have been walking through a minefield. But I can understand why one onlooker came over to say, 'Please be kind to him.'[14]

'Please be kind to him.' The reviewer was, but Jake wasn't. He could no longer command the creative impulse and he was dismissive of himself and his creations. Professionally and personally, he was staring into the abyss.

At this point, however, amid all the darkness, a glimmer of light appeared, to provide a new stimulus for his creativity. It would not bring salvation, but it would perhaps offer a degree of respite, and he would have God's own county to thank.

Jigget • Pip

A Voice from the Bottom

'Dear Ed and Sub ED, I've got all: the spalling, and: punctuation" ded+ , right inthis pieceand and just the right number of words you pay me for so please don't frig it around.'
– Jake Thackray[1]

A week after Jake's reluctant performance at the King's Head Theatre in February 1989, readers of the *Yorkshire Post* were turning to page two of the Tuesday supplement to find a cartoon portrait of a familiar face looking wryly back at them. The paper had a new writer, and he was sharing with them his views on progress:

> As the forefinger stabs the buttons of my pocket calculator (*Plonka-Plonka-Plonka*) and the green digits do this dance in the little window I marvel at myself.
>
> I am a modern man living at high-tech speed-saving time. When the trusty finger hits the word-processor (*Chugga-Chugga-Chugga*) I think: 'This is life. I am cost-effective, labour wise.'
>
> Am I hell-as-like. If I didn't have these blasted machines, I wouldn't bother doing these blasted jobs. I'd have better things to do.[2]

So began Jake's unexpected career as a freelance journalist, writing monthly pieces for 'Yorkshire's National Newspaper', as it proudly styled itself.[3] The people he had to thank for this were Robert Cockroft, its new features editor, and crime correspondent Roger Cross, who had floated his name when they were looking for new contributors. It was an inspired suggestion: Jake had been one of Yorkshire's most famous sons, and his sharp wit and idiosyncratic perspective on life would undoubtedly offer readers something different and amusing. 'It was immediately agreed that it would be good if we could get him,' recalls Robert, and a successful approach was made.

Jake was paid £100 for each piece published – a fraction of what he could earn from a concert, but valuable income nevertheless, given his financial woes. Writing for a newspaper had benefits: it lacked the psychological dread associated with performance, and there was flexibility about when and where he did it. Perhaps most importantly, however, given the demise of his songwriting, it gave him fresh stimulus and an outlet for creativity, with the freedom to write about anything. Almost.

By April 1990, the success of his journalism led to the offer of a weekly column. He sent a note to the features editor, assuring him that he could cope with the increased workload: 'I've got four other pieces ready... So I am well stocked up.'[4] For five years he would entertain readers and, along the way, bring the editorial team great pleasure, and no little frustration.

Getting Jake on-board was undoubtedly a coup for Cockcroft, who was impressed by the distinctive quality of his prose: 'His writing was very musical. There's a sort of rhythm to it that came out very well. Sometimes there would almost be a musical metre to what he had written, it flowed beautifully; it was really very interesting how he wrote.'[5] One early piece about rugby and class illustrates this well:

The Game had of course been invented hundreds of times before by boys in hundreds of other schools.

Lowlier boys in lowlier schools, but for them the Game was a playground commonplace: a sensitive young chap, near to tears, would rebel, pick up the football and – 'I'm taking my ball home!' – set off home with it. The yobs would run after him swearing, grunting and bashing.

It was fun, it was the way things were.

– 'Where you bin our Barry comin''ome in that state.'

– 'Usual, our mam, runnin', swearin', an' bashin' up a snob! Fun, intit, our dad?'

– 'Ant I told yer? Don't say intit and don't bloody swear and don't (whap! wallop!) bash people.'

The Game was simple, skilful, brutal, everyday fun for boys. Had they codified it then and written the rules, picked teams, got jerseys, refs, fixtures, trophies, well the Game could as well have been called, these days Pudsey Infants Football, or Stainbeck Road Elementary Union, or, Tong and Drighlington, or Upper Potternewton Lane Mixed Seniors Union Football, or a hundred other such footballs. Many things would be different now.

– 'Mother, have you cleaned my Pudsey boots?'

– 'Pssst!! Wanna ticket for the Stainbeck Road International, Cuba v Poland?'

– 'Daddy! Guess what! I've got my place in the school Tong and Drighlington First XXXVII!'

– 'Yes, Cambridge is supers! And I've got my Upperpotternewter Blue!'

'Headquarters' would be Hudders or Bradders or Cleckers or Heckers. American Kirkstall Road C of E Mixed Infants would be on Channel 4, Sundays. Farsley Beck Bottom League Football would be played by working men in the depressed Home Counties and weasel scouts from Sevenoaks would be poaching the touchlines of Gildersome, Bramley, Wyke and Shelf.

The Game only really caught on, gave itself a title and a class when The Sons of Gentlemen finally discovered the fun of running, swearing and bashing. Tom Brown, a homesick yob, picked up his football in Rugby School playground and

started home with it, Sons of Gentlemen pursuant. They liked
it.

– 'I say Castlereagh, aintit fun, what! You me, Palmerston,
Salisbury, Disraeli, and Pitt the Younger running, swearing
and bashing a yob! What you say we do it again next
Rupertmas?'

Then came the hols and word spread through St James'
and the counties.

– 'Derbyshire, old chap, we do a dashed spiff of a thing at
Ruggers on the Satters before St Rodney's Day Supper!'

– 'What's that Cumberland-and-Northumberland? Girls
come into it?'

– 'Lor no! Me and Cornwall, Somerset, Kent, Gloucester,
York, Lancaster, Norfolk, Anglesey, Leinster-and-Munster,
the Isles of Bute, and Rum-Eigg-and-Muck Minor run
around with this ball thing and swear and bash a yob! Beats
bunging breadrolls at Quaglino's and even policemen's helmets
on Boat Race Night!'

– 'The deuce ye do! I'll tell the chappers at Eters. All we've
got is the muddy groping thing up against the oppidans' casi
wall every other Sir Godfrey's Quarterday.'

Yes, I am class-conscious. Don't like yobs don't like snobs.
Don't like their class.

Rugby Football is such a lovely game. It is so grand. I was
brought to it when I was very small. My father did some work
for the Earl of Harewood once and in an unlikely, awkward
way they became pally, both shy men but sporting. We met
once at Headingley to see Leeds play Hull Kingston Rovers.
This was when Leeds fielded the Australians Bert Cook and
Arthur '12 across, 1 down' Clues and the Cape-coloured
Verrankamp who went down his wing like a Thompson's
Gazelle leaping high over opponents' heads and the
Welshmen Di Prosser and Dickie 'Ginger' Williams and
Lewis Jones. Anybody reading this ever seen Lewis Jones?
Good Lord he was good! Bald and bandy but strong and
cunning. We watched him set off from under our posts
towards theirs, jinking and ghosting. This was the first and
last time that I heard my Father, or, come to that, an Earl, say

– '****!' (For the sake of my Aunty Betty – '****!' means – 'Blow!'
– 'Well, Blow me pink!' said my father and – 'Blow me gently!'
said the Earl. They jumped, and shouted, and slapped
shoulders and tossed hats as Mr Jones waited, and slid and
drifted, shimmied, dummied, stopped, bullocked and swooped
through all Hull K.R. to put the ball right tidy under their
sticks. Then he converted.

Ever since I've been conscious that the only class is real
class.[6]

This was colourful, amusing, opinionated writing. It prompted
approving letters from readers and caused a buzz among
Yorkshire Post staff. Cockcroft offered Jake his congratulations:
'I thought that your column on rugby was one of the best
things I have read at any time, anywhere.'[7] Two years later, Tony
Watson, the editor-in-chief, would offer his own praise: 'Your
ideas are imaginative, your style highly original and it's all
delivered with a nice mixture of humour and poignancy. A
delight to read. You must pop in for a beer with us next time
you're in this part of the world.'[8] Jake never took up the offer
and he kept at arm's length these journalists who admired his
work so much. As ever, he was uncomfortable when receiving
praise.[9]

He used his column to offer a left-field take on a vast range
of subjects. Readers were left in no doubt as to what he thought
about the foibles of human behaviour, as well as world events,
capitalism and politics, and he was forthright in ridiculing what
he saw as humbug, cant and hypocrisy. He could be erudite,
and was imaginative and playful in his use of language. His
sense of the absurd showed itself in some tremendous comic
writing, such as in the opening to a piece mocking the
proliferation of self-help handbooks:

At last, *The Joy of Sox* (with a foreword by Doctor Scholl and
Doc Marten), a book that openly confronts that most intimate
of relationships between a man and a woman: – sox.

Researched over the years by a team of sociologists, biochemists and laundrette ladies this frank yet tasteful account deals with all the problems we know exist: casual sox, post–odour depression and premature expostulation.

All variations are described: – the golfers, the rugby and cricketing, the fishermen, the Wellington boot position and, most potent of all, the Pennine Way rambler.

Continental practices are explained: – the complicated La Chaussette, the wild Las Plantillas, and the ponderous Einlegeshohle.

Incompatibility is discussed – why some sox do not match and where they get to?

Contemporary thinking suggests that free sox with many partners has a direct connection with that other scourge of modern living: WHABS (we had a biro somewhere!).

Line drawings are explicit but useful. This book is a must for every adult bedside table, tallboy drawer and laundry basket.

This is schoolboy humour, of course, but it is not as tasteless as what slithered through our letterbox on Monday. This was a catalogue from a publishing house in Milwaukee introducing our family (why us?) to their new series *How To Be Happier...*[10]

Sometimes Jake would write about characters and themes developed for his 'talking bits' at concerts, such as Big Black Gilbert, the accident-prone Reggie Sedgewick, or his personal loathing of children's songs. However, most columns were entirely new and, with a weekly deadline to meet, he ranged over every conceivable subject. While almost nothing was off-limits, the editor declined to publish his piece about a man who had three testicles.

Much of the humour was absurdist and observational, and a good deal of it was at his own expense, as in this introduction to a piece inspired by a mis-spelling in a letter from the taxman:

As th editor, the sub-edirots, all od the secretaries, the printer%s and even the tea ladjies at the YOrkk(shire Post will testify to you, I cannot typle.

(Sorry about that, I'l have another go at it.) I canuTe tupe (No.) I cant typ? (Try harder, Jake lad) I annoct pyte. (The letters are all there so let's have one big piush now.) I CANNOT TYPE. (Did it.)

I konn sp*l and rite longhod because my Muommy taugh?t me how to and I wint to grammar school and Uni£ersityl but I cannok typloe.

Every Tuesday I send off my silly words to the Editor and sub-editors and secretaries and printers of the Yorkshire Post and I can hear them laughing from here.[11]

His love of storytelling led him to feature, from time to time, two new comic characters: the doddering Arthur Trubshaw (Wing-Commander, Retd.) and a social pariah, Lionel Bagwell. The creativity of his approach could be remarkable and challenging for the staff setting out his copy on the press: for a piece about the ability of children to look at things differently and spot humbug, he typed portions of the text upside down and asked that it be published in this way, with his column portrait photo also inverted.

Jake's rough drafts offer a fascinating insight into his creative process. Some of his copy was handwritten, but more often than not he used a typewriter and, by the mid-1990s, an early word-processor, which became the subject of one amusing column. Sometimes he honed pieces by typing out several drafts and, without exception, the final version would have further handwritten changes. He was even known to submit his copy twice when he had second thoughts about the earlier version. This was the work of a man who used language with precision and wanted to ensure that he said exactly what he wished to say. Everything he wrote had to get past the eye and pen of a sub-editor and, knowing this, Jake attached messages. Some included requests:

Please, dear sub ed, keep this word in, bastards.

Others made suggestions:

> DEAR SUB EDITOR
> If this is overlong and you've got to cut some fat, please do
> the paragraph on page 1 marked*.
>   But try keeping the rest in, eh?
>
>   J. Thack.

Evidently, he wanted as much control as possible of what was
published. For his piece about rugby and class he had provided
an apt title, 'The Class Game', but this was rejected by the sub-
editor in favour of the less nuanced 'Everyday fun for the boys'.
Jake wrote on his inspection copy 'Why change this?' Later he
made a request:

> Dear Editor,
> Appreciate that you must choose the titles for these pieces but
> I'd like to start choosing my own. Bit by bit, of course, till we
> match up what the YP wants and what I want.
>   May we start this week, maybe, with me asking this to
> be called:
>   WHO? WHO? WHO?
>   TO WIT, WHO? WHO?
>   OR
>   WHO YOU?
>   or, and I'd rather have this one
>   WHO'S WHO?
>   Good on you, thanks.
>
>   J. Thackeroid[12]

The suggestion fell on deaf ears. Cockroft explains why: 'Sub-
editors on the *Yorkshire Post* were renowned for writing very
good headlines. They were imaginative guys themselves. It's
not practice to allow writers to put heads on things. For one
reason, you never know what the size of the column is.'

The best columns were outstanding but, unsurprisingly, given the pressure to produce every week, there was variation in quality. 'At best, they were superb, extremely funny. But sometimes they might be darkly perceptive,' says Cockcroft. 'At best they were very well written. But sometimes they weren't. He might send one in that was pretty average, but we don't remember those. What we remember are the peaks, and there were quite a lot of those. They were extremely impressive.'

Despite the quality of writing, the editor found that, like the poor relative in 'Leopold Alcocks', there was a piece of grit in his life's Vaseline: Jake wasn't good with deadlines. Copy had to be submitted the day before publication – ideally, by post, or by phone or fax, if time was tight. With Jake, it was almost always phone or fax. 'He always went right up to the wire,' recalls Cockcroft. 'Almost inevitably, with Jake, it arrived on the day when the paper was due to go to print that evening, and sometimes it arrived late in the evening, and sometimes he missed and we had emergency columns on hold, written by other people.'

Late delivery of copy caused great frustration for everyone, particularly when it was phoned in. 'One of the problems with Jake – bless him – was that he was eccentric to a fault in how he delivered his copy,' says Cockcroft. 'I might get a phone call, and in the background there would be the sound of the train or an announcement or a whistle blowing, and he would say, "I'm on the train to some place in mid-Wales, but you'll have my copy at the next station." Then he would get off at the station and try and find a phone that worked and phone it in.' His unusual train of thought, turn of phrase and punctuation conspired to present a unique challenge to the copy-takers in Leeds. 'They did their best,' says the editor. 'They were usually taking news and sports reports and most of them were extremely efficient typists. I'm not sure they were always quite attuned to Jake's wit, and so some literals may have crept through, to which he objected.' With the copy being submitted late, and with no opportunity to double-check anything with the elusive Jake, some bizarre errors inevitably got into print: on one occasion, 'he's a proper musician' was heard and published as 'he's a proposition'.

Late copy always came accompanied by profuse apologies and excuses. 'Jake used some amazing excuses,' recalls Cockcroft. 'Anything from a late train, to the weather, to a concert. All sorts. He would ring up with that doleful voice, apologetic. His excuses were always interesting.' The editor could have swapped notes with the singer's agents.

Jake attached brief, amusing notes to late submissions:

Dear Robert,
I bet the worst sin is not to get the words in on time.
   Last week I was snookered at a telephone box in West Wales and couldn't get through. My apologies. I am only now beginning to learn how to do it.

He would also apologise for 'sloppy copy':

Please excuse the sloppy copy.
   You try typewriting on a Red and White Bus from Aberystwyth. I do hope the piece is all right. It is odd and I do not think I have got it right.

And again:

Dear Editor, Sub Editor, Louise,[13]
So sorry about more sloppy copy.
   I write on buses. Not, you know, like ON the sides but insides them, more;
      ED: - is the YP still happy with Wed.'s column?
      SUB-ED: - I shall get the spelling write,
      LOUISE: I shall get a proper typerighter.

In their many phone conversations, the editor was very struck by Jake's tone: 'There was always a sense of irony with him, always, even when he was apologising. Though he was sincere, there would be a sense of irony at the back of it. I think that's how he looked on life. I think that the irony was at himself, almost: "What am I doing, doing this?"'

Irony and self-knowledge were much in evidence when his excuse-making provided the inspiration for another wonderful column, 'Neville outshines the flash flood'. He started by drawing upon his days as a teacher:

'dear, mister fackray my, neville did do his homwork tusday honest sir only, it droped down a drian when, I was running past the coop up cardgn, road oppsit that there lady of lords catholic, place yours respeclty, marjories bink mrs,'

How could I ever have told Neville Binks that I was only too happy not to have to mark his English homework as long as he kept the forged letters coming.

Those prodigal commas that he chucked at the page by the fistful in the hope that some would land in a right place, the dyslexified mother; the wild words, the stream of consciousness and fertile invention of corroborating detail, I cherished them. Gems, Joycean gems. I still have the Collected Works, all hand signed – marjories bink mrs, Priceless.

The only time Neville let me down was when, out of devilment, I set the whole class to write one whole page on 'An excuse note to your teacher explaining why you did not do your homework.' Eager, next day, to read the precious texts I sprinted through the class register but then at 'Binks, N.?' Silence. Oh no! No Nev! Days later I got a sticky letter from marjories that was well below her standard: just a feeble — 'my, neville has, fell purely,' D minus bink mrs, you can do better than this, Nev!

Indeed he could: the night his foot got stuck in next door's mop bucket; the time a brewery horse ran over him on Woodhouse Moor; and who can forget when he was kidnapped?

Then Jake turned to his own behaviour – and offered a fascinating insight:

> When we fail to honour a promise we sometimes feel a need to self exculpate with a touch of unusual colour. The plain unvarnished stuff won't, somehow, do.
>
> I've often been at the batting end to the excuse-bowling of colleagues and acquaintances; most were in the 'sorry, mother's funeral' league; or, 'carburettor packed up at Goole', 'wife has flu'. Colourless stuff.
>
> On occasion I've had the snowdrift gambit, the flash flood at Pocklington, the bolt of lightning and once, (jolly good effort, this), psittacosis. In May 1987 a bass player rang up the theatre and regretted that he was unable to accompany me that evening as he had been held up by a flock of swans in Cardiganshire. (This got the Neville seal of approval).

He ended the piece, appropriately, with his latest offering:

> 'Dear Editor,
> I was unable to submit this contribution to your office on time as I had to jump off the canal bridge by Kirkstall Power Station yesterday morning at 6.30 and when I finally got the old lady out of the water she asked me to go back in again for her rosary beads and then what with the kiss of life and running a mile to ring 999 I must have left my briefcase in the ambulance during the mercy dash because when I regained consciousness a top neuro surgeon had taken it by mistake. Yours, etc.'
>
> I can hear them from here, Neville Binks and the editor, laughing like drians.[14]

Over time, the quality of his submissions declined: the 'sloppy copy' was sometimes harder to decipher, and he struggled for inspiration. There was an air of desperation to some of his rough notes, as he tried to generate ideas:

The disease of the week...
Too many charities it spreads thin...
Looking for a disease... the oceanic flank of Europe...
cultural rabies coming through the tunnel...

Whatever can we write about? Must do it this Monday.

What the hell else is there to write about?

A newsletter from a twinning organisation
Dear member... One small town to another...
In the form of minutes...
Funny features... bit of Franglais from a member...
Extracts from the minutes... got to have some jokes

Ultimately, missed deadlines would be his undoing. 'What did drive us eventually to distraction was the unreliability,' says Cockcroft. 'Jake's pieces were wonderful to get, and amusing to read, but if you couldn't guarantee that the readers were going to get it, the sub-editors really got cross about it.'

Early in 1994, the editor moved on from the *Yorkshire Post*, and Jake's days writing for the paper were numbered: its patience with him was exhausted. When the end came it was abrupt and caught him by surprise. His column on 16th March waxed lyrical on the subject of bullshit (a favourite theme), and he signed off with some reassuring words for his readers: 'Your correspondent has a nose for this sort of thing and you can trust him to keep you in touch.' He was wrong. These were to be his last words in the paper. He received a letter informing him that his services were no longer required and expressing the deep frustrations he had caused the paper's editorial staff. It may have felt brutal and left him smarting but, sadly, he only had himself to blame.

Luckily, as one door closed, another opened, and in the autumn of 1994 he was invited to write a weekly column for the *Catholic Herald*. It was a brave decision on the part of the editor, Cristina Odone, given Jake's irreverent humour and opinionated views. He amusingly acknowledged this in his first 'View from the Pew' column, which took the form of an open letter to the Editor:

Catholic with a small 'c'[15]

Dear Editor,

It was very kind of you, not to say flattering of you and surprising of you, not to say flipping astonishing of you to invite a person like me to write for your paper.

I am a catholic with a very small 'c'. I love my faith and I love my Church, always have always shall, but I use words like flipping. Oh yes, I flipping do.

This is not because I want to show off or to offend people. It is because I am a catholic with a small c and I live in a World with a big W.

So why do you want someone like me to write in the *Catholic Herald*? Most of the time I use good language but there are some days when I use bad language.

Also I don't like St Paul much.

When it comes to epistolisers give me St James. He's my sort of chap is St James. I bet he used to say flipping all the time. He lived in the big W. He'd never have got a job with the *Catholic Herald*.

Now St Paul would have had a regular column blathering on and on every week, boring the backside off us all. And, knowing him, he'd probably have been after your job.

He was pushy, was Saint Paul, see, like a lot of Evangelisers. Some little understanding is perhaps due to that bad mad monster, the Emperor Nero, for finally losing his rag with the old ranter from Tarsus and murdering him.

About both of these people, don't you think, there was a kind of daftness. They were both a bit touched. They were out of touch.

Do you understand, then, dear lady editor, my diffidence

about writing for a paper that is read by our Cardinal, our archbishops, bishops (metropolitan, suffragan and assistant) monsignors, canons, deans (urban and rural), rectors, parish priests, curates, mothers superiors, father superiors, friars and priors and abbots and abbesses, postulants, novices, deacons, nuns, lay sisters, lay brothers, and, well who knows, maybe even the Holy Pole Himself?

Not to mention our altar boys and girls, our little candlestick carriers and bell tinklers, our thurifer swingers and boat bearers and their mothers and fathers and grandmas and sometimes their aunties who comb their hair for them on Sundays to make them look tidy and keep their cassocks and cottas clean and pressed.

Not to mention our ladies who do the flowers without fail every Saturday night and our gentlemen who polish the brasses and floor and furniture of our altars and lady chapels and porches and confessionals.

Not to mention our loyal organists who remember how to play the *O Salutaris* and the *Tantum Ergo* when Father suddenly announces at the 11 o'clock that we will be having a Benediction this evening and there will be a special collection, thank you.

This is the Church as I know it and love it. So, am I right for the job? Am I your man? For instance: along with a lot of other RC's I am ever so worried about the way the Vatican boys went on in Cairo last month; I trust the Holy Father, of course, no question about him, not ever, but I sometimes wonder about his mob. Are they in touch with the same world that most of us are in touch with? Do they read the same gospel that the rest of us read?

'The wisdom that comes down from above is essentially something pure. It makes for peace and is kindly and considerate. It is full of compassion and shows itself by doing good nor is there any trace of partiality or hypocrisy in it.' (James 3:16-4:3).

These are the wonderful words that Louise Armitage read out to us last Sunday from the altar steps at our nine o'clock Mass. She is 12, right black hair, very leggy for a kid. She blushes a lot and she's got these big green eyes. Louise with a big L is one of the reasons why I believe in God with a big G.

My guess is that St Paul would not have approved of this little chick. He was the sort of man who would have frowned.

Whereas old St Jimmy would have told her she was brill and terrif and kissed her for her sheer Catholicism and her holiness and maybe also, knowing his Jimminess, for the big green eyes.

Dear lady editor, you do see my difficulty? If you want a voice such as mine in your grand paper it will not be a Pauline voice, oh no. It will be very Jimmy. A voice from the very bottom.

Yours very faithfully, J. Thackray[16]

He had set out his stall, and this irreverent tone was the hallmark of his writing for the paper. While every column related in some way to the Church, religion or morality, the subject matter was just as diverse as in his work for the *Yorkshire Post*, from which he re-used a piece occasionally. Rather as in his songs, Jake drew inspiration from reality to create a comical, fictional version of his life in which he still spent his Sunday lunchtimes in the Packhorse in Leeds, with Molly behind the bar, and Lionel Bagwell and Arthur Trubshaw on hand.

Readers were quick to show their approval of the paper's new columnist in its letters pages:

Praise the Lord for Jake Thackray. (Mrs Anne Crocker, Bath)

Jake Thackray has brought a ray of sunshine to our household. (John Cullens, London)

Mr Thackray's pieces are now part of a cuttings file I keep of favoured, much-read articles. (Paul Sheehy, London)

But Jake was Marmite, and he provoked some strong negative reactions:

> Please, please, when Jake Thackray asks 'am I right for the job?', 'am I your man?', should 'a person like me write for your paper?', shout 'No, No, No, No, No!' What a load of smug, self-satisfied, mock humility! (Maureen Bell, Gateshead, Newcastle)

Another correspondent was indignant at his amusing description of a congregation in Donegal's supposed behaviour during a tedious sermon:

> Never have I seen behaviour at Holy Mass such as that described by Mr Thackray... The implication is that it is normal behaviour for a Donegal congregation (the word punters is inappropriate) to play cards, feed babies or read newspapers during Mass...
>
> One would also question Mr Thackray's behaviour during Mass. The impression I get is that his thoughts were uncharitable, and he spent the time looking around the church watching other people. (Mrs Mary Long, Southampton)

Fortunately, such letters were rare.

In February 1995, however, Jake was prompted to write his own highly indignant letter to the Editor:

> Dear Ed. Odone,
> A bloke called James from your office rang to ask if I'd immediately write 50 to 60 words about unrequited love for your paper for St. Valentine's Day.
>
> He also said that I would not be paid for this.
>
> Here are exactly 60 unpaid for words as asked and I think I've got them dead right so would you ask your sub-editor to please not shag them up.
>
> If you do not like the words as they are then you've got a wastepaper basket. Also, Odone – you Catholic Heralders, you of all people, should, don't you think, at least offer to pay us

others for what you ask us to do whether you like it or not and whether we want it or not. Tell this James, Cristina, all about what happens to flying doughnuts.

> Regards and God Bless and so on.

Despite his anger at being asked to do unpaid work, at a time when he had huge financial problems, Jake still took the time to deliver a polished piece which met the letter, if not the spirit, of what had been requested:

> Feb. 14, 1779 Captain Cook was stabbed to death in the Sandwich Islands. Feb. 14, 1929 Bugsy Moran and 7 other gangsters were massacred in a garage in Chicago, Feb. 14, 1943 1,400 Jews and gypsies were incinerated in camps in Poland. This St. Valentine, bishop and martyr bloke probably never existed. The other people did exist, once. So why the love letters on Feb. 14, eh?

To the editor's great credit, these 'exactly 60 unpaid for words' didn't go into the wastepaper basket: Jake's alternative view of St Valentine's Day was published, striking a very different note from the more orthodox submissions of other contributors.

A year later, however, his column came to an end. Cristina Odone wrote to him in February 1996, thanking him for the early delivery of his latest piece, but explaining that he was being stood down: the paper had a limited budget, and his column was to make way for one written by Sister Wendy Beckett, a rising television star.[17] Stating her admiration for Jake's humour, the editor sought to soften the blow by suggesting that every columnist sometimes needed a break from writing, and expressed the hope that he would return to the paper in a year or so.

And so two weeks later, in his final piece (the aptly titled 'A feverish month of revolutions'), Jake signed off, leaving readers with news of one of his comic creations:

All important revolutions take place in February: 1917, Tsar Nicholas II abdicates after angry uprising of the common people; 1934, Mao Tse T'ung sets off on the long march to Shanxi. And when did A Hitler's mad stooges set fire to the Reichstag? Feb 1933. And the tradition of revolutionary events will be repeated at St Wilfrid's parish church at the nuptial Mass and wedding of Arthur Trubshaw (Wing Commander, Retd) and Miss Kitty Cadwallader (Master of Foxhounds).

Jake had decided to sign off by having the hapless 'Where are we?' Trubshaw marry the equally clueless 'Who are you?' Cadwallader and, as so often, used comic fantasy to make a political point:

When we all rise, this February, and march upon Whitehall to overturn the establishment, they will be at our head and we will install 'Where are we?' and 'Who are you?' in the marital bed in Downing Street. And who will know the difference?

He had not quite finished with the *Catholic Herald* – he wrote some book reviews a few months later – but he never returned to 'View from the Pew', and his days as a columnist were over. Perhaps Cristina Odone was right. There was a limit as to how much inspiration he could find in the face of a weekly deadline.

It is sad, but inevitable, perhaps, that Jake's late career as a newspaper columnist is largely forgotten. Over the course of seven years his writing was entertaining, imaginative, opinionated, thought-provoking and highly original, but the nature of the medium meant that it was all destined for the dustbin.

Given how little he valued his own talent, it is even sadder to think that he would probably not have wanted it any other way.

Jake Thackray,
25, Monnow Street,
MONMOUTH,
np5 3ef,

0600 71 6869.

Dear Ed. Odone,

A bloke called James from your office rang to ask if I'd immediately write 50 to 60 words about unrequited love for your paper for St.Valentine's day.

He also said that I would not be paid for this.

Here are exactly 60 unpaid for words as asked and I think I've got them dead right so would you ask your sub-editors to please not shag them up.

If you do not like the words as they are then you've got a wastepaper basket. Also , Odone - you Catholic Heralders, you of all people, should, don't you think, at least offer to pay us others for what you ask us to do whether you like it or not and whether we want it or not. Tell this James, Cristina, all about what happens to flying doughnuts.

Regards and God Bless and so on.

" Feb.14, 1779 Captain Cook was stabbed to death in the Sandwich Islands.Feb.14, 1929 Bugsy Moran and 7 other gangsters were massacred in a garage in Chicago.Feb.14,1943 1,400 Jews and gypsies were incinerated in camps in Poland. This St. Valentine, bishop and martyr bloke probably never existed.The other people did exist, once. So why the love letters on Feb.14,eh?"

'Exactly 60 unpaid for words.'
Jake's letter to the *Catholic Herald*, February 1995.   *Thackray family*

Don't Come and Find Me

Think on me kindly,
But don't come and find me.
I'm lost, I've lost heart
And eyes are both crossed,
Now that she's gone,
Now she's gone.

— Jake Thackray, 'The Black Swan', 1967

One thing that made Jake's columns in the 1990s so distinctive was his ability to create a vividly imagined, entertaining, fantasy version of his life. The reality, however, was very different.

Faced with many problems stemming from his alcohol dependency, he was a man in denial, rarely opening up about his feelings, even to close friends, and determinedly keeping up appearances.

On visits to Hillside, Bob and Sue Haverly still found themselves sitting round the table, playing games, as they had always done. 'Once it became apparent that things were really off the rails,' says Sue, 'I remember thinking that games played a huge part in evading a conversation getting to a point where you had to start talking about yourself. You could talk about politics, you could talk about literature, you could talk about funny things that happened, which there were a lot of – all those things you can hide behind, but you never, ever, ever talked about anything personal.'

Jake's problems became harder to hide in May 1990, when he and Sheila separated. For years she had done her best to support him, but the extreme pressures on their relationship caused by his illness and financial problems had proved too much to bear. She would later tell him plainly in a letter: 'You foundered us on the rocks'. Having held on, it seems, until their children were adults, she applied for a legal separation and, although she never divorced him,[1] the marriage was effectively over. Faced with such a devastating loss, it seems that Jake could not bring himself to admit the truth. He avoided telling people about the separation and, when meeting friends, would simply say that Sheila was fine, but couldn't make it. In the fantasies of his newspaper columns, as in his storytelling on stage, the marriage lived on.

Following the separation, the family's precarious hold on Hillside finally ended, and the house was sold. As Jake's study was cleared, a cache of cheques was discovered, fallen down the back of the desk. It was too late to cash any of them, and one was for £1,600. Sheila was understandably very upset.

With little money, Jake moved into rented accommodation and, by 1991, resided in a small flat above a greengrocer's on the high street in Monmouth, where he remained for the next few years. Here he kept the world at arm's length: the flat, like discussion of his marriage, was out of bounds to friends, whom he would arrange to meet on a bench, or in a café or pub.

His marriage wasn't the only relationship to end in the early 1990s: he parted company with Acorn Entertainments too. After more than a decade, his unreliability, lack of communication and anarchic approach to business matters had exhausted Jim McPhee's patience and pushed their friendship to the limit; indeed, the agent hadn't been paid any commission for five years. But Jake, facing financial ruin, seems to have been out of touch with the reality of the situation, even complaining that he was the one owed money. In this sorry situation their mutual friend, Harvey Andrews, has immense sympathy for the agent: 'Jim worked so hard to help Jake. He did everything for him, and covered up for him. Jim was an angel, a brilliant guy.' With no prospect of Jake settling his debt, in March 1993 Acorn Entertainments terminated their relationship 'with great regret'. For months, Jake could not accept the decision and the reasons for it, but there was no going back.

His life was in crisis. In a remarkable turn of events, given his antipathy towards London-centric show business, he at one point swallowed his pride and wrote to Alex Armitage at Noel Gay, admitting he had made a mess of things and asking for help: he wanted to return to the agency. Alex remembers taking soundings from people who knew Jake: 'Every single one said, "Don't touch it with a barge pole". That was probably good advice, but it was also quite sad advice.'

The request was politely turned down.

And so, professionally, that was that. For the first time in his career, Jake was on his own. In desperate need of bookings, but with no agent or telephone, he now had to write to promoters personally. When he contacted the BBC in Manchester, seeking work on Radio 1, he was told that his music was now out of step with the output of the station, but offered help with approaches to Radio 2 and Radio 4.[2] His financial problems were so acute that he was reduced to asking friends for loans. Full of sympathy for his plight, but recognising the serious personal problems which lay behind it, some made a gift of the money and were much surprised when, a couple of years later, he insisted on repaying them.

During this time, with all in such disarray, the Catholic Church stepped into the breach.

Father David Smith, priest of St Mary's in Monmouth, drew Jake into the life of the congregation, where he became a much loved, if somewhat eccentric, member of the community. Rather as in his song, 'The Ferryboat', he lurked in the back

row at services, sometimes smoking, and was known to nip out
to the pub for a quick drink during Communion, making it
back in time for the blessing. The children adored him; after
Mass they would gather around him in the street, chatting.

He supported fundraising initiatives, gave impromptu
performances at church parties and offered to help the cleaner,
enthusiastically sweeping the floor, but then disappearing mid-
job when the pub opened. He was even trusted to assist at
Mass and, clearly anxious to get everything right, made
extraordinarily detailed written notes of procedures he had
carried out hundreds of times as an altar boy. He also rang the
Angelus bell, to call people to worship but, ever the anarchist,
didn't keep to the set pattern of nine chimes. 'He used to let it
rip', says Father David. Jake clearly liked the priest greatly and
enjoyed sharing a pint with him, but never allowed him to buy
the round.

His activities in Monmouth extended beyond religion.
In May 1991, he volunteered to be election agent for his friend
Peter Carpenter, standing as the Unitax Party's candidate in a
parliamentary by-election.[3] 'We had a meeting with the
candidates and a group of town Christians,' recalled Peter, 'and
when asked for a prayer for the other candidates, Jake said,
"Bless thy lambs and make them meat for thy kingdom. Mince
them!"' Despite their best efforts, Peter secured 164 votes, half
the number of the Monster Raving Loony Party, but narrowly
beating Lindi St Clair, the Corrective Party candidate.

In 1993, Jake entered new musical territory when he
appeared on stage in the chorus for Monmouth Operatic
Society's amateur production of Gilbert & Sullivan's *Iolanthe*.
Geoff Webb, a founding member of the group, recalls that he
was keen to take part but, as a solo performer, anxious about
singing with other people. His worries were misplaced. 'He was
very good and enjoyed it immensely,' says Geoff. 'There's a
famous scene in the show where the leading man has to
implore a very grand parade of Peers of the Realm, bedecked

in ermine and coronets. The Peers, played by the chorus, all look down on him with total indifference and turn their back on him, accompanied by some very pompous martial music. When it came to the final performance, the leading man approached Jake who, with a very theatrical swirl, raised his cloak to just below his nose, rather like Bella Lugosi playing Dracula, and, in his inimitable bass voice, at full volume exclaimed "Bugger off!" Needless to say, it brought the house down.'

Jake also joined creative writing groups in Monmouth and Abergavenny. He was at the inaugural meeting of the Monmouth group in 1994 and was an active member for a year. In preparation for their monthly gatherings everyone had to write a poem on a set theme. He responded with hilarious and ingenious writing about his life in the town. Particularly memorable was a poem about a visit to Woolworths, which he made into a comic drama. 'I think that he was an inveterate entertainer really, and that when he came to the writers' group, he partly came to entertain us,' says Michael Mortimer, the group's founder.

It wasn't only Jake's writing that made an impression with the group. He turned up to one meeting with a huge smear of ash on his face, still there from the previous week's Ash Wednesday service. He seemed to Michael to be very proud of it, and to have known that it would invite comment.

Whilst he may have drawn attention to his faith in this way, in other respects Michael found his modesty striking: 'He was a very humble man. There was no aura of the celebrity about him at all. That was completely missing.' The group included a university lecturer in creative writing who treated the subject very seriously, and in the presence of such company Jake was very self-deprecating: 'He would say something along the lines of, "I just write doggerel. I'm not anything like you guys with your creative writing and your expert English. I'm just a doggerel writer."' As so often, dismissive of his talent.

Later in the decade, he got involved with Monmouth's Amnesty International group, and also attended a course of local history lectures, where Geoff Webb from the Operatic Society observed a curious pattern of behaviour: 'Jake would come in before the lecture started, obviously having visited a local pub or two, and setting himself down in the front row he would produce a tape recorder. As soon as the lecture started, he would switch on the recorder, and a few minutes later the faint sound of snoring would be heard, and he would sleep all the way through. At the end, he would switch off the recorder, wish us all goodnight and depart. This happened for the whole ten weeks of the series.'

His life revolved around Monmouth and his favourite pubs, the Punch House and Gatehouse, where, whatever his mood, he kept people endlessly entertained with his sharp, dry wit. On one occasion he set a word-association game going which had the entire pub roaring with laughter. At the Gatehouse he met with other members of the Arthur Peabody Club, a convivial group, dedicated to joke-telling.[4] He was a familiar face around the town, where he was clearly relieved to be simply Jake, a member of the community, rather than Jake Thackray, The Television Entertainer.

During these years he became less and less visible to the general public, for whom his TV and radio appearances were becoming a distant memory. And he had no desire whatsoever to change this. When Alan Franks, a feature writer at *The Times*, wrote to him in the early 1990s, seeking an interview, his letter remained unanswered for three years. When Jake eventually replied, it wasn't to acknowledge the request or the delay, but to invite him to Monmouth to meet Peter Carpenter and write a piece about the berm house. Alan accepted the invitation and an article was published. Thereafter, he became good friends with Jake, and even persuaded him to sing 'Our Dog' and 'Le Cygne Noir' (his French translation of 'The Black Swan') for him. Being a singer-songwriter himself, the journalist and his musical partner, Patty Vetta, sometimes played support for Jake. However, their friendship was founded on an unspoken rule: Alan never again asked for an interview.

Radio broadcaster and lyricist Don Black likewise had no luck when seeking an interview with Jake in 1996 for *I Write the Songs*, a Radio 2 programme celebrating songwriting. 'I tried to track this man down and it wasn't easy,' he told listeners. 'Eventually someone gave me an address in Monmouth, no phone number, so I wrote to him. Two days later I got a call from the great man. I told him I wanted to devote a programme to him on Radio 2. There was a brief silence, and then he said, "You're pulling me plonker!"' [5]

Don did his best to persuade Jake to take part: 'I told him how marvellous I thought he was, and I said that I'm sure he could reach a wider audience if he wanted to.' Despite this recognition, and the obvious financial benefits of greater exposure, Jake point-blank refused to appear, and all Don could do was report their phone conversation to listeners: 'Jake said in a very peculiar accent, something like this: "Oh, I can't be doing with that – all those agents and stuff, and all those preposterous lunches. It's just daft!" He told me that he still performs and that he is writing as much as ever, and promised to send me his latest compositions. He also said that he's got a mortgage and mouths to feed, so he could do with a bit of activity, but not if it involves joining a show-business circus of agents and P.R. people and the like. Oh, Jake! What are we going to do with you?' What the singer had told Don mixed fact and fantasy, but he delivered on a promise, sending him a recently made recording of 'Our Dog'.

It says much that in Jake's final piece of radio work the focus was not on him or his music. In his journalism he had always celebrated Monmouth as a special, unspoilt place, and so when Radio 4 invited him to present an episode of *Going Places* in May 1995 and to choose somewhere to take listeners, he picked the town which had accepted him as one of its own.

In the programme he ensured that it was the people of Monmouth who took centre stage.

The *Going Places* production team had tracked down the elusive singer thanks to the fact that he had a new agent. Throughout 1993 he had struggled on alone, as he tried in vain to persuade Jim McPhee to take him back. Then, in November 1993, after a concert in Worcestershire, he stayed at the house of the promoter, Chris Jaeger, and they talked into the night. 'Jake was always on a high after concerts, sociable and talkative,' says Chris. 'We drank a lot and he revealed that he had recently split with Jim McPhee.' Having just started his own agency, Chris offered to represent him, but Jake turned him down flat, declaring, 'No, no, Jaego. I'm done with agency.' Months later, however, came a change of heart. Out of the blue, Chris's phone rang: 'I had a call from the Theatre Royal in Newcastle, asking to book Jake. I asked them why they were ringing me and they said, "He told us you are his agent."' This was the unorthodox beginning of a successful association which would be unusual in another way, too: the two men never had a written contract.

Chris soon realised three things about his new client: he was broke, hopeless with his finances, and had lots of people pursuing him for money. Faced with this reality, he offered to help. He spent two days getting Jake organised, lent him £500 and constructed a debt repayment plan. He even contacted his creditors to explain the arrangement. For the plan to work, it required Jake to stop taking cash payments at gigs and Chris asked that all the money came to his agency, so that he could ensure the creditors were paid. But sensible as this was, getting Jake to stick to the arrangement proved difficult: old habits would die hard.

Nevertheless, with Chris's support, his performing career stayed on a relatively even keel for several years. He made it to most gigs, helped greatly by the fact that, whenever possible, his agent drove him. If he didn't feel up to performing, he would tell Chris he didn't feel well. The agent would then contact the venue and, finding most people very forgiving, re-schedule the booking: 'Jake was a very loveable bloke. He had an air of vulnerability, so you just wanted to hug him. I have rarely met a man whom people loved so much, warts and all.'

Jake's approach to performance was now resolutely free of 'frig'. When his vocal range dropped and he could no longer reach the high notes with confidence, he simply tuned his battered guitar down several semi-tones and, where necessary, sang the songs differently. His sound checks were memorable for their brevity: he walked up to the mic, said 'Hello... thank you', and then walked off again, without bothering to check the guitar level, to the bemusement of sound engineers. If the audience was small, he ignored the p.a. and stage, and seated people around him. He usually dressed in a baggy jumper rather than a suit, and any sense of separation between him and the audience was completely removed. Indeed, when he appeared at the Wurzel Bush Folk Club in 1995, and someone knocked over a pint during one of the floor spots, to everyone's amazement it was Jake who got a mop and bucket and cleaned the floor.[6]

His informality could be positively wilful, as Chris remembers from a concert in 1994 at The Stables, Johnny Dankworth and Cleo Laine's venue in Milton Keynes: 'There was a fantastic gig at The Stables, the silver anniversary of the venue, broadcast by the BBC. There were many acts on the bill and Jake had been allocated time to do two or three of his songs, when he suddenly decided, during the live broadcast, to do a couple of songs in French. The BBC people were amazed!'[7]

It was en route to this concert that Chris realised the extent of Jake's illness, when he caught him drinking at the motorway services; up until this point the singer had managed to conceal his addiction from him and, when questioned about it, denied he had a problem. As the years went by, however, his condition worsened, and he missed many more gigs. His agent also saw another distressing change: 'Jake lost the ability to recognise that he was unable to perform.' His pace slowed, words were regularly forgotten, songs were repeated. When his old friends Colin and Carol Evans saw the extent of his decline at a concert in Cardiff, they were heartbroken. Whenever Chris wasn't at a concert, he would contact the venue afterwards to ask how it had gone. Increasingly, he would hear, 'Jake was OK in the first half but not so good in the second.' Venues began to say that they did not want to re-book him.

Despite all this, Jake was still capable of some great performances. 'When he was on form he was one of the funniest performers you could wish to see,' says Chris. 'He had superb timing and could have done anecdotal stand-up and been one of the greats.' Indeed, his storytelling could reduce audiences to tears of laughter.[8] He would talk more than ever on stage, and regularly told a long joke about the Battle of Hastings, supposedly to prove that he couldn't tell jokes.[9] Consequently, he would sing fewer songs and, occasionally, when his voice wasn't up to it, no songs at all, but still send audiences away happy, having entertained them all evening with his stories.

As Alex Armitage observes, Jake was always at his best when at his most comfortable. This was the case at Nettlebed Folk Club, where he appeared six times between 1989 and 1996, drawing audiences of a hundred or so. Over time, the relationship changed. 'When we first booked him we did so because he was one of the country's top folk performers, as well as being a TV personality,' says Mike Sanderson, organiser of the club's programme. 'Later, we booked him because he was Jake, one of the club's favourites. Finally, it was a question of supporting him because we knew he was having a hard time and we think he appreciated that.' Nevertheless, in 1995 and 1996, Mike still had to cajole him into accepting the booking by making everything as easy as possible for him, sorting out train times, car transfers and a bed for the night, and ensuring he was met on the platform. Jake never let the club down, which Mike believes is down to the fact that he knew he was in safe hands and would get a good audience. Even so, his lack of communication was nerve-jangling, and Mike had to write to him shortly before each concert to check that he was still coming. Finally, the night before the gig, Jake would phone from a call box to confirm arrangements.

In 1996, he took one of his last big steps outside his comfort zone. Bleddyn Richards, a friend who was helping to organise Monmouth Festival, had eventually persuaded him to go on the bill. However, with a very large audience in prospect, the inevitable happened. 'He was scheduled to play on the Wednesday evening and, of course, didn't turn up,' says Bleddyn. 'Everybody was quite phlegmatic about it, the other performers covered, everything was okay.' But that was not the end of the matter: 'On Friday evening, Jake just suddenly strolled round to the side of the stage and said, "Look, I'm terribly sorry, terribly sorry. I got tied up."' In the midst of these profuse apologies the stage manager, Dick Arkell, arrived, said nothing about Jake's non-appearance, and made a suggestion: 'Listen, I've got a spare ten minutes. Do you want to go on and do a couple of numbers?' Bleddyn recalls how they then trumped the singer's final card: 'Jake brought in his masterstroke: "I haven't got a guitar." And Dick said, "Well, funnily enough, I've got one here." So I pulled him, Dick pushed him, we got him on stage, I introduced him, and he was on for about 40 minutes. Because there were no expectations, there was no build-up, there was nothing, he just went on and did it. And he had a lovely smile on his face when he came off, and we had about 2,000 people who were totally delighted.'[10]

At other times when Jake couldn't face performing, Chris Jaeger found him fabricating weird and wonderful excuses, just as he had done for his previous agents. One evening in the mid-1990s, when he was due to perform a sell-out concert at a 500-seater venue in London, his agent received a call: 'Jaego, I won't be able to make the gig tonight. I've been involved in an accident. I've been knocked down by a taxi at Paddington Station and my leg has been broken. I will have to go to hospital.' Chris knew this wasn't true – his phone display showed Jake was calling from Monmouth – so asked for more details. 'It's true,' said Jake. 'Alan [Williams] is with me. He also got knocked down and he has a broken leg too.' He hadn't worked with Alan for years, and when his agent saw Jake a few days later, there was clearly no problem with his leg. Chris was left wondering whether the singer lived in a fantasy world.

Some friends came to suspect that Jake's self-destructive behaviour was about more than just self-doubt: his attitude bordered on self-loathing, and he appeared resentful of his own accomplishments. Rick Irons wonders if his success led him to believe that he was betraying his own socialist principles: 'It got to the stage where you believed he really didn't want to be successful. It used to drive me nuts. He had all this talent, yet seemed to want to self-destruct.' Alan Franks came to the same conclusion: 'Jake was contemptuous of any esteem, fame or fortune, and I started to wonder if he was actively self-sabotaging.' It was an attitude which would only have been reinforced by his long friendship with, and regard for, Alex Glasgow, a highly principled man who refused to appear on TV variety shows, declaring 'I'm not a bloody commodity!'[11]

Whatever the reason, the reality was that, by the late 1990s, Jake was more and more reluctant to play for paying audiences. 'Towards the end of his life, he didn't do too many gigs,' says Bleddyn Richards. 'He wasn't very keen on it. I don't think it was that he didn't want to perform, I think it was more a question of other people's expectations. He didn't want to disappoint anybody. He wasn't a young man, and he couldn't get up and do the two to three-hour sets that he used to do.'

Singing for friends, however, was different. 'Afternoon parties, if there was no pressure, he would just pick up the guitar and entertain everybody, and it would be fantastic,' recalls Bleddyn. Once, when a power cut interrupted a band performing at a birthday party at the Gatehouse, a guitar was thrust into Jake's hands and he saved the situation. Friends remember him giving phenomenal performances at their barbecues, including his hilarious take on Lou Reed's 'Walk on the Wild Side', sung in a strong Yorkshire accent, with the 'do-do-do' refrain replaced with 'ee bah gum'. They begged him to record it, but he dismissed the idea.

The sight of strangers in the audience, however, could make him freeze. At a pub party he was cajoled into giving an impromptu performance and was just about to pick up the guitar when a coach-load of elderly day-trippers filled the room. It gave him the perfect excuse not to play, declaring that the language in his songs might cause offence to these visitors. After reassurance was offered, his objections were overcome and he sang, to the delight of all.

Other parts of his professional life were now a distant memory. When he entered a recording studio for the last time in 1996, it wasn't to make a record, but to tape two songs as a birthday present for his niece. It was done locally, with the help of his friend Phil Auty, a sound engineer at Rockfield Studios.[12] Jake was evidently nervous, but there was no fuss: in under an hour the job was done, and he wasn't after perfection. 'It was just from the heart,' recalls Phil. 'Whatever we got, we got.' These recordings of 'Our Dog' and 'Lah-Di-Dah' (with a couple of new lines) are charming.[13]

By this time his songwriting days were over. Despite his claims that he was still writing, not a single finished song from the 1990s survives. 'Every time I saw Jake he would be working on a song,' says Alan Franks, 'but it wasn't really happening, rather like the actor who always claims to have the next audition.'[14] His normal working method was to type an idea on paper, and then try to develop it through reiteration:

The suffragan bishop of wellington St... Barry 'Pectoral' Cross
Fingered his ring
Barry 'Pectoral' Cross
The suffragan bishop of wellington St
Fingered his ring
Started things

'For a long time Jake claimed to be writing a song called "The Appalling Mr Kinnell", about a man who would turn up in all sorts of historic situations,' says Alan, 'but it never saw the light of day.' The idea was a very old one – the title first appeared in a concert programme in 1977 – and Jake would sing snatches of it to friends on car journeys. In his papers he left a single tantalising verse:

It was Kinnell, in ludicrous costume
Who lunged around the room
Who gobbled up the bride and goosed the groom
Kinnell Kinnell
Who tried to steal their spoons
Who bought them a spitoon
Who joined them on their honeymoon[15]
He would he would he would he would Kinnell
He would, he would he would, 'kin would Kinnell

He made notes for other ideas for the song: 'It's like inviting Robespierre, he's the fingers in the till, the Johnny on your daughter's window-sill'. It undoubtedly had some potential, if only he could have finished it.[16]

Intriguingly, underneath these fragments he listed the titles of his most recent songs: 'The Dirty Mayor' (a.k.a. 'The Dirty Mare', the song he wrote in 1986 for *Start the Week*), 'Borders', 'Tortoise', 'Daddio' ('Lullaby-My-Daddio'), 'Caroline Digby-Pratte 2' (a sequel or updating, perhaps, of the song he recorded in 1969),[17] 'Children's songs 1, 2, 3' (perhaps yet to be written), 'Elizabeth' (probably another name for 'Our Dog') and 'Kinnell'. This looks rather like the tracklisting for an album that never was. Despite his loathing of celebrity and show business, in the late 1990s Jake was fantasising about a comeback. It was something he discussed with Alan Franks; indeed, following a suggestion from Chris Jaeger that he should get some publicity, he briefly became interested in Alan doing a piece about him but, as with many of his ideas at this time, it never happened.

Chris always found it hard to get cross with Jake, despite his behaviour. However, faced with growing unreliability, he eventually felt the need for an ultimatum: he would only keep the singer on his books if he agreed to go into rehab, which the agent would pay for. Confronted with such a stark choice, Jake continued to deny he had a problem. The two men therefore shook hands, hugged and said their goodbyes. Chris told him that, although they were unlikely to work together again, he would always be happy to help. Jake's parting shot was typically upbeat: 'Never say never, Jaego. I just love it when people say it will never happen, because you never know...'

With his illness untreated, no agent and a reputation for being undependable, bookings soon dried up, and by 1998 Jake had disappeared entirely from public view. In July 1999, he wrote to his old friend Ian Watson, explaining the situation: 'I've been out of sight for a couple of years – was ill, but only a little bit, nothing much. But mainly, was disaffected. I'd never liked the stage much and I was turning into a performing man, a real bloody Archie Rice, so cancelled gigs and pulled out for a bit.'[18] Ralph McTell wrote to him expressing his concern and endorsing his withdrawal from live performance: 'I loved to see you work, but then I like your records and I love to read your words. Perhaps if you decide to change things you should remove the stress of performing from the equation for a considerable time... Whatever you decide to do now will take enormous effort, but you are the man.'[19]

While money had never been important to him, Jake was

now in a desperate situation financially. He had little income coming in, aside from royalty payments which, with his records unavailable and only one compilation CD in shops, amounted to only a few hundred pounds a year. Unable to pay his rent, by the summer of 1997 he had no choice but to leave his flat in Monnow Street. He was re-housed in a one-bedroom council flat in Carbonne Close, on the outskirts of Monmouth.

From there, things only got worse. In late 1998, with the inland revenue claiming it was owed tens of thousands of pounds in unpaid tax, he faced the humiliation of bankruptcy. He was required to cash in his pensions to pay creditors, who would also claim his royalties for years to come. The moment which left him most devastated, however, was when bailiffs took away his cherished books. It was a dreadful year, made all the worse by the death of Alan Williams from a brain tumour. He felt the loss enormously.

Nevertheless, by the time he wrote to Ian Watson a year later, he struck an optimistic note about what the future might hold: 'I'll get twenty or so more songs up to snuff and maybe give it another shot, make a record and try out the theatres again, maybe.'

It was not to be. On 25th September 1999, he performed at the wedding of some friends. He wasn't very confident, but his short set went well enough. Afterwards he stayed overnight with a friend, 'Captain' Mark Philips. Next morning, he had disappeared, leaving only a note: 'Gone badger hunting, boss.' When Mark next saw him in the Gatehouse, Jake had both his arms in plaster: walking in St Dial's Wood he had slipped on a steep, muddy bank, put his arms out and broken both wrists.

He would never play the guitar in public again.

Jigget • Sezer

'We wuz ere. Where wuz u?'

'You can play on my guitar,
And sing my songs,
Wear my shirts,
You can even settle my debts.
You can kiss my little missus
If she's willing then, but
No regrets, boys.'
   – 'The Last Will and Testament of Jake Thackray'

The accident in St Dial's Wood in September 1999 ended Jake's performing career; his retreat into longed-for obscurity was almost complete. But although he had faded from view, friends and admirers were to appear who would give new life to his songs and, briefly, Jake himself.

A few days after his accident, two men sat waiting to meet him on a bench outside the Punch House in Monmouth. His old friend Ian Watson, the tenacious and highly effective arts administrator who had first booked him in 1966, and Roger Stennett, a playwright,[1] had a creative project to discuss with him. For a long time Ian had thought Jake's songs could form the basis of a piece of theatre, and during the 1990s had written to him several times about the idea, but without ever getting a response. In 1999, however, he tracked down Jake's new address and tried again. In July, to his surprise and delight, he had finally got a reply. Jake was upbeat about the proposal:

> My Dear Ian, how absobloodylutely spiffing! How on earth did you track down 75 Carbonne? I'm glad you did, it was grand to hear from you. Listen, if your people like the songs and want to use them, well of course. Whatever they'd like, unconditionally, and I'll do whatever and whenever to help, (just so long as they don't use any of the duff ones and God knows there's lots of them) – let me know what's needed, and I'm your man. So, done!

Further communication followed – always by letter, as Jake had no phone. They arranged to meet outside the Punch House at 10.00am on 30th September. As well as discussing the theatrical project, Jake had an ulterior, altruistic, motive: he wanted Ian to meet some musician friends who needed professional advice. He signed off with: 'I'm looking forward to all this, Watso.'

The last day of September arrived. Jake didn't. Ian and Roger spent hours waiting and searched the town centre before eventually getting directions to his flat in Carbonne Close, where there were no signs of life. After returning to the Punch House for lunch, they bought a postcard of the pub, wrote on the back 'We wuz ere. Where wuz u?', and returned to the flat. 'Reaching Jake's place again, I once again tried the strident bell on his entry-phone and once again there was no response,' Ian recalled. 'So I attempted to post the card through his letterbox. The letterbox was sealed shut.'[2] Utterly frustrated in all their attempts to find Jake, they could do no more than put a stamp on the card and post it, before heading for home; for Ian, this meant a six-hour train journey to Scarborough.

Two days later, Ian was surprised to receive an early-morning phone call. It was Jake.

'"I had an accident," he explained, just coherent. "I've broken both hands and was in hospital." He clearly didn't want a long conversation. "Listen, I've got some Catholic friends – you know, bad Catholics: they use naughty words and that. But they've got hands and they can use faxes and things for me." "Can they play your guitar for you?" I asked, and he grunted. "Shurrup! Look, in the course of the next week – no, dammit, by Wednesday, I'll write you a letter." And he was gone.'

Next evening, to Ian's utter amazement, Jake phoned to say he had sent him an email: 'Jake and email? It was a ludicrous juxtaposition. But he had.' Jake was keen to explain properly that week's events:

My Dear Ian, was it you or me who was half-coherent yesterday morning? I bet it was me. They let me loose late Friday and I was full of silly pills which do indeed stop the pain but also uninhibit the mind something wicked. Lovely. Here's how things went with me last week. Sat afternoon I slipped and fell on a sloping woodside, landing on a stone outcrop like a diver, arms outstretched. I thought I had two bad sprains but by Tuesday it was clear that something was up. The hospital told me that both wrists and one arm were compoundedly broken so must stay in and get them mended. I didn't have my address book with me to let you both know. Directory Inquiries couldn't get anything on you or Roger Stennett from what I could tell them. Next best thing was to leave messages at Punch House, Griffin, Dragon, Vine Tree, Robin Hood. Warned all of Carbonne to keep at the window – they know all comings, goings and doings, always. Also asked Maureen who lives overlooking the square to keep an eye open for two loitering blokes. Also her husband Tom to hang around in the pub. In Monmouth, I tell you, this is absolutely failsafe. Nosiness is the town's principle industry. I am astonished that it so comprehensively did fail. I am so very sorry, Ian, that all that time was wasted for both of you. It is my turn now to do something, and I promise to.[3]

Then, silence. For five months Ian couldn't get Jake to engage in any form of communication, until in exasperation he sent him a terse handwritten note: 'If you want me to bugger off and leave you alone, you only have to say so.' This did the trick. In March 2000, Jake replied:

> My Dear Ian, I do apologise, old love. I am the worst of letter answerers and I'm not saying that with any kind of inverted vanity: it is just not on, it is out of order, bad form, bad mannered, *lèse amitié*, and, well, frigging pig ig [ignorant] to neglect letters from old close friends. Please forgive me.[4]

Having restated his support for the project, Jake arranged to meet Ian outside the Punch House on 22nd September 2000. This time he turned up. At first, Ian hardly recognised him: 'It was a rounder, greyer, more jowly – let's face it, much older – face than I remembered. I had to remind myself it was nigh on 15 years since I had seen him, but it was clear those 15 years had not been kind to him.' He had developed a bit of a paunch, and was no longer the dapper man of Ian's memory. 'To be honest, with unbrushed wispy grey hair (and a bald patch), a slightly grubby Bahamas sweatshirt over a shiny tracksuit and well-worn trainers, he was – by comparison with his former standards – just a touch scruffy; not a man who had completely let himself go, just one who wasn't that bothered any more what he looked like.'

Keen to prove his reason for not meeting Ian a year earlier had been genuine, Jake showed him passport booth photos of his arms in plaster casts. He stressed that alcohol had played no part in his accident, which had brought to light another medical issue that had implications for his ability to perform. 'He was discovered to have Dupuytren's Contracture',[5] wrote Ian, 'which could, he said, have been a result of his period of heavy drinking – and explained that while the left hand could cope with the fret of the guitar, he was having to develop a new technique for playing with his right hand, prompting his son Billy, he said, to observe: "Father, it's taken a major accident to get you to play the guitar properly."'

During the meeting Jake barely mentioned Sheila, beyond

briefly acknowledging their estrangement. He discussed with Ian the effects of age, including the fact that he had recently undergone two operations on cataracts which had left him temporarily long-sighted and only able to read and write with difficulty. As they walked down the high street to the river, he held forth about the undistinguished architecture, self-interest of town councillors and scarcity of local produce in the market. Along the way, he stopped to chat to the locals; he was obviously a well-known and well-liked resident.

The main item of business was discussion of Roger Stennett's written proposal for a play using Jake's songs, putting Big Bad Norman centre stage as the hero and narrator:

> ...a man whose Rake's Progress through life will enrapture and enthral. For you see, in the 2001 version, Norman hasn't been in that Convent for all of 15 years. Far from it. 'On the run' he may have been, but that odyssey (whether with Ulysses the dog or not) took him to all four quarters of the Queendom and brought him into contact with a menagerie of characters who he now recalls as he makes an impassioned plea to us, the audience (and effectively his Jury) for leniency. It's as if the question had been asked "Have you anything to say in your defence before we sentence you?" And back came the answer "Yes, your Honour... Bloody loads". For Norman claims to be a reformed character, and his Everyman journey through the land these past 15 years is a modern Morality play...[6]

Digesting these ideas the night before the meeting, Jake put down his thoughts in a letter which he handed to Ian as he left. He was immensely enthusiastic about the proposal, and also relieved that there was no suggestion that the musical should focus on him: 'I do not like the *Jacques Brel is Alive and Well and Living in Hunslet* thing,[7] I really do not. That was a musical about Brel based on his songs and it was an awful thing. Let's keep the J Thackray thing out of it, eh?' He stressed that he saw the playwright as the senior creative partner in the enterprise: 'So it will be Roger's play, with my music and my characters; but mainly it will be Roger's play.'

The project had energised him and he was brimming with ideas:

> Stennett will write a play of his own. It'll be based on the characters in the songs and they will inhabit their world. Brought to life by Stennett's tale these people will inhabit and light up their/his world. It could take, perhaps, the shape of a morality play; it could perhaps have a revue, cabaret, episodic format... maybe it could have an overall structure – a courtroom setting round it, or some other structure; it would need minimum stage sets. It would also be a proper entertainment, that is, a good show. Punters will have to be made to laugh a great deal and cry a lot, hiss and boo and clap, and so on. Good, lasting theatrical stuff. And commercial.

Despite his own chaotic handling of business matters, Jake offered humorous praise for Roger's attention to detail regarding the need for a formal agreement from the outset:

> Also, I think Stennett says this: It'll have to be a proper business job – Steson, Watray and Thacknet form a company; impeccable business plan; outline, draft scripts... all legal stuff wound up, copyrights, small prints, contracts, agreements all piss tight. Also this all to be an ensemble, egalitarian thing.
>
> I like all this Stennett way of seeing things very much and I'd like to join in, yes please.

For all his enthusiasm, however, he felt he needed to explain his reservations about the theatre, the stage and actors:

> I've only sometimes been bitten by the theatre. I go to it often, and with very serious intent, but I've never been able to suspend my 'disbelief for the moment which constitutes poetic faith'. I got the poetic faith alright, Samuel Coleridge baby,

but the only thing I can usually manage to suspend in the theatre is the suspension of embarrassment, or the suspension of heckling or the suspension of jumping on the stage and kicking the actor up the nuts. I don't like actors. I don't mean luvvies or when-I-was-ins. I simply do not feel at all easy with the stage thing and the people who get up on it. But I am willing to work at this because I do love making up songs. Also I like knocking about with Ian Watson.

Signing off, his attitude towards his meticulously crafted songs was both generous and revealing:

Sounds great fun and larks. Yes, also this – I'm not one bit touchy about the songs, you can knock 'em around as much as you want.

Jake was keen to be given a clear role and offered to write new songs, if needed.

'This eagerness to get to work was a recurrent theme in our conversation,' Ian said. 'I delivered the message I had promised to pass on from Victor Lewis-Smith, to the effect that, as soon as he was ready with some new songs, Victor could guarantee him a one-hour show on BBC2 with a full orchestra...[8] What he really wanted to do was to go into one of Monmouth's recording studios with some musicians and record a new independent album. So had he some new songs ready? I asked. "I've got trunks full of new material," he answered; but there was a hesitancy which suggested to me that much, if not all, of this new material might be half-or-not-quite-finished and that he really needed to be given some specific incentive to work it up to studio-readiness. "What I'd really like," he said, "would be for some local radio producer to say to me: *Jakey baby, can you do us a song on xyz for next Thursday, then another on abc for the Thursday after?*" I said I thought he had decided point songs were not for him many years ago, but it appears it was not point songs that were on his mind: he just wanted someone to show sufficient interest to get him going.'

As the two friends parted, Jake agreed to contact Roger and arrange to meet him.[9] He even suggested that it might be helpful if he got a telephone again. It was a hopeful sign.

Two days later, he was still fired up by the idea of a theatrical project when he met writer and broadcaster Ray Brown, who interviewed him for *Starry, Starry Night*, a short Radio 4 documentary about Georges Brassens's concert at the Sherman Theatre.[10] They got on well and spent hours talking, initially in the pubs of Monmouth and then in Jake's flat where, over bottles of wine, a long interview was recorded. Late that night, Jake took his visitor on a tour of the town in the pouring rain, during which he sang him 'Our Dog' and became keen on the idea of another collaboration. He said Ray should write a radio play about a priest and dog, along the lines of the Father Brown stories, for which he'd provide songs. Next day, he handed over a cassette of 'Our Dog' and several phone conversations followed, but in the end he didn't want to pursue the project.

Ian and Roger were to have greater success, although Jake would still prove elusive. He did indeed get himself back on the telephone, but used three different numbers during the next two years. He also briefly had a mobile, but never answered it. He had an email address, but emails went unacknowledged.

Meanwhile, Roger met up with Jake a couple of times in Monmouth. 'Those meetings were glorious,' he says. 'It was hard to be around him without smiling, and we threw loads of ideas around.' But it was difficult to pin Jake down to anything specific, and he never showed the playwright his fabled 'trunks full of new material'. Even so, he was clearly getting something out of a collaboration which had friendship at its heart: 'Jake was very engaged and enthusiastic. I think it was giving him something that he needed. By then, he wasn't a performing man, as he used to call himself. He didn't see that as being where the next stage of his life was taking him.'

In reality, Jake's life wasn't taking him beyond Monmouth now, and he was content with that. 'I think that for people on the outside, looking on him as a performer,' says Sam Thackray, 'if they're plotting his career as a line on a graph, they see him dropping off the graph. But in his life he experienced the slower decline everybody goes through when they've passed their natural peak. So as a performer and a celebrity there was a massive drop-off, but as a man he found a stable *modus operandi*. He loved Monmouth and he loved the people there; he liked the church and being involved with Amnesty International, and he liked interacting with people. And there was still some connection with family. We all still stayed in touch.' Sam also makes clear that Jake never stopped being Jake: 'I don't think he ever lost his fascination with language, writing and observing people. That was always a real driver for him, his interest in people and characters.' Ray Brown concurs: 'The intelligence and unique perceptions and wordplay, characteristic of his best songs, were still present in his everyday life. He wasn't channelling it into songs, but it was still there.' When Jake arrived late once for a meeting with him, hair still dripping from a sponsored swim, he declared: 'Sorry I'm late, but I've been swimming for the Pope.' On another occasion he dared someone to steal a book that had caught his eye on a shelf in a pub. The title and author which had inspired such thoughts of criminality? *Sin* by H.V.S. Eck. *Sin* by Eck.[11]

Jake had little income – all his royalty payments were going to creditors, along with much of the money from the pensions he had been required to cash in. However, his needs were few, other than money for the pub and cigarettes, and he was still inclined to be generous with what he had. In Chris Jaeger's words, he was always 'the original soft touch'. 'The life he was living was not desperate,' says Ray Brown. 'Jake had a realistic assessment of himself. He knew he had messed up his broadcasting career through drink, but he never seemed to be miserable or unnecessarily self-critical. I don't think the bankruptcy was a really important issue to him. He always wanted to be back with Sheila, but he was okay in his skin, with what he was doing with his time.' Sadly, the relationship was beyond repair.

Sam Thackray doesn't think Jake spent time dwelling upon what he might have done differently or better, and his attitude to life remained optimistic: 'When I was with Dad, I would just feel that there was a force-field around him. He was a master, if there was catastrophe – which he may well have helped create, in Leopold Alcocks fashion – if the world was going wrong, and people were panicking and losing their heads, he would be the person you wanted to be next to, because he was totally used to that environment. His forte was operating in chaos. I don't think he worried too much. He was very comfortable with things going extremely wrong because he was so used to it.'

Although his accident meant that there was little prospect of him performing again, even if he had wanted to, he did start practising and re-learning the guitar. However, he admitted to Ray Brown that he would never again be able to play 'On Again! On Again!'. Ray sensed that he was having to find new ways of being Jake Thackray.

At the same time as Ian Watson and Roger Stennett were plotting new ways to give life to his songs, a group of fans was seeking to rescue his recordings from oblivion.[12] Only one compilation CD of Jake's music was available, and this group, working as The Jake Thackray Project, was intent on changing that. It planned to release, under licence, a limited edition double CD containing all the songs that were unavailable, in the hope that this would raise awareness of Jake's work and persuade EMI to reissue material. All the legwork was done by volunteers and, with no prospect of the record company making the master tapes available, a call went out to fans to share their vinyl and tapes so that the cleanest copies could be transferred to CD.

Jake's music was being revived through the actions of his fans, rather than the industry he loathed, and he would have had it no other way. Even on its limited run of 200 copies, the Jake Thackray Project CD would generate more than £2,000 for him, and the group was keen for him to receive this money. Ian had explained to Jake that EMI wanted to charge the group £500 for the licence: 'He phoned immediately to say that he was outraged by EMI's action and that he would intervene to have the fee waived, as he was only too delighted that people still wanted to hear the songs. He later claimed to have made the call to EMI: EMI denied it and levied the charge.'

By the autumn of 2002, both projects were progressing well and it was agreed that a joint meeting with Jake was in order. 1.00pm on 17th October at the King's Head in Monmouth was pencilled in. Initially Ian and Roger were to be joined by Sarah Willans from the Jake Thackray Project and Victor Lewis-Smith, but getting Jake to confirm the date proved difficult, so the radio producer withdrew, not wishing to risk a wasted day if he didn't turn up. Finally, the day before the meeting, Jake confirmed he would be there.

Whilst he was in good spirits, he revealed at the outset, 'I've been a bit poorly, but I'm fit as a butcher's dog'. Ian noticed the physical changes since they met two years earlier. 'The face was even more jowly than when last I saw it, and there was a slackness to the right-hand side of the face which – I pondered later – could perhaps have suggested a bit of a stroke. There was also a yellowing, which I put down at the time to nicotine staining, but was more likely jaundice, I supposed when I gave it thought. And the voice, whilst totally recognisable, was thinner and failed at moments: it was quite unthinkable that it could cope any longer with a Jake Thackray song – though hopefully this might be a passing phase following illness and the voice would in time be restored to its former strength. All this said, the man stood ramrod straight as ever and when he walked, he walked strongly as though fit for a ten-mile hike.'

Photos taken on the day show how much he had changed over the years: for anyone who had last seen him on television two decades earlier, Jake was almost unrecognisable. However, Ian thought that the decline was only physical. 'The mind was sharp – significantly sharper than at our last meeting,' he said, 'when he had apologised for the fact that the brain cells were taking longer to make the necessary connections: today, it seemed that the memory was clear and the wit spontaneous. He had read Roger's outline paper on *Sister Josephine Kicks the Habit* [the title of the new play] and was excited. "I'm right up for this," he assured me, and went on to outline the sort of contribution he might make, from writing to new songs to jumping in with plotting ideas if Roger hit a wall at any stage.'

Sarah Willans had brought with her a stack of messages of goodwill from fans, as well as a cake, and explained that Jake would soon receive a substantial cheque – his share of the proceeds from the limited edition CDs which would be issued before Christmas. His immediate, entirely predictable response was that he wanted nothing to do with the money, but she insisted that it was his to do with as he wished, even if he gave it all away to charity.

Overcome by this, and with tears in his eyes, he declared: 'All this attention. I'm not sure I'm good enough. I'm not sure I can do it.' When the group sought to reassure him, saying that people simply wanted to show their thanks for all the pleasure his songs had brought, he protested, declaring that some of his songs were really awful. 'It was a line which I had never heard from him before and it caught us all by surprise,' recalled Ian. But Jake was insistent: 'I shall think less of you unless you agree that there was some really lousy stuff amongst it.' Challenged to name one poor song, he picked 'The Lodger', which left Ian feeling astonished and appalled that he was disowning such a superbly crafted, hilarious piece of writing. Eventually, clearly flummoxed that his low opinion of his work was not shared by others, Jake declared, 'Well, I'm whelmed!', before agreeing to sign the inlay cards for the entire 200 edition of CDs when Sarah brought them to Monmouth in a few weeks.

Conversation then turned to the creation of the book for *Sister Josephine Kicks the Habit*. As Roger wanted to get as many of Jake's ideas as possible at the outset, it was agreed that he would spend a day with him and use part of the time to go through his new songs, to see which might be suitable for the show. As for the music, Jake stated that he wanted them to find a 'shit-hot' musical director, and preferred to have his songs accompanied by two guitars and a bass.

As for his availability for meetings with Roger, Jake had some news: he planned shortly to buy a house in France so that he could live near his sister-in-law and her children, while keeping on his flat in Monmouth for visits. Although this was taken at face value by everyone present, what he said didn't connect with the realities of his situation. He had no money to buy a house, let alone run two properties, and he certainly wouldn't have been allowed to keep on his council flat.[13]

What felt like a productive meeting drew to a close and Jake left Ian, Roger and Sarah to their lunch, saying that he wanted to return home to sit, think and write. Everyone said their farewells and vowed to be in touch soon about the various projects. 'As Jake strode off strongly down towards the bridge,' wrote Ian, 'the three of us went back in for lunch feeling that we'd made good progress, but also clear that we needed to push ahead quickly and not allow Jake to fall back out of the loop.'

Ian was conscious that Jake may have found the meeting overwhelming: 'Whatever he had been expecting when we met, it hadn't been a stack of messages bearing witness to abiding respect and affection, the promise of a substantial cheque for songs which he long since gave up singing or, perhaps most of all, a cake specially baked.' Mindful of this, everybody gave him some breathing space. Ian dropped him a line to say how good it had been to see him, and it was several weeks before Roger and Sarah tried to phone Jake to arrange a visit. Neither got through and their voicemail messages went unanswered. 'Soon Roger reported that the answering machine had no outgoing message on it, just a recording of some very laboured breathing and perhaps a groan before the tone,' recalled Ian. Worried, he wrote to Jake in late November, expressing his concern for him and telling him that *Sister Josephine Kicks the Habit* was now pencilled in for a two-week workshop with actors at the Theatre Royal, York, in April 2003; with such a tight timetable, Roger urgently needed to push on with the writing, and he was keen to have Jake's input. The playwright wrote along similar lines in December. Both men wondered whether Jake was in hospital, or perhaps in France.

A few weeks before Christmas, Ian tried phoning Jake once again and, at last, he picked up, as Ian recounted: '"Jake!" I almost yelled. "How are you?" "Not awfully well, old pal," he struggled to say, in a very thin, reedy voice. "I'll give you a ring tomorrow." And the phone went dead.'

He did not phone. His answering machine reverted to the laboured breathing and no message.

Ian never heard from Jake again.

Jigget • Akker

Gather a Bud or Two for Jake

'Death, where is thy victory?
Grave, where is thy sting?
When I snuff it bury me quickly,
Then let carousals begin.'
         – 'The Last Will and Testament of Jake Thackray'

The weeks passed. Jake's silence continued. Might he be in hospital, Ian wondered, or had he perhaps travelled to France for Christmas to see his brother's family? There was nothing he could do but wait and worry about his old friend.

Then, on 27th December, the phone rang. But it wasn't Jake. It was Ray Brown, delivering some devastating news: 'Have you heard? Jake's died. It's just been on the radio.'

On Christmas Eve, Sam Thackray had called in at Carbonne Close to collect his father and take him to a festive drinks party which his friend Peter Carpenter held every year at the berm house. Reaching the flat, he had found the front door ajar, but this was not unusual – Jake had never been great with locks. Sam pushed the door open and called to his father. He then saw his body, lying in the hallway, cold and lifeless. Jake had suffered a heart attack and had been dead for hours.[1] He was 64 years old.

His family mourned in private that Christmas, before

making the news public. Following an announcement on Radio 4's *Today* programme on 27th December, an excerpt from 'The Bull' was played. Someone on the production team clearly knew Jake and his songs very well, and the singer would doubtless have been pleased by the decision to broadcast his brilliant, offensive anthem for anarchists, rather than the comedic 'Sister Josephine'. He had allowed himself little pride in his songs, but 'The Bull' was an exception.

The obituaries followed. In *The Guardian*, Alan Clayson called him a 'founding father of the English chanson', while John Ezard wrote of a man regarded by many as 'the lost genius of British songwriting'.[2] Asked to pay tribute, orchestrator Brian Fahey, who had brought Jake to Norman Newell's attention 35 years earlier, said, 'He was unique. The strength of his lyrics was breathtaking.'

In *The Independent*, Spencer Leigh drew upon his interviews with Jake to provide illuminating insights. But the most moving obituary was provided by Victor Lewis-Smith, who regretted bitterly his decision not to meet his friend two months earlier. Writing in the *Daily Mirror*, he eloquently summed up what the world had lost, and what many people had missed: 'Jake was a rare example of a British singer-songwriter in the troubadour tradition, a satirist who could be darkly vicious, yet could also write hauntingly romantic songs... Had he been born in France, where the singer/poet tradition has been long established, and where little distinction is made between "serious" and "popular" music, he would have been recognised as a major artistic figure. His own hero, the great troubadour George Brassens, straddled both worlds, and was even elected to the Académie française, for writing songs with immense popular appeal. Brassens acknowledged Jake Thackray was his equal, a true British genius. But sadly, most of us just didn't realise it.'[3]

The funeral took place in Monmouth on 6th January 2003, at St Mary's, the tiny Catholic church that played such an important role during the last years of Jake's life. It proved impossible to fit all the mourners in, and so hundreds of people stood in the street, the service relayed by loudspeaker.

Ralph McTell, Victor Lewis-Smith, Ian Watson, Jasper Carrott and Mike Harding all came to pay their respects, and tributes were delivered by Mike and two of Jake's oldest friends, Ian Gliddon and Don Burton. As the coffin left the church to the strains of 'The Last Will and Testament of Jake Thackray', spontaneous applause broke out.

The wake was held at Jake's favourite pub, the Gatehouse, where, in a nod to his song, Victor Lewis-Smith couldn't resist defying him and primly ordering 'a small port wine'. Others, however, dutifully carried out his wishes: the drink flowed freely, a scratch gypsy swing band, made up of his friends, provided the music, and the carousing continued into the early hours. It was the most fitting of send-offs.

His body was cremated. 'Don't bother with a fancy tomb-stone,' Jake had declared in 'The Last Will and Testament of Jake Thackray', and his wish was respected. A small gravestone was erected in the churchyard at Welsh Newton, a few miles from Monmouth. 'No epitaphs', he had sung. His family begged to differ, and the stone bears the simplest of inscriptions:

'In loving memory of Jake Thackray.
27th February 1938 – 24th December 2002.'

Molly would no doubt have approved of the modesty, but not the wording: she brought him into the world as John Philip, and yet he was being memorialised with a name which was his choice, not hers. But it was Jake, not John Philip, whom the world would remember. Perhaps she would have taken comfort from the gravestone's location which, in accordance with his wishes, stands near the tomb of Sir John Kemble, a seventeenth century Catholic martyr. Jake had held onto the faith in which she brought him up, despite all his shortcomings.

Or perhaps because of them.

Acknowledgements

We are hugely indebted to Jake's family for enabling us to tell his story, and to Sam Thackray and Rick Irons for sharing their memories and dealing so patiently with our questions. We would particularly like to thank Sam for entrusting to us Jake's personal papers, which provided countless valuable insights.

We are grateful to all those we interviewed: Richard Abrahall, Tony Adamthwaite, Harvey Andrews, Dick Arkell, Phil Ault, Kath Baker, Phil Beer, Jon Benns, Ann Drysdale, Alan Franks, Alex Armitage, Grant Baynham, Stefan Bednarczyk, Ray Brown, Paddy Burke, Anne Burton, Peter Carpenter, Jasper Carrott, Robert Cockcroft, Dan Cronin, Michael Day, Vince Dobson, Keith Donovan, Elaine Dowson, Murray Edscer, John Etheridge, Carol Evans, Bradley and Penny Evans, Neil Gaiman, Ian Gliddon, Mark Goodall, Roy Goodman, Mike Harding, Sue Haverly, Carol Hawkins, Janet Henfrey, Allan Hunter, Rick Irons, Chris Jackson, Mike Jackson, Chris Jaeger, Victor Lewis-Smith, Ivan Mansley, Stuart Marlow, Ron Miller, Michael Mortimer, Reg Moulton, Stephen Oldroyd, Lin Pass, 'Captain' Mark Philips, Esther Rantzen, John Ryan, Mike Sanderson, John Sharman, Ian Shaw, Bryan Smith, Father David Smith, Richard Stilgoe, Father Don Stoker, Ed Stringer, Graham Stanley, Roger Stennett, Sam Thackray, Trevor Thewlis, Gaynor Williams,

Huw Williams, Tom Wingate, Malcolm and Mavis Yorke. Sadly, several people we interviewed – Michael Bateson, Philip Bonham-Carter, Don Burton, Terry Grant and Vin Garbutt – passed away before the book was completed.

Thanks are also due to everyone else who shared their memories or provided additional information: Michel Ameline, Ian Anderson, Pam Archer, Michael Bell, Kate Booth, Barbara Bret, Ian Burdon, Emma Chadwick, Sarah Cuddon, Mansel Davies, Arie Euwijk, Geoff Fitchett, Joe Fleming, Maggie Garratt, Terry Gilligan, Mike Green, Peter Furbank, Mick Hickling, Father Austin Hughes, Malcolm Jeffrey, Paul Long, Jamie McCoan, Ken McCoy, Bill McMillan, Jim Marshall, Dr Peter Mills, Benedict Nightingale, Father Barnabas Page, John Peat, Dave Pegg, Gerald Sables, Pete Scott, Derek Sharp, Vic Smith, Bob Tabor, Gordon Tennent, Richard Thompson, Carol Timlin, Geoff and Diane Webb, and Sarah Willans.

We are hugely indebted to the late Ian Watson for the rich insights provided by *A Bud or Two for Jake*, his memoir of Jake's involvement with the *Sister Josephine Kicks the Habit* theatrical project. We hope he would approve of its use here.

Many thanks to all those who gave us permission to quote their writing. We are particularly grateful for the generosity of Louis Barfe, Spencer Leigh, John Morrish and Nigel Schofield, who made available the transcripts of interviews they conducted, and Victor Lewis-Smith and Paul Sparkes, who gave us access to all the interviews for their excellent TV documentary, enabling us to hear the voices of Sheila Thackray and others who have sadly passed away. Thanks are also due to Ed Mortimer for sharing with us his 1998 University of Southampton dissertation, *The Performing Artiste – Authenticity and Artistic Responsibility – with reference to the work of Jake Thackray*; this contained the first research into Jake's early career at the BBC, and led to the unearthing of a number of lost songs.

We are indebted to the staff of numerous archives and

institutions: Robert Finnegan at the Roman Catholic Diocesan Archive in Leeds; the BBC Written Archives Centre; Denise Black and Simon Gurney at BBC Licensing and Synchronisation; Angela Graham at the East Anglia Film Archive; Colin Jackson and Barry Walsh at the Police History Society; Grace Norman and the Development Office staff at Hatfield College, Durham; Michael Stansfield of Durham University Archive; the West Yorkshire Archive Service; David Parsons and the North East Film Archive; the British Film Institute Archive; the staff of the British Library in Boston Spa and London. We are also grateful to the *Catholic Herald* and *Yorkshire Post* for their responses to our queries.

Thank you to all those who gave their kind permission for us to publish photos and other illustrative material, and particularly the Thackray family, Ella Murtha, Alex Armitage, Jake and Vicky Carpenter, Carol Evans, Ian Gliddon, Carol Hawkins, Sue Haverly, Adrian Rushton, Burnley Civic Heritage Trust, Mid Pennine Arts, City Varieties Music Hall, Leeds Heritage Theatres and Whitkirk Arts Guild. We are indebted to Edward Walton, Carol Sparkes and Alan Taylor for their expertise, digitising and restoring photos.

We are delighted that the book features photos by the late Tish Murtha, a gifted photographer who became a friend of Jake's in the late 1970s. Much of her acclaimed work focused on the inequalities faced by working-class communities. Her online archive can be found at www.tishmurtha.co.uk

We thank Leola Music Ltd, Noel Gay Music Company Ltd, Hal Leonard Europe Ltd and Harvey Andrews for giving kind permission for us to print lyrics. We are particularly grateful to Ralph McTell and Stuart Ongley for their support, and for giving us permission to publish the lyrics of the lost songs we discovered. The lyrics for works published by Leola Music Ltd are administered worldwide by SGO Music Publishing Ltd (BMG).

Thanks are due to the Khan family for kindly providing an

impromptu tour of their (and Jake's) home at 90 Burley Lodge Road in July 2021; Pam Archer, for sharing her archive of fan memorabilia; Dr Richard O'Brien of Northumbria University for sharing his thoughts on Jake's poetry; Mark Sturdy and Anthony Teague, for helping us to find 'The Tiswas Song' and 'A Ripe Old Age' respectively; and Ian Shaw, whose wonderful memory and musical ability saved from oblivion 'The Lonely Sikh' and verses of other songs Jake wrote for Intake School.

Our family and friends have patiently supported us throughout the project. Particular thanks are due to Jane, Will, Margaret and Richard Thompson, Carol, Alex and Chris Watterson, Jenny Bourke and Linda Hamilton for all their advice; the book benefitted from the honesty of their feedback.

We are especially grateful to Philip Morey and Jamie McCoan for reading the entire manuscript at different stages in the drafting process, and for making countless astute suggestions. The parts of the book dealing with Brassens and France particularly benefitted from Philip's academic expertise in these areas.

We thank Jody Ineson for her expertise in compiling the index, and Carol Watterson, Jamie McCoan and Steve Sheldon for proof reading. Any remaining errors are our responsibility.

Finally, we wish to thank our editor, Tony Hannan, as well as Phil Caplan and the rest of the team at Scratching Shed Publishing, for enabling us to share Jake's story. We have valued their support and advice, and it has been a joy working with people who, like us, felt that this book was long overdue. Given Jake's antipathy towards London and big business, we have no doubt that he would have approved of our decision to work with a small, independent publishing house in Leeds.

Paul Thompson
John Watterson
June 2022

A Tale of Two Authors

Producing this book has been a labour of love, and the authors are both evangelists for Jake. The musical love affair began decades ago, when they saw him at the height of his powers, taking his chances in front of the punters in the small, beer and smoke-filled clubs where he felt most comfortable.

Following Jake's passing, they each began performing his songs in public, which only deepened their appreciation of his genius. It was through doing so that they met and became friends.

The idea of a biography crystallised in 2014. On the back of his reputation performing as Fake Thackray, John was invited to talk about Jake on Radio 4's *Great Lives*. Cast in the role of expert, he decided he needed to live up to this billing and got down to work. Any lack of experience was made up for in energy, enthusiasm and contacts in the folk music world. From early on, he shared his discoveries with Paul, who at first acted as an occasional research assistant.

The project benefitted enormously from the goodwill and generosity of Jake's friends and colleagues: people wanted his story to be told. Undoubtedly, though, the most important moment came when Sam Thackray offered to help. During a series of meetings with John, he not only shared memories, but also entrusted to him boxes of his father's personal papers, bearing a distinct aroma of tobacco, along with a few cigarette burns. This treasure trove of material provided countless valuable new insights, which became known as 'Tutankhamun moments'.

Over the years, those Tutankhamun moments included the discovery of many long-lost songs, leading to a year-long detour in 2016, with the recording of an album, *The Lost Will and Testament of Jake Thackray*. Other distractions – life and work – also slowed progress; finding time to turn research into words on the page proved challenging. Consequently, in 2020, John invited Paul to take the lead on writing, a task he completed 18 months later, with John all the while providing a critical eye and invaluable feedback.

Completing *Beware of the Bull* has taken its authors on a fascinating voyage of discovery.

They hope its readers feel the same way.

Select Discography
and Other Resources

Albums

The Last Will and Testament of Jake Thackray
(Columbia Records/EMI, 1967)
Jake's Progress (Columbia Records/EMI, 1969)
Live Performance (Columbia Records/EMI, 1971)
Bantam Cock (Columbia Records/EMI, 1972)
The Very Best of Jake Thackray (EMI Records, 1975)
On Again! On Again! (EMI Records, 1977)
Jake Thackray and Songs (Dingle's Records, 1981)

The Last Will and Testament of Jake Thackay (1968) and *Jake's Progress* (1969) were both released in America on Philips Records, with different artwork and sleeve notes from the UK releases.

Singles

Remember Bethlehem/Joseph (Columbia Records/EMI, 1967)
Lah-Di-Dah/The Black Swan (Columbia Records/EMI, 1968)
La Di Da (Tra La La)/Le Cygne Noir (Columbia Records/EMI, 1969). Released in France only.
Country Boy/Old Molly Metcalfe (Columbia Records/EMI, 1972)
On Again! On Again!/The Rain on the Mountainside
(EMI Records, 1977)

Jake's records haven't been reissued on vinyl, but secondhand copies regularly appear on eBay.

Compact Discs

Lah-Di-Dah (EMI 'Ideal' Records compilation, 1991)
The Jake Thackray Project (The Jake Thackray Project
2-CD compilation, 2002)
The Very Best of Jake Thackray (EMI Records compilation, 2003)
The Jake Thackray Collection (HMV/EMI Records compilation,
2003)
Live in Germany (The Jake Thackray Project, 2005)
Live at the Lobster Pot Volume 1 (Lobster Pot Records, 2005)
Live at the Lobster Pot Volume 2 (Lobster Pot Records, 2005)
Jake in a Box (EMI Records 4-CD set, 2006; includes all EMI studio
albums and singles, previously unreleased recordings and demos)
Live Performance (EMI Records, 2006; expanded 2-CD version of
1971 album, featuring the entire Queen Elizabeth Hall concert)

Only *Lah-Di-Dah* and *The Very Best of Jake Thackray* are readily
available new. However, secondhand copies of other CDs appear
now and then on eBay. *The Jake Thackray Collection* and *The Jake
Thackray Project* are the only CDs to feature recordings of 'The Bull'.

Streaming

Jake's EMI recordings are available on streaming platforms, such
as Spotify. *Jake Thackray and Songs* is not currently available on
streaming services (as of August 2022).

Jake's unreleased songs

John Watterson's *The Lost Will and Testament of Jake Thackray*
(Kinnell Records, 2016) features many lost songs referred to in this
book. The authors have plans to release their own recordings of
songs which have been more recently discovered. For more
information, or to buy the album, visit www.fakethackray.com.

Other appearances on record

Les Barker and Friends, *Mrs Ackroyd Superstar!* (Free Reed
Records, 1977). Jake accompanies comic poet Les Barker on 'My
Granny's a Wild Flying Dove', playing the guitar and making a
brief spoken contribution.

Various artists, *Where Would You Rather Be Tonight?* (Sunrise Records, 1986). Jake recorded 'Tortoise' for this album, in aid of a charity supporting people with addiction.

Bodywork (First Night Records, 1988). Jake plays the Heart in this cast recording of Richard Stilgoe's musical.

DVDs

Live at the Unicorn (The Jake Thackray Project, 2009)
This is a limited edition release of amateur video footage of a concert Jake gave in a pub in Somerset in 1989. It is out of print, but copies occasionally appear on eBay.

Jake Thackray and Songs (The Jake Thackray Project, 2014)
The DVD features all Jake's performances from his 1981 BBC2 television series, along with the performances of three of his guest artists – Alex Glasgow, Ralph McTell and Pete Scott. It is currently available to buy, brand new, on eBay and Amazon.

Sister Josephine Kicks the Habit – The Jake Thackray Musical (2005)
A limited edition recording of the final performance of the Jake Thackray musical at Leeds City Varieties in 2005. It is out of print, but copies occasionally appear on eBay.

Jake Thackray at the BBC
The Jake Thackray Project is currently working on the release of a new 2-DVD set of Jake's appearances on *Braden's Week*, *That's Life* and other programmes. The release date will be announced on www.jakethackray.com.

Jake Thackray Website

The Jake Thackray website – www.jakethackray.com – has an abundance of information, including interviews and rare video footage. It also has a discussion forum and news section with details of 'Jakefests' and other events celebrating Jake's music.

Jake on YouTube

Numerous clips of Jake performing, plus one or two programmes.

Books
Jake's Progress (Star Books, 1977)
The book, long since out of print, contains the lyrics of most of the
songs Jake released on record, along with some of the anecdotes
and reflections that featured in his concerts. Second-hand copies
turn up from time to time on eBay.

Academic articles
Dr Colin Evans – *Jake Thackray, Translater and Interpreter of
Brassens*. Published in the French journal *Équivalences* in 1992.
The article is largely theoretical, but includes an analysis of
'Brother Gorilla'. It can be found online at www.persee.fr

Dr Colin Evans – *Brassens, Thackray and the French folk tradition*
Published in *Recorded Sound, British Institute of Recorded Sound*,
1977, the article discusses Jake's adaptation of Brassens' writing in
'Over to Isobel'.

Dr Mark Goodall – *When Jake Met Georges: the Chanson Across the
Channel*, in *The Singer-Songwriter in Europe – Paradigms, Politics
and Place*, edited by Isabelle Marc and Stuart Green (Routledge,
2019). Goodall provides an insightful discussion of Brassens, Jake's
adaptations of his work and the Sherman concert.

Dr Peter Mills – *Jake in a Box: Jake Thackray and the Idea of
Northern Englishness*. This essay offers an interesting cultural
exploration of Jake's writing, although with some details of his life
and career now known to be incorrect. Download the essay at
https://www.leedsbeckett.academia.edu/PeterMills

Dr Richard O'Brien – *'I Know My Clay': Some Musical Afterlives of
Hamlet's Gravedigger*, published in 2020 in *Borrowers and Lenders:
The Journal of Shakespeare and Appropriation* Vol. 13, No. 2, 2020).
Online at https://openjournals.libs.uga.edu/borrowers/article/view/2110/2617

Appendix I:
Long-lost Lyrics

Songs written for musicals at Intake School

The Lonely Sikh (1966)
Sung to the tune of 'La Complainte des Filles de Joie'
by Georges Brassens.

I am just a lonely Sikh, I am just a lonely Sikh,
I need a wife, my life is bleak, need a wife, my life is bleak,
But nobody fancies romance with me, romance with me,
romance with me,
Nobody fancies romance with me.

If I ever found a wife, if I ever found a wife
Who'd wash my socks the rest of my life,
wash my socks the rest of my life,
I'd smother my missus in kisses, in kisses, in kisses,
I'd smother my missus in kisses.

If I found a wife who could, if I found a wife who could,
Make a steak and kidney pud, make a steak and kidney pud,
I'd buy her a fridge and a bingo hall, a bingo hall, a bingo hall,
I'd buy her a fridge and a bingo hall.

I love you in every way, I love you in every way,
If you would honour and obey, you would honour and obey,
And fetch my tea in the morning, the morning, the morning,
Fetch in my tea in the morning.

The Lost Property Shop song (1966)

L.O.S.T.
P.R.O.P.
E.R.T.Y.
It's the lost property shop...
If you've left your luggage on the train,
Come around to us and claim it back again.
There's some things that defy belief:
Grand pianos and old false teeth.
It's quite amazing just what some people lose:
Billiard balls and snooker cues.
So...if...you...
Lost a Cheshire cheese,
Please come right away,
It's starting to walk
And it gets bigger every day.

The Bus Conductor's song (1966)

We are the crew of a double-decker bus.
If you want to get somewhere you may depend on us.
Driving round the town all day is simply glorious,
With a 'Ding! Ding!'
'Honk! Honk!'
'Ding! Ding! Honky!'
Yes, it's simply glorious.

We like to give our passengers a pleasant ride around.*
At going slow we pride ourselves, we really do excel.
But if you're sprinting after us we drive like merry...**

With a 'Ding! Ding!'
'Honk! Honk!'
'Ding! Ding! Honky!'
As we drive away like...**

The first line of the second verse is lost. This is actually the first line of the lost third verse.

**The pupils weren't allowed to sing the word 'hell' – it was deemed inappropriate.*

Dog Song (I was a Prince) (1966)

I was a prince,
Then things went wrong,
And ever since
I've been a mongrel.
A magic spell
Changed things around,
Changed me as well,
Into a hound.
I don't sing true,
I don't sing false.
All I can do
Now is my dog waltz.
Around and around
...
Around and around
Slow pirouette.

We are the Royal Knockers-up (1966)
(*Chorus only*)
We are the royal knockers-up,
We are always hail and hearty.
If she is snoring,
We have to break the door in:
We are the royal waking party.

Radio and television commissions

Radio Leeds opening song (1968)
Sung to the tune of 'Miss World'.

If you can't get a sound out of Radio Leeds,
Well, it's not that your set is decrepit;
And you're not going deaf,
It's on VHF,
And there's not many radios can get it.
But come down to Radio Leeds,
Just walk in, you're welcome to enter.
They've a radio car and a budgerigar
In a fish tank in the radio centre.
Well, yes, tonight's the night,
It's frightfully likely
And it's toe-nail-bitingly exciting.
Tonight's the night when we're invited
To cock up our ears to Radio Leeds,
Radio, Radio Leeds.

God Bless Newcastle Fest (1969)

I've made the journey,
Up to the festival
Of arts at Newcastle-up
On-Tyne,
Dressed in my best shirt and suit
And wearing spectacles,
To prove that I
Am no Philistine.

There's Eric Robinson,
There's Sweeney Agonistes,
Hamlet and Ray Charles,
They're all here.

But I made the pilgrimage
Most especially for
The glories of your
Glorious Geordie beer.

God bless the Newcastle Festival,
All the cultural titbits you may choose.
God will bless the Newcastle Festival,
Because Newcastle makes God's own booze.

Don't get me wrong,
I like my bit of classical,
Mister Menuhin
Is sublime,
And my ears and my eyes
Will be glued upon Yehudi,
But only till it's
Opening time.

They've got Semprini,
They've got The Tremeloes,
Così Fan Tutte:
They're all here.
But I made the pilgrimage
Most especially for
The glories of your
Geordie beer.

God bless the Newcastle Festival:
Everything is happening everywhere.
I'm the only Philistine looking in the ale house;
Everybody else is up in Eldon Square.

The Ferry Boat (1969)

If you ever seek to find us and you don't know where to search,
You could try the local prison or the back row of the church.
But 10 to 1 we're in the Ferryboat with cronies of our ilk,
Men of our kidney who've been boozing ever since they came off
    mother's milk.

Big Frank, Sailor George, Sidney and me,
Drinking at the Ferryboat never-endingly.
We won't be in the Duchess's Arms, nor in the Prince of Wales:
We'll all be in the Ferryboat,
Unless we're all in jail.

Come and join us in carousal when we sing and dance and flirt,
Your stomach had better be deepish and you're loins had best be
    girt.
When we leave the Ferryboat we're always cock-a-hoop,
And we never get the whirling pits, we never get the dreaded
    brewer's droop.

Big Frank, Sailor George, Sidney and me,
Drinking at the Ferryboat sentimentally.
We won't be in the Duchess's Arms, nor in the Hare and Hounds,
We'll all be in the Ferryboat
Unless we're in the ground.

The local bishop thought the Ferryboat was where his sheep got
    lost,
So he came along to visit us on the Feast of Pentecost;
And he is still there at the Ferryboat, always toasting one more
    toast,
And we're full of Hallelujahs because all the drinks are on the
Holy Ghost.

Big Frank, Sailor George, Sidney and me,
Dancing at the Ferryboat, not ungracefully.

We won't be in the Duchess's Arms, nor in the Crown Hotel.
We'll all be in the Ferryboat,
Unless we're all in Hell.

And when the Day of Judgement comes, when we've got to answer
	for our sins,
We'll go nipping down the Ferryboat to get a quick one in;
And when the Angel Gabriel has blown the Last Almighty Trump,
We'll be in the public taproom singing hymns and clinging to the
	pumps.

Big Frank, Sailor George, Sidney and me,
Drinking at the Ferryboat everlastingly;
We won't be in the Duchess's Arms, we won't be in the Goat;
We won't be up with Jesus,
We'll all be in the Ferryboat.

God Bless America (1969)

He was only a lonely American,
As American as aftershave and apple pie;
Sitting on the steps of the Albert Memorial,
He started to cry.
'I've done Paris and I've done Copenhagen,
I've done Amsterdam and I've done Rome,
And I've been done by everybody everywhere,
I want to go home.

God bless, God bless America, God bless the biggest and the best.
God save, God save America, God help the rest.

Carry me back to the land of the tranquillizer,
Home of the free and the cut-price gun,
Cradle of democracy and roll-on deodorant,
The land of *The Flying Nun.*
I miss tomato ketchup and sody-pop,
Black-eyed peas and blueberry pie.

I miss the clubs of the coppers in Chicago;
I am a regular guy.

God bless, God bless America, God bless Uncle Sam.
God save, God save America, Vietnam Goddam.

I'm just a red-blooded, decent all-American,
I honour the flag and the great big bomb,
Say my prayers to General Motors, and I love my mom.
People over here don't know how to make a pizza and
Their French-fried potatoes only make me smile,
And they can't grill n*****s quite the way that we do,
Country style.

God bless, God bless America, God will because God's okay.
God will save, God will save America, but check him with the
    CIA.

Carry me back to the land of fraternity,
Where the elks and the buffaloes roam,
Where seldom is heard an unAmerican word:
I want to go home.
He was only a lonely American,
As American as aftershave and apple pie,
Sitting on the steps of the Albert Memorial,
He started to cry.

God bless, God bless America, God bless the Klu Klux Klan.
God save, God save America, He's the only one who can.

When Lucy Comes (1970)

Tell all my cronies when they come around
I've gone to ground,
I've done a moonlight, I'm off.
I've too many debts that I yet have to pay,
I'll stay away;

Too many long knives are sharpening for me,
So keep the door shut, but not if it's Lucy.

Open the door when Lucy comes,
Say where I've gone and she'll follow.
Look how her eyes are tortoise shell,
See how her hair is yellow.

The landlords, the bum bailiffs would, if they could,
Sup up my blood,
But I've not enough to go round.
If the closely cropped coppers should come round to search,
Tell 'em I'm at church;
Tell 'em I go through my rosary each day,
To pray for the souls of all nosing bogeys.

Open the door when Lucy comes,
Say where I've gone and she'll follow.
Look how her eyes are tortoise shell,
See how her hair is yellow.

If the grocer comes trotting round wagging his bill,
Tell him I'm ill;
Say how much I miss his smile.
If the baker complains I have borrowed his bread,
Tell him I'm dead,
But tell him I'll willingly crawl out of hell
To kick his backside, if he can prove that he's got one.

Open the door when Lucy comes,
Say where I've gone and she'll follow.
Look how her eyes are tortoise shell,
See how her hair is yellow.

Open the door when Lucy comes,
Say where I've gone and she'll follow.
Look how her eyes are tortoise shell,
See how her hair is yellow.

You and Your Child (1970)

You and your child,
You and your child,
You watch everything they do,
But don't be surprised
When you realise
That they may be watching you.

A boy at five years old
May wish to be a Cambridge undergrad,
Georgie Best or an astronaut,
Or a bookie's runner like his dad.

You and your child,
You and your child,
You watch everything they do,
But don't be surprised
When you realise
That they may be watching you.

Little girls like to play at housewives,
Princesses or acrobats;
Some play shop and some play nurses,
Sticking sticky-plasters on their cats.

You and your child, oh,
You and your child,
You watch everything they do,
But don't be surprised
When you realise
That they may be watching you.

Rodney St John-Cholmonderley
Is going to be a brigadier, of course.
His little sister, the Honourable Caroline,
Is trying very hard to be a horse.

You and your child, oh,
You and your child,
You watch everything they do,
But don't be surprised
When you realise
That they may be watching you.

Valerie would like to be a dancer,
She pirouettes and strikes a pose,
But where did she learn to finish off her act by
Stepping out of her clothes?

You and your child, oh,
You and your child,
The series now must close.
You may have learned, you may have discerned
The tendencies they show, when they grow up.

You and your child, oh,
You and your child,
Whatever are they going to do?
Don't be surprised
When you realise...
That they may finish up like you.

The Municipal Workers' Strike (1970)

Where have all the municipal workers gone?
The parkies and the men who switch the lamp-posts on?
The mace-bearers, the beadles we held so dear?
Where are the merry rat catchers of yesteryear?

Oh, jolly gravedigger, we miss your professional opinion now
    you've gone:
It's difficult to tell at the Bricklayers Arms just who's passed out
And who is passing on.

No supple public bath attendants guard us while we bathe;
Many a sinking pensioner awaits to be saved.
Your corporation muscles used to loom so large;
Many a female cleavage heaves for your massage.

Lowly sewer men, shovelling sewage, take no notice of sniffs and
     jeers:
We all know that, down at the town hall, they have all been
Shovelling it for years.

Where are the lusty dustbin men with versatile knees,
Strapping shoulders, flashing eyes and eager to please?
There's many a bulging dustbin that craves your touch;
Many a bulging housewife would be glad of half as much.

Hit and Run (1971)
Seven songs written for 'Hit and Run', a radio play by Alfred Andersch.

In the play, a terminally-ill businessman is keen to get away from
his family for the final weeks of this life. However, he knocks
down and kills a shop girl who has just met a horse jockey and is
cycling to meet him at some racing stables. To cover his tracks, the
businessman bribes a petrol-pump attendant, who is reminded of
an encounter with an officer during the war in Italy.

Stuttgart

Slip road,
Autobahn,
Stuttgart on the north side.
Hills are insipid there,
With outcrops of greenness.
July at six o'clock,
Hot in the early morning time.
Insipid greenness
In the white Stuttgart heatwave.
Petrol station,

Gleaming in the summer greenness,
Painted blue and white,
The colour of the firm.
Police car, green, black,
'Morning! Morning!'
Through the heatwave.
Blue light turns and turns and turns...

Slip road,
Autobahn,
Stuttgart on the north side.
Hills are insipid there,
With outcrops of green.
July at six o'clock,
Hot in the early morning time.
Police car that stops
In the white Stuttgart heatwave.

Tuscany

Slip road,
Autostrada,
Genoa to Rome.
Hills are insipid now,
With outcrops of greenness.
July five o'clock,
Hot sun in the morning time.
Insipid green
In the white Tuscan heatwave.
Bombed-out farmstead,
Baking in the summer heatwave,
Ground headquarters
Of a Luftwaffe squadron.
Bombed-out farmstead,
Junction on the autostrada,
Underneath the sunshine in Tuscany.

Slip road,
Autostrada,
Genoa to Rome.
Hills are insipid now,
With outcrops of greenness.
July five o'clock,
Hot sun in the morning time.
Insipid green
In the white Tuscan heatwave.

White Ice and Red Campari

White ice and red Campari,
I'd make more living
If the time was mine.
Oh, white ice and red Campari
Underneath the pitch-black forest pine.
Baden-Baden in the Hotel Rialto,
Expense account, drinking by the swimming pool.
Talking to me contacts in the palm-beach deckchairs,
Keeping up the schedule.

White ice and red Campari,
I'd make more of it
If I had the time.
Oh, white ice and red Campari,
Underneath pitch-black forest pine.
She climbs from the water in a shower of silver,
Daddy is a banker,
She's a sweet little piece.
Rich,
Seventeen,
Exclusively bikini-ed:
'I got people to meet.'

White ice and red Campari,
I'd make more of it

If I had the time.
Oh, white ice and red Campari
Underneath the pitch-black forest pine.

The Café Bristol

In the Café Bristol
On the Kurfürstendamm,
September and five o'clock
On a cool afternoon.
All around about tea-cups
Tinkle discreetly,
Sitting at the next table to Mary-Lou.
Her eyes flicker and phosphorise,
Grey-blue, viable.
Sitting in the Café Bristol
On a cool afternoon.

Shop Window Girl
Sung to the tune of 'The Prisoner'.

In my shop window
Are palely reflected
The street and its chestnut trees,
And its grey sandstone.
The world is a photograph,
Trees and the sandstone,
The jewellery, the leather goods,
Framed in gold.
Coral red is very fashionable.
Everybody's wearing black nowadays.
Reflections in the plate glass
Of my shop window-pane.
In my shop window
The world is a photograph,
The black and the coral red,
The trees and sandstone.

Kentucky Bluegrass

Kentucky grassland,
Where the big red barns
Await tornadoes,
Where the winner of the Saratoga Derby stands
Behind a
White stockade.

And the smells of leather
And the sounds of the mouths
Of the grazing horses,
Pitch-black thoroughbreds,
Dreamily feeding on
Kentucky bluegrass.

And the feel of the smooth black hide
Between your tightening thighs,
And the way that you sway as you ride,
Riding over
Kentucky bluegrass.

Stuttgart (reprise)

Slip road,
Autobahn,
Stuttgart on the north side.
Hills are insipid now,
With outcrops of greenness.
The fear and the heat,
The cancer, the crystal-glass,
Kentucky blueglass,
The chance and the senselessness.

The world is no photograph:
It's red, like Camparis;
It's coral-red, blood-red,

The grey of the sandstone.
The world is no photograph:
It's red, like Campari.
A clear case of hit and run,
A question of a telephone.

Those are the Days (1975)

Those are the days we remember best,
Now we grow older.
Those were the days of happiness,
Made of gold.

Mother shut the suitcase,
Father stood and said goodbye,
We went and took a room in Chapeltown,
Chapeltown.
And we were lost
And we were anxious,
We were eager,
We were shy,
It took some little time to settle down,
Settle down.
Then we were flirting in The Skyrack,
We were boozing in The Ship,
We were fighting in The Fenton,
We were speechless in The Whip;
And in The Eldon we were witty
And superior, of course,
But we were good as gold for Molly in The Packhorse.

Those are the days we remember best,
Now we grow older.
Those were the days of happiness,
Made of gold.

And we were desperately serious,

We read throughout the night,
We argued all the way down Kirkstall Lane,
Kirkstall Lane.
And we beat our fists,
We closed our eyes,
We clutched our foreheads tight;
We understood, we were aflame,
Were aflame.
So it was Shelley in The Skyrack,
Schopenhauer in The Ship,
It was Kafka in The Fenton,
It was murder in The Whip;
And in The Eldon it was Kierkegaard
And Wittgenstein, of course,
But it was Molly, Molly, Molly in The Packhorse

Those are the days we remember best,
Now we grow older.
Those were the days of happiness,
Made of gold.

We got jilted in The Skyrack,
We got legless in The Ship,
We got stroppy in The Fenton,
We got winked at in The Whip;
And in The Eldon we were flippant,
We were cynical, of course,
But we were good as gold for Molly in The Packhorse.

Mother said we talked a little differently somehow,
And Father said we dressed a little strange,
A little strange.
And Kirkstall Road and Woodhouse Lane
Were well behind us now,
We'd gone and left them,
How they must be changed,
They must be changed.

They are flirting in The Skyrack,
They're still boozing in The Ship,
They are fighting in The Fenton,
They're still at it in The Whip;
And in The Eldon they are witty
And superior, of course,
But they are good as gold for Molly in The Packhorse.

Those are the days we remember best,
Now we grow older.
Those were the days of happiness,
Made of gold.

Gritty Old City of Leeds (1980)

Here is the gritty old city of Leeds,
Which is not as it seems
From the tops of the ridges.
It is gaunt and greedy and grim in the face,
Unyielding, unlovely, a flat black place,
And its only merited saving grace
Is the people who live in the city of Leeds.

And here is the arch mathematician of Leeds,
Who by cunning and craft made a grand calculation:
You can square up the mass of the human race
And its energy, time, its motion, its place
If you put twice the number in half of the space.
Who was it squared up the people of Leeds?

And here is the masterful builder of Leeds,
Who slung up so quickly the back-to-back houses.
That they didn't immediately disintegrate
Was a source of surprise and a reason to celebrate,
When he got back to his own home in Harrogate.
Who was it slung up the people of Leeds?

And here is the magical linguist of Leeds,
With his colourful words and his imagination:
Pink and yellow and khaki and black,
And Paddy and Paki and Jew-boy and Polak,
And jungle bunny and daft Anglomaniac.
Who was it conjured the people of Leeds?

So here is the gritty old city of Leeds,
Unyielding, unlovely, with no noble history;
Gaunt and greedy and grim in the face,
And its only future, its one saving grace
Is the people who live in the flat, black place,
The people who live in the city of Leeds

In spite of it all, they are more than alive.
In spite of it all, they'll do more than survive.
In spite of all the twisters and the history of greed,
Count upon the dignity and the grandeur of people in Leeds.

The Tiswas Song (1981)

You're nothing,
You're nowhere,
You're no one,
And nobody knows who you are.
But when Tiswas chucks buckets
Of mucky old yuck on you,
You know you're a star,
You are!
You know you're a star.

The way to the top for a singer
Is not just a question of style or of class.
If you've never been covered in gunk by the Phantom,
You're top of the flops,
You're a pain in the charts.

No!
You're no one,
You're nowhere,
You're nothing,
And nobody knows who you are,
Who you are...
But when Tiswas chucks buckets
Of mucky old yuck on you,
You know you're a star,
You are!
You know you're a star.

You can go on those shows
Where they throw the best grot,
It's the grot what did get you to the fame.
Now Parkinson's parties, and Esther's and Bruce's,
It's pretty hot grot
But it's just not the same...

No!
You're no one,
You're nothing,
You're nowhere,
And nobody knows who you are.
But when Tiswas chucks buckets
Of mucky old yuck at you,
Lobbing those globbering slobs of great glob at you,
Rushing to push mushy pies in your mush on you,
You know you're a star,
You are!
You know you're a star,
You are!
A yucky old star.

Soon Get the Hang of It (1986)

You are sweet, they deem,
Never been pissed,
Never swung a boot or fist,
Never been seen on the missing list,
But you...
Soon get the hang of it.

You will believe whatever I say to you,
Although whatever I say may not be true.
This is to make a man of you
...and you, you, you, you, and you...
Will soon get the hang of it.

You will march to aim, to shoot, to hit,
And talk of tarts and twats and tits,
And maybe, no, not used to it,
But you...
Soon get the hang of it

You will make the bed, clean the kit,
Swear and screw and skive and spit,
And learn to get away with it,
And you...
Soon get the hang of it.

You will sometimes have to die a bit,
With shells or shakes or crabs or squits,
The uniform may not yet fit
But you...
Will soon get the hang of it.

You will believe whatever I say to you,
Although whatever I say may not be true.
This is to make a man of you
...and you, you, you, you, and you...
Will soon get the hang of it.

The Berm House (1989)

He lived below, she lived above,
They were in love and he wanted to show
The extent and the warmth of his deep, subterranean feeling.
'My darling, will you come on down
Into my house? I will show you around.
Feel the heat of my solar panels and gaze at my ceiling.'

'Oh...Oh my heart's desire, I am full of an inner fire:
Come and live with me, feel my never-ending therms.
Oh my pretty, oh my sweeting, I'll give you my endless heating.
Darling, will you come and live with me at Berm
House?'

But she said, 'No, I won't agree:
Though I'm in love, you will never catch me
Making love in a hole in the ground, so you've run out of luck.
I'd live with you in a barn or a shack,
I would willingly bivouac
On Rockall, or Sark, or the islands of Eigg and Muck.'

'Oh...Oh my heart's desire, I am full of an inner fire:
Come and live with me, feel my never-ending therms.
Oh my pretty, oh my sweeting, I'll give you my endless heating:
Darling, will you come and live with me at Berm
House?'

Then came the winter, cold and chill,
And her electricity bill,
She went down and she knocked at his door, she shivered,
    she froze.
'Please take me in, out of the storm;
I am cold and you are warm.
Goodness me, how cosy! I think I'll take off some clothes...'

'Oh my heart's desire, give me more of your endless fire:
Let me rest and nestle in your super-human therms.

I'm your pretty, I'm your sweeting. Please give me your lifetime's
    heating!
Darling, may I come and live in your Berm
House?'

You, too, can live
Happy ever after,
In the warm, and no overdraft,
But there's only one thing that the Berm is unable to do.
It gives you warmth and strength and cover,
But it doesn't include a lover:
That part of design and construction is left to you.

If your heart's desire wants to share your lifetime's fire,
If she wants to live with you forever in your therms;
If your pretty, if your sweeting, wants your never-ending heating,
Take her underground to live in your Berm
House.

The Appalling Mr Kinnell (date unknown)

It was Kinnell, in ludicrous costume
Who lunged around the room,
Who gobbled up the bride and goosed the groom.
Kinnell, Kinnell
Who tried to steal their spoons,
Who bought them a spittoon,
Who joined them on their honeymoon.
He would, he would, he would, he would, Kinnell!
He would, he would, he would, 'kin would! Kinnell!

Appendix II:
Scrapbook

Thackray family

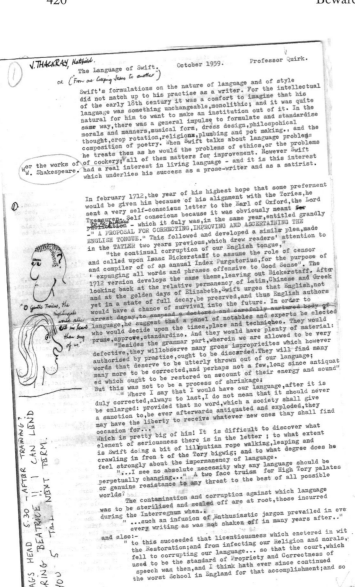

J. THACKRAY, Hatfield.

The Language of Swift.   October 1959.   Professor Quirk.

or ("From one leaping jean to another")

Swift's formulations on the nature of language and of style
did not match up to his practise as a writer. For the intellectual
of the early 18th century it was a comfort to imagine that his
language was something unchangeable, monolithic; and it was quite
natural for him to want to make an institution out of it. In the
same way, there was a general impulse to formulate and standardise
morals and manners, musical form, dress design, philosophical
thought, crop rotation, religions, plumbing and pot making., and the
composition of poetry. When Swift talks about language problems
he treats them as he would the problems of ethics, or the problems
of cookery, all of them matters for improvement. However Swift
had a real interest in living language - and it is this interest
which underlies his success as a prose-writer and as a satirist.

or the works of
W. Shakespeare.

In february 1712, the year of his highest hope that some preferment
would be given him because of his alignment with the Tories, he
sent a very self-conscious letter to the Earl of Oxford, the Lord
Treasurer. Self conscious because it was obviously meant for
publication - which it duly was, in the same year, entitled grandly
-" A PROPOSAL FOR CORRECTING, IMPROVING AND ASCERTAINING THE
ENGLISH TONGUE." This followed and developed a similar plea, made
in the TATLER two years previous, which drew readers' attention to
"the continual corruption of our English tongue,"
and called upon Isaac Bickerstaff to assume the role of censor
and compiler of of an annual Index Purgatorius, for the purpose of
expunging all words and phrases offensive to Good Sense". The
1712 version develops the same theme, leaving out Bickerstaff. After
looking back at the relative permanency of Latin, Chinese and Greek
and at the golden days of Elizabeth, Swift urges that English, not
yet in a state of full decay, be presrved, and thus English authors
would have a chance of survival into the future. In order to
arrest decay, to suspend a doctors and carefully nurtured body of
language, he suggest that a panel of notables and experts be elected
who would decide upon the times, place and techniques. They would
prune, approve, standardize. And they would have plenty of material:
"Besides the grammar part, wherein we are allowed to be very
defective, they will observe many gross improprieties which however
authorised by practice, ought to be discarded. They will find many
words that deserve to be utterly thrown out of our language;
many more to be corrected, and perhaps not a few, long since antiquat
ed which ought to be restored on account of their energy and sound"
But this was not to be a process of shrinkage;
" Where I say that I would have our language, after it is
duly corrected, always to last, I do not mean that it should never
be enlarged: provided that no word, which a society shall give
a sanction to, be ever afterwards antiquated and exploded, they
may have the liberty to receive whatever new ones they shall find
occasion for..."
Which is pretty big of him! It is difficult to discover what
element of seriousness there is in the letter ; to what extent
is Swift doing a bit of lilliputian rope walking, leaping and
crawling in fron t of the Tory bigwig; and to what degree does he
feel strongly about the impermanency of language.
"...I see no absolute necessity why any language should be
perpetually changing..." A two face truism for High Tory palates
or genuine resistance to any threat to the best of all possible
worlds?
The contamination and corruption against which language
was to be sterilised and sealed off are at root, those incurred
during the Interregnum when.
" ...such an infusion of Enthusiastic jargon prevailed in eve
every writing as was not shaken off in many years after.."
and also:-
" to this succeeded that licentiousness which enetered in wit
the Restoration; and from infecting our Religion and morals,
fell to corrupting our language... so that the court, which
used to be the standard of Propriety and Correctness of
speech was then, and I think hath ever since continued
the worst School in England for that accomplishment; and so

"O gentle Trolius, the
Nightingales
would alter
left his heart
than any
of its

NAGS HEAD 6.30 - AFTER TRAINING !
BRING BEATRICE !! I CAN LEND
YOU 5 TILL NEXT TERM.

FOR DINNER. SEE YOU
30 ....?

Left: Jake's
university
essay on the
language of
Anglo-Irish
satirist
Jonathan
Swift –
complete
with his
cartoons
and private
messages.
*Thackray
family*

PROGRAMME PROGRAMME

1.	Opening Chorus	Norman B. Arthur, Michael, Margaret T, Doris, Carol, Suzanne, plus full chorus.
2.	Olive tells the tale	Olive
3.	Romance in Rhythm	Marjorie, Pam, Margaret B, Margaret T, Muriel, Norman B, Norman J, Brian, Leslie Gordon, Arthur.
4.	Meet the Girls	Dorothy, Edith, Mary M.
5.	The Gendarmes	Michael and David
6.	Sketch (The Gypsy's Warning)	Pam, Jean T, Brian and Norman B.
7.	Courtin Days (Duet)	Doris and Ernest Cook.
8.	Swing along with the young ones	Susan S, Susan J, Rosalind, Suzanne, Carol, Mary R, Jean M, Joy, David, Michael, Ian B Ian C.
9.	Dolly and Florrie Forde	Dolly
10	The Christening (musical Sketch)	Pam, Arthur, Muriel, Norman, Marjorie, Brian Margaret B, Margaret T, Olive, Cynthia, Gordon Norman B.
11.	Guest artist	Jake Thackeray.
12.	Musical Comedy Memories	Doris, Jean, Michael, Ernest B, Ernest C. David, Full chorus.

INTERVAL

13.	Army Medley -Do you remember these?	Male chorus with a girl or two
14.	Ragtime	All the girls
15.	Dolly as Vesta Tilley	Dolly
16	The Censor (sketch)	Bon and Norman V
17.	'Travelling along'	Edith, Mary and Dorothy with chorus (Marjorie, Muriel, Pam, Jean T, Carol Barbara, Cathleen Margaret W, Margaret T Margaret B, Cynthia, Pat).
18.	Olive again has a tale to tell	Olive
19.	Music has charms!	Dorothy, Edith, Suzanne, Barbara, Shirley Cynthia, Jean T, Pat P. Mary M, Arthur, Norman B Norman V, Norman J, Gordon, David, Michael, Lesli. Brian.
20.	Operatic Triangle	Doris, Ernest B. Ernest C.
21.	Arthur entertains	Arthur
22.	Family group	Sketch
23	Jean entertains	Jean, with chorus of girls - (Marjorie, Pam, Dorothy, Mary M, Edith, Margaret B, Cynthia, Jean T).
24.	Thanks for the Memory	Dorothy, Marjorie, Pam, Margaret T, Dolly doris, Jean Norman B, Arthur, Brian, Ernest B plus full chorus.
25.	FINALE.	

'I was given one job – to get Jake on stage, come hell or high water.'
Jake on the programme for Whitkirk Arts Guild Music Hall,
September 1966, his earliest attested public performance. *Whitkirk Arts Guild*

Sharing the bill with Leeds legend Vi Tye, 'housewife and stripper'.
Below: The City Varieties programme from the same show.
City Varieties Music Hall, Leeds Heritage Theatres/West Yorkshire Archive

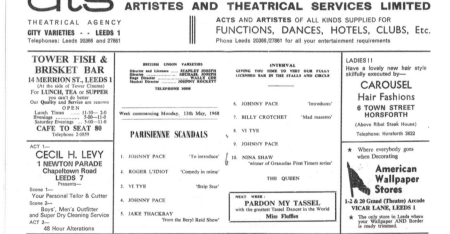

April 9th. 1968,

Dear Kate,

I'm not given to being so familiar with young ladies, but I felt that addressing you as 'Dear Miss Booth' might, by its informality, persuade you that my attitude was aloof and my sentiments less than genuine. The fact is, Kate, I have heard that you are suffering considerable distress over the fate of myself and my dog. I must confess that some time ago Ulysses and I found that our relationship was not developing as richly as it might.

I had indeed decided, in a blind moment, to bring everything to a pretty nasty finish.

But ... oh, but ..... time and kindness being their own solution. He has found a ladyfriend and so I have I and we are waiting for the chestnut trees to blossom when we shall all be united. And so, Kate, we will all accept your kind thoughts and best wishes. Many thanks for your loyal interest.

A kiss from me, and a wag and a wuff from Ulysses,

Yours,

Jake Thackray.

Reassuring words from
Jake for a worried young fan.
Kate Booth

With Sheila, *right*, in The Ferryboat, the pub Jake celebrated in song on
Braden's Week.   *Reading Evening Post*

608

Jake Thackray is a Leeds man, and it was there, singing in the Tap Rooms of Kirkstall Road, that he was discovered by a BBC radio producer. His style of song, and of presentation, however, owes much more to a firmly-rooted French lineage than to any English tradition.

A graduate of Durham University, Jake was working as a teacher in France when he met, and came under the influence of, the brilliant - and extremely popular - French poet/chansonnier, Georges Brassens (cf <u>Georges Brassens</u> by Alphonse Bonnafé; Poètes d'Aujourd'hui 99, Editions Pierre Seghers, 1963). Jake has since adapted a number of Brassens' songs into English, and his own original compositions bear similar stylistic marks.

After travelling widely in Europe, Jake returned to teach in Leeds, and was soon broadcasting regularly in the BBC's <u>Northcountryman</u> series. Television then stepped in, and after several appearances on the regional <u>Look North</u> programme, Jake abandoned teaching, moved south and was quickly signed for <u>The Frost Programme</u> and for the BBC's series of <u>Beryl Reid Shows</u>. He is currently resident on the very popular <u>Braden's Week</u>, a show which has made him one of the most sought-after performers in the country.

The originality and range of Jake Thackray's talent can be sampled on his LP record, <u>Last Will and Testament of Jake Thackray</u>, and on his single <u>Lah-di-dah</u> coupled with <u>The Black Swan</u>.

His present tour for the Mid-Pennine Association for the Arts will be as follows:

Monday 21 April 1969 at 8.30pm: White Hart Hotel, Todmorden

Tuesday 22 April 1969 at 8.30pm: Big Window Hotel, Burnley

Wednesday 23 April 1969 at 8.30pm: Station Hotel, Earby

Thursday 24 April 1969 at 7.30pm: College of Further Education, Nelson

Friday 25 April 1969 at 10.30pm: Century Theatre, Broadway Car Park, Accrington

NEXT WEEK...

The return, by popular request, of T H E   B A R R O W   P O E T S

on tour to Nelson, Bacup, Accrington, Barnoldswick and Burnley.

presented by
Mid-Pennine Association for the Arts   Central Library   Burnley   29513

A week on the road in Lancashire. Mid Pennine Arts programme 1969.
Mid Pennine Arts

Jake performing at the Big Window, April 1969.   *Burnley Civic Heritage Trust*

November 1967. *Record Mirror* article, *left*, introducing Jake and *The Holy and The Horrid.*

More commentary on life, British - style, from across the Atlantic fills "Jake's Progress," second Philips album by Jake Thackray. There is a certain charm and appeal the way the Briton talks-sings in a clipped fashion. While Thackray is not every American's cup of tea, some Anglophiles will find affinity in some Thackray songs, such as "My Family Tree," Toffee-maker," "Grandad" and "Country Girl."

Record review, *above*, for USA's *Jake's Progress*, 1969.

ANARCHY IN THE WEST COUNTRY

JAKE THACKERAY: 'On Again! On Again!'(EMI) "I love a good bum on a woman, it makes my day." WEST COUNTRY RACONTEUR'S ANSWER TO FRANK ZAPPA TURNS MALE CHAUVINIST PIG. "A leg of a donkey is peanuts for her, she could bore the balls of a buffalo." Nice goin' Jake, but will the Beeb play it?

Various clippings – often misspelling Jake's name – from 1960s and 1970s music papers such as *Sounds*, *Record Mirror* and *Melody Maker.*

JAKE THACKRAY, 29, six-footer and single, says he writes two kinds of song: "The Holy and the Horrid". The sacred carol side of his talent comes on his "Remember Bethlehem" single for Columbia, just out. The "horrid" otherwise doggerel ditties are featured on his first LP which is out this month. He's a teacher in Leeds, teaching English but using his own taped "musicals" to get points across. And his record producer, Norman Newell, says of him: "The word 'genius' is completely warranted as far as Jake is concerned. I believe his first single is the most beautiful recording ever made. I urge you to listen to it again and again. He is a brilliant composer but one is so intrigued by his lyrics that not until you hear his songs a second or third time do you realise his great strength as a composer". Jake Thackray—welcome!

JAKE THACKREY: " Last Will And Testament Of Jake Thackrey " (Columbia). Yorkshireman Jake Thackrey is 29, an ex-Rugby League player with a talent for off-beat doggerel that is at times hilarious and at others, obscure. Jake performs in pubs and clubs round Leeds, but a bitter-sweet sense of humour and lyrical talent could bring him to a wider audience.

JAKE THACKRAY "The Last Will And Testament Of Jake Thackray" (Columbia Stereo SCX 6178).

JAKE sounds like a kind of sick Noel Coward. His folk-tinged songs and his unusual songs made me laugh spontaneously (very rare when reviewing LP's). Produced by Normal Newell — a good LP this.

★ ★ ★ ★

JAKE THACKRAY

Bantam Cock. — (Columbia SCX 6506). Quite simply, and not to put too fine a point on it, Jake Thackray is a genius. It's not so much his actual singing as the songs he sings. Even his own brand of sleeve notes stands out. There are some tremendous songs on this one, and even the titles are.excellent. Like: Isabel Makes Love Upon National Monuments.

JAKE THACKRAY: "Live Performance" (Columbia SCX 6453, £2.15). Jake ?.'s acquired taste. He writes and sings his own songs, and plays guitar. And his words are what make him worth listening to. A very perceptive pop paper, Disc and Music Echo, is quoted on the album sleeve as saying his "words are viciously amusing" and we wouldn't argue with that. This is Jake in live performance singing most of his best work, notably "Family Tree" and "Lah-Di-Dah," surprisingly a very perceptive love song. Quality—good. Value f o r money—fine.

from easily. Chart potential.
Jake Thackray: "On Again! On Again!" (EMI). With a face like a surprised bloodhound and a certain off-beat charm, Mr Thackray is one of those well-known personalities — a club performer, a "TV Spot" artist — who it's difficult to place.
He is unlikely to move out of the well-trodden path he's determined for himself. For him, a hit single would be about as unlikely as the sight of Johnny Rotten with waist-length hair. A miss.

JAKE THACKRAY: Remember Bethlehem; Joseph (Columbia DB 8296). With chorus backing, this is a religious slice of philosophy and is unusual enough to attract a lot of attention. ★ ★ ★

A voice not just of France

The late Georges Brassens : a loss to Europe

Sir,—The death of Georges Brassens, last Friday, elicited massive and genuine grief throughout France—on television and radio, and in the entire press. It went pitifully unnoticed here.

I counted a mention on the BBC's 6 o'clock news and, from the six quality newspapers of Saturday and Sunday, a total of about 280 words; some inaccurate, some grudging, some—no medals for guessing which paper—from a different story

from another page. All as if the event were a negligible idiosyncrasy of French life.

In any version of European culture Brassens has a right to a major tribute. He was a prolific and consummate writer, speaking urbanely, bawdily, tenderly, unpredictably about death and love, government, society, the sacredness of life and the individual. The Académie Française thought enough about him to invite him to join its immortal (he declined) line-up. Moreover, he was, popular, 28 million records of his work have been sold, and still sell. When and where else has a complex and serious artistic voice been so comprehensively loved and listened to and understood ?

May I reassure your European readers that there are thousands of people here who recognise his stature, cherish his songs and his memory, grieve at his long suffering and disappearance, and wish to join them in their sense of loss.—Yours etc,
Jake Thackray,
Mitchel Troy Common,
Monmouth, Gwent.

Above: Jake's letter to *The Guardian* on the death of Georges Brassens.
Right: Colin Evans's programme notes about Jake for the Sherman concert.

Above: 'It all had a kind of dream-like quality, really.' Jake and Georges at Hillside, October 1973.
Colin Evans

CONCERT
AN EVENING OF WIT AND MIRTH

IN AID OF THE N.S.P.C.C.

STARRING JAKE THACKRAY

WITH

MAD JOCKS & ENGLISHMEN

WEDNESDAY 2nd JULY 1986   AT 7.30PM
SOLIHULL LIBRARY THEATRE, HOMER ROAD,
SOLIHULL.   TICKETS AVAILABLE FROM
THEATRE BOX OFFICE PROCEEDS TO

Above: 'Jake absolutely hated the cover...'

Left: 'The original soft touch.' One of Jake's many shows for charity.

Jake   Thackray,
25, Monnow   Street,
MONMOUTH,
np5   3ef.,
0600   71   6869.
18th Sept. 94.

Dear Murray White,

          Got your letter. Thanks. Sorry to hear that
Cristina Odone is ill. I did send some pieces some time ago but
they seem to have disappeared They have also disappeared from
my floppy disc due to a playful son of mine. Never mind, I'll
start again.

          Here is a test piece. I'll do a couple more and
get them to you instanter.

          Regards and so on,

          Jake Thackers.

          Jake Thackray.

Above: An early covering letter to the *Catholic Herald*, complete with excuse.

Thackray family

```
It was Kinnelll,

In ludicrous costume

Who lunged around the room

Who gobbled up the bride and goosed the groom

Kinnell Kinnell

Who tried to steal their spoons

Who bought them a spitoon

Who joined them on their honeymoon

He would he would he would he would,Kinnell,

He would he would he would

'kin would,Kinnell.
```

```
       --------------------------------------------------------------
  x------   ----------------------------------------------------------
```

```
It 's like inviting Robespierre

He's the fingers in the till

-

 The johnny on your daughters window-sill
```

```
  --------------
```

```
1   The wedding feast        spoons etc

2 the evillest most malignant man I ve ever known
evil  irritating. abornable  bestial loathsome heinous
depraved corrupt a blight

It is Kinnell,with his appalling grin
pscopath
```

```
      --------
```

```
And then across the wedding cake a crooked shadow
fell
                   gatecrasher spoil the feast
Who was the bogeyman      the beast at the feast the phantom

Tortoise Elizabeth Borders Kinnelll Caroline Digbt Pratte 2
Daddio   The dirty mayor    Childrens' Songs 1 2 3
```

A single verse and ideas for the legendary, unfinished 'The Appalling Mr Kinnell'. Note the list of late song titles at the bottom of the page: tracklist for the album that never was?   *Thackray family*

ODEON New St. BIRMINGHAM

THURSDAY, OCTOBER 29th, at 8.0 p.m.
CLOSED CIRCUIT TV PRESENTATION
LIVE FROM LONDON — ON GIANT SCREEN
The National Playing Fields Association presents,
in the presence of H.R.H. Princess Alexandra,

LOUIS ARMSTRONG   TONY BENNETT

RONNIE BARKER   SANDIE SHAW

JAKE THACKRAY

Introduced from London by

DAVID FROST

HELP CHILDREN EVERYWHERE TO A BETTER LIFE
WITH PLAYGROUNDS AND PLAY SCHEMES.
Tickets £5, £3/10/0, £2 — all bookable.
Booking Office open tomorrow (Friday) 12 noon.
Box Office weekdays (not Sunday) 12-8. Tel. 021-643 0815/6.

Above: In exalted company: on the bill with Louis Armstrong and Tony Bennett, 1970.

BEDFORD COLLEGE
Regent's Park, N.W.1

MIDSUMMER MADNESS
JUNE 30th, 10 p.m.—6 a.m.

M.C.5

BROTHERHOOD OF BREATH

BITCH • JAKE THACKRAY

PEELERS

CHAMPION JACK DUPREE

BLOSSE-ELIOT • BONNIE DOBSON
TIGHT LIKE THAT • DAGON

ALL NIGHT FOLK • FILMS • FOOD
DISCO • BAR
Tickets in advance £1.25. On sale **Virgin Records**

SOLO JAKE

JAKE THACKRAY is to appear in a solo concert at the Queen Elizabeth Hall, London, on November 1.
This will be Thackray's third major solo concert in the London area this year. His previous two appearances were at the Round House and the 1,100 seat Fairfield Hall.

Above: Jake triumphs in London, 1970.

The Boggery Folk Club
IN ASSOCIATION WITH
The Opposite Lock Club
Announce a New and Exciting Venture in the Field of Light Entertainment

BOGGERY FOLK FACTORY

Every TUESDAY at "THE FACTORY,"
(High Speed) Gas St. off Broad St. Birmingham. 1
8.30 p.m – 11.30 p.m.   ADMISSION 6/-

OPENING NIGHT: JUNE 3rd
we proudly present the country's leading solo artist

Al Stewart
Special Guest
Colin Scott

JUNE 10th
from T.V.'s "Bradens Week"

Jake Thakray
plus an outstanding group from London
Magna Carta

Top Artists like these every week with the emphasis on humour and originality. Blues and Country Music will also be featured regularly. Not just a folk club but a new and different format—
TRY IT ! You'll be glad you did

free membership first month

Above: In strange company: on the bill with MC5, American proto-punk pioneers, in 1972.

Right: The Boggery Folk Factory, 1969. This gig was Jake's first appearance at Jasper Carrott's club and the start of a long friendship.

'BORDERS' FOR WDR JULY 23 '86

```
We stand here side by side
We are so near and so divided
We always draw the line
How do we ever come together
Me to your  side you to mine ?


We feel these borders in our bones
We draw these borders in our head
Down the middle of the road
Down the middle of the bed
The north the south the left and right
The orange and green the black and the white
We build more walls than we build bridges.


We stand here side by side
We are so near and so divided
We always draw the line
How do we  ever come together
Me to your side you to mine ?


We ve got these borders in the blood
Under the skin and deep in the heart
We feel the need to keep together
We feel the need to keep apart
The here the there the now the then
The me the you the us the them
We are forever crossing borders.


We stand here side by side
We are so near and so divided
We always draw the line
How do we ever come together
Me to your side you to mine ?
```

Jake's
manuscript
for 'Borders',
written for
German
television.
Thackray family

 J.THACKRAY 1986.

Notes

INTRODUCTION

1   Interview with Spencer Leigh, 1997.

CHAPTER 1 – Up My Family Tree

1   The one truth the song contains is that Jake had a brother called Richard. He may or not have enjoyed the amusing suggestion that, as a boy scout, he offered the Queen a cigarette.

2   Construction at Copley included a church, which alone cost over £100,000.

3   Jake made the claim to his son, Tom, and to Dan Cronin, a university friend. Dan was proud to be half-Irish and, picking up on this one day, Jake said: 'Sorry, Dan. My father was in the police, but he was in the Black and Tans. You can take it or leave it.' It wasn't said to rile or offend him, and Jake clearly believed what he was saying.

4   Most Black and Tans came from Great Britain and were demobbed soldiers. They engaged in reprisal attacks on civilians and civilian property, including extra-judicial killings, arson and looting.

5   During the post-war slump of the 1920s and 1930s, women's chances of employment were also much reduced.

6   This 'shadow' factory was camouflaged using expertise from the film industry: the roof was covered with stone-walled fields, imitation farm buildings and a duck pond, whilst fake hedges and bushes were changed to match the changing colours of the seasons, and dummy animals were even moved around daily. This all proved extremely effective, and the factory remained undetected and undamaged throughout the Leeds Blitz.

7   Ernest's pay was immediately cut by one eighth and stood still for the remainder of his time in the police, in contrast with his pay as a sergeant, which would have continued to rise. In the final year of his police career, his pay was 80 per cent of what it would

have been if he had remained a sergeant. The impact of all this on Ernest's pension was also significant, as pensions were calculated on the basis of the final three years' salary.

8   Talking on television in 1976 to John D Loudermilk.
9   Interviewed for Victor Lewis-Smith's *Jake on the Box* television documentary, 2006.
10   The grandmother of Jake's young neighbour Elaine Howey, who lived two doors down from the Thackrays in the early 1950s.
11   Friends though Teresa and Molly were, they maintained a formality belonging a bygone era, always referring to each other as Mrs Burke and Mrs Thackray.
12   If Ernest had stayed on for a further five years, he would have been on two-thirds salary, so it looks as though a sense of disenchantment lay behind his decision to retire early. However, many policemen serving during the war made the same decision, which may reflect the pressures of the job in wartime.
13   *Leeds Student*, 2nd March 1973.
14   When Jake's schoolfriend, Basil Foot, stayed with him in 1951, he and Jake were sent off by Molly to do the laundry at the wash-house: 'There we were, two young boys among a group of gawping women, trying to make the best of doing the washing.'
15   'I can't see this Heaven and Hell thing, myself', *Daily Telegraph*, 20th August 1995.
16   After serving as a novice in the Order of the Cross and Passion for several years, in December 1950 Michael 'professed' as a Passionist (i.e. made temporary vows), an important step along the pathway to priesthood. However, he left the Order before taking his final vows, and then went to live on the continent, not returning to England for many years, which suggests a concern that his decision might be seen as reflecting badly on the family.
17   'I can't see this Heaven and Hell thing, myself', interview with John Morrish, *Daily Telegraph*, August 1995. That month, Jake also did a TV interview on HTV's *Face to Faith*.
18   Interviewed by John Dunn on Radio 2 in February 1981.
19   *Face to Faith*, 20th August 1995.

CHAPTER 2 – Big Black Gilbert

1   The jazz guitarist, speaking on Victor Lewis-Smith's 2006 television documentary, *Jake on the Box*.
2   He enrolled on 2nd July, and the mid-term start suggests that the family had only just moved, five months after Ernest's retirement.
3   When Jake went to university, he would again be funded by a City scholarship.

4   Taken from a concert recorded for the BBC2 series *Jake Thackray and Songs* in 1981.
5   Published in 1977 by Star Books.
6   Michael's career at St Michael's, like Jake's, was disrupted. He left the College for one year, but the reason for this is unknown.
7   In the 1950s, hitch-hiking was a common way of travelling. Adults sporting a university scarf or military uniform increased significantly their chances of getting a lift.
8   The nose was an allusion to Ovid's full name, Publius Ovidius Naso; 'naso' is the Latin for 'nose'. He was indeed banished, in part because of his irreverent poetry. Ovid's witty writing would certainly have appealed to Jake.
9   Interview with Ann Purser in *She* magazine, April 1969.
10 Interview with John Dunn for Radio 2, January 1981.

CHAPTER 3 – What is a Prof?

1   The verses of the song are distributed throughout the programme, available online via the Yorkshire Film Archive. The programme was written and presented by Richard Hoggart, a distinguished Leeds-born academic and cultural commentator who, like Jake, was working-class and grammar-school educated. He chose 'Castleford Ladies Magic Circle' as one of his *Desert Island Discs*.
2   The Packhorse was Jake's favourite watering hole in Leeds and Molly Heath its formidable chief barmaid. She was a platinum-blonde lady in her forties, cast in the mould of Bet Lynch from *Coronation Street*. Jake would mention her fondly in the introduction to his book of lyrics, *Jake's Progress*, and referred to her frequently in the columns he wrote for the *Yorkshire Post* and *Catholic Herald* in the 1990s. He possibly also refers to her in his song, 'Personal Column'.
3   Whilst there was no formal link between Hatfield and St Michael's, its pupils gained a reputation for doing well there, so a steady stream went each year. The Rector of St Michael's was keen to promote the relationship, and the St Michael's College magazine contained regular reports from Hatfield.
4   Some of the money students paid up-front to the college was used to provide credit at Hatfield's Buttery, where they could buy bottles of pale ale, biscuits and cigarettes. Students who blew their credit quickly were said to 'bust their battels' (*sic*). 'Jake was a leader in that,' says Dan Cronin.
5   Jake's social circle at Durham was unusual – in the 1950s smoking was very popular among men. He always remained a heavy smoker, and this contributed to his health issues towards the end of his life.

CHAPTER 4 – The French Connection

1   Its full name is L'Institut Catholique d'Arts et Métiers.

2   Diploma in Education.

3   Something which Jake narrowly avoided at this point was the requirement to spend two years doing National Service, which was abolished in 1960.

4   *Newcastle Evening Chronicle*, 29th May 1969.

5   Sleeve notes of Jake's 1967 album, *The Last Will and Testament of Jake Thackray*.

6   'I can't see this Heaven and Hell thing, myself', *Daily Telegraph*, 20th August 1995.

7   The interview was recorded in August 1995 for HTV's series, *Face to Faith*. It is remarkable that Jake, who was an intensely private man, agreed to do an interview, especially one covering a topic so personal. However, by this point his profile as someone of faith had been raised by the fact that he was a regular columnist for the *Catholic Herald*. He also had financial problems, so perhaps agreed to do the interview and perform a song because there was a fee.

8   This is a technical term describing its fixed poetic structure.

9   Beckett, who was Irish, wrote many of his novels and plays in French, including *Waiting for Godot*.

10   Interview with John Hall in *The Guardian*, March 1969.

11   Front de Libération Nationale (FLN).

12   *Organisation de l'Armée secrete.*

13   Interview with Jeremy Randall, *Reading Evening Post*, May 1968.

CHAPTER 5 – Tonton Georges

1   *Jake Thackray and Songs* album, 1981.

2   Interview with John Dunn, Radio 2, February 1981.

3   Jake's access to 'teen' culture would have been very limited. Given that his mother had been known to chastise children for going to the cinema, she would not have approved of him seeing *Blackboard Jungle* or *The Girl Can't Help It*. While there may have been what Jake called a 'steam-powered radio' at Burley Lodge Road, the number of stations was limited, as was the amount and range of music broadcast in the 1950s. Even if the Thackrays could have afforded a television (a luxury item at this time), it is hard to believe that Molly would have allowed one in the house.

4   Interviewed in August 1995 on *Face to Faith*.

5   Interviewed by Lance Bosman for *Guitar Magazine*, April 1979. Violinist Stéphane Grappelli and guitarist Django Reinhardt

were legendary jazz musicians who played together in the 1930s and 1940s in the hugely influential Quintette du Hot Club de France. Jake, who got to know Grappelli in the 1970s, admired the playing of both men hugely.

6   Among the important cultural figures who gathered in Paris were writers Jean-Paul Sartre, Simone de Beauvoir, Jacques Prévert, and singer Juliette Gréco.

7   Anyone wanting to hear Brel's songs is encouraged to start with 'Ne me quitte pas', 'Les Bourgeois', 'Le Moribond', 'Amsterdam' and 'Le Gaz', which deal with these themes.

8   Trenet is best known for 'La Mer'. Jake would use one of his melodies for one of his own early songs, 'One-Eyed Isaac'.

9   This led, in art, to the Dada and Surrealist movements which sought to scandalise polite society ('épater le bourgeois') by challenging conventional thinking.

10   Jake would also write adaptations of two of Georges's other songs, 'Marinette' and 'Je Rejoindrai Ma Belle'.

11   *Guitar Magazine*, April 1979.

12   Interviewed by Colin Evans in 1971. Colin Evans was a French lecturer at Cardiff University who shared Jake's admiration for the Frenchman's work.

13   This was probably in Paris in 1962. Jake would later claim, rather fancifully, to have knocked over Edith Piaf in his hurry to get to see him perform.

14   Interview, 25th September 2005.

15   Interview with Colin Evans, 1971.

CHAPTER 6 – A Good Skive

1   Performance at the Medina Theatre, Isle-of-Wight.

2   Helmets, made for a school production, were mounted on the wall, and these would resonate when Gardiner raised his voice.

3   In the 1970s, Charles Gardiner developed a theatre-arts course which brought to Intake young people from all over Leeds and became the blueprint for such courses nationwide.

4   BBC interview, date unknown.

5   Intake's reputation in the performing arts has continued, albeit under its new name, Leeds West Academy. Other alumnae include actress Angela Griffin and Spice Girl Mel B.

6   BBC interview.

7   Facebook group discussion.

8   Interview with Paul Vallely for *Leeds Student*, 2nd March 1973.

9   Interview with Reginald Brace, *Yorkshire Post*, 7th March 1981.

10   The title refers to Thomas Gray's eighteenth-century poem,

'Elegy Written in a Country Churchyard': 'Full many a flower is born to blush unseen, and waste its sweetness on the desert air.'

11   Jake's choice of name is reminiscent of the Akroyd family which owned the mill where his mother's family worked. Likewise, he would often use the names of people he knew in his songs.

12   Interview with Jeremy Randall, *Reading Evening Post*, May 1968.

13   Interview with Rodney Challis, *Yorkshire Life*, November 1981.

14   *Guitar Magazine*, April 1979.

15   One of these churches was The Church of the Assumption of Our Lady in West Park, where Jake and his mother worshipped.

16   The School decided that the pupils were not allowed to sing 'hell'.

17   Interview with Paul Vallely for *Leeds Student*, 2nd March 1973.

18   There doesn't seem to be any connection with the song 'Mrs Murphy' which Jake recorded for his second album.

19   Interview with Spencer Leigh, 1983.

20   Interviewed for the Victor Lewis-Smith television documentary, *Jake on the Box*, 2006.

21   The age difference was eight years.

22   The blundering, accident-prone Monsieur Hulot was the comic creation of the French mime artist and actor, Jacques Tati. Jake had a real fondness for the character and one of his friends, Sue Haverly, believes he was self-aware enough to see something of Hulot in himself.

23   Sheila Thackray, in an email to Michel Ameline, November 2009.

24   Jake explained this in an interview with the *Reading Evening Post* in May 1968.

CHAPTER 7 – Woodhouse Pamela

1   They attended the new Church of the Assumption of Our Lady in West Park, a short walk from Old Oak Close.

2   Like Jake, Howe loved the *Just William* stories, and she was responsible for bringing them to Radio 4.

3   David Heycock, *The Guardian*, 18th March 2004.

4   *Jake's Progress* book, 1977.

5   By the time Jake left Intake in 1968, his teacher's salary was still under £25 a week.

6   'Greasy Joan' was later released on record under the title 'One-Eyed Isaac', a reference to another character in the song. Jake was often rather casual about the titles of his songs.

7   The songs released on record were 'Grandad', 'Isobel', 'Lah-Di-Dah', 'Country Bus', 'Scallywag', 'Jumble Sale', 'Isabella', 'The Last Will and Testament of Jake Thackray', 'Ulysses', 'Greasy Joan' (as 'One-Eyed Isaac'), 'Remember Bethlehem' and 'Family Tree'.

8   Jake loved Brassens's song and took to singing it in French at his concerts in the 1980s. He would tell audiences it was written in archaic language and sent up folk songs 'by writing something better'.

9   Jake sang 'Little Black Foal', 'Kirkstall Road Girl', 'Isobel' and 'Nurses', 'Ulysses', 'Grandad', 'Country Bus' and 'The Cactus'. Sadly, no recordings of these performances exist.

10   Paul Long, in a Folk at the Grove Facebook group post.

11   Jake had recorded the song for the radio on 21st August. In 1983 he told Spencer Leigh, 'I had to finish it by Friday and then go the studio in Leeds and record it for a programme on the Sunday morning. I wrote it very quickly.'

12   Ian Watson, the theatre's assistant manager, also did some radio work for the BBC in Leeds. Pamela Howe grabbed him one day, thrust a tape of Jake's songs in his hand and said, 'You must listen to this boy.' Watson was impressed and immediately booked Jake. It transpired that the two men had much in common: Watson had studied French at Hatfield College, Durham, shortly after Jake had left, and shared his admiration of Georges Brassens. They became friends and, shortly before Jake's death, Ian became the producer and driving force behind a musical using his songs, *Sister Josephine Kicks the Habit*.

13   Nightingale would enjoy a distinguished career in journalism, writing for such newspapers and magazines as *The Times*, *The New Statesman* and *New York Times*, where he was chief theatre critic.

CHAPTER 8 – A Very Valuable Property

1   Jake evidently had no phone at Old Oak Close.

2   Although Pamela did not produce the pilot, she was still well connected with the BBC in Leeds and was involved in commissioning the programme.

3   The songs were 'Grandad', 'Ulysses', 'Lah-Di-Dah', 'The Last Will and Testament of Jake Thackray' and 'Family Tree' (which was written especially for the programme). With characteristic generosity, Jake arranged for the BBC to send his fee for the programme to Dave Blezard, a blind university student who was one of his drinking friends at the Packhorse. By all accounts Blezard was a remarkable man who refused to let his disability stop him doing things like playing darts in the pub. Jake would mention him in the introduction to *Jake's Progress* in 1977.

4   Interview with Spencer Leigh, 1997. In fact, he took greater pride in his work as a lyricist than as a producer. George Martin thinks he 'always wanted to be a Stephen Sondheim [the acclaimed

writer of Broadway musicals]'. Jake and Sondheim have many things in common as lyricists: both are superb storytellers who have a dazzling command of language, a sharp wit and an attention to detail. Norman's own penchant for ingenious rhyme is in evidence in some of his own lyrics, including 'A Portrait of My Love', a huge hit for Matt Munro: 'Anyone who sees her / Soon forgets the Mona Lisa.'

5   Alex Armitage became Jake's agent in 1976, at the age of 18, taking the role over from his father, Richard. Jake was his first client. He would, in time, become the Head of Noel Gay.

6   Richard Armitage's father was composer Noel Gay (real name Reginald Armitage), who wrote such hits as 'Run Rabbit Run', 'Leaning on a Lamp-post', 'The Sun Has Got His Hat On', 'Me and My Girl' and 'The Lambeth Walk'. He co-wrote some songs with Norman Newell. At the time Jake joined the agency, its clients included David Frost, John Cleese, Peter and Gordon and The Scaffold. It would later represent Norman Newell.

7   Interviewed in 1983 on a folk programme on Pennine Radio in Bradford, produced by Nigel Schofield.

8   Sheila Thackray, interviewed in 2005.

9   This is common practice for recording artists: George Harrison went through exactly the same process with producer Phil Spector when preparing to make the *All Things Must Pass* album.

10   Other songs were recorded during the three days, besides the 25 demos released on the *Jake in a Box* CD box set. A demo was made of 'Freda' as well, and 'The Lodger', which was already in Jake's live set, must surely have been recorded. When the box set was compiled it seems that these were left off because the performances were very similar to later recordings.

11   Only four of these 25 songs were never released in Jake's lifetime: 'Dog', 'Slowly Our Eyes', 'The Shepherdess' and 'The KG Girl (The Kirkstall Road Girl)'.

12   Along with the title track, this album would have included 'The Little Black Foal', 'Ulysses', 'Scallywag', 'Jumble Sale', 'The Cactus', 'Lah-Di-Dah', 'Country Bus', 'The Statues', 'The Blacksmith and the Toffeemaker', 'Family Tree' and 'I've Been Left on the Shelf'.

13   The album had a different tracklisting from the version compiled in April. 'Personal Column' and 'The Black Swan' replaced 'The Blacksmith and the Toffeemaker', 'Family Tree' and 'I've Been Left on the Shelf', which were now all kept back for release on Jake's second album (by which time 'I've Been Left on the Shelf' had become 'On the Shelf', and had been rewritten in the third person).

14   The Yorkshire-born son of an African-American dancer and an English actress and singer, Geoff had begun his career as a trombonist, but by the 1950s was an in-house orchestrator for EMI. In the 1970s, he was associated with countless popular easy-listening albums for EMI's budget Music for Pleasure label. Manuel and his Music of the Mountains was a pseudonym under which Geoff recorded many of his orchestral albums.

15   The orchestral sessions all took place at a new studio owned by Chappells, the music publishers, while the songs for which Geoff Love did the arrangements were all recorded at Abbey Road on 25th August.

16   Letter to Carol Hawkins, autumn 1967.

17   Ibid.

CHAPTER 9 – The Holy and the Horrid

1   Letter to Carol Hawkins, 1967.

2   In reality, the balance in Jake's writing was always firmly tilted towards 'the Horrid', and he only recorded one more religious song, 'Country Boy', released in 1972.

3   Petula Clark and Rod McKuen recorded the song as a duet. Hull band Turismo's version is the theme tune for *Meet the Richardsons*, a TV mockumentary series in which comedian Jon Richardson's obsession with Jake's work is a running joke. Arctic Monkeys' Alex Turner was inspired by 'Lah-Di-Dah' to write 'Cornerstone', and pays homage in its retro-style promo video, wearing a red roll-necked jumper as Jake did singing 'Lah-di-Dah' on *Braden's Week*.

4   Compare 'It Was Only a Gypsy' and 'The Ballad of Billy Kershaw', both featuring social underdogs who enjoy surprising sexual success, or 'The Hair of the Widow of Bridlington', which tells the story of a woman who is sexually liberated and enjoys a lifestyle that earns the disapproval of others.

5   These are the words Julius Caesar used to describe his point of no return, when he crossed the river Rubicon and thereby started a civil war. Jake would later use a Latin quotation even more brilliantly in 'On Again! On Again!'.

6   Jake's inspiration may have come from his nights out in Leeds, and his familiarity with the city's Hyde Park, where there was a statue of another British prime minister, Sir Robert Peel. Peel's name would have worked less well than Walpole's in the song.

7   Interview with Spencer Leigh, 1983. Jake's song actually has much more in common with the ideas expressed by Brel and Brassens, and he may have emphasised Henri's influence because the interview was on radio in Merseyside. Adrian Henri was an

important and influential figure on the Liverpool cultural scene in the 1960s. When Jake met him, he liked him enormously.

8   Was 'The Cactus' performed solo because they ran out of time during the session at Abbey Road on 25th August? Jake and the ensemble had already recorded six songs that day. Or was Norman testing the water by allowing Jake one solo performance?

9   Not everyone would agree with this view: the Elvis impersonator Jimmy Ellis (a.k.a. Orion) recorded a country rock version of 'Remember Bethlehem' which owed much to this arrangement. Thankfully, Jake released simpler, more effective acoustic versions of both carols on later albums.

10   *Record Mirror*, 11th November 1967.

11   The launch took place at the company's Manchester Square headquarters, in the building made famous on the cover of The Beatles' *Please Please Me* album.

12   *Record Mirror*, 25th November 1967.

13   *Melody Maker*, 23rd December 1967.

14   *Record Mirror*, 4th November 1967.

15   The show was broadcast as *Follow the Stars* on BBC Radio 1 and Radio 2 on 23rd December.

CHAPTER 10 – Becoming a 'Performing Dick'

1   Introduction to *Jake's Progress* (Star Books).

2   Jake sang 'The Black Swan', 'The Cactus', 'Ulysses', 'The Last Will and Testament of Jake Thackray', 'The Statues' and, in all likelihood, 'Lah-Di-Dah'. (Footage of 'Lah-Di-Dah' and 'The Cactus' has not survived.)

3   The single used a slightly quicker version of the song than the one that appeared on *The Last Will and Testament of Jake Thackray*, presumably in a bid to make it more commercial and increase its chances of getting radio play. Adverts were placed in *Melody Maker* and *The Stage* telling people to save their money and not to buy the album until they were firmly hooked on the single. Doubtless Jake had no hand in this strange marketing ploy, but it matched his ambivalent attitude towards the commercial aspect of his career: part of him would always be puzzled at the idea that anyone should want, or be expected to pay, to hear his songs.

4   *The Stage*, 14th March 1968. This is the trade newspaper of the entertainment industry.

5   *Sunday Mirror* interview with James Pettigrew, November 1968.

6   Mike Kerrigan, *Daily Mirror*, 11th March 1968.

7   *She* magazine, January 1969.

8   *Reading Evening Post*, 16th May 1968.

9   *She* magazine, January 1969.

10   *Sunday Mirror*, 24th November 1968.

11   In his *Catholic Herald* newspaper column in December 1994, Jake expressed a very jaundiced view of London: 'Not that we are any worse or better than London people. We are simply luckier. We don't have to live there. Thus our precious instinctive solidarity and human kindness, our God-given *caritas* ['compassion'], is not in so much danger as theirs is.'

12   *Reading Evening Post*, 16th May 1968.

13   Jake performed 'The Ferryboat' on *Braden's Week* in February 1969. The broadcast is lost and he never recorded the song, but the lyrics were recovered from the BBC archive and set to a new melody by Paul Thompson, a recording of which features on John Watterson's album, *The Lost Will and Testament of Jake Thackray*.

14   In December 1968, to celebrate its 30th anniversary, Noel Gay Artists took out a full-page advert in *Variety*, the American entertainment industry magazine, highlighting its achievements and on-going commitment to developing new talent, citing the successful launch of Jake's career as evidence of this.

15   *Sunday Mirror*, 28th April 1968.

16   Leeds City Varieties was familiar to millions as the home of the BBC's long-running television show, *The Good Old Days*, where audiences, dressed in Victorian-Edwardian costume, watched music hall acts.

17   Leeds City Varieties' burlesque shows often had exotic titles. The programme for *Parisienne Scandals* advertised the following week's entertainment, *Pardon My Tassel*, 'with the greatest Tassel Dancer in the World, Miss Fluffles'.

18   Performing as one of the two headline acts, Jake closed the first half of the show, whilst Nina Shaw, the winner of an ITV talent contest, closed the second. Revealingly, in both senses of the word, the strip act appeared in both halves.

19   *Yorkshire Life*, 11th November 1981.

20   Janet would go on to have a long and distinguished career on stage and screen.

21   This is one of many titles of lost songs registered by Jake's music publishers. No further information survives.

22   Anthony Teague, in an email to Paul Thompson.

23   Jake's music publisher registered copyright for several of the Intake musical songs, including 'Dog Song (I was a Prince)', 'The Bus Conductor's Song' and 'The Lost Property Shop Song', which suggests he may have used them again on leaving teaching.

24   The church is known as the 'Cathedral in the Forest'. Sheila's brother Rick was a choirboy there.

25   *The Guardian*, March 1969.

26   *The Stage*, 28ᵗʰ November 1968.

27   *She* magazine interview in January 1969, published in April 1969.

28   *Sunday Mirror*, 24ᵗʰ November 1968.

CHAPTER 11 – Braden's Week

1   Esther Rantzen had been a fan of Brassens and *chanson* since visiting Paris as a teenager. She and Desmond Wilcox were close, and would later marry.

2   Paul Fox, internal BBC memo, 5ᵗʰ August 1968.

3   Jake's fee was second only to that of Bernard Braden, who was on a TV superstar's rate of £850 per show.

4   The only week Jake was given a rest came on 29ᵗʰ March 1969, when *Braden's Week* made way for the *Eurovision Song Contest*.

5   Peter Kimber, *Reading Evening Post*, 13ᵗʰ February 1969.

6   U.D.I. refers to the unilateral declaration of independence made by South Rhodesia's racist white minority government.

7   The song was broadcast in March 1970.

8   Broadcast in February 1970.

9   Broadcast in April 1969.

10   *Guitar Magazine*, April 1979.

11   In the 26-programme first series, Jake only performed two songs already available on record – 'Personal Column' and 'Ulysses'.

12   Broadcast in December 1968. He had performed it on *Look North* almost three years earlier in March 1966. In 1980 he wrote a song about Leeds for a radio documentary focusing on the history of the city.

13   Letter to Carol Hawkins, 1967.

14   *Guitar Magazine*, April 1979.

15   Like 'God Bless America', the song was set to a new melody by Paul Thompson and recorded on John Watterson's *The Lost Will and Testament of Jake Thackray*. Its metre matches that of a later song, 'Go Little Swale', so Jake may have used the same or a similar melody.

16   *She* magazine interview in January 1969, published April 1969.

17   Interview with John Dunn on Radio 2, February 1981.

18   Sleeve notes of *Jake's Progress*, 1969.

19   Letter to Carol Hawkins, December 1968.

20   Sleeve notes of *Jake's Progress*, 1969.

21   *She* magazine, published April 1969.

22   Interview for *Jake on the Box* documentary, 2006.

23   Interview with Paul Vallely, *Leeds Student*, 2ⁿᵈ March 1973. It was conducted after a concert in the bar of the Civic Theatre, Leeds, with Jake surrounded by friends, former colleagues and pupils.

CHAPTER 12 – Jake's Progress

1   Sleeve notes for *Jake's Progress*.

2   The punning title alludes to *The Rake's Progress*, a series of paintings by 18th-century English artist William Hogarth which inspired an opera by Stravinsky (libretto co-written by poet W. H. Auden).

3   Frank Horrox (piano), Frank Clarke (double bass) and Ike Isaacs (guitar).

4   *She* magazine, published April 1969. The song was 'My Pipe, My Boots and My Lord', which was performed on *Braden's Week* that evening and recorded at Abbey Road the following year, although it wouldn't be released in Jake's lifetime.

5   Whether deliberate or not, the overall effect is reminiscent of the records of Paddy Roberts, an Ivor Novello-winning songwriter, whose comedy album, *Songs for Grown-Ups*, had been a top ten hit in 1959. The most famous of his risqué-laden songs is 'The Ballad of Bethnal Green'.

6   15th, 17th and 18th April 1969.

7   When the album was released it didn't feature any percussion, so either a decision was taken to remove it from the final mix, or the drummer was there, off-microphone, to keep time. The date was probably 18th April, when The Beatles were also in the studio. Jake recorded in Studio 2, The Beatles' favourite, in which the control room at the top of a staircase looks down on the studio.

8   Arguably *Jake's Progress* makes Jake an honorary member of the 'difficult second album' club. If he had wanted to make the record more comic, he had plenty of material available, including 'Miss World' and 'The Lodger', one of his most brilliant and hilarious creations, a staple of his live set. Had these songs been included, they would have shifted the overall balance of the album.

9   When Jake first wrote the song, he took an even more empathetic approach, writing and singing it in the first person: 'I've been left on the shelf...' Presumably he changed this to the third person because listeners might have found it confusing for him to be singing from a woman's perspective.

10   'Débutantes' or 'Debs' were introduced formally into fashionable London society through a series of events, including balls and, at one time, presentation at court. Jake also mocked them and 'all the customary Belgrave balls' in 'Personal Column'.

11   When he first started performing, Jake adjusted his setlist to suit the context. In pubs, he kept to songs earthier and more obvious in their humour. He performed 'Nurse' on *Look North* in 1966.

12   There is no record of the song before Jake's performance on *Braden's Week* in December 1968.

13   Jake is in his trademark roll-necked jumper beneath a jacket. The
      photo is hardly flattering, but he hated having his picture taken,
      and good ones are few. The shoot for the cover produced even
      worse shots, two of which were used for the front of his
      compilation albums in 1975 and 1991. They did him no favours
      at all.

14   *Melody Maker*, 21 June 1969.

15   The US publicity info for Jake's first album all seems to have been
      rather odd. One glossy advert in *Billboard* describes the album as
      'a live-wire, warm performance from the Welsh-born star'.

16   *The Miami News*, 19ᵗʰ November 1969.

17   There are countless examples, and even The Beatles got in on the
      act, recording German versions of 'She Loves You' and 'I Want
      to Hold Your Hand' in 1964.

18   'Tra La La' and both versions of 'Le Cygne Noir' were released
      on *Jake in a Box*, although Jake's translation is a hidden track.

19   John Grace on an internet forum.

CHAPTER 13 – Stepping Out of the Big Window

1   *Welsh Big Issue,* 2003.

2   Remembered by singer-songwriter Pete Scott, who was there that
      night. Change Is was an innovative but short-lived new
      nightclub, owned by comedian Bob Monkhouse.

3   The Lancashire bookings were made by Ian Watson, who ran
      Mid Pennine Arts. Ian had become friends with Jake after
      meeting him at the concert at Manchester University in 1966.

4   In 1956 it became the first public restaurant ever to be dined in
      by a reigning British monarch.

5   Peter Hepple, *The Stage*, 17 July 1969.

6   Jake's fee at the Stanford Arms in 1969 was £28.

7   Might this suggest that 'Country Bus' was Jake's first song?

8   *Newcastle Evening Chronicle*, 29ᵗʰ May 1969.

9   Clearly the hall had no bar, which is consistent with the building's
      use by the YMCA and the Methodists.

10   Alf McCreary, *Belfast Telegraph*, 21ˢᵗ November 1969.

11   *The Stage*, 27ᵗʰ November 1969. Jake was performing in the
      Rainbow Room, at the Manor House.

12   *The Stage*, 9ᵗʰ July 1970.

13   Rosemary Say, *Financial Times*, 29ᵗʰ June 1970.

14   This was Armstrong's final performance in Britain, and Jake is
      said to have featured in an American documentary about his visit
      to London. Years later, Jake would write amusingly in the
      Yorkshire Post about a brief conversation he claimed to have had

with Armstrong at a Buckingham Palace reception after the show.

15   Spencer Leigh, in his obituary for Jake in *The Independent*, 28th December 2002. Spencer was well-placed to know. He had interviewed both Norman and Jake, and the singer had stayed with him on occasion while performing in Liverpool.

16   *Record Mirror*, 20th March 1971. The album, released in 1971, included 14 of the songs from Jake's performance, but a limited edition, double album of the entire concert was also produced for promotional purposes. The full concert was eventually released on CD in 2006.

17   He misses out a verse of 'Remember Bethlehem' and, at one point, uses the wrong name in 'The Lodger'.

18   'Grandad' and the brief, amusing 'Romance'.

CHAPTER 14 – Jake's Scene

1   Interview with Spencer Leigh, 1983.

2   Live Performance, 1971.

3   Decades later, with inspiration hard to find, Jake would admit to his friend Ian Gliddon that writing to order had provided him with much needed discipline and forced him to remain productive. Indeed, in the 1980s he would seek more commissioned work as a way of kick-starting his writing again.

4   The fee for this radio work was £20, far less than the 85 guineas Jake received on *Braden's Week*.

5   Jake had a busy and productive week on regional television, also appearing on the BBC's *Look North* on 17th October, performing 'The Castleford Ladies Magic Circle'.

6   'God Bless Newcastle Fest' survives in the North East Film Archive, whilst 'You and Your Child' is in the collection of the British Film Institute.

7   As Abbey Road was one of London's most prestigious and sought-after studios, using it was not cheap, and nor was hiring an orchestra.

8   On the CD box set, *Jake in a Box*. The album included 'Leopold Alcocks', 'The Policeman's Jig', 'The Shepherdess', 'Pass Milord the Rooster Juice', 'The Vicar's Missus', 'The Ladies Basic Freedoms Polka', 'My Roly Poly Girl', 'My Pipe My Boots and My Lord', 'The Kirkstall Road Girl', 'Freda' and 'The Lodger'.

9   Journalist Ann Purser witnessed Jake rehearsing this song for *Braden's Week* when interviewing him for *She* magazine in January 1969.

10   Jake's performance remains in the BBC's vaults. John Watterson

made a recording of the song on his album *The Lost Will and Testament of Jake Thackray*.

11   *Belfast Telegraph*, 21ˢᵗ November 1969.

12   Jake and Sheila were apparently required to put down a 50 per cent cash deposit, an indication of how much money Jake had been making, and also of the bank's anxiety about the unpredictability of his future earnings.

13   Don had become friends with Sheila at university, and first met Jake in 1966, when he called round to see Sheila in her flat and was put out to find the singer in his chair. He would remain one of their closest friends.

14   Jake wasn't someone to let such injuries stop him. With foot in plaster, he once went by train to perform in the Manchester area, where he had arranged to stay with fellow performer Mike Harding. When the two men climbed into a taxi and the driver asked, 'Where to?', Jake replied, quick as a flash, 'Lourdes!'

15   *Newcastle Evening Chronicle*, 4ᵗʰ September 1971.

16   The director of the series, Ken Stephinson, had worked with Jake on the programme about the Newcastle Festival. He had a history as an innovator, which included being the first person to add humour to news items by setting them to popular music. He almost got the sack for accompanying footage of Prime Minister Harold Wilson visiting a miners' gala with 'Dancing in the Street' by Martha Reeves and the Vandellas. Doubtless such irreverence struck a chord with Jake.

17   'The Girl in the Window' was released on the *Bantam Cock* album, but 'Uncle Arthur' and 'Fashion' had no life beyond *Jake's Scene*. 'Uncle Arthur' appears on John Watterson's album, *The Lost Will and Testament of Jake Thackray*.

CHAPTER 15 – Bantam Cock

1   Interview with Spencer Leigh, 1983.

2   Jake emphasises that Jesus put himself on the same level as the people he came to save, and years later he would express the same idea more flippantly in 'The Bull'. He would soon use the tune of 'Country Boy' for another song, 'The Girl with the Fragile Eyes'. Melodically, its opening line is similar to the Beach Boys' 'Heroes and Villains'.

3   The album was recorded in three days on 7ᵗʰ January, 7ᵗʰ February and 29ᵗʰ March. One reason why it sounded different was that Abbey Road had moved over at the end of the 1960s from valve to transistor technology, which gave everything a warmer sound. The Beatles' final studio album, *Abbey Road*, benefitted from this.

4   Sadly, the identities of the session musicians have never been published, but the guitarist is likely to be jazz legend Ike Isaacs, still accompanying Jake on *Braden's Week*. Jake liked and admired enormously the amiable guitarist, who taught guitar, and is likely to have had a big impact on the development of his playing.

5   Jake later offered simple advice to Grant Baynham, a singer-songwriter who became a presenter on *That's Life!*: 'Distrust anyone who sings nicely!'

6   Brassens was admired for his songwriting rather than his voice, and was sometimes criticised for singing out of tune.

7   The approach taken in 'Bantam Cock' is reminiscent of the 'Catalogue aria' in Mozart's *Don Giovanni*, in which Don Giovanni's servant, Leporello, enumerates his master's innumerable romantic conquests throughout Continental Europe of women of all shapes, sizes and ages.

8   His friend Jasper Carrott recorded the song, and in concert parodied his delivery. It is a measure of Jake's fame in the 1970s that the parody was readily recognisable.

9   Aqua Velva is both an after-shave and a cocktail – a neatly ambigious touch, suggesting smooth charm and cocktail parties.

10   Jake's brother-in-law Rick remembers telling him both jokes, which were doing the rounds when he was at school and university.

11   For part of the verse Jake reused the melody of his early, earnest love song, 'Slowly Our Eyes'. The tune is put to much better use here.

12   Interview with Spencer Leigh, 1983. Jake would go on to tell him, 'I lobbed in a couple of things that Georges never mentioned and I made a couple of jokes of my own. I changed the chorus a little bit. Before I put it on record, I sang it to Georges and he said, "Absolutely bloody wonderful".'

13   E.g. 'The Hole', 'When Lucy Comes' and 'The Policeman's Jig'. Of course, Jake's own behaviour towards the police could be less than respectful, such as on the night when he was caught swimming naked. Perhaps his father was a source of inspiration for the character in the song: the court reports in the *Yorkshire Post* testify to how seriously Ernest Thackray took the business of law enforcement.

14   Interview with Spencer Leigh, 1983. The song was performed on *Braden's Week* in December 1970, but not in Jake's setlist at the Queen Elizabeth Hall a month earlier, which suggests that it may have been completed shortly after the concert.

15   In 'Sœur Marie-Louise' the police arrive at the convent when the nuns are celebrating Marie-Louise's 40th birthday, and she/he is

hauled off to be sentenced to 40 years' hard labour. The song contains a few rather weak jokes. In its most celebrated version it was performed on stage by a quartet, Les Quatre Barbus.

16   It would eventually see the light of day in 2006 on the *Jake in a Box* CD box set.

17   *Record Mirror*, 23rd September 1972.

18   *Reading Evening Post*, 6th October 1972.

CHAPTER 16 – Rachmaninov and Charley Farley

1   Charley Farley, played by comedian Ronnie Corbett, was the diminutive sidekick of Ronnie Barker's Piggy Malone in their spoof detective mini-series, 'Done to Death', from the BBC sketch show *The Two Ronnies*.

2   Interview with Ray Brown, 24th September 2000.

3   The interview with Ray Brown was recorded in preparation for a short Radio 4 documentary *Starry Starry Night*, broadcast on 22nd August 2001. Only brief excerpts were used in the programme. All quotations of Jake in this chapter are taken from this interview. An hour of his conversation with Ray can be heard on www.jakethackray.com.

4   *Jake Thackray and Songs* album, 1981.

5   Colin Evans' translation of his own French article in *Les Amis de Georges* number 70, 2002.

6   Ibid.

7   Colin was actually Welsh, but the quote is from his translation of an article he originally published in French. 'Anglais' can be used to indicate that someone is British or English. Colin was so fluent in French that he was often assumed to be a native speaker. His fluency would undoubtedly have impressed Georges.

8   *Les Amis de Georges* number 70, 2002.

9   Loïc Robinot, who worked with Colin at Cardiff University, wrote about Georges's first trip to Cardiff in his book, *Sur Ma Route, Un Certain...Georges Brassens*. Carol Evans introduced Colin to Georges's songs. She had fallen in love with them as a teenager, hearing them in the house where she was staying on a French exchange. At the end of her visit, the family gave her a copy of his first album which she later lost. When Georges heard the story, he sought to replace it for her.

10   Sheila Thackray, email to Michel Ameline, 12th July 2009.

11   The concert was on a Sunday evening. The theatre was formally opened by the Duke of Edinburgh the following month.

12   The concert in Italy was in 1958.

13   Antony Terry, *Sunday Times*, 28th October 1973.

14   It is inconceivable that the self-effacing Jake would ever have made the suggestion.
15   Email to Michel Ameline, 12ᵗʰ July 2009.
16   The recording of Jake's excellent performance has never been released.
17   Colin Evans, *Les Amis de Georges* number 70, 2002. He wrote the album's informative sleeve notes and provided the cover photograph of Georges at Caerphilly Castle (in Colin's hometown), taken during his stay with Colin and Carol in 1970.
18   Ibid.
19   Email to Michel Ameline, 12ᵗʰ July 2009.
20   Radio 4, *Starry, Starry Night*, 22ⁿᵈ August 2001.
21   Ibid.
22   Jake is referring to a short item about the concert that featured on 3ʳᵈ November on Bragg's BBC2 arts programme *Second House*. Two years later, in May 1975, the BBC broadcast Colin's documentary about Brassens and the concert, which featured footage of Brassens's performance and a brief interview with Jake.
23   *Daily Telegraph*, 30ᵗʰ October 1973.
24   Both newspaper pieces emphasised it was friendship that led to Brassens performing in Cardiff, a view only confirmed by the fact that the event went completely unreported in the French press.

CHAPTER 18 – The Camera and the Song

1   Interview with John Dunn, Radio 2, 13ᵗʰ February 1981.
2   Ibid.
3   Mike Jamieson, *Newcastle Evening Chronicle*, 30ᵗʰ May 1981.
4   One of the myths perpetuated online is that Jake appeared on *The Frost Report*. He never did. This seems to have been his only performance on a TV show hosted by David Frost.
5   Alex Glasgow, Ralph McTell, Jeremy Taylor, Ian Campbell, David Campbell and Max Boyce were the other songwriters involved. Jake became good friends with many through meeting them on the folk club circuit and at festivals.
6   Philip Bonham Carter would go on to have a long and distinguished career in television, and his credits included filming the Queen's Christmas broadcast for many years.
7   Performing with a quintet on a hillside was hardly practicable, and it is unimaginable that Jake would ever have agreed to mime.
8   Southgate, a classically trained musician from New Zealand, went on to become an eminent conductor and composer, and received a knighthood. He was the musical arranger for the entire series, and the recording sessions with Jake may have taken place at SB Independent Radio Studios in London: this is where

Southgate recorded the songs for Alex Glasgow's episode in the series, which were released on an album in 1973. Sadly, Jake's recordings weren't released.

9   The lines mocking the film crew and Jake were replaced when he came to record the song for his next album.

10   A recording of the song features on John Watterson's album, *The Lost Will and Testament of Jake Thackray*. There is also an excellent acoustic version on YouTube, performed by Ian Burdon and Hugh Bradley.

11   *The Guardian*, 29th December 1973.

12   *Birmingham Daily Post*, 12th August 1974.

13   *Sunday Times*, 25th July 1976.

14   He sings 'Bantam Cock', 'Sister Josephine', 'Lah-Di-Dah', 'It Was Only a Gypsy', 'Brother Gorilla', 'Fine Bay Pony' and 'The Poor Sod'.

15   *Sunday Times*, 25th July 1976.

CHAPTER 19 – A Singer's Place

1   Sleeve notes of *Jake Thackray and Songs* album.

2   *East Kent Times and Mail*, March 1973.

3   *Kent and Sussex Courier*, 26th March 1971.

4   *The Stage*, 29th June 1972.

5   *Melody Maker*, 1st July 1972.

6   *Birmingham Daily Post*, 27th April 1973.

7   *Belfast Telegraph*, 25th November 1972.

8   It is hard to imagine a more unlikely combination, but Jake usually enjoyed performing for university students.

9   Review of a concert at the Sheffield Crucible, *Sunday Times*, March 1972.

10   Interviewed by Pam Archer at Henley College Folk Club, Coventry, for BBC Radio Birmingham, February 1977.

11   Interviewed by Ed Doolan for BRMB (former name of Free Radio Birmingham).

12   A 150-mile drive.

13   This was in contrast with his television work, where he was normally accompanied by other musicians.

14   Interview with Ray Brown, 24th September 2000.

15   Performing at the Medina Theatre, Isle of Wight, 18th November 1983.

16   Alan showed this on one memorable occasion in his orchestral work. While the string section was rehearsing a particularly challenging avant-garde piece, he picked a quiet moment to whisper loudly to a friend, 'Fucking nice tune, Henry!' The music

came shuddering to a halt, and the conductor was left attempting to stop the laughter and identify the culprit.

17   A concert was broadcast by British Forces Broadcasting Service on the *Forces Folk* programme; it was eventually released on the CD, *Live in Germany*, in 2005.

18   *Yorkshire Post*, 26th September 1990.

19   Taken from Jake's performance on *Jake Thackray and Songs*, January 1981.

20   Catherine Comerford, *The Stage*, 4th August 1977.

21   Recalled by John Pearce in the book of condolences on www.jakethackray.com.

22   Transcript of a performance at The Stables near Milton Keynes, released in 1981 on the live album, *Jake Thackray and Songs*.

CHAPTER 20 – On Again! On Again!

1   Sheila Thackray, email to Michel Ameline, 2009.

2   Brassens's output likewise decreased over the years: in his final decade he released only two albums of new material, the result of years of work carefully honing his songs.

3   'Silly song! Silly song!' he would declare. He would dispense with the guitar introduction to 'Bantam Cock' so that audiences wouldn't recognise it, and he would do 'Sister Josephine' early in his set 'to get it out of the way'.

4   Vic Smith, who regularly booked Jake to perform at his folk club, remembers talking to him about their shared love of Brassens: 'I suggested that he was the English Brassens and he said that was blasphemy – no songwriter could hold a candle to Brassens.'

5   Jake's playing on the entire album is nimble, inventive and accomplished. Particular highlights include the clever, unorthodox introductory riffs on 'On Again! On Again!' and 'The Kiss', which many a guitarist has admired and puzzled over for years.

6   This studio would be used a few weeks later by the Sex Pistols. Jake's album was a Noel Gay Production, meaning that the agency managed the project for EMI.

7   Jake creates a double entendre using a Latin philosophical phrase: proof that God exists comes 'a posteriori' ('from what follows later'), which, in the song, is from her beautiful behind.

8   Interview with Spencer Leigh, 1983.

9   Interviewed by the *Newcastle Evening Chronicle*, 30th May 1981.

10   Interview with Spencer Leigh, 1983.

11   Speaking in the BBC TV documentary, *Jake on the Box*, 2006.

12   *Southwest Arts Magazine*, 1977. Nightingale was the critic who gave Jake his first national review in *The Guardian* in 1966.

13   Speaking in an interview with Colin Evans in 1971; quoted in
            Colin's article *Jake Thackray, Translater and Interpreter of Brassens*,
            published in the French journal *Équivalences* in 1992.
14   Interview with *Guitar Magazine*, 1979.
15   Interview with Spencer Leigh, 1983. He may have been thinking
            particularly of the country rock version of 'Remember Bethlehem'
            recorded on the legendary Sun Records label by Orion, an Elvis
            Presley soundalike.
16   The most famous gravedigger in English literature is in *Hamlet*.
            For a comparison of Shakespeare's character with Thackray's and
            Brassens's, see the paper written by Dr Richard O'Brien: *'I Know
            My Clay': Some Musical Afterlives of Hamlet's Gravedigger*
            (published online by Northumbria University, 2021).
17   As with the other out-takes, released in 2006, on *Jake in a Box*.
18   Jon Ford, *Leicester Chronicle*, 11th February 1977.
19   *New Musical Express*, 26th February 1977; *Sounds*, 19th February
            1977.
20   *Melody Maker*, 19th February 1977.
21   Noel Gay would have had little difficulty persuading *That's Life!*
            to book Jake. Esther Rantzen, its lead presenter, was, of course, a
            huge fan, and also happened to be another of the agency's clients.
22   *South West Arts Magazine*, 1977.

CHAPTER 21 – Lots of Beans, No Songs

1   Interview with *Guitar Magazine*, April 1979.
2   Utterly overwhelmed at such generosity, the Haverlys politely
            declined.
3   Peter had worked as a biology teacher in Monmouth and had
            taught Jake's brother-in-law, Rick. He first met the singer in
            1969, and the two men and their families became great friends.
4   Jake's youngest son, Tom, at one stage worked for Robert Plant
            as an assistant gardener. One daily task was to move the singer's
            plastic pink flamingos into different positions in the grounds.
5   The Wimpy burger bar chain was ubiquitous in 1970s Britain.
6   Interview with *Guitar Magazine*, 1979.
7   Radio 4, *On the Town*, broadcast 9th January 1980. The song is
            not given a title, but could be called 'Gritty Old City of Leeds',
            a phrase which appears in most verses. A recording is preserved
            in the British Library sound archive.
8   The final verse is reminiscent of the ending of Homer's epic, *The
            Iliad*, where the Trojan king, Priam, and his enemy, the Greek
            hero Achilles, meet and recognise that it is their suffering and
            mortality which unite them.

9   He had been working on the song for some time. Although he would not perform it until 1979, it is listed in a 1977 concert programme under the early title 'This One'll Kill You', which is similar to a line in the final version of the lyric.

CHAPTER 22 – Jake Thackray and Songs

1   Quoted by Colin Godman, BBC producer, in an interview with Louis Barfe in 2015, used throughout this chapter.

2   Ibid.

3   Colin's background was in drama, and he was only available to make *Jake Thackray and Songs* because a strike had grounded his other projects. No doubt Jake was also pleased that Colin was based at the BBC's studios in Bristol rather than London.

4   Ralph McTell, who enjoyed a huge hit with 'Streets of London' in 1975, first met Jake in Sheffield in the early 1970s. After appearing in *Jake Thackray and Songs* he returned the compliment by inviting Jake to perform on his radio series. Jake often stayed with him when performing in London. His sons once stayed with the McTells while he and Sheila went to a concert in Paris.

5   Jake saw Pete Scott, a young singer-songwriter from Tyneside, perform at the Hare and Hounds, Birmingham. Hugely impressed, he phoned him personally to invite him to be on the programme.

6   Richard Thompson, in an email to John Watterson, 2021.

7   A DVD of *Jake Thackray and Songs*, featuring Jake's performances and those of Ralph McTell, Alex Glasgow and Pete Scott, was released by the Jake Thackray Project in 2014 to excellent reviews.

8   *Southern Rag*, 1981.

9   The concert took place at The Stables, a venue owned by jazz legends Johnny Dankworth and Cleo Laine. Jake often played there. He and Alan were accompanied by jazz guitarist John Etheridge.

10   *Southern Rag*, 1981. Sadly, the album is out of print and has not, as yet, been reissued in any format.

11   Jake received the news in a call from Brassens's housekeeper, Sophie, whom he got to know during visits to Georges in Paris.

12   Whilst Jake's criticism was accurate at the time his letter was published, within a month the *Sunday Times* rectified matters, with a glowing tribute from Julian Barnes.

CHAPTER 23 – The Glowing Red Phone

1   Interview, *Welsh Big Issue*, 2003.

2   Letter to Ian Watson. Archie Rice (a character in John Osborne's

	play and film, *The Entertainer*) is an angry, middle-aged, failing music hall performer.
3	Radio 2 interview with John Dunn, February 1981.
4	Agutter was one of the child stars of the 1970 film *The Railway Children*, which was a huge success.
5	Jake still managed to get occasional bookings on regional TV. On London Plus in 1984 he sang 'The Jolly Captain', provoking mild criticism from the presenter about how out of step with the times the song's sentiment was – a sign of growing political correctness.
6	The song didn't appear in Jake's live set, and seems to have had only one outing on radio which survives through a low-grade home recording of the broadcast. John Watterson recorded a version for his album, *The Lost Will and Testament of Jake Thackray*.
7	Jake recorded the song at Wormwood Studios, founded by the Fairport Convention bassist, Dave Pegg, and his then wife, Christine. The session offered up a memorable Leopold Alcocks moment when Jake was bitten by the Peggs' dog. 'I was away on tour at the time,' says Dave, 'and when Christine offered him a cup of tea on his arrival at the studio, while reassuring him the dog wouldn't hurt him, he replied that the bugger already had!'
8	Decades later, Jaconelli would be identified as part of a paedophile ring that included Jimmy Savile. He died in 1999, before he could be brought to account for his activities.
9	Jake's recordings are unavailable. Both songs feature on John Watterson's *The Lost Will and Testament of Jake Thackray*.
10	Many aspects of Jake's contribution to the programme are odd. Although Jake was in the studio for the broadcast, the song was pre-recorded. The presenter, Russell Harty, explained to listeners that Jake couldn't perform live because his hand was bandaged. However, at the end of the programme, to Harty's surprise, Jake took the bandage off and performed 'The Remembrance'. Perhaps he was nervous at the prospect of performing the new song, so came up with the excuse, but felt more confident playing the older song live. 'The Remembrance' clearly had some tangential relevance to the programme's focus, only serving to reinforce the anti-militarism Jake expressed in 'Soon Get The Hang Of It'.
11	Sue Haverly, who was an anti-nuclear campaigner, featured in the programme devoted to nuclear power.
12	The song is better known as 'Side by Side'. Jake performed it on Radio 2 in 1990, but never released a recording. John Watterson recorded a version on *The Lost Will and Testament of Jake Thackray*.
13	In addition, the lyrics were analysed in the accompanying course book, together with the lyrics of 'The Jolly Captain', which also featured in the series.

CHAPTER 24 – It Doesn't Get Any Easier

1   Review of concert, King's Head, Islington, 23rd February 1989.

2   Letter, January 1985.

3   Interview with Ray Brown, 24th September 2000.

4   While outwardly supportive, Jake seems to have been resentful and embarrassed about Sheila having to get a job.

5   Jake was once invited to do an advert for Penguin biscuits, as Rick Irons recalls: 'He told me with obvious scorn that they asked him to "pick up a fxxxxxg Penguin!" Needless to say, it didn't happen.'

6   Jake's first trip abroad as a performer was to Kenya in 1974. In the 1980s, he regularly went overseas, to the Gulf States (1980), West Germany (1982) and Cyprus (1983), Canada (1984 and 1986), Bermuda (1984 or 1985) and Hong Kong (1984, 1989).

7   Further recognition of this had come in 1985, when he was one of the judges of a songwriting competition; on the panel he was joined by Melvyn Bragg, Victoria Wood (who often found herself being compared to Jake) and Kirsty MacColl.

8   There would be a strong sense in Jake's final radio appearances that he was singing whatever took his fancy: alongside familiar favourites, listeners heard obscure songs, such as 'Borders' and 'The Cenotaph', and an immaculate rendition of Brassens's 'Dans L'Eau De La Claire Fontaine'.

9   Richard had also written a topical song about the Festival for the Tyne Tees television programme in which Jake sang 'God Bless Newcastle Fest'.

10   It is hard not to believe that Jake's poor organisation played a part in this. Sometimes Sheila Thackray seemed to have a better idea as to where he was meant to be performing than he did ('Aren't you supposed to be playing a gig tonight?').

11   The album was released in 1988, but vinyl copies are hard to find. It never had a CD release, but is available via streaming services.

12   For a couple of years Jake had his caravan office parked on Peter's land. Peter became a leading figure in the underground-house-building community, and Caer Llan, his award-winning 'berm house', was the result of years of research on his part, credited at the time as the second most energy-efficient building in Europe.

13   Radio 2, *I Write The Songs*, July 1996.

14   *The Stage*, 23rd February 1989.

CHAPTER 25 – A Voice from the Bottom

1   Note to editor attached to copy for one of his newspaper pieces.

2   *Yorkshire Post*, 28th February 1989.

3   Founded in 1754 as the *Leeds Intelligencer*, the *Yorkshire Post* is
       one of England's oldest and best-known regional papers, and in
       the 1980s and 1990s had a large circulation across the north-east.
4   Note to Cockroft on Jake's copy for 3rd April.
5   Cockroft, who had a degree in music and a career in music
       journalism, was well-placed to make this observation.
6   *Yorkshire Post*, 25th April 1989.
7   Letter to Jake from Robert Cockroft, 28th April 1989.
8   Letter to Jake from Tony Watson, 24th July 1991.
9   He even objected to having his photograph taken to advertise his
       column on the front page: 'No. I don't like pictures of myself'.
       He eventually relented, the end-result an immensely characterful
       and lugubrious portrait.
10   *Yorkshire Post*, 27th June 1990.
11   *Yorkshire Post*, 19th June 1991.
12   On another occasion Jake signed off as 'J. Thackratty'.
13   The editor's secretary.
14   *Yorkshire Post*, 30th April 1992.
15   This title replaced Jake's suggestion, 'A voice from the bottom'.
16   *Catholic Herald*, 7th October 1994.
17   Sister Wendy presented a series of hugely popular programmes
       on art history.

CHAPTER 26 – Don't Come and Find Me

1   This may have been in recognition of Jake's Catholic faith, or to
       avoid him the embarrassment of Sheila having to prove the
       grounds for divorce in court.
2   Letter from John Leonard, Editor Radio 1 North, 27th May 1994.
3   The party proposed a single energy-based tax to replace all other
       taxes.
4   The group's name was a reference to the supposed inventor of the
       hokey cokey, and an old joke about the difficulty of getting his
       whole body into the coffin: 'You put the left leg in...'
5   *I Write the Songs*, Radio 2, 23rd November 1996
6   *Coventry Evening Telegraph*, 1st January 2003.
7   Jake sang 'Tortoise', 'Our Dog', Dans L'eau de la Claire Fontaine'
       and 'Bantam Cock'.
8   Bob Ross, who ran the Paysanne restaurant in Deganwy, North
       Wales, remembers 'several hilarious anecdotes which left the
       audience in tears' when Jake performed there in a dinner concert.
9   He had heard the joke from singer Vin Garbutt, when Jake was
       due to perform at the Monmouth Festival, but had got himself
       double-booked. Garbutt agreed to perform in his place, and Jake

drove to Birmingham to collect him. Hearing the joke on the journey back, Jake laughed so much he started swerving.

10   *Jake on the Box*, TV documentary, 2006.

11   Alan Plater, writing his obituary in *The Guardian*, 17th May 2001.

12   The world-famous studio, constructed in a set of farm buildings near Monmouth, has been used by countless artists, and is where Queen recorded 'Bohemian Rhapsody'.

13   For the aunt, 'I'll be civil to your appalling Auntie Beryl...'; for the mother, 'although she's always so bloody vague'; for the father, 'although he always bores me with his boats' and 'the tries he used to score...'

14   Similarly, during the last years of his life Jake told his son Sam several times that he was writing an autobiography or something based on his life, but no evidence of it was ever seen.

15   There may be some self-irony in this line: Jake and Sheila had joined several other couples on their honeymoons.

16   The authors took Jake's verse and the ideas he left and created a full song, writing a tune and additional verses. 'Kinnell' appears on John Watterson's 2016 album, *The Lost Will and Testament of Jake Thackray*.

17   Stuart Marlow, who commissioned Jake to write 'Borders', remembers hearing him singing an acerbic song on the radio in the late-1980s about a girl, in which he mocked the language and attitudes of Yuppies. This sounds like it might have been an updated version of 'Caroline Digby-Pratte'. Apparently the song didn't really fit with the rest of the programme and wasn't well-received by the studio audience.

18   Letter to Ian Watson, 14th July 1999.

19   Undated letter from Ralph McTell to Jake.

CHAPTER 27 – 'We wuz ere. Where wuz u?'

1   Roger, whose father was music-hall legend Stan Stennett, was good friends with Ian, having been his assistant for ten years running South West Arts. He was based in Gloucestershire. He had first seen Jake perform at the Casson Theatre in Cardiff (the concert where the singer met Colin and Carol Evans), and Ian later introduced them at a concert in Bristol.

2   Ian Watson, *A Bud or Two for Jake*, 2003. Except where otherwise stated, all the recollections quoted in this chapter are taken from this memoir of his work with Jake on his theatre project.

3   Jake, email to Ian Watson, 3rd October 1999.

4   Jake, letter to Ian Watson, 10th March 2000.

5   The condition causes one or more fingers to become permanently

bent in a flexed position. Alcohol and smoking are known risk factors.

6   Roger Stennett email to Ian Watson, 19th September 2000.

7   The actual title is *Jacques Brel is Alive and Well and Living in Paris*. An essentially plotless stage visualisation of Brel's songs, it made no direct reference to him, other than in its title. Jake's point was that he did not want his name to be given such prominence.

8   An in-joke based on the fact that Victor had always pressed Jake for new songs, and knew that he would hate the prospect of his own television show and performing with an orchestra. It was Victor who had provided Ian with Jake's address.

9   Jake also told Ian that he would contact William Hinshaw, webmaster of the American Georges Brassens Fan Club website, who wanted him to attend the Brassens Festival in Vaison-La-Romaine, France, the following spring.

10   The 15-minute programme was broadcast on 22nd August 2001. In a letter to Ian Watson in September 2000, Jake complained about how little attention Brassens received in the British media: 'Don't you think, Ian, that it is sickening and typical of B.B.C. creeps, "philistins, épiciers", that twenty years after the event – which like pig-ignorami Presspeople [*sic*], local and national, they comprehensively missed...they finally allow a mention of the one appearance in Britain of a major European artist (yeah, let's be fulsome about it, that's what the bastard was, and is).'

11   When it was suggested that he should steal the book himself, Jake protested that he couldn't do so because he was a Catholic.

12   In the 1990s, The Unofficial Jake Thackray Page, run by Edmund Chattoe, was an essential early online resource. The Jake Thackray Project began as an email discussion group and went on to become www.jakethackray.com, run by Gordon Tennent.

13   Odd, too, that he made no reference to his brother Michael, at the time alive and well in France. Communication between the Thackray brothers was by now sporadic. Michael's daughter, Wendy, invited Jake to a surprise 70th birthday party for her father in France in 1998, but had no contact details for Richard. When Richard died in 1999, Jake didn't attend the funeral.

CHAPTER 28 – Gather a Bud or Two for Jake

1   Coronary artery thrombosis and coronary artery atheroma were recorded as the causes of death. His heavy smoking was a significant risk factor.

2   *The Guardian*, 28th December 2002.

3   *Daily Mirror*, 28th December 2002.

A singer's place: Jake performing in London in 1983

Index

Jake Thackray   *Tish Murtha © Ella Murtha. All rights reserved, DACS/Artimage, 2022*

The Last Will and Testament of Jake Thackray

I, the under-mentioned, by this document,
Do declare my true intentions,
My last will, my testament.
When I turn up my toes,
When I rattle my clack, when I agonise,
I want no great wet weepings,
No tearing of hair, no wringing of hands,
No sighs, no lack-a-days,
No 'woe-is-me's and none of your sad adieus.
Go, go, go and get the priest
And then go get the booze, boys.

Death, where is thy victory?
Grave, where is thy sting?
When I snuff it bury me quickly,
Then let carousals begin.
But not a do with a few ham sandwiches,
A sausage roll or two
And 'a small port wine, please'.
Roll the carpet right back,
Get cracking with your old Gay Gordons
And your knees up, shake it up, live it up, sup it up
Hell of a kind of a time.
And if the coppers come around,
Well, tell them the party's mine, boys.

Let best beef be eaten, fill every empty glass,
Let no breast be beaten, let no tooth be gnashed.
Don't bother with a fancy tombstone or
A big-deal angel or a little copper flower pot.
Grow a dog rose in my eyes or a pussy willow
But no forget-me-nots, no epitaphs no keepsakes,
You can let my memory slip.
You can say a prayer or two for my soul then,
But make it quick, boys.

Lady, if your bosom is heaving, don't waste your bosom on me.
Let it heave for a man who's breathing,
A man who can feel, a man who can see.
And to my cronies: you can read my books,
You can drive around in my motor car,
And you can fish your trout with my fly and tackle,
You can play on my guitar,
And sing my songs, wear my shirts
You can even settle my debts.
You can kiss my little missus if she's willing then but –
      no regrets, boys.

Your rosebuds are numbered
Gather them now for rosebuds' sake.
   d if your hands aren't too encumbered
      a bud or two for Jake.

(
Anc
Gathei